Nick McKenzie is one of the nation's most decorated investigative journalists, having been named Australian Journalist of the Year on four occasions. Over two decades, he has worked for the Australian Broadcasting Corporation's *Four Corners* program, Nine's *60 Minutes* and the *Sydney Morning Herald* and *The Age* newspapers. His reporting spans politics, defence, foreign affairs, the criminal justice system, corporate crime and social affairs. He has been awarded the Walkley, Australia's highest journalism award, a record fourteen times.

CROSSING THE LINE

NICK McKENZIE

hachette
AUSTRALIA

hachette
AUSTRALIA

Published in Australia and New Zealand in 2023
by Hachette Australia
(an imprint of Hachette Australia Pty Limited)
Gadigal Country, Level 17, 207 Kent Street, Sydney, NSW 2000
www.hachette.com.au

Hachette Australia acknowledges and pays our respects to the past, present and future Traditional
Owners and Custodians of Country throughout Australia and recognises the continuation of
cultural, spiritual and educational practices of Aboriginal and Torres Strait Islander peoples. Our
head office is located on the lands of the Gadigal people of the Eora Nation.

A catalogue record for this
work is available from the
National Library of Australia

ISBN: 978 0 7336 5043 7 (paperback)

Cover photography courtesy of NewsPix; Fairfax Photos
Author photograph courtesy Nine Entertainment Pty Ltd
Typeset in Sabon LT Std by Kirby Jones
Printed and bound in Australia by McPherson's Printing Group

MIX
Paper | Supporting
responsible forestry
FSC
www.fsc.org
FSC® C001695

The paper this book is printed on is certified against the
Forest Stewardship Council® Standards. McPherson's Printing
Group holds FSC® chain of custody certification SA-COC-005379.
FSC® promotes environmentally responsible, socially beneficial
and economically viable management of the world's forests

To my family

CONTENTS

AUTHOR'S NOTE

If Shakespeare had stumbled upon the story of Ben Roberts-Smith, he may well have considered it worthy of a play. He likely would have dismissed any claim it was true. But what you are about to read is a work of non-fiction. In mid 2017, I embarked on an investigation that would change many lives. Exposing the involvement of Australia's most famous and revered soldier in the nation's worst war crimes scandal has been the most difficult undertaking of my twenty-year career. I still shake my head in wonder at the rollercoaster ride this story has taken me on. Much of it I, too, wouldn't believe if I hadn't lived it.

This book aims to tell the Roberts-Smith story from my own perspective, as well as capturing the thoughts, conversations, feelings and actions of other key characters: SAS witnesses, Afghan victims and villagers, politicians, lawyers, investigators and Roberts-Smith's friends, foes and lovers. And, of course, Ben Roberts-Smith VC, MG.

But this book is not only about Australia's most infamous war crimes scandal, and the soldier at the centre of it. It is about Australia's media, its justice system and its defence force, and how history can be hijacked by vested interests. It is about how power and money can threaten truth and justice, and how Australia's hunger for military myth created a monster. It is also about how the pen can be mightier than those elite and powerful Australians who have never stopped backing Roberts-Smith, even when it seemed clear he wasn't the man he claimed to be.

Telling my own story was relatively easy. It was and remains burnt into my brain.

I have recreated the conversations, thoughts, feelings and actions of others, including SAS soldiers and Roberts-Smith, as faithfully as possible from multiple credible sources.

Roberts-Smith's decision to sue Chris Masters and me provided a wealth of material. Most of the key SAS characters in the book are trial witnesses whose stories I have recreated from trial transcripts and other court documents. Entire chapters are sourced from the witness box, as SAS soldiers recounted, blow by blow, their dealings with Roberts-Smith and their recollections of key missions, conversations and incidents.

I have supplemented this with extensive briefings from confidential sources, including SAS insiders or other informants.

The extensive report by another character in the book, war crimes investigator Justice Paul Brereton, helped me tell some of the story as it relates to the judge, as did other public source documents authored by him or about him or his father. So too did briefings from sources who had direct dealings with Justice Brereton, including in Afghanistan.

Some of the characters I interviewed at length or on multiple occasions, including defence force consultant Samantha Crompvoets, SAS medic Dusty Miller, SAS captain turned politician Andrew Hastie and the Afghan family members of one of Roberts-Smith's victims. I conducted many other interviews with sources I can never name to protect their safety or livelihoods.

Roberts-Smith was grilled on the stand for days, and I have used this testimony, along with his speeches and media interviews, to write about him. I also had access to more than two dozen sources who have dealt with him at various periods of his life, including his days as a young infantry soldier, as an SAS patrol team member and commander in Afghanistan, as a media executive and as a friend, family man, comrade or confidant. Some of the conversations I have recreated are based on actual covert audio recordings made of Roberts-Smith. These, too, have been provided to me by confidential sources.

Further notes about sourcing for each chapter is in an endnotes section.

I have no doubt Ben Roberts-Smith will deny much, if not all, of my account of his descent from famous to infamous but Federal Court Justice Anthony Besanko has made it clear Roberts-Smith cannot be believed. The judge concluded he is a liar, bully and war criminal.

The timing of some of the events I have described has been truncated or may be out of sequence, but is otherwise told faithfully. For instance, my dealings with Dusty Miller occurred over a far greater period than reflected in the book. I have had hundreds of conversations with my lawyers, but only very few are described.

I have also only written about certain key moments in the defamation trial. One could write an entire book just on the court case, but this story is a far broader telling of events that happened well before the trial was underway.

To protect legal privilege or the identity of some sources, some of the contents of certain conversations or events as they pertain to legal or source dealings have been altered. However, nothing deviates from the essential truth of the journey I lived and breathed for more than five years.

Some Australians will ask, justifiably, why I have written this book given Roberts-Smith may yet face a criminal trial. If Roberts-Smith is criminally charged, then it will be for a jury to weigh the evidence put before it in deciding whether he is guilty to the criminal standard of beyond reasonable doubt.

This book is not about whether Roberts-Smith will or should be convicted of any crimes. Only a jury of his peers can decide that.

Yet it should also be said that my decision to tell this story is partly based on the fact that it was Roberts-Smith who forced so much of it into the public domain by suing me. It was he who chose to put a vast amount of detail about his own activities before a civil court for a judge, and the nation, to hear.

Having done this with the intention of using our nation's defamation laws to suppress the truth, and having been declared by a judge (to the civil standard of 'balance of probabilities') to have engaged in the very war crimes and cover-ups I accused him of in my original reporting and again in my trial defence, it could hardly be said that I should now fall silent.

Ben Roberts-Smith tried to defeat the truth. This book tells the story of how the truth triumphed.

–Nick McKenzie

National security laws and court suppression orders require that certain people be given a number or a pseudonym. They include members and support staff of the SAS. Some names in the text have been changed in line with court orders or for national security reasons, or for security concerns. The following names attributed to a 'Person number' are not real names.

Jason Andrews – Person 4
Neil Browning – Person 5
Tim Douglass – Person 35
Vincent Jelovic – Person 11
Amanda Jones – Person 17
Boyd Keary – Person 7
John Langmore – Person 41
Brian McMurray – Person 18
Keith Nueling – Person 31
Nick Simkin – Person 6
Jimmy Stanton – Person 16
Dean Tilley – Person 14
William Tindell – Person 1

I do not have authorisation to waive legal privilege. In order to protect legal privilege, the contents of certain conversations or events as they pertain to legal dealings have been changed. I have also altered the content of some conversations to protect my confidential sources.

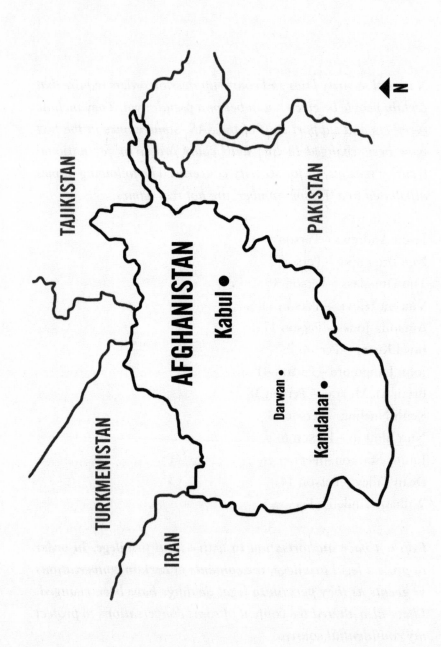

DARWAN, AFGHANISTAN

11 September 2012

The rising Afghan sun had yet to warm the chill of the morning air as the heavily armed men raced towards the helicopters at the Tarin Kowt military base runway. In the distance rose the foreboding mountains of southern Afghanistan, silent and monolithic sentinels of a country famed for swallowing up the men and morale of invading armies.

If the soldiers boarding the helicopters held any misgivings about their own role in Afghanistan that morning, they betrayed no sign of them. Most wore an expression of steely intent, along with the markings of Australia's most elite and secretive fighting force, the Special Air Service (SAS) Regiment. But an SAS translator later observed something else about a few of the soldiers: 'Their blood was up.'

Fifteen minutes later, the choppers settled on the outskirts of Darwan, a farming village adjacent to the Helmand River and consisting of mud and stone compounds. From the sky, Darwan looked like an ancient civilisation, but as the soldiers swept through the village, the fusion of modern and rustic was apparent. Some of the men who lived here rode motorbikes and wore watches. Mobile phones peeked out of the pockets of the colourful tunics they wore over Afghan robes.

Ali Jan didn't own a phone or a watch. The farmer and father of seven had arrived in Darwan by donkey the night before, bunking down at the village mill owner's home. Ali had come to Darwan to collect flour, firewood and shoes for one of his children.

At Ali's own home, a mud hut on a ridge three hours away, his wife, Bibi, cooked on a small open fire. Ali's life turned not with the tick of a clock but with the seasons, the impoverished cycle of many Afghan farmers. Ali had told Bibi to expect him back by around midday, when he'd planned to eat with her and their children, but the arrival of the helicopters delayed his return. Ali instead decided to bunker down at a relative's mud-walled compound until the soldiers had departed.

As with the seasons and weather that governed Ali's life, avoiding men with guns had become an entrenched feature of his existence. As a child, he'd seen the American-armed Mujahidin drive out the Russians. The intermittent violence that flared in his country had not stopped; it was replaced by some of his own countrymen: warlords, bandits and Taliban schooled in the *madaris* over the border in Pakistan. At first, at least, the arrival of armed men to Darwan on 11 September was nothing to be too alarmed about.

As an SAS soldier pointed out much later, well after teams of federal police agents, military investigators and investigative journalists started making inquiries about that day, Ali's trip to Darwan should have been as insignificant as any dad popping out to buy some bread and milk. His was a longer journey, but just as unremarkable.

This was why Bibi initially wasn't worried when Ali didn't come home at the time he'd said he would. Lunch could be served cold and there were kids and animals to tend to. She could wait. And it's why she couldn't at first quite comprehend what had happened to her husband when she was told of his fate by Darwan villagers.

The descriptions came through in nightmarish fragments from different eyewitnesses, an unfolding horror story Bibi couldn't believe and then, later, could never forget. The villagers told her that Ali had somehow earned the ire of the biggest soldier in a patrol team, perhaps by denying the accusations hurled at him after the soldiers had entered the compound where Ali had been sipping warm tea with his nephew. Or maybe it was Ali's decision to smile that had sparked the rage of the large soldier. Perhaps the soldier had interpreted insolence and contempt in what was Ali's anxious and bewildered facial expression.

Whatever the reason, sometime after that, the Australian soldier described by locals as strikingly tall and wet from the chest down, had positioned Ali at the edge of a small cliff a few metres from his relative's compound. By this point, Ali's hands were manacled behind his back with plastic cable ties.

The soldier had taken a few steps backward. And then he had lunged at Ali. Bibi couldn't repeat what happened next to anyone without fighting off emotion.

Ali's widow wasn't alone. A member of the small SAS patrol team that had encountered her husband would suffer a similar, visceral reaction when retelling his own version of events to comrades. He could also never forget.

This Australian soldier was, like some of the villagers who had spoken to Bibi, also an eyewitness to events at the cliff's edge. His account matched the detail provided by the locals. Like them, he had seen Ali spinning over the precipice, ten metres or more down. And he'd seen Ali strike rocks, face first, teeth broken in an explosion of blood and pain.

One difference between this soldier's story and that of the villagers was that while he didn't know the name of the handcuffed Afghan, he could identify the tall, hulking figure who had kicked the prisoner. In fact, he considered the large soldier – the cliff kicker – like a brother.

He knew other things about him, too. He knew him to be Australia's most famous war hero, the most decorated soldier in the military and a man regarded by prime ministers, historians and generals as an ideal candidate to become the noble face of modern Australia at war. The big man, whom the villagers of Darwan would come to curse, was increasingly seen in his home country as the contemporary embodiment of the Anzac legend born on the beaches of Gallipoli during the Great War that, a century before, helped define a young Australia's identity.

This SAS eyewitness knew something else about his comrade. He knew the famed fighter had become accustomed to keeping dark secrets and making sure men like him stayed quiet. He knew he would be expected to cover up what had happened on the cliff edge, and in the dry creek bed below it. And he knew that if he didn't fall into line, his brother soldier would ensure there was hell to pay.

PART 1

PART 1

CHAPTER 1

A NEVER-ENDING STORM

Federal Court, New South Wales, June 2021

I felt a hand grip my shoulder and a voice whisper into my ear as I sat in the Federal Court room.

'Nick. Come with me now. Something bad has happened.'

The whisperer was Dean Levitan, a thirty-year-old media lawyer who, through a combination of timing and circumstance, had come to lead the small legal team representing myself and journalist Chris Masters in what the press had dubbed the defamation trial of the century: *Ben Roberts-Smith vs Fairfax Media Publications*, owner of my employer newspapers *The Age* of Melbourne and the *Sydney Morning Herald*.

I turned my head, and Levitan indicated that I should follow him out of the courtroom. His face looked pale and, as I noticed this, a surge of panic felt like it was twisting up my stomach. At that very moment, Ben Roberts-Smith was in the witness box, his deep and authoritative voice rebuffing question after question from our counsel that even I had to acknowledge was in a manner both impressive and believable. He'd already testified for days, with barely a trace of exhaustion or concern.

'I'm looking forward to finally setting the record straight,' he'd told a reporter before he'd first entered the witness stand. Each morning, as he'd walked into court past a throng of journalists, he radiated confidence, his suit impeccably pressed, his chin held high.

When I had caught Roberts-Smith's eye, he would coolly hold my gaze. If I cocked my eyebrow, he would do the same. This had made me wonder if Roberts-Smith was enjoying the contest unfolding in courtroom 18D and if it would destroy his reputation – or mine.

As I rose to follow Levitan out of the court, every fibre in my body was telling me that it would be the latter. If Levitan was saying that something bad had happened, it meant we were in deep trouble.

When I'd first met Dean Levitan in 2018, I'd pushed back at the suggestion from his legal firm, MinterEllison, that this 27-year-old lawyer should play a key role in a case that was not only threatening to swallow up my career but my mental health. He seemed far too junior, too inexperienced. As short as a jockey, he had a boyish face with glasses that were part hipster, part Harry Potter.

'He's very, very good,' Levitan's boss had told me. 'Give him a chance.'

Three years on, I was glad I had. He was ferociously intelligent and intensely serious. Even more, Levitan had given up his life for the Roberts-Smith case, becoming as invested in it as Chris Masters and I were. As I watched him grow, not just as a lawyer but as a human, a dynamic had emerged between us that I had not anticipated.

Three years of trial preparation had taught me that I was a natural catastrophiser. During the months and months of pre-trial research, my deep inclination to high anxiety and perfectionism had morphed into an overbearing attention to detail and unsurpassed ability to believe that every positive legal development would be enveloped by disaster.

This was probably part genetic. I'd always been an intense investigative journalist, running on a mixture of adrenalin, insecurity, passion and ideals. I was also the son of a Polish Jewish migrant whose extended family had been killed in Nazi gas chambers, and whose resting state was one of worry, a characteristic my siblings and I had inherited in rich quantity.

My working environment also fuelled the fire. My career had been a rollercoaster of exhilarating highs and debilitating lows. I'd broken stories of which I was intensely proud and that I deeply believed had helped, in tiny but tangible ways, to make our society a fairer and more just place.

But this work had also led to regular lawsuits, death threats and witch-hunts for my confidential sources. A businessman suspected by the mafia to have helped me expose the alleged bribery of politicians by Italian organised crime bosses had been murdered, prompting homicide detectives to advise that I move house. An anti-corruption official, concerned that their meeting with me had been subject to surveillance, had sent me a bunch of flowers with a greeting card that simply said: 'You are being watched by three sets of eyes. Take precautions.'

To protect those in government and defence agencies who spoke to me, I had taken to driving to distant phone boxes to make calls. Encrypted communication apps had eased this burden, but not the weight of paranoia that I was, or my sources were, being watched by those who wished for certain information to be suppressed.

My decision to investigate Ben Roberts-Smith and rumoured allegations of war crimes had sent this anxiety into overdrive. When I told my former newspaper editor that Chris Masters and I were coming close to corroborating allegations of battlefield misconduct that we believed the public deserved to know about, he'd responded: 'Do you really want to shoot Bambi?'

As I'd pressed on with my inquiries, Roberts-Smith and his team of high-powered lawyers had urged the federal police and the Department of Defence to investigate how it was that I was seemingly finding out so much about highly classified SAS missions in Afghanistan.

The decision to carefully publish stories, that at first didn't even name Roberts-Smith, had led to Masters and me being pilloried by politicians and radio shock jocks. We'd both received threats of violence from veterans who didn't know Roberts-Smith but believed our reporting amounted to a treasonous attack on the Anzac legend itself.

We had countered publicly that the concern about alleged war crimes wasn't the product of our twisted imaginations, but of hundreds of conversations with defence force insiders, including men who had served on the ground with the SAS in Afghanistan. A public relations company hired to protect Roberts-Smith had drowned out this response, briefing reporters from conservative outlets all too willing to attack us.

My anxiety had reached fever-pitch with the commencement of the trial and the realisation that our defence against the lawsuit launched by Roberts-Smith might be going south, and fast. No one outside our team of lawyers, barristers and newspaper editors knew it, but, in my mind at least, our trial preparation had been marked with setback after catastrophic setback. Key SAS witnesses had refused to cooperate. The defence department and military investigators had fought to keep critical documents secret. Our brilliant senior counsel, Sandy Dawson SC, had been diagnosed with brain cancer on the eve of the trial, prompting a mad scramble to find a replacement. There had been wins, too. We had found new and vital witnesses and documents and, on paper at least, our barristers had charted a course to victory as long as cooperating witnesses performed well and those still yet to commit showed up. But if they didn't, we were done for.

I had reacted to our growing list of problems with despondency, despair and endless exasperated calls to Levitan, during which I would urge new legal strategies, suggest ways to engage with hostile witnesses and demand to know why certain things hadn't been done quickly enough. He would respond with a calm assurance belying his age. He refused to panic, even when the news was unambiguously bad. He'd politely shut down my loopier legal suggestions and embraced the few that held promise. I'd come to appreciate Levitan in a profound way. This junior lawyer, ten years younger than me, had become a calming influence in a never-ending storm.

But at this moment Dean Levitan didn't look calm; he looked as panicked as I felt.

The news was grim. Our key witness, the man upon whom the fate of a large part of the trial would likely rise or fall, would not be coming to testify. Without this witness, we would have no chance of proving the war crime allegation at the centre of the case. The risk now looming was that Australians would in time be left with a singular, inescapable conclusion: Ben Roberts-Smith had been stitched up by the media, a war hero unjustly tarnished.

'We're fucked,' I told Levitan. 'We are totally fucked.'

The young lawyer didn't reply and I followed him out of the room and back into the court, making sure I didn't catch the eyes of Ben Roberts-Smith's parents or legal team. If they were watching me, they would surely see that something was terribly wrong. I sat back in my seat as everything in the courtroom – the lawyers, the barristers, the government officials – turned into a blur, a sea of eyes that needed avoiding.

Was I having a panic attack? I could feel sweat running down my back. I tried to write in my notebook but couldn't think of any words to put down. All I could hear was Roberts-Smith's voice, calmly dismissing each question from our counsel.

I forced myself to look at him, but immediately looked down before his gaze could meet mine. Ben Roberts-Smith sounded like a man sure that he was winning. I couldn't let him know I thought he was right.

CHAPTER 2

WHISKEY 108

Kakarak, Afghanistan, Easter Sunday 2009

Was today the day he was going to die?

Crack-thump.

Dean Tilley breathed in sharply as a bullet thudded into the ground a few metres away.

Crack-thump.

Another round came closer and his body tensed up even further.

The SAS scout had woken up as the Afghan dawn had broken a few hours earlier, splashed his face with cold water and begun preparing for an uneventful trip back to base. His SAS troop of a few dozen men had spent the night before Easter Sunday on a dry, rocky outcrop overlooking Kakarak, a typical Afghan village made up of mud-walled compounds ringed by large fields of verdant crops.

Crack-thump. Another round whizzed by.

The insurgents firing at the SAS knew what they were doing, thought Tilley. They were clearly battle-hardened, bold and well-armed.

As the Australians readied to confront them, Tilley perched on the edge of the outcrop in sniper position, scanning the crops and compounds for men who appeared and disappeared like startled ghosts. Coalition aircraft circled the sky like predatory birds looking for prey.

The SAS had been ordered to raid a likely insurgent stronghold they had named compound Whiskey 108, but one of the birds would drop their payload on this target first, a massive bomb obliterating part of the mud-walled structure in a cloud of dust, fire and smoke.

It wasn't until the light began to fade that Tilley and his fellow SAS soldiers advanced towards the damaged Taliban hideout. By then, the weather had closed in and the sky was a patchwork of greys, growing darker as the air grew thicker with drizzle.

Tilley's six-man patrol team was responsible for finding the stealthiest path to lead the other small teams of SAS fighters towards the hidden enemy. As the scout of his patrol team, Tilley would be the first man forward, the tip of the spear. It was a job the pugnacious soldier with a broad, boyish face relished. He was built like a classic old-school SAS operator: six foot and with a physical presence that belied his lithe build and mischievous grin.

Tilley strode forward in the direction of the insurgent hideout, his mind willing his body towards an enemy he'd assessed as not only formidable but willing to die for their cause. He felt a pang of fatalism, a sensation he'd felt on previous missions but which he'd usually been able to quickly counter by telling himself: *Not today*. But this feeling was different. It was sharper, more vivid.

Today, Tilley found himself thinking, *may well be the day.*

Before he could further analyse this black thought, he glimpsed an aqueduct splitting the earth between him and the target compounds ahead. Now, he focused only on gaining enough speed to make it across the lengths of rotting wood the locals had placed over the water and mud below. He leapt, one foot racing after the other, until he felt the relief of hard ground.

Glimpsing behind, he watched patrol team members follow his path and bolt across the makeshift bridge, then trained his eyes forward and strode into a poppyfield. The poppies stood tall and strong. A few metres in, Tilley realised they were also wet, a sea of upright red-tongued snakes surrounding him and soaking his uniform.

Blocking out any discomfort, he moved on to a mud-walled alleyway system next to the poppyfield until he heard a sound and froze. It was the creak of a door.

Was this the moment?

Tilley was already on one knee, rifle raised towards the opening door, his finger ready to squeeze. His eyes were focused ahead, but he sensed his comrades behind him halting, a backwards baton relay of danger and unease. The door opened wider and an Afghan walked out. Even though every cell in Tilley's body was trained on the Afghan, the man didn't notice the Australian soldier or the gun pointed at him.

Tilley counted the seconds – ten, twenty, thirty – as the Afghan walked away from him and into the poppyfield, oblivious to the shadow of death stalking him. Only then did Tilley relax his trigger finger, draw breath, stand up and stride onwards.

The poppyfield, sodden ground and drizzle mirrored the conditions in the jungle reconnaissance training Tilley had undergone years before. This was a textbook SAS operating environment for the camouflaged line of advancing soldiers, thought Tilley, as he dipped into the aqueduct. This thought didn't last either, as the sound of two shots fired from the rifle of one of his patrol team members rang out.

Tilley felt another rush of adrenalin and, with his view obscured by the aqueduct walls, he raced up the mud embankment to find his patrol team commander training his weapon in the direction of a clump of dense, twisted trees. Before Tilley could settle his breathing, machine-gun fire exploded near him and he plunged forward into the mud and grass, waiting for the pain. But there was no heat, no blood, so he popped his head up and looked behind him.

'Okay ... that is our gun,' he said to himself as he got back to his feet and continued closing in on the suspected enemy stronghold. A few feet out, he dropped again to his knee and scanned the compound walls for any openings that might allow a glimpse inside.

It was then that he noticed the very top of a man's head. It was bobbing above the wall towards a large gap that would soon bring its owner into complete view. He appeared to be carrying something. If the man exited and turned towards Tilley, he would see the Australians and possibly engage them. If he moved the opposite way, Tilley could avoid taking his life.

'Don't fucking turn our way,' Tilley whispered to himself, heart racing.

'Don't ...'

It was too late. His finger squeezed the trigger and the man fell. Tilley felt his heart pounding as he waited for the body to move, but it lay still. (Later, a communication device was found on the Afghan, indicating he was Taliban.)

Tilley calmed himself, taking up a cordon position outside Whiskey 108 as his SAS comrades moved in, guns raised. He watched them silently advancing, and wondered what was waiting for them inside. Minutes ticked by as Tilley scanned the compound perimeter, looking for any sign that could signal an attack from insurgents hiding in the surrounding fields. There was only stillness.

As the sky grew darker, Tilley's attention was drawn to three Australian soldiers. The trio were part of the assault teams that had entered Whiskey 108. For some reason, they had walked a few feet outside one of the compound walls.

As Tilley turned to observe them more clearly, he saw a dark mass being thrown towards the ground by the largest of the three Australians. As the shape hit the ground, it made a sound. It was a man exhaling, as if he'd been badly winded.

That noise was followed quickly by another, much, much louder sound. Tilley recognised it instantly. It was the burst of an Australian F89 Minimi machine gun. Before the man could rise, the soldier who had tossed him into the mud had fired into his body. Now it was Tilley who felt winded.

'What the hell?' he said to himself.

The man had been tossed by the large Australian soldier like a garbage bag, only to have his body ripped apart by bullets. The soldier who had fired was wearing distinctive camouflage paint, and was unmistakeably large, strong enough to handle a machine gun with one hand.

But it was too dark for Tilley to make out his face. He turned to another soldier within earshot.

'What the hell?' he hissed.

He walked over to the man who had been machine-gunned. Lying on his back was an unarmed Afghan with a short, dark beard, flowing robes, and a white prosthetic leg. The man's bloody, empty face confirmed to Tilley what he already knew. The man was dead.

'*What the hell?*'

The question would stay with Tilley for weeks, and then months, and then years.

As time went by, new snippets of information emerged at SAS headquarters, including a claim the dead man with the plastic leg was actually an armed insurgent who'd been shot as he'd brazenly raced towards an SAS soldier.

The fact that this story was being peddled as truth served only to underline the question he'd asked when the Minimi first erupted.

'*What the hell?*'

CHAPTER 3

TO LONDON TO MEET THE QUEEN

November 2011

Queen Elizabeth was dressed in a bright blue dress, pearls worn elegantly on her neck and ears. A photographer captured the moment as she looked up at the giant Australian soldier standing before her.

Thanks to the Queen's guest of honour, everything in the palace room appeared shrunken, including the monarch. During her reign, the Queen had seen many knights, officers and brave men of battle, but Ben Roberts-Smith was likely the tallest and widest. Standing 202 centimetres and weighing more than 100 kilograms, photos show the 33-year-old's hands clasped in front of his immaculately pressed military dress uniform, his back straight, neck arched slightly forward. His face was lean and handsome, his dark brown hair neatly cut and styled.

His jacket buckles had been polished into a glistening gold, his dress shoes shined to resemble two black mirrors. Even with the few extra centimetres the monarch gained care of her grey permed hair, she didn't quite reach

Roberts-Smith's shoulders. Yet it was the 85-year-old royal who commanded the room in Buckingham Palace, not the war hero.

Roberts-Smith's wife, Emma, standing in an adjoining waiting room, knew why, for she was feeling exactly the same as her husband at the prospect of meeting the Queen. Ben Roberts-Smith, son of a Supreme Court judge, and Emma, a Queensland girl born with few of the privileges of her husband, were both nervous. 'Shitting ourselves,' was how Emma had described it to a friend. The monarch seemed to sense it.

Back in the meeting room, the Queen dropped her handbag on a double-seated couch and motioned for Roberts-Smith to sit down. Rather than sitting opposite him, she sat right next to him, a gesture that seemed designed to relax her guest.

The two had already met a few weeks before, at the Commonwealth Heads of Government Meeting in Perth, and the Queen chatted warmly of this earlier encounter. She then moved to more serious business: the Afghan mission for which Roberts-Smith was awarded the Victoria Cross, the heroism decoration created by her great-great grandmother Queen Victoria in 1856, and the most prestigious military medal in the Commonwealth.

A palace adviser had already refreshed the Queen on the details of the SAS mission at Tizak, in the Kandahar Province of southern Afghanistan, a June 2010 operation in which Australian SAS soldiers searching for a Taliban commander had been pinned down by a machine-gun nest. Roberts-Smith's Victoria Cross citation described an 'extreme devotion to duty' paired with 'a total disregard for his own safety' as he 'stormed the enemy position killing the ... machine gunners'.

Shortly after the guns fell silent at Tizak, the shoes Roberts-Smith had worn during the battle were photographed. They told their own story. The size 15 Brooks Beast sneakers were splattered with blood, evoking the image of a man racing towards danger, risking all.

As he addressed the Queen, Roberts-Smith spoke quietly but eloquently, hitting the notes his wife knew he'd practised before. Appearing humble, he paid tribute to his SAS comrades and described the privilege and sacrifice of serving.

Eleven months before, during an earlier investiture ceremony in Australia, Roberts-Smith had also been modest and talked up his fellow SAS soldiers. 'I am so very proud to have taken part in the action with my mates,' he had said. 'This award also belongs to them.'

He used the same words with both the Queen at the palace and with the British and Australian press waiting outside. 'It obviously was a great opportunity for me to tell her about what everyone else in my patrol did that day,' Roberts-Smith told the reporters about his private audience with the Queen. 'I got to explain to her a bit of what everyone did as opposed to just myself.'

Emma watched him as he spoke. She would later tell confidantes that she instantly recognised the show her husband was putting on. It was part of something she'd described as 'the brand' – her husband's attempts to commercialise his status as a war hero, creating and enhancing the image of a man to be both loved and respected.

The notion of 'Brand BRS' was hidden from all but a very few. New friends and casual observers interacted with a man who, on paper at least, appeared not only to have it all, but to have taken life's rewards in his stride with class and composure. There was no obvious hint of insecurity or uncertainty about Roberts-Smith's public persona. And why would there be? His medal rack was heaving. In addition to his Victoria Cross and other distinctions, he also had a Medal for Gallantry in connection to a 2006 mission.

By the time Roberts-Smith arrived at Buckingham Palace, he was the father of twin baby girls and married to a beautiful, vivacious woman who had given up her career to support his ambitions. He strolled the palace grounds as one of the most decorated Afghan veterans in the Commonwealth, early steps in a journey that all but guaranteed fame and fortune back home.

Many Australians revere their military heroes and a national identity forged by the Anzac legend of the sacrifice of its underdog soldiers in World War I and the idea that 'nations and men are made in war'. Others prefer a more nuanced approach, recognising much of history has been contested, shaped by those with the power to do the telling and re-telling. Hence Brand BRS.

The man calmly answering the press pack's questions was nothing like the Roberts-Smith that 23-year-old Emma had met at an army ball in Sydney when he was a 19-year-old junior infantry soldier. Back then, Emma had encountered a chubby, self-conscious and shy young man with few close friends. At the ball, Emma's friends joked he was following her around like a puppy, something he'd do again and again in the coming weeks as he tried to convince her that he was worth a go. Her friends called it 'love bombing'. And it worked. Emma fell for the young soldier.

After she began dating him, he opened up about his life. His father, Len, was a senior Western Australian judge and high-ranking military figure who stood at the top of the

Perth establishment and who had enrolled his sons, Ben and Sam, in the Western Australian capital's top schools. He told Emma that his father was a stern patriarch who had wanted him to become an officer rather than a soldier. The elite schools he attended should have been a springboard into officer training college, but Roberts-Smith didn't find this to be an easy path. He had struggled academically, leaving one Perth college after a friend was busted with pot and achieving average grades at another, Perth's exclusive Hale School.

In the schoolyard, Roberts-Smith developed a reputation for standing over those who were smaller than him, which by his later high school years left an entire student cohort to intimidate. Those on the receiving end tell of an outsider who appeared to use his size to feel in control.

Emma would learn that, for Roberts-Smith, joining the army was all he'd really ever wanted to do, all he'd ever imagined himself doing. His was a decidedly uncomplicated, old-fashioned dream. And the army not only welcomed his size and demeanour, but offered structure and purpose.

It helped that the 3rd Royal Australian Regiment (3RAR), the infantry battalion Roberts-Smith was assigned to after basic training in 1996, was a place where bullying was rife. The eighteen-year-old thrived in this environment.

Other soldiers recount how Roberts-Smith's specialty was bastardising new recruits. Twenty-five years later, a former infantry recruit would tell journalists of being king-hit by Roberts-Smith on his first night at the 3RAR base in Townsville, as part of a twisted initiation regime.

The alleged incident contributed to the young soldier leaving the army, his dream shattered. But Roberts-Smith's journey was just beginning.

* * *

After deploying to East Timor in 1999 with 3RAR, Roberts-Smith set his sights on something bigger. His Timor postings had been formative, but he ached for action.

More than anything else, the decision to attempt to join the Special Air Service Regiment was Roberts-Smith's most significant sliding doors moment. It meant training for the gruelling selection course designed to weed out weaker, regular army soldiers from those with the mental and physical prowess to perform 'special operations like reconnaissance, strike operations, counter-terrorism and training indigenous forces', all in enemy-controlled territory and war zones.

If he hadn't been selected, Roberts-Smith may have lived the ordinary life he'd told confidants his teachers thought him destined for. Of the 150 men who would seek selection, fewer than thirty would finish, and only fifteen would be chosen by a panel of mostly grizzled SAS veterans. Roberts-Smith wanted more than anything to be in that fifteen.

He'd taken 'leave and spent three solid, solitary months training'. He considered this preparation regime the hardest he'd ever done in his life, but he wasn't going to fail. His aim was to fashion himself into the perfect soldier: exceptionally fit and strong, calm in combat, and able to endure extreme hunger, fatigue and psychological duress.

He knew the SAS selectors would be watching for any sign of weakness, any indication of whether he would break when it mattered most. When he hadn't eaten for three days and had only a smidgen of sleep in twenty-four hours, would he be the soldier who would pull his weight or let someone else carry the can?

And yet, Roberts-Smith wasn't surprised when, in 2003, he was told he'd made it.

Put simply, he'd earned it. His new military home, at Campbell Barracks in Perth, was regarded as a place for the exceptional, a fact that observers in the SAS felt appealed greatly to Roberts-Smith. His new comrades were quick to perceive in the recruit an arrogance not evident in other junior soldiers. It was as if joining the nation's most lionised military regiment wasn't so much a challenge overcome but an overdue restoration to his rightful place. They detected his simmering resentment towards life forces that had previously conspired to deny him his rightful place among the rarefied few. Finally, the military had worked out what he had always known.

Ben Roberts-Smith was special.

Those wary of the cocky corporal figured it didn't help that Roberts-Smith was assigned to the water troop. The men of the SAS specialised as either water operators, who gained expertise in amphibious missions; free-fallers, who would attack from the sky; or the vehicle-mounted troop. The 'wateries' were renowned for being the most self-assured and aggressive men in the regiment.

Some of these same observers glimpsed something Roberts-Smith couldn't or didn't want to see. It was the shadow of the high school student who never quite fitted in but didn't know why, an unspoken animus he seemed to harbour towards his early failures and unrealised potential.

Despite his best efforts, Roberts-Smith remained a divisive figure within the regiment and, outside of a small clique of mates, was increasingly considered a bully with a brittle ego, a big man somehow inflicted with 'little man syndrome'. He was one of the lads, downing beers and comparing tattoos at the boozer, but adopted his private school airs in the company of senior officers. It seemed that the real Roberts-Smith was always just out of sight. Few really knew what he stood for, beyond his own advancement. His most notable deployments to Afghanistan, those in which he'd won his major decorations, had, among many of his comrades, evoked eye rolling rather than back slapping.

Some soldiers spoke openly about the claim that his role in the 2006 battle with the Taliban for which Roberts-Smith had won his Medal for Gallantry had been aggrandised or exaggerated. Members of Roberts-Smith's own patrol team there that day confided in other soldiers that they were deeply uncomfortable about how he had conducted himself, not just on the mission but in the weeks afterwards, when the bully of old had resurfaced. The smallest member of Roberts-Smith's patrol team had seemed on the verge of tears when recounting how Roberts-Smith had threatened to shoot him in the back of his head after the pair had fallen out.

After Roberts-Smith had been awarded his Victoria Cross, but before his name had been publicly released, an article in the *Sydney Morning Herald* reported on concerns that the unnamed war hero was in fact a controversial figure in the regiment. Some argued that jealousy fuelled the negative chatter, however, the SAS's other recent Victoria Cross recipient, Mark Donaldson, had attracted none of the same ire.

All this was the backdrop to Roberts-Smith's polished Buckingham Palace performance. Given his name was now public, the meeting with Her Majesty would begin to shape the outside view of Ben Roberts-Smith. Any rumours that there was a more complicated story than that of the tall, gracious hero, beloved by his comrades and who had charmed the Queen, were yet to spread beyond the soldiers who had been there during battle.

But it wasn't just the bullying allegations that were swirling. There were secrets Roberts-Smith was keeping that even Emma wasn't privy to. One comment he'd sometimes make would cause her to wonder aloud to friends about what her husband wasn't telling her.

'You know I'm going to be famous,' he had told her. 'Or if not famous, I'm going to be infamous.'

CHAPTER 4

PREMEDITATION

Lancelin Training Facility, March 2012

'What's the John Dory?' The troop sergeant with a fondness for rhyming slang climbed to the top of a shipping container to query a mate about the training scenario about to play out below. Sergeant Boyd Keary was told it was a prisoner-handling exercise. 'Good as gold,' he said as he took up his position.

Eleven years into the Afghanistan conflict, mission rehearsal training could often seem as arduous as the mission itself. For five months a squadron would practise: live fire, helicopter insertion, dog-handling, detention management, drill after drill, at the massive Cultana complex in South Australia, set up as a mini-Afghanistan, and at Lancelin, the heavy weapons facility north of Perth.

For Australia and the coalition partners ensnared in the war in Afghanistan, detention management had become a hot-button issue. Rough handling of anyone detained and locking up Afghans for no proven reason was hardly the way to win hearts and minds, and procedures were now in place to ensure humane treatment and collection of evidence to decide if a prisoner was an innocent farmer or a committed Taliban warrior.

Those procedures were meant to be practised on days such as this.

A few metres below Keary, Corporal Ben Roberts-Smith was bedding in his new hand-picked patrol team, the soldiers who would accompany him to Afghanistan on rotation number 18. Keary had completed SAS selection in 2001, two years ahead of Ben Roberts-Smith, but the pair were far from close.

To anyone who would ask, Roberts-Smith said that Keary, who was about to chalk up his eleventh deployment to Afghanistan, was jealous of his success. The young corporal despised the older soldier's quiet confidence and self-resolve. Keary had never wanted to be popular, caring more for soldiering than socialising, a focus that many blokes on the base respected him for.

In contrast, Roberts-Smith appeared eager to be admired, which made some of his fellow soldiers wary. Keary had Roberts-Smith pegged as a vicious bully after he'd joined Keary's sabre squadron in 2010 and they'd deployed to Afghanistan together. Before that, he'd heard the whispers that Roberts-Smith threatened smaller soldiers and was a big-noting and blustering presence. But they were only rumours until Keary saw the way he used his size and strength on a mission in the Deh Rafshan area of Oruzgan.

There, Keary and an SAS colleague had been trying to handcuff an unarmed Afghan in a compound when Roberts-Smith unexpectedly strode in. The Afghan wasn't threatening Keary or his comrade. Rather, the man was in the foetal position, terrified and whimpering. Keary was giving the Afghan a moment to calm down, when

Roberts-Smith launched into him, punching the Afghan three or four times in the side of the head with fists covered in Kevlar gloves. He'd then kneed the man twice in the guts.

A stunned Keary had barked at Roberts-Smith: 'Woah, woah, woah, what are you doing? We're looking after this. Get out of here.'

The Afghan's face began to swell and turn purple. Keary watched Roberts-Smith leave without uttering a word.

His respect for Roberts-Smith plummeted after this incident, but it was his lack of care and attention to the junior soldiers in his patrol team that had begun occupying Keary's thoughts in early 2012. Rotation 18 was to be Roberts-Smith's first tour as a patrol commander, and members of his patrol team were new to the regiment; one had no Afghanistan experience.

In Keary's mind, Roberts-Smith should have been training his soldiers, but instead he was attending to his Victoria Cross duties. His patrol team were often training without the man who would lead them on the ground. This wasn't how things should be done.

Keary had heard enough disquiet about the 2006 Medal for Gallantry action from others in the SAS to harbour serious doubts about the war stories built around Ben Roberts-Smith.

Both men had fought at the famous battle of Tizak in 2010, the fight that had seen the Victoria Cross bestowed on Roberts-Smith. Both Keary and Roberts-Smith fought bravely, at close quarters. Both had killed their enemy. The fact that Roberts-Smith and his team came away with the medals would later be seen by some as a root cause of envy that in turn fuelled untrue stories about Roberts-Smith. Others would say there was no jealousy, only anger at a false narrative surrounding an undeserving hero.

But, in the lead-up to rotation 18, for now at least, differences between the pair were at simmer rather than boiling point. Keary and Roberts-Smith were still getting on, if only just.

The year before, Keary had joined Roberts-Smith on a speaking tour to different military facilities to recount the Tizak battle to groups of soldiers.

Roberts-Smith had asked Keary to accompany him, and he'd done so begrudgingly, recognising that if they were to again fight together, they would need to put up with each other. So on this day at the Lancelin training facility, Keary was not expecting drama. But then, from his elevated vantage point on the shipping container, his attention was suddenly drawn to a command issued by Roberts-Smith.

'Fucking kill him,' he heard Roberts-Smith order.

Keary, alarmed, looked towards Roberts-Smith's patrol team.

They were assembled in a courtyard designed to replicate a typical Afghan compound. An SAS soldier, role-playing as a prisoner, was on his knees facing a wall. Roberts-Smith and several of his subordinates stood in a semi-circle around him, armed with M4 assault rifles.

The order to kill the pretend prisoner was directed towards the most junior soldier in Roberts-Smith's patrol team and it was momentarily stunning, not just to Keary but also to the rookie. Keary saw the soldier hesitate, confused. The manacled SAS soldier playing the 'prisoner' twitched.

'Shoot him,' Roberts-Smith repeated.

Perplexed, but beginning to catch on, the young trooper pretended to carry out the order.

'Bang, bang,' he said.

Even from a distance, Keary sensed the fake prisoner's relief as Roberts-Smith placed his hand on the rookie soldier's shoulder.

'Are you good with that? Because that's how it's going to be when we get over there,' Roberts-Smith told the young trooper.

To no one in particular, Sergeant Keary fumed.

'Geez, he's a fucking idiot.'

After climbing down from the container, Keary went looking for Corporal Ben Roberts-Smith VC, MG. As Troop Sergeant, he had oversight of the patrol commanders. Keary was not one to stand in awe of the uber alphas in Roberts-Smith's water troop.

At a nearby carpark, he caught up with Roberts-Smith. 'Hey, RS, you got a second?' Roberts-Smith appeared annoyed to be stopped. They came face to face.

'What was that shit all about?'

'What shit?'

'You know what shit I'm talking about. Pull your head in. Grow up and wake up to yourself.'

Roberts-Smith turned and walked towards his car.

As he did, Keary heard him mutter something under his breath.

The only words he caught were: 'fucking war'.

CHAPTER 5

A WOLF IN SHEEP'S CLOTHING

Village of Darwan, Southern Afghanistan, September 2012

Even before the mission on 11 September 2012 had begun, the soldiers of the SAS appeared more animated than usual. There was a palpable intensity, a human-generated electricity, in the air. The men in Boyd Keary's patrol team felt it; so did some of those in Ben Roberts-Smith's four-man team.

They were hunting a killer, but not just any killer. A wolf in sheep's clothing. A fortnight earlier, an Afghan partner force soldier who was meant to be willing to die alongside his Western allies, had turned his weapon onto Australian soldiers as they played cards at patrol base Wahib, north of Tarin Kowt.

The base was ringed by barbed wire and sandbagged concrete walls, designed to make it one of the few places a coalition soldier could drop their guard within the badlands of the country's south. The enemy, however, was lurking within.

Sergeant Hekmatullah was a Taliban operative in disguise, the ultimate symbol of the problem facing Australian soldiers, be they SAS or regular army. In Afghanistan, differentiating between friend and foe, farmer and jihadi, was often impossible. After eating, training, fighting and shitting alongside his Australian compatriots, Hekmatullah drew his M16 and fired more than thirty rounds from close range at Australian troops, killing three of them: Lance Corporal Stjepan Milosevic, forty; Sapper James Martin, twenty-one; and Private Robert Poate, twenty-three.

Hekmatullah had then escaped the base and rendezvoused with the Taliban, who spirited him into the Afghan wilderness. He was now Australia's enemy number one.

Yet, in the days after he fled, Hekmatullah had remained beyond the reach of the eavesdropping satellites and drones the Australian military had mustered to help find their quarry. Pressure on the Australian Defence Force was building.

In Canberra, the sombre-faced Australian Prime Minister, Julia Gillard, and the Chief of the Defence Force, David Hurley, had vowed justice would be done.

The SAS soldiers needed no inspiration from political or military top brass. Hekmatullah's blood-soaked betrayal was motivation enough.

* * *

Mohammed Hanifa Fatih was on his knees praying softly when he heard a deep vibrating noise in the air growing louder and louder. Looking up, he spotted military helicopters heading towards his village.

The sight spelled trouble. He had begun his morning in the village of Darwan with no more apprehension than the day before. The almond trees and corn crops were well watered and healthy, and his uncle, Ali Jan, had arrived the previous evening from his home in the nearby village of Baag and spent the night at the home of the local mill owner. Hanifa planned to accompany Ali to the mountains with donkeys to gather firewood after morning prayers.

Like Hanifa, Ali was lean and deeply tanned from a life spent in the elements. Both men were fathers who eked out a meagre existence from farming and foraging, and who regarded the Taliban as suspiciously as Western soldiers. For Afghanistan's dirt-poor farmers, nothing good had ever come of men with guns.

Hanifa quickly rolled up his prayer mat and, as three of the helicopters landed nearby and men in fatigues with guns spilled out, he watched his neighbours gathering nervously. They all knew a wrong move during a raid could mean death. Days before, a man had arrived in Darwan bearing pamphlets that promised a reward for information about a bearded Afghan National Army soldier with a name and face Hanifa didn't recognise: Hekmatullah. Perhaps it was him the choppers were looking for?

Before Hanifa made his own move, Ali appeared, leading a donkey draped with a rug of deep red, with another donkey a few feet ahead of him.

'Quick ... let's head to the mountains now,' Hanifa said to his uncle, believing the soldiers would ignore a pair of nomads. Hanifa, Ali and the two donkeys had travelled about 100 metres when a bullet struck the ground near them. Hanifa froze.

'We must go back.'

The pair turned the donkeys around and, somewhere between a walk and a run, headed towards a guesthouse Hanifa shared with a neighbour, Man Gul. It was one of several mud-and-wood structures comprising the furthest compound on a ridge on which sat a series of other homes and which overlooked a dry creek bed. To move too fast would invite suspicion, but to walk too slowly, more bullets.

As he drew close to the guesthouse, Hanifa yelled at his daughters to help tie up the donkeys. He and Ali were then joined by Man Gul and the trio sat together on a colourful, faded carpet, hands clasped around small, steaming cups. As the heat of the tea warmed Hanifa's skin, he willed time to pass and for the foreign men with guns to disappear.

As Hanifa waited nervously, so too did the second-in-command of the patrol team led by Ben Roberts-Smith on the other side of the village. Despite being his deputy, Jason Andrews was older than Roberts-Smith, having been in the army for more than two decades. Andrews had joined the SAS several years after his younger colleague and deployed to Afghanistan for the first time in 2009, three years after Roberts-Smith's first Afghan trip.

Andrews was quieter and more considered than his patrol commander, more naturally inclined to follow rather than lead. He was also kinder, quicker to laugh and more popular. As a result, he was often torn between loyalty to Roberts-Smith and his own desire to cultivate quiet friendships with those in the SAS he knew disliked and distrusted the war hero.

Andrews' connection with Roberts-Smith extended well beyond his role as his patrol team second-in-command in 2012, or the fact the pair had almost died together in the famous battle of Tizak two years earlier. Andrews had received a Medal for Gallantry for his actions that day, a decoration not as prestigious as Roberts-Smith's Victoria Cross but significant nevertheless. The pair's bond was a brotherhood forged not just through their shared valour and war experience, but also with secrets and shame.

As Andrews waited that day in Darwan, surveying the Helmand River and the rocky embankment on the other side, more than three years had passed since the SAS mission on Easter Sunday 2009.

Andrews knew what had really gone down that day, when the Afghan with a prosthetic leg had been machine-gunned near compound Whiskey 108. Andrews didn't just know it. It was burned into his brain.

Now, on the banks of the Helmand forty-two months and many missions later, Andrews was waiting for Roberts-Smith to reappear. Each passing second was longer than the one before. Minutes earlier, Roberts-Smith had waded across the river, emerging soaking wet as he chased down a 'squirter', a suspected insurgent who had raced away from the Australian soldiers and hidden behind some large rocks.

Roberts-Smith had disappeared too. He had no other soldiers to back him up, having ventured across the Helmand alone, a decision some of the soldiers watching believed foolhardy, but others thought brave. The bolter could have been Hekmatullah, and Roberts-Smith obviously thought it a risk worth taking.

As he re-emerged from the boulders, Roberts-Smith lifted up a limp body for his deputy to photograph from his vantage point on the opposite bank. No one witnessed the exact circumstances of the Afghan's death except Roberts-Smith, but Andrews noted the man was armed with an AK-47 and a radio, the hallmarks of a Taliban fighter. Under the rules of engagement, soldiers were allowed to use lethal force against Afghans who posed a serious risk

to Australian lives. In certain circumstances, a man with
a radio alone could be lawfully engaged due to the risk he
could communicate with insurgents and call in an attack.
Because of what the bolter carried, he was a legitimate kill.
But he wasn't Hekmatullah.

The SAS's target was still a ghost. As a wet Roberts-
Smith, Andrews and their two subordinate patrol team
members moved westward along a ridge dotted with
compounds and which overlooked a dry creek bed, Boyd
Keary's patrol team was corralling scowling, handcuffed
Afghans. Since landing in Darwan that morning, the
SAS had swept through most of the village, arresting
several dozen men. As each man was briefly examined,
disappointment grew. Hekmatullah was nowhere to be
found.

Andrews and Roberts-Smith's destination was one of
the few areas not yet searched: a compound cluster on the
end of the ridge. The pair's patrol team headed towards it,
along with a translator and dog handler.

As his team drew nearer, Andrews thought little about
the Afghans they found waiting. He simply clocked some
bearded men, including an Afghan near a donkey draped
in a red blanket. Their presence was unremarkable, a few
more village men to be detained and grilled.

Hanifa's reaction was different. He was scared. He
called his daughters over, hoping the foreigners might
go easier on them if children were nearby. To Hanifa,
Andrews could not be differentiated from the other
fearsome-looking fighters in identical uniforms. But one of
the soldiers stood out.

Hanifa's gaze locked on a huge man who moved with
aggression and purpose. Within seconds, Hanifa felt a hand
grab his neck and push his head into a mud wall. As pain

shot through him, a military dog lunged at his daughter. She raced towards her father, and Hanifa shielded her with his body, protecting her from the men with paint-smeared faces and their snarling animal.

Ali Jan was also surrounded, his jacket and turban ripped off, his hands bound behind his back. Hanifa felt plastic cuffs gripping his wrists as he was pushed towards a nearby compound wall and lined up next to Ali and Man Gul, who was also handcuffed.

Andrews stood a few feet away. As second-in-charge of the patrol team, his focus wasn't on the detainees but on detecting any threat in the area surrounding the compound. He scanned but saw nothing.

It was becoming clear that if Hekmatullah had been in Darwan, and that was by no means certain, he was long gone. This didn't stop Roberts-Smith from trying to extract a fresh lead. As patrol commander, his responsibility was on the new detainees. Hanifa watched the giant soldier, wet and covered in river sand, as he barked questions in a foreign language, his anger palpable. Alongside the soldier was his interpreter, a wild-eyed young Afghan with a scrappy mullet haircut, an American accent and dressed in the same Australian military fatigues worn by the other soldiers. As the large soldier's fury grew, it was mimicked by the interpreter translating his questions.

'Where is Hekmatullah? Are you Taliban?'

Hanifa's protestations that he knew no one called Hekmatullah and was no friend of the Taliban further enraged the big blue-eyed soldier and his Pashto mouthpiece. Hanifa saw a flash of the pistol in the interpreter's hand, then felt it pressed into his head.

'Show me Hekmatullah, or I will shoot you,' the interpreter hissed.

As the pistol smashed into the side of his head, Hanifa felt another searing bolt of pain.

Now the questioning of Hanifa focused on Ali Jan. What did his uncle do for a job? Was he Taliban? His answers brought no respite. With every response, the large soldier punched him in the head.

Whack. Whack. Whack.

The soldier then turned to Ali, yelling at Hanifa's uncle in English as the interpreter translated. The answers again failed to please the interrogators, who kept hurling questions, as if asking with more force could somehow conjure up a fugitive who neither men knew.

Instead, it led to something no one expected. Whether through terror, exhaustion or defiance, Ali stared at the tall Australian soldier and smiled.

'Ya Allah,' Hanifa whispered to himself, watching on in terror as the soldier turned incandescent.

Several metres away, Andrews turned his attention back towards the compound where the Afghan detainees were being interrogated. He had moved from his earlier position and now had a clear view of the small cliff on which the compound sat. Andrews watched as one of the handcuffed Afghans was marched to its edge. He recognised the detainee as the man he'd earlier seen near the donkey. The donkey man now stood facing Roberts-Smith, who had in turn walked maybe 3 to 4 metres away from his prisoner.

Another member of Andrews' patrol team was holding the man by his shoulder, preventing him from moving. What the hell was going on?

The thought was answered with action. Roberts-Smith spun around, strode forward and kicked the man square in the chest with the power of a stomp designed to break a length of thick wood.

Andrews watched in horror, his mouth dry and heart racing, as the Afghan catapulted backwards, off the edge of the ridge and down the slope. As he fell, Andrews saw the man's face strike a large rock.

Reeling with confusion and shock, Andrews found himself numbly following Roberts-Smith and the second soldier down a goat track to the bottom of the small cliff where the donkey man was lying. His face was disfigured, teeth shattered, and he was covered in dust and blood.

As Andrews approached him, the man attempted to sit up, only to fall back down again.

'Drag him,' Roberts-Smith said to Andrews.

Andrews followed the order, helped by a second member of his patrol team as Roberts-Smith looked on. The pair pulled the detainee towards a large tree, his arms still handcuffed behind him. At the base of the tree, the man gingerly tried to stand again. He managed to get upright. He looked like a lone, thin river reed making a futile stand as a flood rolled towards him.

Andrews looked away. He did not want to see what he thought would happen next, but he heard it nevertheless. A number of shots were fired in quick succession. It was the sound of Australian M4 rifles.

When he looked back, the donkey man was lying on the ground.

'Get the camera,' Roberts-Smith told Andrews. 'We need to take some photos.'

As the other patrol member photographed the body, Andrews noticed two things. The dead man's handcuffs had been removed and a radio had been placed near his body. Its screen was fogged up with water. It was the radio that Roberts-Smith had found on the Taliban insurgent across the river, thought Andrews.

It was a 'throw down': the term for items that soldiers plant on people they have executed. The Afghan was now lying dead in a fake crime scene designed to make it appear he was an insurgent killed to prevent him calling in a Taliban ambush.

Roberts-Smith spoke into his radio to the other SAS patrols: 'One enemy, KIA.' The cover-up was almost complete.

Andrews knew that Roberts-Smith's version of events would likely go unchallenged. As a general rule, the men of the SAS, even if they encountered things that made them feel uncomfortable or suspicious, didn't ask questions, and certainly not of the soldiers responsible.

In the more than three years since the Easter Sunday 2009 mission, no one in command had challenged the story invented by Roberts-Smith and repeated by Andrews. No one had asked him about the handcuffs placed on two men detained in the compound Whiskey 108, only to be removed once they were shot dead.

No one had asked Andrews about his own role in ending one of those two lives, that of an older Afghan who'd been detained alongside a man with a prosthetic leg after the pair were discovered hiding in a tunnel. No one had asked him about the throw downs.

No one had asked him anything.

A similar cover story was now forming about the dead man in Darwan, a fable of an enemy threatening the lives of brave Australians.

But there were exceptions to this unwritten ask-no-questions policy. Boyd Keary wasn't on the Easter Sunday mission with Roberts-Smith and Andrews, but he was standing a few hundred metres away at Darwan when Roberts-Smith's voice entered his earpiece and transmitted the news an enemy soldier had been killed in action.

Keary had a lot of questions.

The Darwan mission was minutes from ending, the helicopters on their way to pull the Australians out. Yet none of the circling aircraft or other SAS patrols had spotted the mysterious enemy soldier Roberts-Smith was claiming as a EKIA.

What were the chances of an enemy appearing hours after the SAS had swept through the village and were preparing to depart? Had the helicopters' thermal scanners missed an armed insurgent hiding in a cornfield just metres from one of the helicopter extraction sites?

* * *

Hanifa waited until he saw the soldiers racing towards their helicopters before he dared to move. He asked a neighbour's daughter to cut off his plastic cuffs then raced down the goat track towards the dry creek bed, where he followed a trail of blood to a large tree. Ali lay at its base. As Hanifa leaned over his body, he heard women sobbing. Ali's front teeth were missing, his eyes lifeless.

Hanifa noticed his uncle's cuffs had been removed. He knew why. The soldiers had tried to cover up the death of a man whose only crime may have been to smile at the wrong time. He tried to brush the dust and blood off Ali's face, but if it was a gesture aimed at restoring some hint of life, it was pointless.

Still, he kept at it. As he did, he heard someone telling one of the children to run to the village of Baag. The child's job was to tell Bibi that her husband, the father of their children, was never coming home.

CHAPTER 6

SUPERMAN

Late August 2013

It is quite the title: Father of the Year.

Corporal Ben Roberts-Smith might have been the most decorated Afghan veteran in Australia, but being named the nation's best dad rounded out the war hero's public persona. Here was a man who it seemed could do it all.

Australia's former defence minister Brendan Nelson had first encountered Roberts-Smith in late 2006. Back then, Nelson was the minister reviewing citations for soldiers nominated for decorations. He had been captivated as he'd read the description of Roberts-Smith fighting the Taliban atop a barren mountain range. According to the official military record, Roberts-Smith had put his own life on the line to help save his fellow soldiers.

The citation described the Corporal acting with *'courage, tenacity and sense of duty to his patrol'* while *'under heavy Anti Coalition Militia fire and in a precarious position, threatened by a numerically superior force'*. Nelson read it a second time and then a third, and with each rereading he found himself further confronted by the notion that a man could be so courageous.

It wasn't just courage. To Nelson's thinking, Roberts-Smith had class. This view had been reinforced five years later, when Nelson met Roberts-Smith after the soldier's trip to Buckingham Palace. At the time, Nelson was serving as Australia's ambassador to the European Union and the North Atlantic Treaty Organization (NATO) and he'd taken Roberts-Smith on a tour of Flanders, the Belgium region whose fields were soaked with the blood of young Australians killed during the Great War.

He had later been deeply touched when he'd received a card from Roberts-Smith. Roberts-Smith had written that of all the things he had done on his overseas trip, including meeting the Queen, the most moving and meaningful was the time he spent in Flanders.

After Nelson was appointed in late 2012 to run the Australian War Memorial, he championed the 34-year-old as the poster boy of the nation's modern military. Nelson saw in the towering soldier a figure he believed would inspire all Australians, a man with qualities that parents would encourage their 'children to strive towards'.

This character judgment firmed after he observed Roberts-Smith profoundly move audiences at war memorial events. Strangers would ask him for a photo, or to simply shake his hand, but others, mostly veterans, would fall into his arms, emotionally describing their experiences of war.

Nelson had felt it fitting when Roberts-Smith was named Father of the Year by the Shepherd Centre, a non-government organisation for deaf children set up by Nelson's political mentor, Bruce Shepherd. Nelson was a member of the Shepherd Centre's board of patrons.

Super soldier. Super father. Superman. And everyone who visited the war memorial should know it.

When Nelson first arrived at the hallowed complex as its new boss, he had asked out loud: 'When are we going to present Afghanistan?'

Preserving and extolling the foundational touchstone of Australian identity – the Anzac legend forged on the beaches of Gallipoli in 1915 – was at the memorial's core. The sombre halls and spaces echoed with spirit and memory, the ghosts of those who died long ago 'on some hill-top still, beautiful, gleaming white and silent'.

Guides would tell school groups, tourists and visitors that while the Gallipoli campaign failed militarily, the Australian soldiers' display of 'courage, endurance and mateship' had helped to define the very essence of what it was to be Australian.

Yet the centre was also meant to teach its visitors about modern military service. Equally brave Australians were still fighting and dying in Afghanistan. Far fewer diggers had died there – 41 compared to 62,000 in the Great War – and the Afghan War was being fought by professional soldiers rather than volunteers. But Australia also needed to acknowledge its modern military heroes, the contemporary representations of the Anzac legend who could inspire future generations.

That the Afghan conflict was mired in political controversy, a symbol of the strategic miscalculations of America and its allies, didn't matter. Politics wasn't the concern of the soldier. Roberts-Smith stood for individual service and sacrifice and the notion that a digger would risk their life for their mates, whatever the debate back in Canberra.

When Nelson asked the memorial's staff why there wasn't a greater focus on Afghanistan, they told him it would be a few more years before the conflict would be told in detail.

A few years?

'We're doing it now,' he told them. Nelson saw his job as educating Australians about what had been done in their name recently, not just in the wars of old.

In Roberts-Smith, Nelson had found the perfect teacher. Tall, broad, strong and humble. Victoria Cross. Medal for Gallantry. Commendation for Distinguished Service. And now, the dad of three-year-old twin girls was the nation's Father of the Year. The press lapped up this bookend to a perfect story.

New Idea gushed about the 'modest' war hero who informed their reporter he was 'just an everyday Aussie bloke'. Roberts-Smith told the Murdoch tabloids he was accepting the award on behalf of all the parents who had served in the military, 'so that other families in Australia can live in safety'.

If anyone had suggested to Nelson that Ben Roberts-Smith's family or war history was more complicated, it is fair to say that he would not have believed them.

* * *

Among those who knew the Ben Roberts-Smith not manicured for public consumption, the news of him winning the title of Australia's best dad sparked a markedly different reaction from that of Brendan Nelson. Emma's friends' phones had begun buzzing with the reports of the award.

Some had thought the gong was a bad joke.

'Father of the year. No friggin' way,' was the general theme.

A number of Emma's friends considered Roberts-Smith a frequently shitty husband whose hands-off parenting was hardly father-of-the-year material.

Emma had confided in her mates that much of her marriage had been a struggle. They had wed in 2003, the same year Roberts-Smith joined the SAS and, ever since the move to Perth and her decision to put her blossoming career in marketing on hold, things had changed. Everything was about Roberts-Smith's ambitions. Emma had been slowly wilting in his shadow while his career had grown bigger and bigger.

There had been some bleak times, including a period when Emma had separated from Roberts-Smith and lived with her best friend, the wife of a veteran SAS soldier nicknamed Turtle. The separation didn't last long.

There was also an added pressure. For seven years they had tried to have children.

In 2006, after Emma had fallen pregnant, she had almost died after an undetected ectopic pregnancy caused a catastrophic haemorrhage. This was the year Roberts-Smith was on his first tour of Afghanistan and was subsequently awarded the Medal for Gallantry for his bravery on a mountain ridge far from home.

For most of the pregnancy that would produce the twins, he had been fighting overseas. It was the lot of most army wives, but at least some of them felt cherished when their partners came back home. This wasn't the case for Emma. Her friends would instead see her endure snide comments and sneers.

When she'd put on weight during IVF treatment, Roberts-Smith would tell her she was fat. 'Lucky you've got a nice face,' he'd say.

A tiff would end with a put-down – you're really fucking stupid – followed by hours of the silent treatment.

The birth of their daughters in 2010 was a blessing and Turtle's wife became godmother to the girls. A year later, the Victoria Cross, and the prospect that Roberts-Smith would quit the army and hit the lucrative speakers' circuit, held the promise that the family's finances could balloon. After taking long service leave in late 2012, Roberts-Smith had begun fielding inquiries from corporates prepared to pay up to $20,000 to hear from the war hero.

But the promise of fortune hadn't brought happiness on the home front. Emma's friends learned that Roberts-Smith was becoming paranoid and controlling. After he found out that Turtle had taken the side of a junior soldier who'd accused Roberts-Smith of bullying after the 2006 operation in which he'd received the Medal for Gallantry, he'd demanded Emma cut ties with Turtle's wife. She agreed without a fight. His new-found fame had also led to admirers frequently approaching Roberts-Smith in public, but he told Emma and her friends he loathed having to make conversation with these well-wishers. His fans weren't in his league, he'd say.

Emma told confidantes she was worried about the man her husband had become. She stayed in the marriage for family and loyalty rather than love.

* * *

Nelson knew little of the true inner workings of Roberts-Smith's private life. He'd met Emma at various events and found her delightful and charming, an ever-gorgeous and supportive army wife.

All his interactions gave Nelson confidence that the Victoria Cross recipient was the right choice to help Australia's premier war museum speak to the nation about its modern Anzac heroes. Roberts-Smith started appearing at event after event. He'd been the war memorial's ambassador for the Anzac Day celebration in April 2013. An enormous and striking painting of him was nearly finished and Nelson had plans to place it centre-stage at the museum. One commentator even mused that if the museum was to name its mascot, it would be Ben Roberts-Smith, VC.

But this was a mutually beneficial relationship. The war memorial would help transform Roberts-Smith's life, and not just because of the role Nelson had envisaged for him. The memorial's most powerful benefactor had also taken an interest in the tall soldier. If Roberts-Smith had a bigger fan than Nelson, it was the memorial's chairman, Kerry Stokes. The billionaire media mogul would help propel the Victoria Cross recipient up the ladder of Australian business and society. And, unsurprisingly, Ben Roberts-Smith seized the opportunities that came his way. If he could excel in the dust and blood of Oruzgan, there was no telling how far he could rise in the ruthless world of Australia's media industry.

CHAPTER 7

DISCLOSURE

Campbell Barracks, Swanbourne, Perth, 2013

Nothing had sat right for Sergeant Boyd Keary since the mission to the village of Darwan months before. He had an awkward feeling about the last shooting that day, the Enemy Killed in Action of the man whose bloodied body lay under a tree, but not much else to go on. That was until Keary bumped into another SAS sergeant, who recounted the most unbelievable story. The sergeant, an affable soldier called Brian McMurray, knew Roberts-Smith well, as the pair had served in the same patrol team in 2009 and 2010.

Unlike Keary, whose growing antipathy towards Roberts-Smith was well known throughout the SAS, McMurray was friendly with the towering soldier. He was even closer with Jason Andrews, who'd served as the second-in-command of Roberts-Smith's patrol team in 2012, including at Darwan. It was a disclosure by Andrews that McMurray wanted to talk about.

'Andrews reckons RS kicked a prisoner off a cliff,' said McMurray.

His friendship with Roberts-Smith and Andrews made it unlikely McMurray would be bullshitting. Still, Keary asked McMurray to repeat himself, so he did.

'Andrews said he watched the bloke fall. Even saw his teeth come out,' McMurray said.

No bloody way. There was no way in hell Roberts-Smith had kicked a prisoner off a cliff, Keary thought. McMurray saw the incredulity on Keary's face.

'That's what Andrews said. You don't believe me, ask Andrews yourself.'

Rightio, Keary thought. *I bloody well will.*

Keary had joined the Army in 1994 after reading an Anzac Day newspaper supplement that included an account by a German soldier of Australians who had fought at Tobruk. The story caught his imagination. The German spoke of being in terror of bayonet-wielding Australian soldiers who appeared merciless. But having been wounded himself and lying helpless, he told of an Australian crawling up to him, applying first aid and effectively saving his life.

On an early deployment to Afghanistan, when Keary came upon a wounded Taliban fighter, he pulled out his medical kit and did the same as that long-ago Anzac.

In Afghanistan, Keary could sometimes be overheard counselling his men. 'We are not Genghis Khan's raiders; we are Australian soldiers.'

But Keary didn't go around judging tough blokes doing a job that needed tough blokes. He hadn't reported Roberts-Smith for bashing the Afghan prisoner in 2010, even though it had made him deeply uncomfortable.

Keary knew that war is ugly. If his eleven deployments to Afghanistan had taught him anything, it was that.

The job of the SAS was to capture or kill, provided it was done within the rules of engagement. Hundreds of

Taliban insurgents had ended up on formal capture or kill lists, and many of them had rightly been taken out. Keary was no squib when it came to killing by the book. But even those marked for jail or death couldn't be kicked off a bloody cliff. That was a bridge too far.

Keary would later wonder about a comment Roberts-Smith had made shortly before their first mission on the 2012 deployment. An SAS comrade had just been killed and Roberts-Smith had approached Keary, saying, 'Hey mate … I'm going to talk the talk. I want you to make sure I walk the walk. Before this trip's over, I'm going to choke a man to death with my bare hands. I'm going to watch the life drain out of his eyes.'

Maybe, instead of choking someone, he would take inspiration from the Spartan war movie *300*, which includes a scene involving a fearsome warrior kicking a man over the edge of a pit.

Keary spotted Andrews in the barracks and walked briskly up to him. 'Hey, mate. I've got a question,' he said.

Andrews looked at him: 'Yep.'

'Did RS kick a bloke off a cliff?'

'Yeah, bro.'

Keary listened as Andrews quietly explained what he'd witnessed at Darwan, near the end of the mission. He recounted how Roberts-Smith had kicked a man with his hands bound behind his back off a steep ridge and how Andrews had felt a wave of panic as the Afghan man's head hit a rock and some of his teeth flew out.

It was in that moment, Andrews told Keary, he realised he had to get out of Roberts-Smith's patrol team. Keary looked at Andrews square in the face, speaking slowly and forcefully.

'This is a very serious allegation that you're making here. Is this 100 per cent accurate? Are you telling the truth?' Keary asked the question twice.

Each time, Andrews responded: 'Yeah, bro. I am.'

This couldn't rest, thought Keary. Someone up the line had to be told.

'We're going to take this somewhere. This just can't be left here,' he told Andrews.

This time, Andrews said nothing. His face appeared worn out and weathered as he looked at Keary and nodded.

CHAPTER 8

MEMORIES AND MEDIATION

November 2013

In the quiet before the spring dawn broke, Roberts-Smith woke at 3am. Lying in his bed in his new Brisbane home, a feeling of fear invaded his body. Perhaps his unease was due to his decision to announce he was quitting the SAS, but that didn't quite explain it. On the surface, his future looked bright, in the finance and business departments at least.

He'd been working on a documentary with the Seven Network about the Victoria Cross recipients, *The Power of Ten*, that had drawn him closer not just to Brendan Nelson but to Kerry Stokes, the war memorial chairman and owner of Seven West Media, the company that owned both Seven and the *West Australian* newspaper.

Roberts-Smith had met Stokes in 2011 when he and another SAS Victoria Cross recipient, Mark Donaldson, attended the relaunch of the Australian War Memorial's Hall of Valour. The Hall displayed sixty-seven Australian VCs, of which at least seven had been purchased and donated by Stokes, at an estimated cost of $14 million.

It appeared that Stokes was at one with Nelson on the glorification of Roberts-Smith. Stokes' previous VC medals belonged to men who had died. In Roberts-Smith, he had access to the life-size thing, in flesh and blood.

After meeting the two VC recipients, Stokes had met again with Roberts-Smith in Perth and discussed potential job opportunities within his business empire.

The Power of Ten documentary had been conceived as a stunning television event, depicting Roberts-Smith as the humble legend paying tribute to his own heroes: the ten Anzac soldiers who'd won a VC during the Great War. The film was going to cost Seven a fortune, but it would most likely resonate with the one person who mattered: Stokes. The network would build a replica Anzac trench system, hire actors to play the Anzac soldiers and fly Roberts-Smith around the world to retrace the VC winners' stories.

If the documentary was primarily about the Anzac VCs, it was also about Roberts-Smith. In telling the stories of long-dead soldiers, he'd embarked on a personal quest to find out how other heroes had displayed such incredible bravery. Like much in the ex-soldier's life, it all came back to him.

The program wasn't the only major development for Brand BRS. His company, the RS Group Australia, was taking off, not least because other companies were now lining up to hear him talk.

He'd signed off on his speakers' circuit biography, one of the few arenas he could shelve modesty without fearing judgment. If groups of CEOs and surgeons were going to fork out to hear him speak, it wasn't just a hero they would be paying for, but a leader who could 'manage by example and motivate high-performing and diverse teams to respond effectively to complex and high-pressure situations'.

In September, Roberts-Smith had bought a $1.6 million Brisbane home with five bedrooms and a pool. There was talk of a full-time job at Seven. Things were definitely looking up.

And yet he had found himself waking at 3am to confront a creeping fear. Something wasn't right. He'd left the SAS, but it hadn't left him.

* * *

On the spring morning of 22 November 2013, the ghosts of an old battle had come back to haunt him. Not just any old mission, but the 2006 operation for which he'd won his first major award, the Medal for Gallantry.

Roberts-Smith had been summoned by a senior SAS officer to discuss the fall-out from the eight-year-old mission. The man he had been asked to mediate with was William Tindell, a soldier from his 2006 patrol team. Tindell had long been agitating to open a box that Roberts-Smith thought needed shutting. Today, he intended to close it.

The core elements of the operation at the heart of the dispute were not contested. The battle of Khoran Gar had unfolded atop a barren mountain range in southern Afghanistan in June 2006 after Roberts-Smith, Tindell and four other SAS patrol team members had set up a hidden post to observe the movement in and out of a Taliban stronghold called the Whitehouse, which lay in the Chora Valley below.

It was meant to be a classic SAS stealth surveillance mission by soldiers able to endure hardship for days, to piss in a bottle, chew dry rations and concentrate, concentrate, concentrate. Tindell was one of two junior Australian soldiers concealed behind rocks, wearing desert camouflage and bush hats. Behind the pair's observation post were the four other SAS soldiers, including Roberts-Smith, then a junior trooper.

On the morning of the second day, his muscles still strained from hauling 70-kilogram packs up the steep slope on a ten-hour trek through the night, Tindell had spotted a young, unarmed Afghan male about 75 metres away. He had disappeared behind rocks, only to reappear with a small bag and walk away. Tindell and the second observation post soldier both believed the Afghan had not seen the Australians, but Roberts-Smith disagreed and, with a second soldier, raced after the man and killed him. The gun fire had drawn other Taliban, and insurgents swarmed the mountain. Soon, the members of the small patrol team were fighting for their lives.

Roberts-Smith maintained fire on fleeting images while the most senior SAS soldier in the patrol team, Sergeant Matt Locke, slung his M4 assault rifle, climbed a rock face and attacked a fighter trying to outflank them. Calm and assured, Locke killed the man, during a 'persistent one on one fight'.

Recognising an imminent risk of being overrun, the SAS patrol team had called for air support, a radio Hail Mary. A shriek of jet engines and the ripping canvas sound of 30-millimetre chain-gun cannon fire sounded in the air. More terrifying hours followed before the patrol team, under cover of darkness, were extracted to safety.

Tindell and Roberts-Smith were at one on most of these points. Tindell had also conceded something else. He had forgotten his machine-gun oil, causing his weapon to jam during the firefight with the Taliban. It was a soldiering failure Roberts-Smith had felt was unforgivable, and he'd complained the reduced firepower almost got them killed.

Roberts-Smith hadn't just complained. He wanted to hold Tindell to account. Tindell was an easy target: he had joined the SAS from the derided 'choco' ranks, the 'chocolate soldier' reservists, was short of stature, from Sydney's north shore, had no tattoos and didn't talk shit.

Tindell had complained to other soldiers that Roberts-Smith had begun a merciless campaign of bullying that included a violent threat he believed Roberts-Smith could well carry out. Roberts-Smith, Tindell had sworn, had told him: 'If your performance doesn't improve, you're going to get a bullet in the back of the head.'

This comment, Tindell suspected, was prompted not by his failure to oil his weapon or some other performance issue, but by Roberts-Smith's unease over the myriad other concerns Tindell held about the mission. Was Roberts-Smith trying to shut him up because he was worried these festering concerns led some to question the judgment to decorate Roberts-Smith for gallantry for his actions upon the mountain top?

For starters, Tindell had disagreed with the decision to kill the unarmed Afghan. It wasn't because of his belief the man hadn't seen the Australians, although that had long played on his mind. It was because the decision to fire upon him had prematurely ended what was meant to be a silent surveillance operation, likely drawing the Taliban to attack the patrol team.

The radio reporting from the mission was also at odds with the reality. Someone other than Tindell had radioed back to base to claim that the young unarmed Afghan was killed after the patrol had observed him moving aggressively while carrying an AK-47. Tindell knew this claim to be false. It seemed someone was trying to justify his killing.

There was another inaccurate claim in the official reporting: that the man killed had a smoke grenade that exploded after he was fired upon.

When Tindell complained to an SAS officer about Roberts-Smith's threat to shoot him in the back of the head, he'd copped yet more abuse. Roberts-Smith had approached Tindell outside the mess, loomed over him and growled: 'If you're going to make accusations, cunt, you better have some fucking proof.'

He'd spit on the ground in front of Tindell when he got the chance, and if Tindell was walking into a building, he would hold the door only to let it slam in his face. It was hardly a fair physical face-off. Tindell weighed just under 70 kilograms, Roberts-Smith close to 100.

Tindell was losing sleep. It was why he'd finally decided to complain to the most senior soldier on the base, the Regimental Sergeant Major. Yet, when Tindell had asked ten soldiers who had witnessed the bullying to put their observations in writing, only four had done so. Few wanted to be seen as a snitch, and certainly not by Roberts-Smith. His complaint fizzed out, replaced by an offer of mediation. In Tindell's mind, this was at least something: one last attempt to get his tormentor to leave him be, especially since Roberts-Smith had just resigned from the SAS.

If the mediation was meant to thaw relations, it started poorly. Tindell asked Roberts-Smith to explain the campaign of bullying. Roberts-Smith had responded with denials: his wasn't inappropriate behaviour, he'd said. It was Tindell's fault because it was Tindell who had poorly performed back in 2006.

Realising an apology would not be forthcoming, Tindell requested a lasting détente. If Roberts-Smith was no longer at Campbell Barracks, could he at least agree to cease speaking ill of him? Roberts-Smith nodded. The pair stood up and shook hands. In Roberts-Smith's mind, a niggling problem had finally gone away. The Victoria Cross recipient had much bigger things to focus on than a puny soldier he believed lacked the guts to admit he was inferior.

CHAPTER 9

PASTOR'S SON, FIGHTER, POLITICIAN

Perth, 2014

Andrew Hastie woke up with a start, straining to see through the darkness. It wasn't just the lack of light. He felt enveloped in an emotional fog, sapped of energy, stomach churning. It had happened again. Another dream where he was back in Afghanistan surrounded by chaos, flashes of a dead Australian soldier, faces of his comrades and voices whispering about covering up the death. This was one of two recurring dreams the blond-haired captain was having. The other also involved Afghanistan, but it featured a face staring at his own: that of Ben Roberts-Smith.

The 32-year-old Hastie wiped the sleep from his eyes as the objects in his room took familiar shape. Light was creeping in from a streetlamp outside, illuminating his wife's body next to him. This brought him more relief. Ruth was the only person he'd told about the dreams because she would listen and not judge.

She'd seen him struggle before. She'd been with him since before his SAS selection course in July 2010. She'd told him not to come back from the course unless he was finished, and he'd been selected, or it had broken him. It was her advice he had recalled when he'd faltered, wondering whether he had it in him to pass.

He'd begun questioning himself about the point of it all. 'Why are we walking around with no food, with fifty kilograms on our back, with no sleep?' His dream to become a young officer in Australia's finest fighting force was slipping away. And then, as he confronted the realisation the regiment was testing his ability to endure pain and fatigue, Ruth's words had echoed again in his head.

Don't come back unless you're finished or you're broken.

Lying on his bed, his mind drifted back to the image of the dead soldier. In his dream, this faceless man had been felled by friendly fire and the SAS had covered up his death. This had not actually happened in Afghanistan, but Hastie figured the dream was the product of the lingering unease he now felt about the regiment he had strived so hard to join. The SAS of his teenage dreams may not be the regiment he had come to know. His anxiety about this had been steadily growing, a distant drum beat getting louder.

When he'd deployed with the SAS to Oruzgan, briefly in late 2012 and then for a longer deployment in 2013, Hastie had begun encountering Australian special forces soldiers who seemed not just worn out, but damaged. Perhaps it was the repeated deployments to a war with no end in sight, he had told himself.

The successive rotations to Afghanistan had bred in some a preference for what the manual called 'direct action', and they called 'killing bad guys'. For others, more likely old-school SAS, this went against the grain. For them, staying in the shadows, collecting intelligence, suppressing violence was more the go. As was often said, 'The shot not fired can be more important.'

Other factors weighed on Hastie. As the strategic objective of installing a stable Afghan government with a domestic security force able to suppress violence and rid the country of terrorists became a distant hope, success had come to be measured by one of the few tangible metrics: kill count. The Afghan justice system would release Taliban bomb makers and insurgents far too quickly after the SAS had captured them, further incentivising Australian soldiers to kill rather than capture enemy fighters.

This was why Hastie had become increasingly worried that the rules of engagement, which permitted a coalition soldier to fire on a person posing a risk to the life of an Australian, perhaps weren't just at risk of being interpreted loosely. His foreboding in Afghanistan, fuelled by disparate comments, dark glances and disjointed observations during missions, was that some Australians might be tempted to throw out the rule book altogether.

There were small signs, things like the excessive drinking by SAS troopers at a makeshift bar called the Fat Lady's Arms. The so-called 'hands' mission solidified the captain's concern. This was an incident where one of his troopers had cut off the hands of a dead insurgent, arguing it made it easier to fingerprint him and that a Defence official had earlier endorsed the practice. War was messy, but this had felt like something else.

Hastie's troop sergeant had evidently sensed the same thing. 'I'm not going to Afghanistan to put dirt farmers on their knees and shoot them in the back of the head,' he'd said.

The Australian politicians who had visited Afghanistan seemed unaware of the strain their policies were putting on those they were deploying again and again. They seemed more interested in photo opportunities than understanding the strategic and military policy failures that were not only losing the war but eating away at the men fighting it.

This is why he joined the Liberal Party of Australia when he'd returned from Afghanistan and began seriously considering a tilt at parliament. Ever since watching vision of the planes fly into the two towers in New York he had wanted to contribute. At first it was to fight as a soldier. But Afghanistan had left him wondering if he could have more impact through politics than through the military.

Hastie checked the clock. It was 2am. It was quiet, save for Ruth's breathing. If the dead soldier conjured up in his sleep was an allegory for his discomfort about Afghanistan, why was Ben Roberts-Smith appearing in dreams laced with dread? He had once held his comrade in high regard. In 2009, when he had still been an officer in the regular army, he'd encountered Roberts-Smith while on a tour of the SAS base. The giant soldier was wearing footy shorts, pistol on his hip, fit and physically imposing. Hastie had thought at the time: the SAS is the unit I want to be part of.

But after joining the regiment, he'd heard another growing drum beat of concern. This was about Roberts-Smith himself, but it was nothing solid. Yet again, it was fuelled by a jigsaw of whispers and encounters. During a mission in southern Afghanistan in October 2012, Hastie met a rookie SAS trooper seconded into a patrol team with Roberts-Smith and his second-in-charge, Jason Andrews. This rookie was usually a happy-go-lucky soldier, bursting with g'days and grins, but during this mission he'd transformed into a shadow of his former self, like a man who'd seen a ghost.

Hastie was told Roberts-Smith's patrol team had killed two enemy fighters out of sight. Minutes later Roberts-Smith strode past the men, staring at Hastie as he did so.

'Just a couple more dead cunts,' he had said, eyes gleaming.

Boyd Keary, whom Hastie regarded as a thoughtful and experienced soldier, had also raised concerns. At the SAS barracks, he'd bumped into a distressed Keary, who'd blurted out how another soldier had described watching Roberts-Smith kick a prisoner off a cliff. Keary had no proof of anything, but the comment had stuck with Hastie.

There were other remarks that left an impression, from one of the oldest SAS soldiers on the base. Nick Simkin, a short, strong and wiry SAS veteran with a patch of spiky grey hair and an easy laugh, held the record for the oldest patrol commander to deploy in Afghanistan. Simkin was an old-school operator who loved soldiering and had literally written the memo on the art of performing stealthy reconnaissance, the SAS's truest calling. He relished a beer and a dirty joke, was loved and loathed in equal parts in the SAS, and never missed an opportunity to speak his mind.

Simkin had taken Hastie aside in 2013 and warned him that before deploying, he needed to tell the soldiers under his command not to cross any lines. Simkin muttered darkly one name more than others: Ben Roberts-Smith. Hastie could still remember Simkin's exact words. 'People are doing stupid shit overseas. Don't do it. Don't be that guy. Don't ruin your life.'

* * *

Half an hour's drive away, in another Perth suburb, a letter of complaint sat in the drawer of Nick Simkin's desk. It was neatly typed with a heading: 'Sensitive: the Special Air Service Regiment, Campbell Barracks, Swanbourne, 6010'. The subject of the letter was Corporal Ben Roberts-Smith.

Simkin's note was not about a war crime, although he was all but certain Roberts-Smith had murdered a Taliban fighter on the Easter Sunday mission in 2009. Simkin was on the ground that day and both he and his scout, Dean Tilley, had glimpsed the machine-gunning of an unarmed Afghan insurgent with a prosthetic leg. In his war-hardened logic, Simkin could live with a comrade executing a Taliban insurgent, as long as this murder was done on the soldier's own accord. It wasn't something Simkin would ever do, and he'd have had the balls of any member of his patrol team who tried it on.

Simkin had mates who'd served in Vietnam and he'd sense them carrying an unspoken burden that had grown like a tumour as they had aged. Hard men could be broken by a decision made in just a few seconds many years before, in a jungle far away. It wasn't the fog-of-war stuff that left the darkest stain, it was those conscious decisions to leap over a moral line: to summarily execute an unarmed prisoner. Or put a dirt farmer on the ground and shoot him in the back of the head. But Simkin wasn't about to judge other men or break the SAS code of silence. If Roberts-Smith's patrol team members were intent on knocking off Taliban prisoners, that was their business. They could live with the burden of knowing what they had done.

The general concept of death didn't bother Simkin, and certainly not the death of an enemy fighter who would have just as soon cut his throat as look at him. He wasn't naïve to the pressures placed on the SAS in this seemingly endless war, and the dilemma every soldier faced when they encountered an insurgent who for reasons of practicality or necessity – the helicopters were full, or a mission was rolling on – couldn't be handcuffed and taken to a prison. Did you leave them on the battlefield to pose an ongoing risk to your brother soldiers? Simkin would tie them tightly to a tree, perhaps with a firm whack in the guts to say goodbye, and hope this would delay their return to the battlefield until the Australians were back at base.

If this same insurgent prisoner had posed any genuine threat, trying to grab a weapon off his captors or reaching for a hidden knife or explosive device, Simkin wouldn't hesitate to do what needed to be done. He hadn't felt any lasting moral revulsion at the machine-gunning of the Afghan with the prosthetic leg on Easter Sunday. As he walked past the bloodied corpse, he'd spotted the white plastic leg. *You won't be needing that anymore*, he'd thought. Taking battlefield trophies from the dead was against the rule book, but he'd thought nothing of it as he'd grabbed the prosthetic limb, attached it to his backpack and, later, installed it at the Fat Lady's Arms. 'Das Boot' had become the biggest beer vessel in Afghanistan.

If he could shrug off some battlefield events, there were other things Simkin couldn't so easily let go. Since 2009, he'd quietly stewed on rumours that a junior soldier in Roberts-Smith's patrol team had also been caught up in something sinister on Easter Sunday. The whisper involved a rookie trooper called Jason Andrews and a term Simkin had only heard after that fateful mission: 'blooding'. To be blooded was to be bullied into getting your first kill by executing someone. If it had happened, Simkin viewed it as the vilest of all initiations by the sort of senior soldier who thought loyalty or brotherhood could be extracted with blood-stained coercion.

PASTOR'S SON, FIGHTER, POLITICIAN

He'd watched on from a distance over a few years as Andrews and other junior soldiers in Roberts-Smith's patrol team had become changed men. William Tindell had copped bullying for a decade only to end up in a miserable mediation with his tormentor. Others had been physically assaulted. The only time Simkin had directly confronted Roberts-Smith was when he king-hit a soldier half his weight and twice as drunk during a boozy night out at the Fat Lady's Arms. 'He's half your bloody size, RS,' he told him, watching Roberts-Smith's face burn red with anger.

And then there were the rumours of blooding. Although he had no proof of the practice, Simkin reacted by reminding his own patrol team members to never cross that battlefield line.

None of it, not the bullying or the battlefield misconduct, had ever made its way to a formal complaint until now. But it wasn't any war crime that had led Simkin to type up his letter. What prompted his missive was the New Year's Honours list announcing that Roberts-Smith would be getting a military commendation for his 'outstanding' leadership of junior soldiers. Leadership? The term alongside Roberts-Smith's name had left Simkin fuming, his anger building as he read and reread the award citation.

It described a June 2012 mission that had been led and planned by the Victoria Cross recipient, but the words in the citation didn't match Simkin's memory of that day. He recalled a mission so poorly conceived and executed by Roberts-Smith that one SAS patrol had fired upon another, a 'blue on blue' incident that risked Australian lives. In the wash-up, Roberts-Smith had blamed the most junior soldier on the ground for the fiasco and, in a patrol room out of sight of the officers, punched the rookie in the face.

Worried the young soldier might report him, Roberts-Smith had later threatened to implicate him in a concocted allegation that the rookie had fired at women and children. The soldier had become the latest young trooper left broken, his career and mental health in tatters. This was why Simkin had typed up a formal complaint about Roberts-Smith's leadership commendation, put his name to it and resolved to send it up the chain of command.

He'd kept the contents to what he knew he could easily verify. There was no mention of war crimes, but rather a 'cover-up' to hide a bungled mission, followed by the bullying of a young soldier.

'As SAS soldiers, we are responsible for accurate reporting and honesty, in the field and in camp,' the complaint stated. *'This citation is a contradiction of those values.'*

For the moment, the complaint sat in Simkin's desk drawer. It would take courage to send it. Simkin didn't know it, but his decision to do so would ultimately set off a series of unexpected events. It would lead to phone calls from journalists accusing Simkin of gun smuggling, a raid by armed police and, ultimately, an unmistakeable message: no one messes with Ben Roberts-Smith.

CHAPTER 10

AN UNUSUAL RESEARCH TASK

Australian Defence Force Headquarters, Canberra, June 2015

Samantha Crompvoets, a sociologist with a fierce intellect, bright eyes and a loud, warm laugh, sat in the office of Major General Jeff Sengelman, the most senior special forces officer in the country. While Sengelman addressed her, she scanned his shelves and wondered how many others had sat in the deep leather couch and studied the book spines as the Major General delivered one of his famous monologues.

The general looked and sounded the part of the modern military leader. With closely cropped, sandy grey hair and a fit, lined face, Sengelman was ferociously smart, deeply principled and hard working. He was ominously nicknamed the 'dark lord' in military circles. His monologues were not known for their brevity.

The briefing this day involved a piece of consulting work Crompvoets had been asked to do by Sengelman, who had assumed the mantle of Special Operations Commander

Australia (SOCAUST) six months earlier, on 15 December 2014. That was the day of the Lindt Café siege, in which a terrorist had taken eighteen hostages in Sydney's CBD. After a seventeen-hour stand-off and the execution of a hostage, café manager Tori Johnson, the terrorist was killed by state police. Shrapnel fragments fired by police accidentally killed a second hostage, Katrina Dawson, a respected solicitor and sister of well-known defamation barrister Sandy Dawson.

The perceived shortfalls of the police response to the siege had sparked fierce debate about whether Sengelman's special forces, comprising the Perth-based SAS and Sydney-headquartered Commandos, should have intervened. Crompvoets had monitored the ensuing debate.

Former SAS captain Andrew Hastie, who had announced himself as a Liberal Party candidate in Western Australia, was among those arguing for greater military involvement in domestic counter-terrorism events. He was vocal in saying he 'felt instinctively that the Commonwealth should take over where an attack is made by a listed terrorist organisation in Australia'.

Crompvoets concluded Sengelman thought the same. Since 2009, after she'd conducted an inquiry into the incidence of domestic violence in the Australian Defence Force, she'd become a go-to consultant and investigator for the Chief of Army, Angus Campbell, and a year earlier Sengelman had commissioned Crompvoets to study the culture of an army division devoted to modernisation and strategic planning. That was when she'd first found herself sitting in Sengelman's office, scanning book titles as he held court. In time, she had memorised the titles of almost every book on his bookshelf, tomes on military history, leadership and ethics.

As a Canberra consultant specialising in diagnosing cultural problems in closed and secretive government agencies, Crompvoets had become expert in building rapport with the mostly men who ran Australia's national security agencies. It wasn't about knowing military schemes of manoeuvre or the history of the Five Eyes intelligence network. It meant positioning herself as a trusted outsider. She had become a master at massaging the egos and insecurities of those hiring her and they in turn knew that while she wasn't afraid to call out systemic problems – domestic violence, gender inequity, bureaucratic malaise – she would do so in a manner that ensured whoever had hired her could still position themselves as a champion for change.

People had always liked Crompvoets, even when she bore bad news. She could deliver fierce criticism about a person in a way that was disarming rather than rude, leaving them sometimes apologising for their foibles while praising her sincerity. Her hearty laugh would soften cold silence, her natural warmth lessen the blow of a report delivering conclusions that would end careers.

She was an outsider who felt comfortable on the inside, confident and resourceful, at once self-deprecating and self-assured. She'd always walked her own path. When she arrived as a country girl at an elite boarding college at Melbourne University, she'd made friends easily, partied hard but also left fellow boarders with the impression that she was going somewhere. While she was earmarked as the student bound to make an impression in later life, she never expected to find herself working so closely with the military. Defence chiefs had begun to increasingly call on her when they sensed something was wrong and that change was needed and they required evidence to make the case.

Sengelman was calling on her on this day because he wanted more power and autonomy within the military, but needed a vehicle other than himself to recommend reform. Sengelman's ultimate aim was to ensure his special forces could be called on in a future terrorism crisis and that he, or someone of his rank, would be calling the shots, when they were.

'You'll need to canvass the leaders of the national security community,' Sengelman had instructed her, reeling off the names of military, police, diplomatic and intelligence agency chiefs. She'd also be assigned helpers – or were they minders? – in the form of two mid-ranking officers who answered to Sengelman and would open doors to the who's who of the nation's defence and security world.

Crompvoets was to collect their impressions of Australia's special forces. Australia's homebound spies at ASIO worked with SAS soldiers on domestic surveillance jobs, while the nation's overseas spooks at ASIS worked alongside the Commandos and the SAS in Afghanistan, Iraq and Africa. Spies were keen observers, so they would know plenty. In the small pond of Canberra, senior officials prepared to drop their guard might be a wellspring of information about the effectiveness, or otherwise, of Australia's elite fighting forces.

As the meeting wound up, Crompvoets' eyes settled momentarily on a book on Sengelman's shelf. It was titled *Dust, Donkeys and Delusions*. The book was about the story of Private John Simpson and his donkey. According to accounts from Gallipoli, Simpson had risked his own life to save fellow Anzacs. The word 'EXPOSED' was imposed over the title in large red letters, a none-too-subtle reference to the book's desire to challenge military myth and propaganda. People were still calling for Simpson to be given a posthumous Victoria Cross, despite historians arguing his heroic deeds had been vastly overstated by a nation in search of a hero. Even though many knew the truth, the myth was too big to overcome.

The special forces had their own myths, thought Crompvoets as she walked out into the Defence headquarters carpark and felt the icy Canberra wind sting her cheeks.

What were they hiding?

* * *

On the other side of the country in Perth, in a house a short drive from Campbell Barracks, one of Ben Roberts-Smith's closest friends in the SAS had stored away a USB for safekeeping. Had Crompvoets known of its existence, the USB's contents would have given her an immediate glimpse into the darker corners of the SAS. The small storage device contained several folders, titled with the dates of the three last deployments to Afghanistan undertaken by Roberts-Smith's patrol teams: 2009, 2010, 2012. Within each folder were sub-folders titled with mission place names or descriptions like 'Smithy's 40th birthday party'.

All up, the folders contained hundreds of photos of Roberts-Smith and his closest comrades at war. Many of them were unremarkable: soldiers grinning post-mission or on patrol, Afghan children with their thumbs up, or bearded and scowling Afghan elders displaying no interest in paying false tribute to the foreign invaders and their digital cameras.

But some of the photos were more interesting. There were dozens of pictures of SAS soldiers and officers swigging beer from a white prosthetic leg at the Fat Lady's

Arms, the bar at the SAS quarters at Camp Russell in Tarin Kowt.

One of the photos captured Roberts-Smith grinning, hands draped over the shoulder of a US special forces soldier who had just downed a can of beer that had been poured into the leg. Another showed the Victoria Cross recipient cheering on another American soldier while he drank from the same prosthetic leg. A third photo was a group shot of two dozen or so soldiers posing at a Fat Lady's Arms dress-up party. In the foreground was one of Roberts-Smith's closest friends in the SAS, one of the few to regularly socialise with Roberts-Smith outside of work. He'd gone to the party as a member of the white supremacist group, the Ku Klux Klan. He wore a white robe, a pointed white hood, and was holding a burning cross and a noose. The cross was literally on fire.

In the background of the photo was a celebratory Roberts-Smith holding up one hand to display a shaka, his curled middle fingers clenched while he extended his thumb and little finger. He had a huge smile on his face.

Tucked away in a subfolder was another series of photos taken on a 2012 mission that took soldiers back to Tizak, the location of Roberts-Smith's Victoria Cross battle in 2010. These were photos that never should have been taken. Military rules only allowed army-issued cameras to be used on the battlefield to create a formal record of dead enemy, potential evidence to identify more insurgents, and the identity of prisoners. Taking battlefield snaps for personal kicks was banned.

But on this mission, known as Tizak 2 to distinguish it from the 2010 operation that transformed Roberts-Smith into an Australian legend, a member of the SAS had been busy taking pictures for their own photo album. These unofficial photos revealed red flags about how an Afghan man shot dead on the Tizak 2 mission had been treated.

One frame showed the dead Afghan on his back a short time after he had been killed. The boots of an unknown member of Roberts-Smith's patrol team could be seen near the body. The man lay on a colourful woven mat, the sort that poor farmers perched on when sorting almonds.

On the man's eyes rested two coins. One was engraved with the winged dagger of the SAS. The second coin bore the logo of the SAS 2nd Squadron, which boasted Roberts-Smith as its most famous alumni. This coin depicted the famous Australian bushranger Ned Kelly holding two pistols and standing in front of that other icon of Australia, the Southern Cross. In ancient Greece, coins were placed on the eyes of the dead to pay the ferryman to take them to the underworld. But the laws of modern war dictated that the dead must be treated with respect, not mocked or desecrated.

The soldier who had placed the SAS souvenir coins on the dead Afghan's eyes had perhaps wanted to send a message to the unlucky locals who found the body, or maybe capture a macabre image for private viewing back in Australia. Whatever the motivation of the coin placer, the photo spoke for itself.

It told of a human body robbed of dignity in a celebration of his killing. And it told of Australians who wished to leave their mark in Afghanistan, no matter how ugly it looked.

CHAPTER 11

AUSTRALIA DAY CELEBRATIONS

January 2016

A few minutes into his speech before an audience that included women in Muslim head scarves and men wearing the skullcaps he'd seen in Afghanistan, Ben Roberts-Smith touched on the key theme of his presentation to the Australia Day event: what it meant to be an Australian. He told the small crowd that it was about posing a question. 'How do we ensure that the things fundamental to human dignity are the same for all of us?' His answer was to make sure that everyone, regardless of their religion, skin colour or ethnicity, was treated with respect. That's what Australians do

Wearing a dark blue suit, white shirt and navy tie and flanked by the Australian and Aboriginal flags, Roberts-Smith addressed the audience of local multicultural leaders in Bankstown, in south-west Sydney, with a studied solemnity. He'd been asked to speak in his capacity as Chairman of the Australia Day Council Board, an appointment made by Prime Minister Tony Abbott fourteen months earlier.

In a baton swap between Aussie legends, Roberts-Smith had replaced cricketer Adam Gilchrist as chair of the organisation dedicated to promoting Australia's national day of celebration. His role was also symbolic. Abbott had intended Roberts-Smith to be the face of the nation.

After opening his speech by paying respect to traditional owners of the land, Roberts-Smith had noted that Indigenous Elders had for thousands of years issued an 'acknowledgment of country' when visiting foreign lands. Non-Indigenous Australians had only recently followed this lead, a long overdue move that had helped the nation come to terms with its ancient roots. Refugees had also changed Australia for the better, he opined. They were drawn to Australia because of the 'hope and promise this country offered' to those escaping 'conflicts in their homelands, the unbearable limits of fear, despair and poverty'.

As he delivered this paean to cultural difference and diversity, Roberts-Smith at times spoke too fast, racing through points he should have emphasised. It was as if the words weren't his. As it turned out, they may well have belonged to someone else. Roberts-Smith had begun paying a speech writer, who had worked for Governor-General Quentin Bryce, to help craft many of his public talks.

One line, though, did ring true. It was when Roberts-Smith spoke of what he had learnt as a soldier on the front line in Afghanistan, far away from the politicians and generals trying to solve the intractable problems that troops faced up close every day when they ventured out past the barbed wire.

For a moment, he appeared to slow down ever so slightly as he spoke words that carried a particular resonance for his own life.

'What matters is the strength and resolve of individuals,'
he told the crowd.

* * *

On the other side of the country, the newest federal
member for Canning, Andrew Hastie MP, was reading
through words he'd written for his own Australia Day
message. The public statement he'd prepared was also
plump with rhetoric. Since winning the Western Australian
seat at a by-election four months earlier, Hastie had been
careful with his tongue. He was known to be passionate
and intensely idealistic, qualities that could get a rookie
politician into trouble.

Shortly after signing up to his local branch, the pressure
for him to make a tilt at parliament had begun building.
With his military background, conservative bent, flair for
public speaking and good looks, Hastie was viewed in the
party as having vast potential. Among his greatest backers
was the then prime minister, Tony Abbott.

Hastie had learnt quickly that not everyone supported
his rise and that politics and the media were vicious and
unforgiving businesses. After he'd been announced as
a candidate, *The Age* and *Sydney Morning Herald* had
splashed with an article about the 'hands' affair. It made
no mention of the fact that it was Hastie who'd reported
the misconduct.

It wasn't just the media and the vipers in his own party
that he needed to worry about. Perth was a small town
with powerful business titans who loomed large over its
politicians. If this is true, then Kerry Stokes, owner of the
local paper and Western Australia's highest-rating television
channel, was seated at the top of Perth's power apex.

Political elders had advised Hastie that if he were to effect change, he needed to play the long game and try to keep powerful people on side. Since he'd been elected, however, some old whispers about the integrity of one of Australia's soldiers had been growing louder. Now it wasn't just those in the SAS raising Ben Roberts-Smith's name, it was journalists as well. Because of his time in the regiment, reporters had been asking Hastie about rumours that Roberts-Smith was a bully, or worse.

Hastie had been careful to keep his suspicions to himself. He had told nobody of the cliff-kick allegation involving Ben Roberts-Smith, or of his concern at the way more junior soldiers had appeared to change after entering Roberts-Smith's orbit. He wouldn't trade in hearsay. It was a policy he'd abided by a few months earlier, when Major General Jeff Sengelman had asked SAS soldiers and officers to confide in Sengelman in writing about any of their concerns

Sengelman's request was included in a report that documented three troubling incidents: an SAS member had been caught stealing explosives; another had been arrested for armed robbery; and a third had lost weapons. The Major General had avoided direct reference to a deeply troubling fourth incident, which involved an SAS soldier drawing a pistol on an Australian spy in Afghanistan.

Hastie was on his way out of the SAS, but he had still responded to Sengelman's call by writing a short letter, in which he described the reason he was drawn to make a change to politics: 'the appalling lack of strategic direction from our military and political leaders, and the pressure it placed on tactical elements'. He hadn't held back when describing his fear that the special forces had been infected by a 'gradual erosion of leadership and accountability across the full span of command responsibilities'. He also outlined certain behaviours at the regiment he'd seen up close, and which he believed pointed to something more sinister at play that had remained just out of view of young officers. These indicators included excessive SAS drinking at the Fat Lady's Arms, and trips to see strippers back in Perth, a looseness 'tacitly endorsed by the senior leadership of SOTG [Special Operations Task Group]'. Hastie had refused to go to strippers because of his 'religious convictions' and concern for 'my wife's commitment to me and her sacrifice in supporting my long absences on training operations and operations with the ADF'. As a result, he'd been pushed further away from the SAS inner circle.

While he had no definitive proof, he knew that something was off. Something was lacking in the culture of special forces, and it wasn't just the absence of adequate capability, equipment and mandate. Hastie was convinced that the values system of the SAS was also way out of kilter. Perhaps Sengelman could look further. He finished his letter to the general by writing: 'We have carried ourselves no better than an infantry battalion from a bygone era military, where binge drinking and other reckless behaviour was commonplace ... During the last decade, we have therefore lowered our moral obligation accordingly.'

Hastie could only guess what this had truly meant on the ground in Afghanistan when diligent officers and soldiers were not looking.

* * *

Samantha Crompvoets sat at her computer on that Australia Day preparing to send the most incendiary report she had ever written. She felt a vulnerability she'd not experienced before. She was a woman who had never been to war, and here she was, casting judgment on men who'd risked their lives to serve their nation. As she reread her words, she reminded herself that she was merely the messenger. It was SAS soldiers themselves, and those who had served with them, who had described what she was now preparing to email to Chief of Army Angus Campbell and Major General Sengelman.

The stories had trickled in slowly at first. She had canvassed defence, diplomatic and security leaders about their perceptions of the special forces. They offered up different perspectives, but their observations coalesced around a singular concern: something had happened within the SAS in Afghanistan that needed further scrutiny. Crompvoets then turned to soldiers in the regiment and their mission support staff. These SAS 'insiders' initially spoke to her 'sotto voce', in quiet tones. Over time, these voices grew louder and 'more difficult to ignore', as their concerns moved from the intense rivalry between the SAS and the Commandos and stories of drug use, stripper parties and boozing, to hints of 'extremely serious breaches of accountability and trust' on the battlefield.

Crompvoets contacted Campbell in late 2015, warning him that the general culture observation piece commissioned by Sengelman was at risk of morphing into something else.

'Write it all down,' Campbell told her. When she'd next warned Sengelman of her findings, he asked her to go directly to him for anything sensitive.

'I can't trust anyone anymore,' he said. 'There are leaks everywhere.'

As Crompvoets met more and more SAS insiders, the stories grew worse and their telling more visceral. Adrian

Norton, an SAS chaplain, sat with Crompvoets in his office, a stuffy demountable at an army barracks in Far North Queensland. Norton was dressed in camouflage, like the soldiers who'd come to respect him.

When the padre had first arrived at the SAS, many of the elite troopers sneered at men of the cloth: how could they understand the soldier's lot, let alone the rigours of war? The vibe was clear enough. Priests were soft, and so were the soldiers who sought their pastoral care. Norton, a former boxer, had responded by challenging anyone in the regiment to fight him in the ring. The SAS soldiers weren't so sneering after that.

As they'd learnt to trust him, a small number of soldiers sought his counsel after returning from missions in Afghanistan. As Norton told Crompvoets what some had confessed, his eyes welled up with tears. It wasn't just soldiers who were broken, she had thought. The padre was also hurting.

Norton had encountered stories of battlefield trophy hunting, of soldiers drinking from a dead Afghan's prosthetic leg and of killings outside the laws of war.

'They shot him in the back of the head,' a distressed SAS soldier had kept repeating to the priest.

Soldiers also reached out directly to Crompvoets. One told her how he'd witnessed special forces soldiers slitting the throats of two teens. Others told her of Afghans shot for no good reason and of killings covered up with claims that the dead were 'EKIA', Enemies Killed in Action. It was easy to turn an innocent farmer into a hostile combatant, they told Crompvoets. The SAS patrol team that had killed someone simply had to claim the dead Afghan was engaged because they had bolted from soldiers while holding a radio that could be used to communicate to armed insurgents in hiding. Just like that, the deceased was marked as a 'squirter' or 'spotter': a legitimate target under Australia's rules of engagement.

After weeks of meetings, Crompvoets realised that many who had served in or with the SAS were repeating the same phrase over and over again: 'It happened all the time.'

In consultation with Sengelman and Campbell, Crompvoets resolved to write two reports. One would be a generalised cultural assessment of the special forces that could be widely disseminated. The report – 'Special Operations Command culture and interactions: Perceptions, reputation and risk' – wouldn't pull any punches, but its assessments would be sweeping rather than specific.

Her second report would go only to Sengelman and Campbell, and would document the war crimes allegations. This was the report she was finalising on Australia Day. It had taken her a few days to compile, and as she slowly typed up her findings she grew increasingly anxious. The incidents she was describing were not a couple of 'fog of war' events, but deliberate and repeated patterns of behaviour.

Crompvoets had promised her informants confidentiality. She would take their names to the grave. This meant that if the top brass wanted to bury her report citing a lack of verifiable evidence and her own inexperience with war, they could do so. It was why she had chosen her words so carefully. Whatever she submitted to Campbell and Sengelman had to be shaped in such a way as to compel them to deliver the accountability and scrutiny those who'd confided in her were demanding. Crompvoets would put it all down: the good, the bad, the ugly and the *very* ugly.

The conduct disclosed to her, she wrote, had been described by military insiders as on par with the Abu

Ghraib affair, the Iraq prisoner torture scandal that enveloped the US military in 2004, triggering inquiries and jail terms. Australian special forces had engaged in 'competition killing and blood lust' extending to the 'inhumane and unnecessary treatment of prisoners'. Allegations from special forces suggested that some soldiers were 'glorifying these crimes' and were involved in the 'cover-ups of unlawful killing and other atrocities'. After sweeping through a village, Australian special forces 'would take the men and boys to these guesthouses and interrogate them, meaning tie them up and torture them'. Some would later be found executed.

'These are corroborated accounts' from SAS soldiers, Crompvoets had written. 'Soldiers would do bad stuff to fit in. It becomes part of the banter,' one special forces insider had told her. Another stated: 'Guys just had this blood lust. Psychos. Absolute psychos. And we bred them.'

Another of her informers had painted his own picture. 'If they didn't do it, they saw it. And if they didn't see it, they knew about it. If they knew about it, they probably were involved in covering it up and not letting it get back to Canberra ... and to make it even harder, if they didn't know about it, the question will be: why didn't you, because you should have.'

Crompvoets had simultaneously encountered 'countless references' from the special forces insiders 'to exceptional soldiers and officers who upheld Army values and whose character was unquestionably upstanding'. She found this bewildering. It seemed clear atrocities had occurred, but also that many in the SAS were repulsed by bad behaviour. For weeks she had been asking the obvious question: Why did they not intervene or do anything to stop what was happening?

She detailed in her report the 'various answers' provided by special forces insiders to this question: 'they were too high up the chain to see it; the tempo was so high the priority was just to keep everything ticking over; they did try to do something but were dismissed/ marginalised/moved on; they only saw one incident not the pattern over time; eventually they left quietly'. Ultimately, special forces soldiers felt they needed to 'conform to survive'.

In drafting her report, Crompvoets also decided not to spare the chain of command. Senior officers had, in some cases, encouraged high body counts while failing to act on suspicious 'killed in action' post-operational reports and briefings. And generals such as Angus Campbell, who'd previously served as commander of the Australian forces in the Middle East, had backed the deployment of special forces again and again on capture and kill missions in what by 2012 had become a hopeless war.

The year 2012 was singled out by an Afghanistan veteran as the period in which he had seen conduct he rated as 'by far the worst' of that he'd witnessed in all his many deployments. 'He mentioned that the Afghan interpreter they worked with kept reporting that Australian SF [special forces] were executing farmers, but no one ever followed anything up.'

Crompvoets read her report one last time. She was as confident as she could be that its contents could not be ignored. Still, the words of some in the SAS, her insiders, were echoing in her head. They were convinced their concerns would, in the end, be denied, dispelled, downplayed and dismissed. It was these insiders who had warned Crompvoets about the 'diaspora of SOF [special operations forces] alumni'. For good measure, she had referenced these warnings in the report intended for Campbell and Sengelman.

Once it hit their inboxes, both men would be on notice that they, too, would face blowback from ex-soldiers and officers from SAS ranks who were 'powerful, have a great deal to lose, and will no doubt fight to protect their personal reputation as well as the SF [special forces] brand should they be implicated'. If the SAS had produced a batch of men who were leading by example in business and politics, a small cabal of SAS veterans were also intent on ensuring what happened at war stayed on the battlefield.

It was this small clique of soldiers who were 'responsible for the worst of it. A core group of people who wield so much influence that officers find it very difficult to manage ... They are hero worshipped and unstoppable.'

* * *

For weeks, Samantha Crompvoets waited to learn how Campbell and Sengelman would react. The initial signs were promising, if surprising. After digesting its contents, Sengelman had asked to meet her.

She'd felt nervous. Nothing she'd ever delivered to the defence force, or, for that matter, any agency she'd ever worked for, had been so undeniably shocking. Crompvoets knew that ever since she'd started digging, Sengelman had faced intense pressure to shut her work down. Powerful defence establishment figures were willing him to fail, or at least to stop her lifting up rocks. But Sengelman appeared energised when they had met.

'I want to hug you right now,' he'd blurted out. 'You have given me a gift.'

Crompvoets was immediately struck by the realisation that Sengelman viewed her report as a means of driving his agenda to reshape the special forces into the fighting force he wished to lead. Reforms were clearly needed and Sengelman was a fine leader. But what was also desperately needed was a further investigation and a guarantee that, at some point, the concerns outlined in her report would see the light of day. If her work remained classified and circulated only among the top brass, then it would be as good as dead and buried.

In early February, Campbell and Sengelman had both requested she provide harder evidence to back up the bombshells littering her report. Implicit in the request was the concern that her report was full of smoke, but perhaps lacking in fire.

Could this be the start of the subtle cover-up her informants had feared?

She'd written again to Sengelman and Campbell, telling them that even she did not know the names of some of her informants. Those who identified themselves as SAS soldiers had begged her to remain anonymous. These war-bitten men were scared. They feared 'for their safety, their family's safety, their career in the ADF'. And even if the defence force wanted to hear the men's interviews, she could not help. She had deliberately not tape-recorded any person and her written files did not detail names.

In May, she heard the news that a senior judge was to be appointed by the Defence Inspector-General to investigate the allegations she'd documented. Crompvoets was flooded with relief. She'd met Justice Paul Brereton before, and had instantly connected with him. Sure, judges, let alone judges with military rank like Brereton, were part of the establishment. But the genial Brereton was known for two things: intelligence and integrity. This was a far better outcome than handballing her report to the defence minister, who would surely face political pressure to keep it in-house. Sengelman and Campbell hadn't decided to bury her grenade. They had loosened the pin, and rolled it down the road.

A judge could still cover things up, but that wasn't in keeping with Brereton's nature. He was the sort of man who would pull at the threads she had loosened. Brereton wouldn't hesitate to pick up the grenade, Crompvoets reckoned. Exactly who it would blow up if the pin was ever pulled was the unknown. The only certainty was that in the viper's nest of military and political vested interests Brereton was entering, there'd be plenty hoping for the judge and his inquiry to self-detonate, blowing up Crompvoets' reputation along the way.

PART 2

CHAPTER 12

A METEORIC RISE

Brisbane, Queensland, 15 February 2017

Ringed by palm trees and with a massive bright red '7' statue overshadowing its entrance, the Channel Seven building in Brisbane was usually a hive of reporters wearing suits and powdered faces, camera operators in jeans and t-shirts and editors cutting one-minute-thirty stories about car crashes, rugby league and local politics.

But on this day, the corridors were empty. The staff had been told to assemble in the auditorium. Months earlier, Ben Roberts-Smith had been named General Manager of Seven West Media's Queensland operations, the latest leap in his meteoric rise through the Australian media company with the help of his mentor and now ultimate boss, Kerry Stokes.

It was a job he'd decided to fashion in his own image, despite some briefly nagging doubts about one undeniably important thing. As he'd told a magazine journalist: 'I know nothing about the television industry.'

A few months earlier Roberts-Smith had attained a Master of Business Administration from the University of Queensland and had performed a six-month stint as Seven's deputy general manager. When his promotion to general manager was first announced, some staff joked that it would have been difficult to find a less suitably qualified person than Roberts-Smith. Even he had confessed to being 'shocked' when he was offered the top job.

The little Roberts-Smith knew about the business of television was what he'd learnt fronting and appearing on shows on Seven about Australian war heroes, including the prime-time Sunday evening specials on himself and other VC recipients.

From the start, it was obvious that Roberts-Smith was going to do things at Seven his own way, relying on one very special attribute: the fact he was Ben Roberts-Smith, VC, MG, MBA, Father of the Year, modern Anzac legend and, thanks to the backing of Kerry Stokes, now a media executive.

Roberts-Smith believed that the man he'd replaced at Seven, Neil Mooney, had nailed it when he'd told him: 'Mate, I can teach you television, but I can't teach character. And character is what you have in spades.'

Roberts-Smith had told a journalist that those who doubted his leadership abilities were forgetting something: he'd led teams of subordinates when it was a matter of life and death, not ratings or revenue. Anyone who doubted him needed to reflect on the fact his SAS unit was 'probably one of the most high-performing teams in Australia'.

When Stokes had first brought him into Seven as a consultant, Roberts-Smith had realised very quickly that he couldn't 'consult on a business level because he wasn't a businessman'. What he could deliver on were those buzz words he'd learnt from his MBA and from the military: culture and leadership.

He'd put the Roberts-Smith theory of leadership on the public record during a speech the previous year. Forget the tomes about leadership on business school bookshelves, he'd told the audience. Leadership was 'best explained in action': in 'the physical and mental sharpness, the resilience and steadiness that come with pressing on through hard stuff day in day out, doing the best you can over and again, never even whispering "can't"'. Leadership involved 'impeccable timing', knowing 'what needs to be done and when'.

On this morning, at the Seven office, he had decided to do things a little differently. A drumline marching band from an elite Brisbane private school arrived, walked past the giant red '7' statue and made their way towards the auditorium and waiting staff. The twelve high school boys in red blazers and striped ties then assembled in formation.

If the students could feel the awkwardness in the room, none of them let on. But even before a single stick had cracked a drum skin, Seven staff were exchanging expressions ranging from bemusement to bewilderment. A marketing employee mouthed the words to a colleague: 'What the fuck?', just as the cacophony erupted, a whir of staccato drumbeats that continued for an inordinate length of time as stares transformed into eye rolls.

The reason for the annoyance was obvious to many in the room. Lunch was eaten on the run in any busy commercial media office. Journos had stories to file, camera operators had events to film. Sales staff were flogging advertisements, producers plotting programs.

Some in the newsroom would crack a beer or down a glass of cheap wine after the bulletin on a Friday night, but even that tradition was lapsing. Yet, here they were, enduring some faux military drum display when they had work to do.

As the students continued their furious drumming,
the staff watching Roberts-Smith observed no sense of
discomfort. He stood with what was interpreted as a stiff,
satisfied smile on his face, somewhere between a proud
father and, as one staff member whispered, a wannabe
Tony Robbins. This comment was informed by Roberts-
Smith's other efforts to implement military lingo and
culture in the office. Staff were told to 'fight every day' but
also to 'hot wash your guns', which meant leaving work
in the office after they'd given it their all, but not before
preparing for the next day's combat.

In the lead-up to the drum performance, a few of the
staff who'd interacted with Roberts-Smith started to twig
that he had no desire to bring his employees willingly
along with him on his career march at Seven. They were
junior soldiers and he was the aggressive drill sergeant.
He divided staff into different camps. There were those he
favoured, including a few young blonde women, whom he
offered career advice and advancement. His favoured few
also included 'the lads', men he had personally recruited
and whose loyalty was guaranteed. One of them told a
newspaper reporter that Roberts-Smith was 'the most
remarkable man he'd ever met'.

'He could walk into any job he wants. He could be a
scientist, he could go into politics, he could be a world-
class athlete,' the mate said. He also explained to the
journalist that he had trained Roberts-Smith to box. If
Roberts-Smith had wanted to, he could have been 'fighting
for a world title in two years'.

Roberts-Smith's rebuilding of his workforce at Seven
reflected his style as an SAS patrol commander. His
supporters in the office would prosper, invited to long
lunches where Roberts-Smith bought expensive bottles of

wine, drank heavily, told war stories and talked shit about female employees.

During one long lunch, he lambasted Seven's hiring of high-profile sports presenter Mel McLaughlin: 'You know the worst thing? I just don't think she's that good looking.'

At another, he told a stunned table that he used to get paid 'to shoot cunts in the head'.

Those on the outer at Seven, whom Roberts-Smith didn't rate or who didn't fit into his corporate plan, soon knew about it. He had gone about cutting what he perceived as fat, no matter if it meant removing people who had served for years at Seven or had joined the network with promises of longevity. A much-loved, long-time make-up artist was removed. So too was a local newsreader.

Roberts-Smith displayed little obvious interest in what drove many under his watch, the employees who came to work for relatively paltry salaries because they loved being news reporters, or producers, or creatives. Roberts-Smith had levelled with a trusted colleague: 'I'll be frank with you ... I don't really like this industry, to be honest. I don't see myself staying.'

Those who dared challenge his style of leadership learnt not to do so. When a marketing employee complained that another colleague had been subjected to unchecked workplace bullying, Roberts-Smith called the complainant into his office. He towered over her and told her she was weak as piss.

'He's a creep and a bully,' a Seven employee complained to friends. 'I used to feel honoured to work in the media. But under him, Seven became a dark place. He's just a really shady guy.'

In a conversation with one of the other 'lads', Roberts-Smith derided 'the smiling assassins' he believed were intent on undermining him or causing office unrest. 'I hate this shit where people go, "Oh, you know, this person is a bully, this person is this, that person's that and there's sexual harassment", and you throw these things out there.

'I go, "Okay, that's fine, but if we are going to do that then I want to know dates, times, places. I want stat decs on the fucking lot. I don't want your fucking opinion, I don't want people's bullshit rumours. If you say that to me again, make sure you come with the fucking proof. Otherwise, it impacts on you."'

Roberts-Smith told the lads that his fellow executives were also not at his level. He told one of his confidants, 'As a businessperson, or inside the business, you just sit there going, "What the fuck?" … If I was actually in charge … like they fucking pay me to do, then I would be able to actually do a job. But I'm not in charge.'

He'd fronted one executive he learnt had badmouthed him and said, 'You'd better watch yourself, cunt.'

Roberts-Smith was particularly derisive of the way Seven executives, including the CEO Tim Worner, were jealous of his relationship with Stokes. The former soldier had shared holidays at Stokes' Beaver Creek, Colorado, resort and countless hours discussing the media mogul's passion, military history.

It was BRS and KMS, as they called each other, the mega-rich mogul and the mega hero, with their own in-jokes and ability to wheel out the other in a crowd to provoke awe, fear and excitement. Roberts-Smith never considered that Stokes was favouring him for a reason other than the ex-soldier's exceptionalism. It never occurred to him, as it did to others close to Seven's top executives, that there might be something more complex lying behind Stokes' fondness of him.

Was it Stokes' obsession with military history and heroes? Did Stokes feel Roberts-Smith had qualities missing in others he had propelled up the company ladder? Or did Stokes, who'd made his fortune from nothing, see in the corporal who'd become a military hero a similar story of brute determination conquering all?

After bandying around their own theories, a small group of disaffected staff at Seven settled on a shared truth: whether Stokes knew it or not, the new Queensland boss was aloof and arrogant, scowling and unpleasant, a self-styled leadership guru who thought it a good idea to bring a high school drumline band to a workplace full of busy, underpaid newsroom staff.

Despite his bravado, MBA talk and increasingly expensive suits, Roberts-Smith brought another unique attribute to his role as Queensland GM: paranoia. This was why he had called on a private investigator to do him a favour. John McLeod, a balding, husky-voiced ex-cop, had met Roberts-Smith while overseeing security for a major hotel where the media executive was staying. Impressed by the war hero's military achievements, McLeod offered to provide personal security and run special errands for Roberts-Smith if the need arose.

One task Roberts-Smith had set McLeod was snooping. When he hosted drinks at his new Sunshine Coast home, complete with a roundabout driveway and pool, McLeod was installed as a bartender. His real task, though, was eavesdropping. Roberts-Smith wanted to know what people at Seven were saying about him. These drinks and nibbles events looked and felt to some attendees like a scene from a show on how to project success. Even his supposed closest associates would mutter about the awkward vibes. Try as he might, to many, Roberts-Smith never seemed totally comfortable in his own skin. It didn't help that, after a few drinks, he would casually drop the number of enemy he killed in Afghanistan.

Those who knew him well felt something of a dark shadow following Roberts-Smith around, a force that would suck the life out of a room. They knew he was struggling to get to sleep and drinking too much after work. Emma told friends she often overheard him mumbling in the shower or in front of the mirror, giving himself pep talks. At restaurants and bars, a few drinks in, he would rage against his enemies back at SAS headquarters. Certain blokes had been talking shit, he would fume. The word was that some of them had also been talking to Chris Masters, a veteran journalist working on a book about the special forces in Afghanistan.

They were no doubt jealous of all he had accomplished in the military and then at Seven. These haters were deliberately fuelling a whisper campaign, perhaps in an attempt to stir up some interest from Masters. Or perhaps they were hoping to excite interest from an inquiry announced the year before. All anyone needed to know about that particular waste of time was that it was, as Roberts-Smith described it, overseen by a judge who had never so much as stepped foot in Afghanistan and probably never would. Who was Brereton to judge those who put their lives on the line?

But the whispers were getting louder.

CHAPTER 13

THE TWO REPORTERS

June 2017

I recognised Chris Masters before he noticed me. The 68-year-old walked up Elizabeth Street in Sydney's CBD, his face furrowed in intense thought. A brown leather satchel hung over his shoulder. It was raining gently but I wasn't sure Masters had noticed.

He looked older than I remembered, but there was still something of a boyish quality about the famed reporter. Maybe it was the way he leant forward as he walked, like a schoolboy carrying a backpack twice his size, or maybe it was his slight awkwardness in certain social situations.

I wondered just briefly if his satchel contained what Masters had alluded to over the phone: documents that could cast light over the military secrets he'd hinted at. The allure of getting one's hands on files marked classified, official, protected, commercial-in-confidence, was like a drug for most journalists. It certainly was for me.

If there is an art to investigative journalism, it is the dance done with the source to reveal such files, sometimes without feeling like they had revealed anything at all. The more resistant a person is to sharing something secret, the more you have to appeal to their sense of idealism, or injustice, or stoke whatever darker motive may have led them to you in the first place.

It is comparable to asking a boss for a pay rise in the knowledge you almost certainly won't end up with what you have requested but still hopeful you'll be offered something worthwhile. And so you ask a source for a copy of a classified report hoping they will at least tell you the name of the title page and perhaps summarise its contents. Rarely do you actually get a classified report and even more rarely from another journalist.

Masters greeted me outside the Royal Automobile Club with his usual quiet courteousness. Was it cautious warmness? Or just wariness? I had sensed for days that this would be no ordinary meeting, just as it was the last time we'd shaken hands. That had been to say goodbye and I remembered it well. Back then, Masters had what I'd imagined was the hint of a tear in his eye, as had I, and I'd wondered if we'd meet again.

At that last meeting, some seven years before, Masters had been hours away from flying to report on the war in Afghanistan, but his impending trip wasn't the source of our emotion. Perhaps fittingly, we'd had a bust-up over secrets. Our falling-out had ostensibly been about the handling of sensitive information deriving from an organised crime investigation we'd been working on for the ABC television investigative program *Four Corners*.

In time, I'd come to believe that our clash was simply the product of mixing two fiercely focused journalists with their own inbuilt insecurities that were in turn shaped by being at different ends of their careers. But when it happened, it felt personal and gutting.

As an ambitious university journalism student, Masters was my hero, a near-mythical figure who had revealed some of the most consequential stories in Australian history. His *Four Corners* story 'The Moonlight State' had not only exposed systemic police and political corruption in Queensland in the 1980s, but had captured a moment in which the distrust of state institutions began to seep into middle Australia.

His program about the French spy service sinking Greenpeace's ship the *Rainbow Warrior* was the sort of journalism that was brimming with the ideals, impact and adventure romanticised by the Watergate film *All The President's Men*. Masters wasn't dashing in the style of Robert Redford playing Bob Woodward, but he exuded a raw and authentic passion for his craft that was tangible. I'd found it intoxicating.

When I was assigned as his researcher in 2004 as a 23-year-old, I'd locked myself in an edit suite and watched Masters' *Four Corners* programs from the 1980s and 1990s. With his large glasses, serious face and sonorous voice, the unspoken moral outrage at the corruption and abuses he was uncovering felt as loud as his carefully chosen words.

Reporting on the road with Masters to meet gangsters, hitmen and police, I'd witnessed his uncanny ability to engender trust. Senior police, high-ranking public servants and crime bosses would call him, eager to spill their secrets. Detectives who had worked in Queensland would often find a quiet moment to self-consciously tell Masters how he had restored their faith in policing.

That was the journalist I wanted to be, I'd told myself. I'd also caught glimpses of the Masters that some colleagues warned me about. He could be obsessive about his work, to the point where those around him felt invisible. He didn't suffer those he considered fools.

He wasn't alone in drawing such criticism; I'd hear the same thing said of myself, followed by the observation that I was so obsessive, perhaps I had no clue how I appeared to others. This would injure my insecure self, but I learnt in time to push it away, building a few deep friendships at work, but keeping my social life mostly outside the newsroom.

My mates called Australia's most esteemed journalism awards, the Walkleys, the Wankleys, and that played fine with me. And the fact was, I *was* obsessive about investigative journalism, just like Masters.

Once Masters let you in, there was a gentleness to him that many people missed. He seemed to enjoy being my mentor and was generous with his time and advice. Around those at work he truly trusted, mostly the cameramen and sound operators, he could be self-deprecating. When he was awarded an honorary university title, he nicknamed himself the 'fat professor'.

But with passion comes conflict. In 2010, when he'd been asked by the *Four Corners* executive producer to help me as lead reporter shape a story on organised crime and corruption, Masters and I had clashed over how the secrets in the story would be shared and with whom. I was too enamoured with my own story, believing it to be far better than it was and believing the classified files that informed it juicier than they were. Masters was at the other end of the scale, the product of seeing so much for so long. Information about the program had made its way out of the *Four Corners* office and I'd reacted with the righteous fury of a young reporter. In response,

I'd seen, for the first time, the flash of Masters' anger I'd been warned about. We had made amends as he'd left for the war.

'Let's put this behind us,' I'd written to him that same day. 'And do not let it cloud your mind in Afghanistan.' He'd written back politely but in the next seven years, we'd had only fleeting contact.

That was until mid-2017, when I began to poke around the whispers growing louder in media, political and defence circles that Australian special forces may have engaged in misconduct in Afghanistan. A military Inspector-General's inquiry overseen by a little-known NSW Supreme Court judge, Paul Brereton, had been announced. Some old friends and colleagues of mine at the ABC, Sam Clark and Dan Oakes, had also published a story relying on leaked classified Defence files detailing the suspicious deaths of Afghans during Australian raids. There was no smoking gun in their story, but Oakes, in particular, was convinced that much more lay beneath the public narrative of the Afghanistan conflict.

It was Oakes who had told me that Masters was writing a defence force vetted book chronicling the history of Australia's special forces in Afghanistan. Some reporters were sceptical of the venture, wondering aloud if the defence force had sought to trade access for positive spin. If Defence had done so, it would be for nought. The reporter I knew in Masters would never bury a secret.

And that's how I had found him when I called him up. He was bristling with annoyance at his publisher for having removed content from his manuscript in fear of a defamation lawsuit. The offending material involved a soldier I had heard of but knew little about. As Masters talked, I googled the man's name: Ben Roberts-Smith.

This was why we had agreed to meet at the Royal Automobile Club in Sydney, a musty, formal venue which strived to project the air of a British establishment club without the expensive fees or captains of industry prepared to pay them.

'It's cheap, private and quiet,' Masters told me as we made our way to a table covered in a crisp white cloth. We ate and drank, talking journalism, family and Masters' upcoming book. I opened up to my old mentor, telling him that after fifteen years of reporting, I felt tired, full of self-doubt and was thinking about leaving the profession. I was sick of worrying about making mistakes, about being sued for defamation, about copping threats from the powerful and pernicious, about seeing colleagues made redundant as media companies fought to stay alive. I told Masters that sometimes I would double over the toilet in the morning, dry-retching from stress. My vulnerability appeared to strike a chord with him. He'd lived through all my worry and more and I wondered if he felt his younger self in me.

'Death by a thousand courts,' was how he described the way investigative reporters faced constant litigation threats due to Australia's plaintiff-friendly defamation regime.

Over his second glass of red wine, he spoke of the challenges he was facing in handling some of the information he'd found out about Roberts-Smith. Defamation risk had once again reared its ugly head. The contested allegations involved claims of bullying of fellow SAS soldiers and a disagreement in a small patrol team in 2006 about an Afghan man shot dead on a mountain ridge. Masters had no hard proof of any war crimes, but he had heard enough whispers to be greatly troubled.

All signs suggested that Australia's most famous soldier was a more complex character than his public persona.

Fearing negative coverage, a lawyer for Roberts-Smith had sent a letter warning of the consequences of defamation to Masters' publisher. This was all stock-in-trade for Masters, but this time something was different. The same lawyer had also written to two SAS soldiers, threatening them with defamation action and accusing them of leaking adverse information to Masters.

Offering to help Masters, I said, 'Maybe *The Age* and the *Sydney Morning Herald* can step up. And if there is more to find, let's go digging.' Masters seemed energised by this. As I stood to leave, he unzipped his satchel and handed me a manila folder.

'I can't use these for the book, but you might find them useful,' he told me. I felt a twinge of excitement as I placed the folder in my bag.

In the back of a cab to Sydney airport, I opened the folder, making sure the blank cover shielded whatever was inside. I was immediately glad I had done so. The folder held various military documents, each with markings denoting the secrecy of their contents.

My eyes were drawn to a defence department report about special forces culture which had been marked up with a pen by someone unknown. The author's name was foreign to me: Samantha Crompvoets. One paragraph had been underlined more heavily than elsewhere. I read it once, and then again, and felt a surge of excitement. Masters had been sitting on a small gold mine.

There were no individual soldiers named in the Crompvoets' report, but she had disclosed concerns about the 'unsanctioned and illegal application of violence on operations, disregard for human life and dignity, and the perception of a complete lack of accountability'.

My mind flashed to something Masters had now mentioned several times. There were rumours about a mission in a village called Darwan where Ben Roberts-Smith's patrol team had taken a prisoner whose treatment had sparked ructions within the SAS. Sydney's busy traffic flashed by my cab window, and the rain was falling heavier as I sat in silence, scanning the secrets in the files before me and feeling more alive than I'd felt in months.

CHAPTER 14

THE JUDGE AND THE INQUIRY

March 2017

On the wall of Justice Paul Le Gay Brereton's chambers in the Supreme Court of New South Wales hung a piece of Japanese calligraphy which translates to: 'True heart is the core of everything.' Japanese Lieutenant General Baba Masao, the Supreme Commander of the Japanese Army in Borneo had given it as a gift to Brereton's father, Russell Le Gay Brereton.

Brereton Senior was a lawyer and officer who'd served during the war in the Middle East and Pacific Islands before being appointed to try Japanese war criminals. In a tent in the shade of palm trees near the Australian camp in Borneo, Brereton had prosecuted Sergeant Major Sugino, a murderous Japanese soldier nicknamed the Jersey Bull because of his aggression towards Australian prisoners of war. In his last act of resistance and honour, Sugino had yelled '*banzai*' three times before he was executed by a military firing squad.

It was Brereton's honour that Sugino's commanding officer, Lieutenant General Masao, had recognised in gifting him the calligraphy. Even as the Australian press had been baying for blood, Brereton Senior displayed unflinching fairness towards enemy accused of the most heinous of war crimes. Baba faced death by hanging a short time later, but his gift had travelled with Russell Brereton back to Australia and was displayed in his chambers when he was appointed a judge of the NSW Supreme Court.

Paul Brereton was just sixteen when his dad passed, but he knew already he would follow in his father's footsteps as a lawyer and military man. He'd hung the calligraphy in his own chambers when he'd been appointed as a judge to serve the same court as his father.

'True heart is the core of everything.'

Brereton supposed it meant that only with a fair and honest heart could one deliver justice. His father could have easily been swept up in nationalistic fervour, but instead he'd done things by the book, establishing facts and applying the law regardless of public sentiment. At his judicial swearing-in ceremony in 2005, Brereton invoked his father to explain his own passion for the law. Justice would only prevail while 'lawyers of ability and conviction can and will fearlessly act for unpopular causes'.

As a judge, Paul Brereton had presided over a mix of controversial and difficult cases, including those involving the fate of children adopted out of dysfunctional homes. Compared to cases in which the wealthy battled the wealthy, adoption disputes often involved people with little except hardship and love for a child they couldn't care for. Brereton was quietly proud that his work as a judge had helped change the court's stuffy attitude towards such cases. He'd also felt the glare of the media from the bench when he'd presided over an acrimonious battle over family money and promises, pitting Australia's richest and arguably most powerful woman, mining magnate Gina Rinehart, against her own children. In his judgment, Brereton had scolded Rinehart for using tactics bordering on intimidation. 'I have never seen such pressure exerted, so persistently, on a litigant, as has been apparent in this case,' he'd said in court. His comments were reported around the world.

It was a year after the Rinehart case that Brereton had received a call to head an inquiry that, if it actually bore fruit, would face media and public attention of a sort he'd never experienced before. Where his father had resisted popular sentiment demanding the Japanese face revenge rather than due process, he was facing something of a reverse dilemma.

Many Australians instinctively rallied against anyone who hadn't been to war but dared scrutinise the conduct of our military personnel, condemning scrutineers in ivory towers like academics and journalists. Or judges.

Brereton had risen up the part-time military chain of command to become a senior officer overseeing the defence force reserves but, in his time in charge, the judge had not been deployed to combat. So it wasn't war fighting experience that had prompted Army Chief Angus Campbell to request Brereton head up an Afghanistan war crimes inquiry to examine the allegations laid out in the Crompvoets reports. Brereton guessed it was because he was trusted to be painstakingly fair, relentlessly thorough and unfailingly discreet. His job was to conclude if there was 'any substance to persistent rumours of criminal or unlawful conduct' involving the SAS or Commandos in Afghanistan.

Now, a year into his inquiry, many in the military community were already muttering about the armchair general with the arrogance to be delving into the fog of war. Brereton was acutely aware that he wasn't, as yet at least, at risk of facing any real public backlash. Nobody knew it, but he had found no hard evidence to back up the most serious of Crompvoets' assertions. He hadn't discounted them – it was too early for that – but he wasn't convinced they were true, either. There was every possibility that his inquiry would go nowhere, and he'd soon be back on the judicial bench full-time, hearing cases about adoption, bankruptcy and business disputes.

All Brereton really knew for certain was that the SAS and the Commandos were a closed shop. Few soldiers appeared eager to talk to him, seemingly scared of being labelled a snitch, a betrayer of the special forces' secretive brotherhood. Or maybe there was nothing to report: no prisoner executions, no blood lust, no soldiers gone rogue. Maybe it was Crompvoets who'd gone rogue.

Brereton was assigned a small team of staff, some of whom he'd selected or who'd come recommended due to their legal or investigative skills. He told his team that perhaps the only way to break the special forces code of silence might be to use the unique powers given to him as part of his inquiry. They enabled the judge to order soldiers and officers to appear before him and answer questions, forgoing their constitutional right to silence. In return for telling the truth, his witnesses would be guaranteed immunity from criminal or military prosecution. Lie to Brereton, and he could threaten to have a soldier charged.

The interview he had lined up for that day, though, wasn't with a soldier. Brereton wanted to talk to the woman who had caused all the fuss.

* * *

Samantha Crompvoets greeted Judge Brereton with a smile.

When she'd previously mingled with Brereton at military events, Crompvoets had been struck by his warm and engaging manner. They were not descriptors usually applied to judges or generals, and Brereton was both. But today, Brereton had a stern demeanour. It took Crompvoets a few minutes of listening to realise that the judge was not only frustrated but looking to her to break an impasse. His inquiry had clearly stalled.

'We have found no one in the SAS or Commandos to back up your report,' he told her. 'Perhaps we are speaking to the wrong people, but no one has said anything of substance.'

Crompvoets immediately felt a wave of unrest. Had she overreached, or misjudged the motives or credibility of those who told her of Afghan prisoners being tortured and murdered? She had always told anyone who asked, including Campbell and Sengelman, that she had never kept any recording or notes of the special forces informants who had assisted her inquiry. She had promised them anonymity, knowing that if they were outed within their own ranks as rats, their careers would be finished, or worse.

Brereton watched her intently as she again explained this. The friendly jurist was now a steely-eyed judge. He wasn't threatening or intimidating, but he was unflinchingly resolute.

'We have the power to compel people to talk to us, be they civilians or military,' he said, before pausing.

The judge had already resolved not to use his powers on Crompvoets but he wanted to ensure she knew he was nevertheless determined to lift up every rock he could.

Crompvoets repeated that she had kept nothing. In some cases, she didn't even know the names of those who had confided in her. She had made a pledge to men who'd put their livelihoods on the line and wasn't about to break her word.

A few minutes later, she walked from the inquiry office into the open air. She ached to her core. *I feel like shit*, she thought to herself.

It seemed obvious Brereton doubted her findings would ever be corroborated. Maybe the soldiers who had trusted her were right. Maybe the truth would never come out.

CHAPTER 15

WORDS AND THREATS

October 2017

I slipped my shoes on and crept out of the house. It was still cold and dark, but I couldn't sleep. As I ran past Californian bungalows and fifties red-brick houses towards the creek, I was reviving an old tradition. Whenever a story I'd written that had already sparked legal threats and editor intervention was about to hit newsstands and porches in Melbourne and Sydney, I'd lie in bed, legs sweaty and restless, mind racing with the question: What have I got wrong?

As if searching for a slip-up, I'd log on to the newsroom's online system at 2am and reread my copy, cursing grammatical errors as I searched for anything more seismically flawed. My copy would have already passed through three or so sets of editors' eyes, but I'd log in again at 3am and check. Just in case I'd stuffed up.

When I still couldn't doze off, I put on my sneakers and a hoodie and ran into the dark morning, a ghostlike figure pounding his worry out of existence. That morning I headed out at 5am. My story about Ben Roberts-Smith was short, less than 1000 words, carefully penned and even more carefully legalled. I had written about Roberts-Smith's 'first seminal battle' and 'first major decoration, a Medal for Gallantry' for what the official record described as 'courage, tenacity and sense of duty to his patrol'. My story also detailed how Roberts-Smith's medal citation had not dealt with all of the events of that historic day.

The article described how Chris Masters had, while researching for his book on the Afghan war, uncovered conflicting accounts from Roberts-Smith's own patrol team about the death of an Afghan teen spotted by two SAS soldiers who were hiding in an observation post. According to Roberts-Smith, jealousy was the reason for his colleagues' misgivings over the teen's death, the subsequent battle and his supposed bullying of a fellow soldier. He believed his comrades were bitter that he had won not just a Medal for Gallantry, but a Victoria Cross.

'The bullying is what they do to me,' he told Masters in a tense interview for *No Front Line*, Masters' book that was due to be released in October 2017. 'Bullies are cowards. They stay in the shadows. This is about group cowardice. I don't like bullies. I am sick of it.'

As I ran, the pre-dawn light illuminated my path. Warehouses lay to my left, the creek, swollen from heavy rain, to my right. My story wasn't overly controversial. It didn't link Roberts-Smith to any war crime. The article contextualised the dispute over the 2006 mission as an example of 'the moral ambiguity of battle and questions over when and when not to fire'. It described Roberts-Smith as 'iconic and polarising' but also described how 'for those grumbling about the decorated soldier turned successful businessman, jealousy looms as an obvious motive'.

As I ran, I wondered why Roberts-Smith had reacted so defensively to my earlier attempts to engage with him. Weeks earlier, I'd sent him a LinkedIn message requesting a meeting or interview. My message was polite and respectful, but had also flagged the fact of the ongoing Brereton Inquiry into rumours of unlawful conduct in Afghanistan. I'd also written that it was 'clear' that Roberts-Smith was 'a target for some complainants'.

With Masters' help, I had made contact with several defence force insiders, including one who'd leaked me a complaint about Roberts-Smith written by a sergeant called Nick Simkin and signed by a small number of other patrol commanders. This complaint had nothing to do with war crimes or the 2006 mission that had split Roberts-Smith's patrol team, but rather detailed concerns from a 2012 mission about Roberts-Smith's bullying and attempt to cover up and blame a bungled mission on a junior trooper.

My LinkedIn message was a genuine attempt to speak to Ben Roberts-Smith. Journalists often spend far too long circling the subject of a story, having their confirmation bias fed by a coterie of critics only to have the target of their investigation dispel claims with facts at the last minute. I wanted to meet Roberts-Smith and tell him straight up about the concerns I'd learnt of, including the formal complaint written by Simkin.

My view was that Simkin's complaint was as much about one soldier as it was about the officers who wrote up citations and handed out awards, such as Roberts-Smith's leadership honour. I'd written this in the story now landing on readers' front porches: 'The complaint's ultimate beef, though, is not with Roberts-Smith but with those up the chain of command.'

Roberts-Smith never responded to my request. Instead, I'd received a blistering email from a defamation lawyer, Mark O'Brien. O'Brien was known for his fierce attacks on reporters to shut down their articles about his clients. On his website, he had republished a line from an article describing O'Brien as one of the 'most feared' defamation lawyers in the country.

While I could see the merit in his approach if the journalism was shoddy, I hadn't written a single word about Roberts-Smith when O'Brien had launched a legal salvo via email. 'Yesterday you contacted my client through LinkedIn,' O'Brien wrote, noting Roberts-Smith had 'had no knowledge of any suggestion he is in any way involved in the year-long investigation by' Justice Brereton. 'It is apparent that you are attempting to falsely link my client, as Australia's most decorated soldier, with the year-long investigation purely for a headline grabbing purpose.'

Any hint in print that Roberts-Smith was under investigation for 'any alleged misconduct or breach of duty in Afghanistan will be a most despicable and indefensible defamation'.

On behalf of his client, O'Brien had not only threatened to sue me for defamation 'without further notice' but wrote that if his client learnt I had made 'false allegations' while talking to people in the course of my journalistic research, I'd also be in legal trouble.

I'd found O'Brien's letter bewildering. Was this grenade the product of O'Brien's legal advice to Roberts-Smith, or was it the ex-soldier seeking to shut down any journalist who dared ask questions of him? I'd written back to O'Brien politely, hoping that if my response made it to Roberts-Smith, he might rethink his decision not to engage with me.

'The fact that I sought to speak to your client about

these issues should be read only as evidence of my desire to thoroughly research the matter,' I'd written. 'This is sound journalistic practice and done in the interests of fairness and accuracy ... I'll take it that Ben doesn't want to have a confidential chat. I would, however, ask that you send him this email.'

With Masters' help, I had also kept on researching. I'd heard nothing from Roberts-Smith directly in the weeks that had passed since then, but O'Brien resurfaced. He fired off another missive filled with yet more legal threats and accompanied by a full-blown assault on the credibility of the author of the 2014 complaint, Sergeant Simkin.

Roberts-Smith, through O'Brien, claimed that Simkin had 'smuggled unregistered automatic rifles into Afghanistan by falsifying customs documents', breaching the criminal law. The letter also alleged that Simkin had asked Roberts-Smith to cover up his crime, which Roberts-Smith had 'rightly refused to do'.

The intention was clear: Roberts-Smith wanted to convince me that it was Simkin who was the soldier deserving of scrutiny. Simkin's complaint was no more than a malicious smear. Repeat it and I would be sued to kingdom come.

O'Brien then sent a letter on behalf of his client to my senior editors and, unusually, to Greg Hywood, the chief executive of the media company employing me. His intention in doing this also seemed clear. O'Brien wanted my bosses to know that I was at risk of costing the company dearly, both in dollars and reputation.

* * *

I stopped running, gathered my breath and opened up *The Age* on my phone. The story was halfway down the page: 'The fog of war and politics leads to controversy over Afghan war mission', the headline stated. I read the copy for what must have been the thirtieth time. With my editors breathing down my neck, and O'Brien breathing down theirs, I'd been careful to differentiate between the concerns about Roberts-Smith's leadership in the SAS, and the war crimes rumours focused on by Justice Brereton.

The judge, I'd written, was probing 'allegations that have nothing to do with Roberts-Smith'. This wasn't strictly true. Masters and I had by now spent weeks hitting the phones. In whispered conversations with SAS insiders, including soldiers and support staff, the conduct of Roberts-Smith's patrol team had come up again and again.

It was evident that these opaque tales were eating away at some SAS members, fuelled by stories told in jumbled snippets at barbecues, pubs and, increasingly, during veterans' debriefings with psychologists. None of our sources were direct eyewitnesses to any execution, but many had expressed a genuine concern that Roberts-Smith, or those close to him, had crossed moral lines on the battlefield.

The persistent rumours had ranged from the sinister to the shocking: a training exercise during which one SAS member instructed a junior soldier to practise executing prisoners of war; 'kill' competitions that encouraged soldiers to chalk up head-counts; pistols planted on unarmed Afghans to justify their deaths; junior soldiers subjected to a 'blooding' ritual involving the execution of a prisoner to enable the rookie to chalk up their first kill.

I was initially deeply sceptical of all these claims. None of them was firm enough to put into questions that could be sent to Roberts-Smith through O'Brien. Far more journalistic research was needed.

'He says you're just jealous of his VC,' I'd fire back at sources when they urged me to look more closely at the war hero. The response to this was mostly the same: 'Why are none of us talking shit about Donno?' This was at least one fact beyond doubt: the other SAS recipient of the VC, Mark Donaldson, was subject to none of the same scuttlebutt.

As I placed my phone in my pocket and turned to run back towards home, my thoughts turned to the loudest whisper about Roberts-Smith. It involved a story about an Afghan prisoner who had been pushed, thrown or kicked from a great height. I was even more sceptical about the truth of this allegation, even if our sources in the SAS seemed convinced it was more than a tall tale.

To me, it seemed too far-fetched, too ugly, too brutal, even for soldiers who'd endured endless deployments to an endless war.

* * *

Just before midnight the night after my story had run, my editor called me. 'He's responded in *The Aus*,' he said. *The Aus* was *The Australian* and *he* was Roberts-Smith. 'And it's not just him. It's a pile-on. Nelson is quoted. So is Stokes.'

The article read like a free kick for the famed soldier, a press release that had been polished and published. The paper had given him an uncritical platform to dismiss the inconsistencies apparent in the different accounts of the 2006 mission that Masters had dug up during his book research. They were no more than the product of the recollections of a 'bitter' former SAS member, Roberts-Smith told the reporters.

The article didn't mention the 2014 complaint by Simkin or anything else adverse to Roberts-Smith, and it allowed him to savage Masters' book for scrutinising the 2006 mission on the basis that it involved Sergeant Matthew Locke, an SAS member later killed in action.

'(Masters) is really affecting the legacy of an Australian hero killed in action ... His son is in the army now. That's not fair,' Roberts-Smith had told the paper. 'There's an agenda there against Matt Locke and, for whatever reason, because I've got the profile, it's better to throw my name into the mix because you know it's going to be a headline and that's essentially why I'm being dragged into it ... I've been under the microscope for the last six years and, you know what, my record is spotless.'

I'd spoken to Masters earlier in the day, after *The Australian* had asked him a series of questions. He sounded tired and upset, especially at the allegation he was smearing Locke or had been insensitive to grieving families. His book, like my article, had done no more than document the fact that Roberts-Smith's patrol team was deeply divided about what had gone down in 2006 and that this dispute had burned on ever since. There was no suggestion that Matthew Locke wasn't a brave soldier or had committed a war crime.

I heard the strain in Masters' voice as he'd explained how he'd written to Defence to notify any families of dead soldiers who were named in the book about its impending publication. He'd even offered to 'personally background any family members'.

The Australian had capped off its attack on Masters with Roberts-Smith's claim that he was seeking to profit from the war service of others by writing a book about Afghanistan: 'The only thing that matters to me is that people who have served their country in Afghanistan ... their legacy is never detracted from, just simply because of someone's attempts at personal gain.'

The war memorial director and ex-defence minister Brendan Nelson had been interviewed, as had the billionaire businessman Kerry Stokes, Roberts-Smith's boss. Stokes called for the SAS to be 'applauded and respected'. But it was Nelson's comments, as the custodian of the nation's war history, that echoed in my head as I lay in bed in the pre-dawn hours.

'It's my very strong view that the alleged controversies involving special forces, unless involving the most egregious breaches of the laws of armed combat, should be left alone,' Nelson was quoted as saying. 'The average Australian is not generally stupid and they know that things don't always go according to plan in war and that armchair lawyers and others on their sanctimonious thrones should not be shaping our attitude to what in the end are very serious military actions necessary to deal with people that threaten our freedoms and our values ... Where is the national interest in tearing down our heroes?'

Nelson and Roberts-Smith appeared to me to be sending the media a warning. Up until that point, I hadn't seriously wondered if it was worth pushing on with our investigation into Roberts-Smith, even after the legal threats from his lawyer. We were simply undertaking public interest journalism. It was our job to tell the public what the armed services were doing in their name, but only if and when we found compelling evidence to justify publication. If this was the public relations response Roberts-Smith had mustered for an article that had ultimately said very little about him, what forces would he unleash if we corroborated anything more serious?

CHAPTER 16

RAIDED

Late 2017

On 20 October 2017, just hours after Ben Roberts-Smith's blistering response was splashed on the front page of *The Australian*, Andrew Burrell, a journalist at the paper, received an anonymous email. The sender was a person calling themselves Blowerw2 and their message was both urgent and alarming, unlike anything Burrell had ever received while covering state and federal politics.

Blowerw2 was portraying themselves as a whistleblower with information from deep within the ranks of the SAS, the elite fighting unit stationed a short drive from *The Australian*'s Perth bureau, where Burrell had moved after spending years at the Canberra press gallery. Blowerw2 made it clear in his email that unless action was taken quickly, people could die. The subject of Blowerw2's concerns sent to Burrell was a serving sergeant in the SAS.

According to Blowerw2, Sergeant Nick Simkin was a gun nut who in 2012 had smuggled into Afghanistan an 'untraceable fully automatic machine gun' by 'falsifying customs documents' in a manner that could have enabled battlefield misconduct to go undiscovered. And now, five years later, Simkin was keeping a fresh stash of illegal guns in Perth. Blowerw2 warned that Simkin might use these weapons to cause grave public harm, and highlighted this threat by citing the Las Vegas massacre, a reference to the recent murder by a crazed gunman of fifty-eight innocent civilians at a country music festival.

The email to Burrell also revealed that Blowerw2 had, weeks earlier, sent their warning about Simkin to the commissioner of the Australian Federal Police, Andrew Colvin, and to a federal politician known to use parliamentary privilege to air serious allegations. These earlier missives were clearly written to jolt the police into action and to force the SAS to sack Simkin.

Whoever was behind Blowerw2 desperately wanted Simkin to be investigated and wouldn't rest until he was. 'This matter is time sensitive and a critical public safety issue due to the high level of specialised training the nominated individual has received over many years and his current ability to access untraceable automatic weapons,' Blowerw2's email to police stated. Blowerw2 also warned the AFP that they wouldn't hesitate to take other 'courses of action' if the police commissioner should 'fail to perform your duties in actioning this information'.

Contacting Burrell was just one of these courses of action. Blowerw2's strategy seemed obvious. If the police wouldn't act on the anonymous tip-off, then perhaps they'd respond if the same information appeared in a national newspaper.

Intrigued, but with no means of confirming the accuracy of anything in the anonymous message, Burrell replied to the mysterious emailer by asking them if they were a member of the SAS. A short time later, this was confirmed.

Burrell had no proof of the accuracy of this claim, but he wasn't flying completely blind. His editor at *The Australian* had been contacted about the same allegations, although this time not by someone from the SAS. On this occasion, it was a Sunshine Coast paparazzo who'd been asked to do a favour and tip off the media about Simkin. The photographer was a 'cut out', a middleman doing the bidding of someone else who wanted to remain in the shadows. Blowerw2 was possibly the same. Or perhaps they were what they purported to be: a concerned member of the SAS, worried that Simkin would turn his guns on the innocent.

Burrell knew something else, too, something Blowerw2 had failed to disclose in their emails to police, the politician and the reporter. Simkin was the author of an internal military complaint about Ben Roberts-Smith, the contents of which *The Age* and *Sydney Morning Herald* had revealed just a day before. This was the same story that had already prompted Burrell's own paper to provide Roberts-Smith a front-page platform to attack his critics.

This background information raised another distinct possibility. Perhaps someone supportive of Roberts-Smith was behind the Blowerw2 email and was feeding Burrell as part of a more sinister plot to silence Simkin by having him named in the media and investigated by police and by the SAS. After all, the bulk of Blowerw2's email was about alleged gun-smuggling into Afghanistan five years earlier. Why hadn't Blowerw2 raised these concerns previously? Why only now, after Simkin's complaint had hit the press in the shadow of the Brereton Inquiry?

Days later, *The Australian* published two articles leading with the allegation that Simkin had 'smuggled automatic weapons from Perth to Afghanistan in an attempt to evade responsibility for incidents on the battlefield'. Burrell's reporting flagged that Simkin had made a formal complaint about Roberts-Smith, but the possibility that it was Simkin's complaint, rather than any genuine concern about gun-smuggling, that had led to Blowerw2's tip-offs was flagged only in the last line of one of Burrell's articles.

If Blowerw2 believed that press coverage might prompt law-enforcement action, they were right. A week after Burrell's story was published, detectives at a Perth police station held a brief planning meeting and then headed towards the headquarters of the SAS. The most senior detective was carrying a search warrant.

* * *

Nick Simkin had dropped his son off at school, driven to SAS headquarters at Campbell Barracks and was walking towards his office when he spied a colleague looking ashen faced. A few minutes later, he discovered why.

Four military policemen had arrived at the barracks to search storage areas and offices used by Simkin. They read him his rights and explained their ultimate intent: they were looking for unlicensed guns. At first, Simkin didn't know whether to be bemused or enraged. He quickly settled on the latter. He had no doubt why the search was taking place. This wasn't about unregistered weapons. Someone was sending him a message.

Simkin had felt uneasy for days now, ever since Burrell called him and told him about the emails from a person calling themselves Blowerw2. Simkin told Burrell that it was beyond obvious that the journalist was being used and that he suspected the anonymous whistleblower was motivated by his challenging of Ben Roberts-Smith's citation. But Simkin never expected much to come of it, and certainly not a search of his workplace.

After it turned up nothing, the military police told Simkin they needed to escort him to the barracks gate. He arrived there to find two unmarked police cars manned by several armed detectives. Now it was the turn of the state authorities.

'Are you Sergeant Nick Simkin?'

He nodded.

'We have received an anonymous complaint about firearms. We have a warrant authorising the search of your home.'

Simkin's anger now ratcheted up a notch. Did the police really want to raid his family home? Was he really about to be bundled into a cop car like a common crook?

In the back of the police vehicle, he broke the silence. 'My wife will not be very happy,' he told the two detectives in the front seats. 'She is South American and she has a temper. There will be fireworks.'

Simkin's wife was with one of their children at an orthodontist's appointment. If he could at least break the news to her that they were about to be raided, she wouldn't have to deal with the shame and shock of discovering it from a neighbour.

'Can I ring her?' he asked.

'No worries, mate,' one of the detectives said.

As he arrived at his house, there were eight police waiting. One of them read Simkin his rights. He opened his front door, watching them file in. A female officer began filming as her colleagues searched through drawers.

'You know you won't find anything,' he said to the detective who appeared to be leading the search. The cop looked embarrassed, so Simkin kept talking.

'You know this is a malicious complaint. This is nothing to do with me being a nutter.'

The cop nodded.

'We gathered that might be the case, mate. That's why we didn't come knocking at three am. But because there has been a serious complaint about guns and public safety, we had no choice.'

Simkin's attention was suddenly diverted. His wife was at the door, and he heard her demanding to know what was happening. 'This is my family house,' she pleaded to a policewoman. 'I'm here to support my husband.'

Simkin could see the distress on his wife's face as she walked towards him. 'It's okay,' he told her. 'They'll be gone soon.'

The police had found no pistols, no machine guns, no weapon of any sort, nor would they. There was nothing there.

As the search wrapped up, the senior detective signalled to Simkin to follow him outside.

'We know you are good people, but we just have to do this,' he said apologetically.

'This is a joke,' his wife said to the most senior cop. 'This is part of a campaign. It's part of people trying to denigrate my husband for standing up to someone powerful.'

'What's going to happen to whoever cooked up this bullshit?' Simkin asked.

The policeman shrugged.

'You're free to put in your own complaint.'

Simkin swore under his breath. He had little doubt his complaint about Roberts-Smith was the real reason for the raid.

But he had no way of proving anything. All he had was an anonymous email address which would no doubt lead nowhere: Blowerw2@gmail.com.

CHAPTER 17

A CALL AND A COVERT RECORDING

28 January 2018

Ben Roberts-Smith dialled a number and, as he did, he readied a covert recording device. He was paranoid, unsure of who he could trust. Ever since he'd learnt some of his old comrades were speaking ill of him, he had resolved to target them. Defamation threats had been sent to his ex-patrol members via his lawyer, Mark O'Brien. Nick Simkin had copped a raid.

'What happened to Simkin will scare the others,' Roberts-Smith texted his wife.

Now, he was readying to secretly tape the ex-soldier who had worked hand-in-glove with Simkin in Afghanistan.

Roberts-Smith hit record as the phone rang.

'Keith Nueling speaking.'

'Nuelo. It's RS, mate.'

The words were friendly but the tone was not. In the recording, Roberts-Smith sounded defensive and tense. He wasn't quite sure where Nueling sat in the hierarchy of Roberts-Smith haters, but he'd sent him a legal threat via Mark O'Brien, just in case. He had added some extra spice, too. Nueling was related by marriage to the family of Australia's richest woman, Perth mining magnate Gina Rinehart. So Roberts-Smith cc-ed Rinehart into his legal threat to sue Nueling. Roberts-Smith called it 'going loud'. This was military slang for taking off the suppressor from your rifle before you fired. He wanted Nueling to watch his mouth, and bringing Rinehart into the game would help.

The legal threat seemed to cause the desired ripples. Nueling had sought an audience with Roberts-Smith, leading to today's phone call. His voice piped out of the speaker phone as the tape recorder rolled. If Roberts-Smith sounded combative, Nueling sounded calm, if slightly exasperated.

'Emailing Gina Rinehart with that document was pretty uncool,' he said.

Roberts-Smith had no hard proof that Nueling was spreading information to the media or the war crimes inquiry. But, at the very least, Nueling's mates were stirring up the past.

'I think you very well know what has gone on in the last couple of years and particularly what has happened with that inquiry,' Roberts-Smith shot back at his former comrade. 'I know you have talked shit about me. I know that. I know you are mates with all those guys … Just remember, I was minding my own fucking business one day and I get attacked by all these fucking journalists … People got together and deliberately fucking targeted me by colluding on a lot of shit which is fucking … I find it pretty hard to take.'

Roberts-Smith continued: 'I was going to sue. Absolutely have no doubt that is what was going to happen if I had any inkling or thought that you were involved.' As he spoke, his tone shifted from accusatory to self-pitying. 'I'm so fucking over it, it's not funny.'

Nueling remained calm, saying he hadn't given the Brereton Inquiry or any journalists any information. 'I don't know where this inquiry is at or where it is going. I haven't had anything to do with that,' he insisted.

The mention of the Brereton Inquiry triggered something in Roberts-Smith. He appeared ever-so-slightly to change gears, his words tumbling out as he denigrated the investigation. 'I have never spoken to them and have never been invited. So if nothing has happened by now it is going to be a fuckin' whatever it is ... Which is some ridiculous, broad sweeping thing that really fucks everybody over. And has no purpose. And is not necessary.'

His attempt to dismiss the Brereton probe rang hollow. The inquiry hadn't stalled, or at least not completely. Soldiers in Roberts-Smith's old patrol teams had been handed subpoenas to attend secret hearings before Justice Brereton. The inquiry was working like a stealthy submarine that very occasionally broke the surface, only to submerge again. Those close to Roberts-Smith sensed an increasing fixation on the question of whether it was him it was circling.

For the first time in the conversation, it was Nueling who sounded like he had the upper hand. 'Well, whatever comes of it, I don't know,' he said, before casually tossing a grenade into the conversation. 'Part of it has actually come from your own patrol,' Nueling told him. He was suggesting it was those Roberts-Smith considered loyal who might be talking. The comment appeared to momentarily infect Roberts-Smith's voice with a trace of panic.

'What are you talking about, from my ... [are] you talking about 2012 or 2010?'

Just as quickly, Roberts-Smith appeared to steel himself. No one in his crew had broken ranks. He'd spoken to his patrol members 'again and again', he told Nueling. They had his back.

The only people who were breaking the code were those in the SAS who Nueling ran with. They had 'done what we don't do ... which is fucking talk out of school,' Roberts-Smith said icily. 'And say a lot of shit that isn't fuckin' real.'

CHAPTER 18

THE HUNT

February 2018

With the cabin lights dimmed, and most of those aboard the Qantas flight asleep or watching movies, I opened my laptop. Chris Masters was across the aisle, deep into a book. Masters was sixty-nine to my thirty-eight, but he still seemed to thrive on the journalistic quest, the hunt for an elusive truth. The prospect of our mission to Perth had enlivened him. We spent days attempting to line up meetings with serving and former members of the SAS. A dozen or so had agreed to consider meeting over coffee or a beer. Some seemed willing, but most were wary.

It hadn't helped that defamation threats had been sent to at least three SAS Afghan veterans by a lawyer representing Ben Roberts-Smith, warning them that to even talk to a journalist could land them in court. But the story we had written in November delving into the discord in the regiment about Roberts-Smith had helped our cause. It had marked us as journalists willing to take risks by asking questions Defence insiders themselves had been pondering.

Masters' deep relationships reached all the way up the chain of command, and his willingness to hand me his contact book had been invaluable. The more veterans I spoke to, the more I realised that some considered Masters not just a journalist and military historian, but someone who spoke their language, understood their culture and respected their service.

Masters' inclination to furrow his brow and intellectualise stories in search of a deeper meaning could give him an aloof air, but once he relaxed, his warmth and boyish humour would emerge. Junior soldiers and senior officers enjoyed his company, and he enjoyed theirs.

The aim of the Perth trip was to see if there was any substance to the stories about Roberts-Smith and alleged war crimes. We had no corroboration of any prisoner execution, just some jigsaw pieces forming an incomplete puzzle.

On most long-haul plane flights, I had taken to guessing the occupation of those around me. High-vis shirt meant mining or construction. Suits were corporate lawyers or bankers. Parents with kids were holidaymakers. Short back and sides hairstyles meant police or military. Tonight, I played my guessing game until the plane lights signalled I could open my laptop. I had another puzzle to solve.

It involved a task of comparison. I was trying to uncover the person behind the Blowerw2 emails, which had landed in my own inbox after they had been sent to *The Australian*. I cut and pasted the contents of the emails into one of two columns on a blank page. In the adjoining column, I pasted the contents of the legal threat emailed to me by Roberts-Smith's lawyer, Mark O'Brien.

Working on the assumption that O'Brien had written his email to me based on information given to him by his client, the nearly identical phraseology had stirred my suspicions.

O'Brien's email had sought to ensure I wouldn't place any weight on the formal complaint about Roberts-Smith that Simkin had sent up the military chain of command in 2014.

O'Brien had done this by describing how Simkin had 'smuggled unregistered automatic rifles ... by falsifying customs documents' in 2012. I underlined these words in column one.

In column two, I underlined the words Blowerw2 emailed to police, a politician and journalists: that Simkin had undertaken 'smuggling' involving an 'untraceable fully automatic machine gun' by 'falsifying customs documents' in 2012.

Next, I performed some more cut-and-paste comparisons. O'Brien had written that Simkin had asked Roberts-Smith '... to provide a statement ... that Simkin's conduct was a sanctioned trial of weapons, which my client rightly refused to do.'

Blowerw2 noted that Simkin had asked 'squad members to provide supporting statements ... that the weapons were a trial ... most refused to provide statements'.

O'Brien described Simkin's actions as 'a federal offence'.

Blowerw2 described them as a 'breach of federal law'.

Lined up against each other, the content of Blowerw2's emails and O'Brien's message to me appeared strikingly similar.

I was now leaning towards a singular possible conclusion. Could it be Roberts-Smith who had penned the content in the Blowerw2 emails? If this was true, it would suggest that Roberts-Smith was trying to scare off anyone willing to talk to reporters or Justice Paul Brereton.

Sitting in the dull light of the plane cabin, I drafted an email.

'Mr O'Brien. This concerns an email you wrote to me in October 2017.' As I described the similarities between his client's legal threat to me and the Blowerw2 email, I knew what I was doing was pointless. I'd never get approval to send it. The case was circumstantial.

Writing a story that suggested it, or merely sending an email that did the same, would only generate more legal heat from O'Brien. I stared out of the plane window.

My editors were already wary of lawsuits. The year before, the Australian Broadcasting Corporation had aired my *Four Corners* program about large donations given to political parties by a billionaire property developer. The developer had promptly hired O'Brien as his lawyer and sued me, while *The Australian* gave the donor a front-page berth to criticise my reporting.

Australia's defamation laws made it hard for journalists to run a defence when reporting was informed by confidential sources, no matter how credible they were. It was looking likely the property developer would win his case against me. Given I was already on the legal ropes, my newspapers would be beyond hesitant to take on another billionaire-backed litigant in the form of Ben Roberts-Smith.

I knew that if I wrote anything more about Roberts-Smith, we'd have to have some damn good material to back it all up in court.

Masters and I made a start, digging up hard evidence of Roberts-Smith's past history of bullying. We could prove that some of the official record about his war service was incomplete, telling a partial story and obscuring ugly truths. The still-secret Crompvoets war crimes report was also in our possession. Its contents were dynamite, but it didn't identify a single individual.

We'd need a lot more on the Victoria Cross recipient if we expected the newspaper to publish anymore allegations.

I glanced over the plane aisle. Masters was writing intently in his small red notebook. I shut my laptop screen, my email to O'Brien unfinished, and stared back out through the plane window, into the dark unknown.

* * *

Five days later, I ran without any sense of direction except forward, the Swan River on my left guiding me. Then, drawn to a steep path that veered right, I climbed up Mount Eliza to an expanse of exquisite green that led to a cenotaph erected in honour of the ANZACs who died in World War I. Next to it, an eighteen-metre granite obelisk stood sentinel, solemn and imposing. I remembered that Andrew Hastie, one of those we'd met over the last week, had told me this was his special place, a site he'd visit to remember those lost in past wars, and in his own. He'd come here just to think. Standing in this spot basking in the sun, I could see why.

The trip to Perth started as a resounding failure. We tried to speak to members of Roberts-Smith's patrol teams from 2009, 2010 and 2012, and those who had served closely with them. Our intent was clear. We wanted to find eyewitnesses to back up the allegations we'd heard.

Responses ranged from gruff hang-ups to polite nos. 'I know exactly what you are talking about,' one soldier had stammered. I knew he was close to Roberts-Smith and I had, seconds before, explained I was investigating allegations of war crimes. 'But I can't talk to you.' The conversation lasted less than thirty seconds.

Others simply ignored text messages.

For hours, we waited for a call back, only to hear nothing. Masters and I felt like two men stuck in quarantine, too contagious to meet.

But on day three, our phones began to buzz. A junior officer who had deployed to Afghanistan on multiple occasions agreed to meet us at a café overlooking the Indian Ocean. He arrived, covered in sweat, carrying two weights he'd held tightly as he'd run several kilometres to meet us. He appeared on edge as he described his concern about rogue SAS patrols.

This officer believed the problem had begun during SAS selection, with men chosen in a process that favoured 'lung capacity over mental resilience'. When selection worked well, the archetypal elite soldier would be left standing: smart, hard, quiet, determined, ruthless, moral.

When it went wrong? 'They are selecting fuckwits,' he told us.

What was most troubling, this officer said, was the mental state of a small number of soldiers who appeared to relish killing. 'Attack dogs' and 'light switches that can't turn off', he called them. To illustrate his point, he recalled a patrol commander who had deployed despite being arrested by police for domestic violence and who carried a home-made war hatchet with him in Afghanistan.

Those with truly dark interiors were in the minority, outnumbered by the honourable. But these few 'functioning psychopaths' had embedded themselves in the regiment, forming cliques that operated like 'bikie gangs, black holes that had sucked in junior soldiers'.

He'd encountered men in Tarin Kowt, grinding their teeth and whispering: 'I don't want to be here.' When soldiers hinted at witnessing atrocities committed by their own, the officer had told them to alert the chain of command. But most 'did not want to dob in mates'. Higher ranking officers had taken a 'don't know, don't care' attitude, fuelling an absence of oversight and accountability.

Masters finally mentioned the elephant in the room.

Roberts-Smith had come up in 'plenty of hushed conversations', the officer responded. The Victoria Cross recipient was polarising – loved or hated, a legend to some but to others a walking embodiment of entitlement and arrogance.

'Have you ever heard of a mission to a village called Darwan?' I asked him. He nodded. He had heard something bad had been 'covered up'. But he knew no more.

Different versions of our conversation with this officer were repeated over the next two days in meetings at homes, pubs and coffee shops. One Afghanistan veteran spoke as his wife served us tea and biscuits. Another downed wine after wine.

The picture they painted was complicated. Many were proud of their own service and that of their mates, of missions conducted with bravery and honour. But as some dropped their guard, dark descriptions and memories tumbled out.

He wasted three dudes – What for? – Just for being dudes.

Some blokes carried throw downs. – Throw downs? – Shit to plant on those who'd been wasted to legitimise the kill.

RS's patrol blooded blokes – Blooded? – That's what they called it. They got junior soldiers to get their first kill by shooting prisoners. Sick fucks called it 'blooding the rookie'.

Nearly all the men we met had their own Roberts-Smith story, but some of their recollections about him and his patrol team amounted to no more than suspicions. A serving SAS soldier described how a member of Roberts-Smith's patrol team had shown him unofficial photographs of dead Afghans with SAS coins placed over their eyes and cigarettes jammed in their lips.

'Get rid of those fucking pics,' our source said he had told the patrolman. 'We don't mock the dead.'

Soldiers had witnessed a kill board tally on Roberts-Smith's patrol-room door in 2012. Whenever Roberts-Smith or one of his patrol team members killed an Afghan, the tally would be updated.

'They were trying to get to twenty,' one SAS insider told us.

Competition killing or chalking up a body count didn't equate to war crimes. But it was an indicator of a culture that Andrew Hastie described to me over a beer and in which kill count became the only measure of success.

Several sources also described conversations they overheard involving Roberts-Smith's patrol team after a mission on Easter Sunday 2009. The sources said patrol members had described how a then junior soldier, Jason Andrews, had been directed to kill one of two prisoners discovered hiding in a tunnel in a compound named Whiskey 108. On the same mission, it was said that Roberts-Smith had executed the second tunnel prisoner. In a macabre twist, the dead prisoner's prosthetic leg was later souvenired by Roberts-Smith's chief antagonist in the SAS, patrol commander Nick Simkin.

Masters and I couldn't firm up the story of the Easter Sunday executions, but the taking of the prosthetic leg wasn't a myth. Sources told us of the leg being used to swill beer back at Camp Russell in Tarin Kowt.

Hastie was one of several SAS veterans who had also heard whispers about the mission to Darwan. As our week in Perth neared its end, the story of what had taken place at the village in September 2012 had slowly firmed. It wasn't yet fully corroborated, but there was a consistency to the accounts disclosed by SAS soldiers who were on the ground that day.

During the mission, Roberts-Smith had waded over a river and shot dead an insurgent. He'd waded back through the water and continued the operation. At the very last compound perched on a ridge in the village, shortly before the SAS was due to fly back to base, Roberts-Smith's patrol team had been keeping watch over a small number of Afghan prisoners. One of the men had annoyed Roberts-Smith. He'd been taken to the edge of a small cliff above a dry creek bed and, without warning, kicked over the edge and summarily executed.

After this, Roberts-Smith's patrol team had agreed to cover up the crime by claiming the prisoner was an insurgent with a radio. But the cover-up had been compromised. One patrolman in particular had been left traumatised by the incident, unable to let it go. We were told but couldn't yet confirm the patrolman was Jason Andrews, the man who was allegedly blooded on Easter Sunday 2009 and who had risen to become Roberts-Smith's deputy patrol commander by the time of the Darwan mission in 2012.

Andrews was one of those who held the key to unlocking the secrets of Darwan and Easter Sunday, but he was one of those who hadn't taken our repeated calls. Still, there were other ways Masters and I could seek to corroborate details about Andrews and the Darwan mission.

'Roberts-Smith is the Lance Armstrong of the Australian military,' one of the SAS soldiers who'd become a confidential source told me. This source suggested that by 2012, Roberts-Smith was so confident he'd never get caught, he'd begun to do things without checking who might be watching. Others may have seen the kick. Accompanying most SAS missions were medics, translators, electronic warfare specialists and Afghan partner force soldiers. Drones guided by faraway pilots watched from the sky. Our SAS source suggested that Afghan villagers from Darwan may have also witnessed the cliff kick.

As I headed back down the hill towards the Swan River, I resolved to track down as many people from the mission to Darwan as possible. I reached for my phone and called my editor. I skipped hello when he picked up.

'What are my chances of flying to Afghanistan?'

CHAPTER 19

A BLACK EYE

Sunshine Coast, Queensland,
April 2018

Emma Roberts-Smith had dropped her twin girls off at art class and was at the supermarket when her phone began buzzing. The number on the screen belonged to Di, the family's housekeeper, who was back at home.

'Hi, Dizy,' Emma said.

'It's not Di,' a woman's voice replied. Emma had never heard this voice before. 'I'm a friend of your husband. I'm at your house and I need to speak to you.'

Emma felt her heart racing as she asked the woman for her name.

'It's Amanda.'

'Tell me now on the phone what you need to tell me,' she told the stranger.

'No ... I need to see you in person.'

Emma walked to her car, shopping bag in hand, head spinning, stomach churning. A few months before, she'd received a letter from someone claiming to be from the

Seven media company alleging Roberts-Smith had been
having an affair. When she'd challenged him, her husband
claimed that SAS Sergeant Nick Simkin had sent it, but
that made no sense. Their marriage had been in crisis for
months – or was it years? – and Simkin had no role in that.
She'd long suspected Roberts-Smith had strayed, but he'd
denied it again and again.

The signs were everywhere. He was cold and withdrawn;
he'd switch his phone off when he was away; she discovered
he was keeping a second mobile phone; she'd spied him
taking selfies that never landed in her inbox. He'd brushed
off her accusations and instead suggested counselling and
a holiday.

In the car, her voice laden with distress, she called Di's
number. This time she heard the housekeeper's familiar
voice.

'Is it what I think it is?' she asked.

'Yes.'

As she drove, she dialled Roberts-Smith's number.

'Who's Amanda?' she asked him.

'Who are you talking about?' There was panic in his
voice.

'Ben, she's on our doorstep.'

As she drove down the driveway of the Roberts-Smith
family home, she spotted an unfamiliar car and then a
woman in a pink and black dress sitting with Emma's ashen-
faced parents in the front garden. Amanda was wearing
sunglasses and when she took them off, she revealed a large
black eye. She had tears pouring down her face.

Emma wondered if her husband had struck her.

Amanda's phone was also ringing over and over again. It
was Roberts-Smith, no doubt in a panic, trying to wrestle
back control, to plug a volcano that had already exploded.

'Don't pick it up,' Emma said.

'Do you want to see his messages?'

Emma nodded, and began scrolling. There were hundreds of them.

She scrolled. And scrolled. And scrolled.

Whoever Amanda was, she wasn't a one-night stand. Roberts-Smith had a full-time girlfriend with whom he was planning to start a life. Now the woman was weeping in front of Emma on her family's front lawn.

The woman spoke again: 'I fell pregnant. It's Ben's.'

* * *

Emma watched the woman's car disappear before she walked gingerly to her own vehicle and headed out to pick up her twin girls from art class. Her mind whirled. *My life is imploding and I need to protect myself.*

She stopped at a bank and withdrew $1000. Next, she transferred $50,000 from a joint account to her parents.

* * *

A fortnight later, in their bedroom, Emma faced her husband. For days, he'd begged her for a second chance, and apologised both to her and her parents. She'd agreed to give him another go.

Now, he wanted something else from his wife. 'Brand BRS' was at risk of damage. If the affair was made public, it could cost the Father of the Year's reputation dearly. Corporates wanted a clean-cut war hero for paid talks, not a cheater.

He wanted her to pretend that they were separated when he was having his affair.

Emma breathed in. 'There have been enough lies, Ben. I'm not going to lie.'

She watched her husband carefully as she spoke. Then it was his turn. His voice laced with malice, Roberts-Smith pointed to the loungeroom where their girls were sitting and told her if she didn't lie she would lose her children.

CHAPTER 20

TURNING UP THE HEAT

Campbell Barracks, Swanbourne, Perth, 8 May 2018

As Justice Paul Brereton sat inside a makeshift interview room at the SAS barracks in Swanbourne, two soldiers waited outside. The two Afghan veterans were unaware that the other had been ordered to attend a separate interrogation session with the judge. They arrived within minutes of each other and after a brief encounter, they sat apart, keeping a wary distance. The tension between the pair was palpable.

While Brereton had subpoenaed the two soldiers to attend his inquiry, it wasn't either man the investigators were most interested in. Brereton's war crimes investigation team had made the five-hour flight from Sydney to Perth the previous evening, aiming for a low-key arrival at the base. The surreptitiousness was partly due to the laws under which Brereton's inquiry operated.

All interviews were to be held in secret, and no SAS soldier was to tell another they had been called to testify, or what they had been questioned about by Brereton.

These rules, punishable by criminal charges if broken, were designed to aid Brereton's unambiguously arduous task: to break the SAS code of silence and find out if dark secrets had been left hidden in the fields and compounds of Oruzgan, as Samantha Crompvoets' investigation had claimed.

Brereton and his team of military lawyers were in hostile territory. If Sydney's law precinct was their home ground, Campbell Barracks most certainly was not. It was one of the finest military training sites in Australia, equipped with indoor and outdoor firing ranges and areas where soldiers could practise in close-quarter and urban battle scenarios.

The barracks was also where the soldiers of the SAS undertook the resistance-to-interrogation training they could rely on if they were captured by enemy soldiers seeking their secrets. For some in the SAS, Brereton was the enemy. Resistance to interrogation before the judge was non-negotiable. The men of the SAS didn't talk out of school. Brereton had come to realise that if he was to have any prospect of loosening lips and breaching the SAS 'culture of silence', he needed to wield the full extent of his powers, including forcing soldiers to answer questions honestly or face criminal charges.

Brereton wasn't running a police investigation, nor was his role similar to his day job as a judge of the New South Wales Supreme Court. He was effectively working as a Royal Commissioner running a fact-finding mission. If he found credible information about war crimes, he could refer it to the federal police, with one vital caveat.

As a safeguard to soldiers who would be forced to give up their usual right to refuse to answer a question – a right they could ordinarily rely on in court or in a police interview – Brereton had to marry his demand for truth-telling with a powerful protection. This involved Brereton making a promise he could never break. Any confession of their own wrongdoing by a soldier could never be used against them in any future investigation or prosecution of war crimes.

The legal term was a 'derivative immunity'. In lay terms, this meant soldiers could tell Brereton about committing the most nefarious of crimes, safe in the knowledge the judge could never give this confession to the federal police or the International Criminal Court. However, there was still a catch to Brereton's offer of a get-out-of-jail-free card.

Brereton could pass to the federal police any testimony from an SAS soldier about another comrade's conduct. If a soldier decided to forgo the promise of immunity and instead tried to cover up their involvement in wrongdoing in the hope Brereton would never discover it, they faced the risk that one of their comrades could still implicate them.

Brereton knew this created a precarious dilemma for SAS soldiers who had served in the same tight-knit, four- or five-man patrol teams. If three soldiers from a five-man patrol had gone rogue, they would need to ensure the two other patrol team members, and anyone in the near vicinity, didn't witness anything and choose to speak out. The trio would also need to trust each other. Each man would need to stick to the same cover-up story if ever questioned. There could be no inconsistencies. If they did that, Brereton would likely never get to the truth.

But if one of the trio reached for the get-out-of-jail-free card and confessed not only to their own wrongdoing but that of their two comrades, then Brereton could confront the duo with this testimony and call in the police to probe everyone but the confessor. His task was to divide and conquer, holding out the promise of immunity in one hand, and the threat of prosecution in the other.

The judge had one other means of getting to the truth. Crompvoets' report told of soldiers tortured by their knowledge of war crimes. If her conclusions were true, and that was a big if, then Brereton would be facing off with soldiers 'torn between loyalty to their comrades; and their own sense of morality'. Even if they were 'fearful of the consequences' of being labelled a snitch or implicating themselves or others in a battlefield atrocity, the hope was that at least a few might succumb to 'a crisis of conscience'.

Brereton needed not only to wield his legal power to extract the truth. The judge could also hold out the hope that confession may bring 'atonement'. At least that was the experience of investigators in other historical war crimes investigations.

Then there was the reality of cracking Campbell Barracks. The two men sitting outside the interview room on this morning had both undergone the training to withstand interrogation. The SAS headquarters was their turf. So, too, was Afghanistan. Brereton was trampling where he wasn't wanted.

One of the two soldiers he intended to interview was Neil Browning. Browning had been Roberts-Smith's patrol team commander during the Easter Sunday 2009 mission to the compound named Whiskey 108. There were rumours swirling that two Afghans had been pulled out of a compound tunnel and executed by Roberts-Smith and a third patrol team member, Jason Andrews. If the rumours bore any truth, Browning would know about it. He'd also know if there was any truth to the allegation that Andrews had been blooded that day. But Browning was also a man Roberts-Smith considered a close mate and mentor, a brother he knew would have his back. The two men spoke every other day.

Browning had been steeling himself for this confrontation with Brereton. 'They've got fucking nothing,' he'd been overheard snarling at a regiment barbecue weeks earlier, in reference to the war crimes inquiry. Now, Browning would finally discover if this was true.

* * *

On the evening of 8 May, on the east coast of Australia, Emma Roberts-Smith watched her husband descend into a state of deep anxiety. The pair's relationship was in chaos after the discovery of the affair, but this wasn't what was causing Roberts-Smith's distress. He'd received a call from his old patrol commander from 2009. Browning had revealed how he'd just been grilled by Justice Brereton.

Despite the Brereton Inquiry's warnings that those summoned before the judge were not to breathe a word of anything – even the mere fact they had been questioned – Browning didn't hold back. He told Roberts-Smith that Brereton had 'drilled' him 'for hours', peppering him with question after question. He revealed something else too. The subject of much of Brereton's interrogation was the Victoria Cross recipient.

'Prepare yourself,' Browning told his old patrol team member. 'Brereton is on a witch-hunt.'

Browning also told Roberts-Smith the identity of the other soldier summoned, the man Browning had bumped into outside the interview room. It was Brian McMurray. In 2009, McMurray was the fourth member of Browning, Roberts-Smith and Jason Andrews' patrol team. McMurray was also someone whose loyalty Roberts-Smith had increasingly begun to question.

Whatever McMurray had revealed to the judge that day was known only to Justice Brereton and McMurray. But if he'd chosen to, McMurray could have disclosed plenty. During the Easter Sunday mission in 2009, McMurray was assigned the official task of photographing any Afghans killed by the SAS, as well as recording in a logbook the details of where their bodies had been found. If two men had been executed by Roberts-Smith and Andrews near a compound tunnel, there was every chance that McMurray not only knew about it, but might have preserved key forensic evidence of the crimes.

McMurray's relationship with Roberts-Smith had soured, but he remained close mates with Jason Andrews. This was why McMurray also knew of the story circulating about what had gone down three years after Easter Sunday, in the village of Darwan.

Even though McMurray had left Roberts-Smith's patrol team by then to head his own patrol team, it was McMurray to whom Andrews turned to after the Darwan mission. Andrews had wanted to disclose a vision he couldn't put out of his mind. This vision was of the face of a handcuffed Afghan man striking a rock after he had been kicked over the side of a small cliff.

* * *

Several hours after the phone call from Browning, confident that Roberts-Smith wasn't watching, Emma sent a WhatsApp message to a childhood friend detailing Browning's disclosures, as well as Roberts-Smith's agitated response.

He 'didn't get much sleep', Emma texted her old friend. 'It's obvious that someone has said a hell of a lot about Ben.'

CHAPTER 21

BREAKTHROUGHS

Melbourne, May 2018

'Ali Jan. His name is Ali Jan.'

I sat at my desk as Afghan journalist Rashid Ghulam spoke excitedly.

'His wife is Bibi. His children are seven in number. He farmed the almonds, and was shepherd to the animals and picked the firewood.'

'Are you sure,' I asked. 'Are you sure that's him?'

Rashid responded fiercely, proudly. 'Of course I am sure. I am a journalist just like you. The villagers told me many times. Ali Jan is the one who was kicked. Ali Jan is the one who was killed.'

Days before, with my editor still considering my request to fly to Afghanistan, I'd been introduced to Rashid by our paper's war photographer. 'I'd trust him with my life,' she'd said, before adding: 'I literally trusted him with my life. He kept me safe in Oruzgan during the war. He's smart and well connected.'

When I'd asked Rashid if he could find locals from a tiny village visited by Australian forces almost six years before, the Kandahar-based freelancer responded cautiously. The Taliban's influence in southern Afghanistan was growing again, and journalists were not welcome.

By the time I called Rashid, Chris Masters and I had mapped out far more detail about the mission to Darwan by talking to those from the SAS who'd been on the ground that day along with other confidential sources. We pinned down the mission to 11 September 2012, thirteen days after Afghan National Army sergeant Hekmatullah shot dead three Australian soldiers.

By the time of the operation at Darwan, our sources had observed two distinct personalities emerging in the SAS. Each four-month deployment had begun to blur into the next. The regiment had honed its ability to capture or kill militants placed on what was known as the coalition's Joint Priority Effects List (JPEL). It was the modern version of a wanted poster.

One source told us that some soldiers sought redeployment because they were addicted to the hunt. Others had come to feel uneasy as an escalating enemy body count was not matched by progress in achieving the US-led NATO mission.

The patrol team Roberts-Smith belonged to appeared unburdened by such introspection. In this group, sources told us, junior members were pushed to kill rather than detain. We'd already learnt that at the start of the 2012 deployment, Roberts-Smith's patrol team tacked a 'kill board' to the wall of their patrol team room. Members of another patrol team heard Roberts-Smith urging on his fellow patrol team members – 'only two more to go, boys' – a suspected reference to reaching a desired kill count to record on the board. We'd now confirmed the target was twenty kills.

The patrol team's aggressive approach drew some admirers, including officers who believed it was needed on Afghanistan's asymmetrical battlefield. Roberts-Smith, too, had fierce backers, those who believed his assertive soldiering was setting an example for others in the regiment. Those bagging Roberts-Smith, they said, were jealous of his courage and resolve.

It also seemed that less aggressive patrol teams risked unofficial sidelining. One patrol team commander was regarded by his peers as overly cautious after he told his soldiers they had to be comfortable with everything they did in battle.

'He told us we needed to be able to get to sleep at night when we were grandparents,' a patrol team member told me. Subsequently, his team started being overlooked for missions.

When satellites intercepting phone calls gathered intelligence that placed Hekmatullah in the vicinity of Darwan, the Australians moved fast. For them, he was the most wanted man in Afghanistan.

Near the end of the mission, the realisation had dawned on our SAS sources that Hekmatullah was not in the village. If the day's manhunt had started with promise, it was ending with failure. As helicopters thundered into the village to take the SAS back to Tarin Kowt, dozens of Afghan detainees were crammed into a compound and issued a blunt warning by SAS soldiers. 'If you come outside before the helicopters are gone, you'll be shot.'

The Afghans waited, some with their heads bowed, listening for the whir of rotor blades that would signal the end of their ordeal. Then a radio communication crackled into SAS earpieces, relaying a message from Roberts-Smith. The famous soldier was with his patrol team at a compound cluster on the end of a steep ridge overlooking a dry creek bed, out of sight of most of the other soldiers: 'One spotter EKIA,' he had said over the radio.

One of the SAS members on the ground, a respected and experienced operator, described feeling a distinct pang of suspicion. 'I thought to myself, something's not right.' The soldier who felt something was awry had a clear line of sight up the dry creek bed. If a spotter – an enemy surveillance operative who reports coalition soldiers' movements to militants – had emerged, the soldier reckoned he would have seen him. It also made little sense, the soldier reasoned, for an active spotter to approach the Australians so late into their Darwan mission.

'We didn't require any spotting – we had come in like an elephant and made our presence well known,' the SAS soldier recalled. As his helicopter lifted off, he remembered glancing down and seeing what looked like a body and asking himself a question: If it wasn't a spotter who was EKIA, who was it?

A short time after the mission, another SAS soldier had approached two senior regiment members separately with an answer. Chris Masters and I had finally found the multiple sources to confirm this soldier was Jason Andrews, a member of Roberts-Smith's patrol team. We'd also confirmed the names of the two men he'd separately confided in: Sergeant Boyd Keary and Sergeant Brian McMurray. Both Keary and McMurray had relayed Andrews' disclosures to others, who had in turn told us.

Andrews had told Keary and McMurray of a scene he'd witnessed which was playing on an endless loop in his head, haunting his dreams. It involved an irate and frustrated Roberts-Smith grabbing one of the handcuffed prisoners from a compound at the furthest end of the ridge.

The Afghan was then walked to the edge of a rocky cliff, perhaps 10 metres high. According to Andrews, Roberts-Smith gave himself a short run-up, then kicked the detainee off the edge. As the man plunged, his face smashed into rocks. Then the injured man was executed.

* * *

The reason I asked Rashid to find any information on the ground in Afghanistan was twofold. I was searching for further corroboration. And I wanted to put a name to the victim, to hear his story.

After a few days, Rashid told me he'd contacted a network of tribal elders to locate villagers who'd been at Darwan on 11 September 2012. It was dangerous work. Rashid repeatedly warned that, as an Afghan helping a Western journalist, he faced an even greater threat from the Taliban.

A group of villagers had agreed to meet at a safe house. According to Rashid, the villagers described how Ali Jan, a farmer from a nearby village, had arrived in Darwan on 10 September to collect flour, firewood and shoes for one of his children. The villagers who spoke directly to Rashid hadn't witnessed what had happened to Ali Jan, but they insisted others had. I'd been careful to tell Rashid little about the precise allegation. If Afghan witnesses had seen something, I wanted to collect their testimony untainted.

As Rashid continued, I felt a surge of adrenalin. I was hearing again what I'd heard from soldiers in Australia. The Afghans had claimed Ali had been kicked by a foreign soldier over a 'manda', a small cliff, next to the compound where he had been held. Ali had then been executed.

The hearsay accounts of the villagers tracked down by Rashid matched the accounts circulating at Campbell

Barracks back in Perth. What were the chances that SAS soldiers had made up a story of a man being kicked off a cliff and that villagers on the other side of the world had conjured up the same story?

'Was Ali Jan a member of the Taliban?' I asked Rashid.

Rashid said the villagers had scoffed at this suggestion. 'He was a poor farmer with nothing to do with the Taliban,' they had insisted.

While they weren't eyewitnesses to his last moments, those who spoke to Rashid claimed to be among the villagers who had attended to Ali Jan's body. They described how a young boy was dispatched to a neighbouring village with the grim news. Expecting her husband to return home to the hills with the goods and gossip from Darwan, Bibi instead received word that he was dead.

'Then the screams started,' Rashid said.

Ali Jan's brother, Abdul Ahmad, was among the villagers Rashid had spoken with. He had comforted Bibi and her children after the news arrived. 'His two elder daughters were screaming and running after their grandmother' in a state of bewilderment, pleading to be told their father was alive, Ahmad recalled.

'Ali's mother was crying day and night for a week,' he said. Six years after Ali's death, Ahmad still struggled to comprehend how 'a person who went to get flour' could somehow end up dead. He told Rashid that Ali's death had left Bibi struggling to put food on the table. His family could no longer afford meat or to send the children to school.

I asked Rashid to tell me the ages of Ali's children. When he came to the youngest child, I felt a pang of doubt. The timing seemed awry. Ali's youngest child was born after his death. I immediately challenged Rashid and he could tell by the tone in my voice that I was sceptical, testing both him and his information. I could also tell by the tone of his voice that he was offended.

'Of course I asked about this,' Rashid said.

When Ali died, Bibi was pregnant. After death had come life. Three months after the man fitting the description of Ben Roberts-Smith kicked Ali Jan off a cliff, Bibi gave birth to a baby girl. Ali's youngest daughter was now five.

* * *

The story of what happened at Darwan was definitely taking shape. But it wasn't enough. 'I need an eyewitness,' I said to Rashid. 'And I'd like to meet his family.'

We agreed that I would travel to Afghanistan if we could find a witness or convince Bibi to meet me and be interviewed. The information from Rashid was enough to prompt me to make my next phone call. I'd been holding off dialling this number for days. It belonged to someone who'd served with the SAS and who I'd been told was with Roberts-Smith in the last hour of the mission to Darwan.

I dialled and held my breath.

CHAPTER 22

THE LAWYER AND THE POLITICIAN

May 2018

At seventy years old, Mark O'Brien had lost none of the charm, aggression and swagger that had enamoured him to many when he worked for the Nine Network, the commercial television giant controlled by billionaire Kerry Packer before he died and then his son, James, until he sold it off.

O'Brien had robustly defended Nine against those claiming the company had defamed them, employing a legal style that to observers appeared underpinned by a defining principle: take no prisoners.

If O'Brien could be ferocious in legal combat, he was also endearing and erudite to those on his side.

O'Brien's embrace of Ben Roberts-Smith was not just about fighting for a war hero. It placed the lawyer at the tip of the legal spear in a battle that had the potential to pit Australia's biggest media players against each other and define how the history of Australia's longest war, and its most famous soldier, would be told.

O'Brien was convinced Roberts-Smith was being unjustly targeted by the *Sydney Morning Herald* and *The Age*, the newspapers owned by one of the other legacy media giants of Australia, Fairfax Media. O'Brien had also once boasted the *Herald* as a client, but was better known for helping the wealthy and powerful sue the paper and its investigative reporters at the sister papers. Over time, he'd filed writs against the most decorated journalists in Australia.

When famed *Herald* journalist Kate McClymont exposed Labor Party politician Eddie Obeid as corrupt, he hired O'Brien to sue her. Obeid won the case, along with a hefty payout and hundreds of thousands of dollars in legal costs. Years later, when Obeid was jailed for graft, he'd kept his legal winnings.

McClymont told colleagues of bumping into O'Brien, dressed only in a pair of Speedos and a towel, near one of Sydney's eastern suburbs beaches. She'd offered him a brisk hello.

'I'm not finished with you yet,' he'd replied cordially.

O'Brien was already acting for another of his clients who had me firmly in their sights, the property developer turned political donor I'd reported on. I was set to be trounced in court. If a developer with little public profile was set to win, then a beloved war hero would have a field day if I published anything that even slightly resembled a criminal allegation.

No wonder O'Brien was confident he'd secured a winner with his latest client.

For months now, Chris Masters and I had been circling Roberts-Smith. O'Brien's carriage of the war hero's legal brief placed the lawyer firmly in the camp of Roberts-Smith's employer, the Seven Network, Australia's other

major commercial television behemoth. The Kerry Stokes–
controlled Seven was the traditional corporate enemy of
O'Brien's client, the Nine Network. Nine was also poised to
merge with the target of so many O'Brien lawsuits, Fairfax
Media. Nine's managers would soon be my new bosses.

Nine's legal executives had resolved to present O'Brien
with a choice. Given Nine's pending acquisition of the
newspaper company he was helping Roberts-Smith sue,
the lawyer would need to either retain the war hero as
his client, or stay on the books of Nine. O'Brien couldn't
represent both. The lawyer ultimately chose the hero.

In defending Roberts-Smith, O'Brien could again go to
war with his old nemeses in Fairfax, while also assisting
Seven's Kerry Stokes to take on Nine, O'Brien's new bête
noir. Stokes not only owned Seven but the *West Australian*
newspaper. Stokes was also close to senior figures in the
Murdoch stable, who loathed both Nine and the Fairfax
press. If the Roberts-Smith case ended up in court, it would
be a *Game of Thrones* meets *Succession* style of battle,
with media armies attacking from all sides.

Few people outside of his inner circle knew it, but Seven
was paying for Roberts-Smith's fees at Mark O'Brien
Legal. This was a most unusual arrangement: Seven was
a public company listed on the stock exchange. Under
corporate rules, it was meant to use company money only
on things that would benefit Seven and its shareholders.
Helping Roberts-Smith fend off war crimes allegations
may have been in the ex-soldier's interests, but it wouldn't
benefit Seven's bottom line.

Seven's legal support of Roberts-Smith didn't stop with
the ex-soldier.

Throughout May, SAS soldiers who were close friends
with Roberts-Smith had contacted the former soldier

with information they shouldn't have shared about their interactions with the war crimes inquiry conducted by Justice Brereton. On at least one occasion, Roberts-Smith briefed O'Brien of the soldiers' concerns. This meant that Roberts-Smith and his lawyer knew the direction of Brereton's inquiry with respect to a key allegation being investigated.

In late May, a soldier very close to Roberts-Smith had called him in a panic. Vincent Jelovic was a member of Roberts-Smith's four-man patrol team on the mission to Darwan. He was at the compound on the ridge, along with Roberts-Smith and Jason Andrews, when the mission had drawn to an end.

Brereton had already grilled Jelovic once, and now he was demanding he reappear before a secret hearing. Jelovic had turned to Roberts-Smith for help. As a serving member of the SAS, Jelovic was entitled to request that the defence department pay for an independent lawyer to represent him at his next hearing. But instead of pursuing this offer of help, Roberts-Smith put Jelovic in touch with Mark O'Brien.

When Brereton learnt of this, the inquiry warned O'Brien that it may be a conflict of interest for Roberts-Smith's lawyer to also be representing Jelovic. Roberts-Smith provided Jelovic with the name of a company called Addisons, another legal firm of choice for Seven. Roberts-Smith's patrol team commander from the Easter Sunday mission, Neil Browning, also chose to forgo defence department legal advice and use Addisons.

Neither Browning nor Jelovic had ever heard of Addisons before, but the firm had something else in common with O'Brien and Roberts-Smith. It was not only one of Seven's preferred law firms, but Roberts-Smith had ensured that

Seven would pay for any legal costs that Jelovic and Browning racked up in appearing before Brereton.

There were two ways to look at this. As a senior Seven executive, one could have argued the case for the network to pay for Roberts-Smith's lawyers to battle Brereton or investigative journalists about his time in Afghanistan. If this was deemed acceptable, then stumping up for the legal fees for two of Roberts-Smith's mates could similarly be excepted.

The contrasting view was much uglier. If one believed Roberts-Smith might have turned rogue and executed prisoners, there was every chance Browning and Jelovic had knowledge of these crimes. If this were true, this meant that one of Australia's best-known media companies was now using shareholder funds to pay the legal bills for three war crimes suspects. (After public disclosure of this payment, Seven arranged for ACE, a private Kerry Stokes company, to repay Seven West Media.)

* * *

Wearing a blue suit and tie, his brown hair neatly parted, Andrew Hastie had risen to his feet in the chamber feeling decidedly nervous. An Australian flag hung limply on the opposite wall, near the country's coat of arms.

What Hastie planned to do threatened to blow up his short political career. But, as he told the fellow politicians in the chamber on 23 May 2018, it was a risk worth taking. Hastie had decided to speak on a matter of principle. His speech concerned a client of Mark O'Brien.

'I have considered closely my responsibilities as a member of the Australian House of Representatives. The beauty of our political tradition is that we protect the free speech of our parliamentarians.'

By speaking in parliament, Hastie couldn't be sued for defamation for anything he said. He intended to use this power and privilege

'I raise a matter before the House that is of great importance to the Australian people,' Hastie said, speaking slowly and carefully.

'My duty first and foremost is to the Australian people and to the preservation of the ideals and democratic traditions of our Commonwealth. That tradition includes a free press.'

Hastie's speech finished just before 7pm, but even before he sat down, his words were racing through Parliament House. He'd risen in the parliamentary chamber to raise his own questions about the wealthy property developer and political donor suing me. It wouldn't impact on the outcome of the legal case – which O'Brien's client would win – but his speech would underline the way defamation cases could muzzle the media.

Press gallery journalists dashed back into their offices to punch out copy. Prime Minister Malcolm Turnbull was briefed by his advisers.

'Hastie's gone rogue,' one of them said.

Hours later, Opposition Leader Bill Shorten took to the floor of parliament to suggest Hastie may have used confidential information from authorities about the political donor without proper clearance.

O'Brien joined the fray. 'Mr Hastie purports to be acting in the interests of Australians, but it seems he has forgotten or disregarded the right all Australian citizens have to a presumption of innocence,' he said.

Hastie was inundated with journalists' phone calls after his speech, but he let them go to voicemail. He didn't need to say anymore. Media outlets across Australia were already reporting both his claim that defamation law was being used to silence scrutiny as well as O'Brien's counterattack.

The ex–special forces officer suddenly became the story. The *Australian Financial Review* profiled Hastie, describing him as an 'uber-patriot' who 'takes his duty to Australia seriously, first as a soldier then a lawmaker'. 'This is a guy who decided as an eighteen-year-old that he was going to join the army the day after the September 11 terrorist attacks,' the paper wrote. 'Hastie, a devout Christian, has a strong sense of right and wrong, and is not afraid to stand up for his values.'

Hastie later scanned the coverage, only to realise much of it failed to report parts of his speech – some of which he'd laboured over for hours. His own side of politics hated the *Herald* and *The Age* as they were seen as progressive platforms, more aligned to Labor than the Coalition. Despite that, Hastie had put his career on the line to defend the papers' right to investigate.

To the young politician, it felt both uncomfortable but worthwhile. Afterall, he'd deployed to Afghanistan in service of ideals such as a media that didn't fear to report on the rich and powerful.

'Our democracy works only if we have a free press that can publish information that serves the public interest,' he'd said in his parliamentary speech. 'We don't always like what the press writes, but they are essential to a free and flourishing democracy. The Australian people deserve the truth.'

In his Canberra bed, Hastie scanned his phone one last time before turning it off. As he shut his eyes, he wondered if visions of Afghanistan would visit him again in the night.

* * *

Samantha Crompvoets watched me walk towards her, past the graffiti and skip bins on Little Collins Street. She felt somewhere between suspicious and curious. I'd called her, offering to brief her on a story Masters and I were hoping to publish about her secret investigation.

'You might soon be in the headlines,' I'd said over the phone, dangling what seemed like an obvious carrot to get her to engage. She'd hardened her resolve to keep her guard up but had still agreed to meet. The coffee hadn't yet arrived when I cut to the chase. I told her I had the entire copy of one of the reports she'd sent to generals Campbell and Sengelman and was considering publishing it.

Crompvoets later told me she immediately felt herself withdrawing, while simultaneously trying not to let on that she was concerned. If the contents of her report hit the papers, where would she be left in the wash-up? The good news for Crompvoets was that it appeared that the less damning of her two research reports had been leaked. The bad news was that even though she wasn't the leak, she'd inevitably be blamed.

Ever since she had emailed Campbell and Sengelman her findings, she had encountered more and more dark stares and whispers.

'Well, look who it is ... the most influential person in the building,' a senior special forces officer had remarked coldly while she was waiting in the foyer of Defence headquarters. Crompvoets interpreted these words as a warning – while she had the ear of the chief of the army, she was upsetting others down the chain of command, including senior officials who might seize on any attempt to undermine her.

'There are no names in your report,' I said, before hesitating. 'Did Ben Roberts-Smith's name ever come up?' I was on edge as I fished for information, every inch the journalist in search of a story. But I also felt tired and worried. Most investigations took time, but I'd poured almost a year of research into the Roberts-Smith story and still wasn't sure I would convince the lawyers and editors we had enough to publish.

Now it was Crompvoets' turn to ask questions. She'd heard plenty of rumblings about Roberts-Smith. One SAS soldier had labelled him a 'morale vampire'; another 'just a bad guy'. But no one had provided further detail about any specific incidents.

'Why are you asking about him?' Crompvoets quizzed me.

I paused again, before deciding to trust her. 'Some in the SAS believe he committed war crimes. And we have Afghans saying the very same thing. But I don't know if we can ever tell the story. We've been threatened by Roberts-Smith's lawyers and my bosses don't want to see me dragged into court again.' I was now the one withdrawing, momentarily lost in my own thoughts. I spoke again. 'It is pretty horrifying. They say he kicked a handcuffed prisoner off a cliff.'

To call him just a prisoner felt like it denied him his humanity. 'We have tracked down his family. He was a father. His name was Ali Jan.'

* * *

After she returned to Canberra, Crompvoets asked a friend, a high-ranking female military officer, for advice.

'You have to report the leak of your report,' the officer told her. 'You must escalate it.'

Before she realised what was happening, Crompvoets was directed to meet with a senior military official and pass on everything I had told her. I had revealed nothing about my sources, but I had mentioned that an unnamed person had challenged some of the contents of her report in the margins.

'McKenzie said the copy he obtained has someone's handwriting on it.' This was a useless clue – it could have been Masters' writing for all she knew – but Crompvoets found herself passing it on so she could give the official at least some crumbs. An investigation would soon be underway.

A day later, I called Crompvoets again. She hesitated before answering.

'I thought our meeting was confidential,' I said quietly. I felt deflated.

Masters and I were facing an investigation for obtaining leaked defence force files before we'd even published a word of our intended story about Roberts-Smith.

* * *

Twenty-four hours later, I sent Roberts-Smith an email. I had heard he was on holidays, but didn't know where. I was certain of one thing. He wouldn't like its contents. Emma later told friends she had watched her husband turn pale as he read my message.

Mr Roberts-Smith. I have sent you two emails and a further email to Channel 7 corporate affairs to get in touch with you. I have had no response to date.

A week has passed. I'm not sure if you are away, but I know that as an executive in charge of many journalists,

*you will appreciate that I am trying to talk to you to hear
your views on various issues.*

Over the last fortnight, Roberts-Smith had been in his
comfort zone. He'd met the Queen again in London, but
this time it was a more self-assured war hero who appeared
before Her Majesty. Of all the Victoria Cross and George
Cross winners invited to Buckingham Palace, Roberts-
Smith had built the most sparkling post-military career.

It helped that the reporting Masters and I had published
in October had little lasting impact. The fact that it was
Fairfax Media's *The Age* and *Herald* who had dared
scrutinise Roberts-Smith appeared only to energise the
papers in Rupert Murdoch's News Corp stable as they
rushed to his defence.

Roberts-Smith had even been asked by the *Courier-
Mail* to lead a campaign for Queensland to secure a
$5 billion Defence contract. One of the paper's stories had
opened with: 'Prime Minister Malcolm Turnbull says he
has tremendous regard and affection for war hero Ben
Roberts-Smith ...'

Still, I wasn't going away. My email suggested that, if
anything, I was firing up.

*I have been researching the involvement of a very small
number of SASR personnel in alleged serious breaches of
the Geneva Convention in Afghanistan. I am willing to
come and meet you in Brisbane whenever you wish to
interview you, or talk to you, about these issues.*

As Roberts-Smith read on, it was clear the legal threats
hadn't worked to shut me down. In my email, I described
'tracking down first-hand witnesses and other primary
supporting material', sending researchers to the 'village of
Darwan' and interviewing 'persons who worked with you
in Afghanistan'.

We understand these allegations are extremely serious. We would not put them to you without having gathered corroborating material.

We wish to put them to you fully and without varnish, and with reasonable notice, to allow you to consider them and respond.

I then outlined the allegations of him having kicked a man called 'Ali Jan' from the top of a 'small cliff' before conspiring with other soldiers to execute the Afghan.

What is your response to this allegation?

I also asked if Roberts-Smith had teamed up with Neil Browning to direct Jason Andrews to execute an Afghan prisoner.

On Easter Sunday 2009, along with your then Patrol Commander, you are alleged to have encouraged another patrol member to shoot dead an unarmed man in a practice known as 'blooding'.

Roberts-Smith had killed a second prisoner that same day, I alleged in my email.

It is alleged that as part of the same assault on a compound, you shot dead an unarmed man with a prosthetic leg.

Roberts-Smith's response was threefold. At first, he panicked. Next, he called Mark O'Brien. And then, after speaking to the lawyer, he began to seethe.

People were piling on. His jealous, embittered enemies appeared to have sniffed 'blood in the water' and seemed to be hoping Roberts-Smith just might be 'going down'.

It wasn't just 'pieces of shit' in the SAS like Simkin who were probably 'chiming in'. Andrew Hastie was likely stirring the pot from Canberra, promoting himself as the arbiter of morality in the military for his own political benefit. If they were all counting on Roberts-Smith rolling over, they could forget about it.

Ben Roberts-Smith didn't cave in.

Ever.

Ben Roberts-Smith had always fought, and when he did, he always won. He was a winner with a billionaire media mogul in his corner.

'Bottom line' was that Roberts-Smith would probably be 'fucked without' Kerry Stokes in his corner, but Stokes was backing him 100 per cent and was 'prepared to run down his bank' in doing so. The media mogul wasn't 'an idiot' and Stokes wasn't going to back 'a loser'. There was a reason 'politicians' were 'scared of guys that own media networks'.

I would find out later that Roberts-Smith believed Masters and I had badly underestimated him. By coming after him despite being already warned off by his lawyers, we had made it personal. In doing so, we had made a massive mistake. From this moment on, Roberts-Smith would embark on a 'sole fucking mission in life'. He would 'do everything' he could to 'fucking destroy' us.

CHAPTER 23

AN UNEXPECTED SOURCE

Late May 2018

I walked under the giant chandeliers and past the display of opera costumes and giant, gilded mirrors in the Sofitel lobby, towards the reception desk.

'Is there a package for Nick McKenzie?' I asked the concierge, who eyed me warily before handing over an envelope. I felt the hard edge of a hotel card inside.

Days before, an anonymous person had contacted me via the encrypted and disappearing communication channel used by *The Age*'s investigative team. I didn't know if this informant was military or civilian, but they claimed they held information about Ben Roberts-Smith and had directed me to meet them in Melbourne's CBD. Instructions would be left with the receptionist at the Sofitel.

The envelope contained a note instructing me to use the card to get access to level 27 and to then knock on door 12. As I travelled upwards in the hotel's glass elevator, I felt a gnawing suspicion. Could this informant be a double agent working for Roberts-Smith?

It was a crazy thought, yet I felt I knew enough to justify my paranoia. A former *Age* reporter had reached out to me a few days before, saying he'd heard I was sniffing around Ben Roberts-Smith and warning me not to underestimate the steps people might take to shut this scrutiny down.

An SAS source suspected to be helping Masters and me was worried that he might find his dog murdered or car brakes tampered with.

If this new informant waiting at the Sofitel was a genuine source with real information, maybe it could break the impasse preventing Masters and me from going to print. The delay in publishing wasn't for lack of trying.

We felt like we had more than enough corroboration to identify Ben Roberts-Smith as a suspect in two incidents on Easter Sunday 2009: the execution of an unarmed Afghan with a prosthetic leg and a second execution carried out as part of a blooding ritual involving SAS soldier Jason Andrews. I was also confident that we could identify Roberts-Smith as a suspect in the brutalisation and murder of Ali Jan at Darwan. Both Masters and I had independently gathered crucial, credible eyewitness testimony implicating Roberts-Smith in these crimes.

The Age's lawyers and editors were far less sure. Our most senior legal adviser, Peter Bartlett, had fielded an aggressive call from Mark O'Brien, who had also emailed me directly warning that the allegations detailed in my questions to Roberts-Smith were '*false, constitute a gross and indefensible defamation, and provide further evidence of a malicious smear campaign against Australia's most decorated soldier*'.

'*My instructions are to commence immediate defamation proceedings in the Federal Court of Australia, against Fairfax Media, and those directly involved, if the same or similar allegations as outlined in your email are broadcast or published.'* To amplify his threat, O'Brien demanded I *'retain all text messages, emails (including emails to Fairfax editors, management and internal legal counsel), telephone records, drafts and notebooks relating to my client'*.

On the phone to Bartlett, O'Brien had apparently been sceptical of the suggestion that Masters and I had carefully corroborated our allegations.

'No one is going to believe a bunch of Afghans,' he had said.

O'Brien had also raised the issue as to whether Masters or I had been leaked military information. It was almost certain that Roberts-Smith was planning on reporting us to authorities for receiving classified information, in the hope of sparking a raid.

Still, the door wasn't completely shut on publishing. Bartlett and my editors were warming to my suggestion that perhaps I could use a pseudonym instead of naming Roberts-Smith.

Andrew Hastie remained supportive. I had begun to consider the conservative politician a friend. He'd also revealed to me that he was one of those who had written to Major-General Jeff Sengelman, helping to kick off the Crompvoets investigation.

In addition to exposing the Darwan and Easter Sunday allegations, the third plank of our war crimes reporting was to be the revelation of the Crompvoets' report. Yet even the preparation of that story had not been easy.

When I'd met Crompvoets in Melbourne, I'd found her wary but seemingly supportive. A day later, a military source tipped me off that she had relayed our confidential conversation up the chain of command.

'There's a good chance you'll be raided,' my military source had warned me.

In the hours before I'd walked up Collins Street to the Sofitel, I'd confided in Hastie that our efforts to cast a light into the dark corners of his former regiment's Afghanistan history may have hit a wall. I was also becoming more and more nervous about a police raid.

I tried not to sound despondent, but he'd gently inquired about my mental health.

'You okay, mate?'

I'd brushed it off but after I'd hung up from him he'd sent me a Bible quote. It was Corinthians 16:13: 'Be on your guard; stand firm in the faith; be courageous; be strong.'

Hastie was urging me to keep going.

* * *

I knocked on Sofitel room number 2712 and waited for a person I guessed would be a grizzled Afghan SAS veteran. When a woman opened the door, I was momentarily taken aback, wondering if I had the wrong room.

'My name is Amanda Jones. It was me who made contact about Ben,' she said quietly. She appeared nervous, even scared, as she ushered me into the room.

'I was in a relationship with him,' she said hesitantly.

'I'm worried what he might do. I'm hoping you can tell me if he's capable of ...' Her voice trailed off and I thought I saw her hands shaking.

I realised this woman had reached out not only to give me information, but to find out if Roberts-Smith was dangerous.

Amanda detailed how she'd met Roberts-Smith when he was the VIP at a charity event. A one-night stand had morphed into a fast-moving and all-consuming months-long secret love affair. He'd told Amanda he wished he'd met her twenty years earlier and how he didn't want to stay in an unhappy marriage for the rest of his life. Roberts-Smith had promised her he'd leave Emma and start a new life.

She'd told him she was falling in love too.

I listened to her, scrawling a few sentences down on a Sofitel notepad as she showed me messages that seemed to back up her story. Although jittery, Amanda appeared clever and articulate.

Amanda said Roberts-Smith was using multiple phones not subscribed in his own name to contact her, as well as encrypted phone applications. She also described a man who muttered about intense pressure brought on by dark forces, including journalists.

Amanda also revealed how she had travelled to Roberts-Smith's house and told his wife, Emma, about their relationship. She deserved the truth, she had explained. It was also Amanda's way of ending the affair.

She then asked if she could show me a photo. I nodded and Amanda brought up an image on her phone. It was a photo of her face with a large, purplish black eye.

'Did he do that?' I asked her. 'Did he hit you?'

Amanda nodded, before explaining how as their relationship was in its final, tumultuous throes, he'd invited her to a veterans' event at Parliament House in Canberra. Roberts-Smith was to take the stage with Prime Minister Malcolm Turnbull during the evening. He'd taken Amanda to a winery beforehand and then to the event, where she'd kept drinking.

According to Amanda, near the end of the evening, he'd become irate at her as she'd chatted with senior military officials and politicians in Parliament's Grand Hall. He'd wanted to leave, and he had grown increasingly frustrated.

When Amanda finally walked towards the Parliament House carpark where a driver was waiting, she'd slipped on a stair and fallen, hitting her head in front of several onlookers. Roberts-Smith was furious.

She said that back at the hotel room, he'd berated her about her behaviour. She then alleged he'd punched her in the eye.

The next day, Amanda claimed Roberts-Smith had instructed her to lie about him striking her face and blame it on her fall down Parliament House stairs.

'Have you gone to the police,' I asked.

She nodded, describing how she'd entered a local police station but had been too scared to name her alleged perpetrator. She said Roberts-Smith had told her he had contacts in various police forces, and had ways of monitoring her, even accessing her bank account.

'I can give you the number of someone trustworthy,' I told her.

I thought briefly about which senior officer from the federal police – the agency that would have jurisdiction in Canberra – I regarded as the most professional, before giving her the number of a superintendent who led the AFP's counter-terrorism team.

Even after an hour and a half of telling her story, Amanda seemed guarded and on edge, as if someone could leap into the room from the darkness outside the window at any moment. As their relationship came to an end, Roberts-Smith had threatened her, she said.

'As long as we're on the same page, we've got nothing to worry about, but if you turn on me I will burn your house down,' Amanda claimed he had told her. 'It might not be you that gets hurt. It might be people you love and care about.'

* * *

As I left the Sofitel and walked into the Melbourne night air, my head was ablur with thoughts. If it passed legal muster – and that was still an unknown – our draft copy about Darwan and Easter Sunday would have no reference to what Amanda had alleged about Roberts-Smith striking and threatening her. But her allegations had painted a new portrait of Australia's most famous soldier.

Since the only way we might publish a story about the war crimes allegations was by giving Roberts-Smith a pseudonym, I was tossing up between the legendary Spartan soldier Leonidas or the mythical fighter Achilles. Sources in the SAS said he was known as both. I preferred Achilles, a feared warrior with a fatal weakness, but Leonidas worked too. Leonidas was also the main character in the film *300*.

Maybe, in time, Amanda's allegation of domestic violence might also be aired. In a country reluctant to hear about tarnished modern Anzac legends, perhaps it wouldn't be SAS whistleblowers who would threaten to expose the fallacy of 'Brand BRS'. Were Amanda's allegations his weak point? Would it be a woman, not a war crime, that might collapse the house of cards Roberts-Smith had built for himself and was now fighting to protect?

CHAPTER 24

REACTION

Early June 2018

On the partition wall of my desk at *The Age* was a photo of renowned veteran political correspondent Michael 'Mickey' Gordon. When the sixty-two-year-old had died unexpectedly earlier in the year during an ocean swimming race, I'd lost a friend, mentor and surfing companion.

'Go, Nicky, go!' Gordon would yell at me while bobbing in the water at Woolamai, urging me to paddle harder for a wave I was unsure I would make.

'Go, Mickey, go!' I would yell back when it was his turn.

It was out the back, behind the breakers waiting for the Southern Ocean sets to roll in, that I'd regularly sought Gordon's advice about journalism. He'd worked at *The Age* back when it was located in a tired brown-brick building in Melbourne's CBD that our competitors in the Murdoch press liked to call the 'Spencer Street Soviet' in a nod to the paper's history as a left-leaning broadsheet. In truth, *The Age* was historically a grand old paper of record, internationally acclaimed as one of the finest outlets in the world.

Back in the day, the men who ran *The Age* smoked in the office and legend had it that the men's toilet had a fridge stocked with beer nicknamed 'the bog bar'. The bar and the smoking were gone when I arrived at the paper in 2008, but Gordon was there, a testament to *The Age*'s storied past and commitment to journalistic ideals that the financial decline of the industry and advent of the internet had, at times, placed under severe strain.

Gordon, almost as anxious as me, had a slight stutter that enveloped his speech at the most inopportune of times. He was also brilliant, idealistic and fearless about his beliefs, having grown close to the refugees who'd fled the Taliban in Afghanistan, only to be locked up in detention centres by Australia. His legacy as a reporter was humanising asylum seekers, reminding readers that they had the same hopes for their children as they did.

It was why he'd urged on my reporting of war crimes and encouraged me to keep pestering my editors to fund a trip to Afghanistan.

'The victims have no voice,' he'd tell me.

'It's our job to give them one.'

Gordon's view of the craft of reporting was the same as his belief about surfing. Only once you had done the work could you go for it. With surfing, it meant swimming, running, studying weather reports and regular 5am starts. With reporting, it was making those extra calls to the sources you'd already spoken to five times before, just to make sure you had the facts and context down right, and then getting someone, such as Gordon, to read and question your copy.

How do you know that? You sure? How many sources? You sure that's enough?

Then it was about having the courage to go for it, be it the wave or the words.

Since he'd died, I had a habit of touching the photo of Gordon's face at my desk before I'd publish a risky story.

'Go, Nicky, go,' I'd whisper to myself, as if the words might stave off an unknown disaster I feared lay buried somewhere I couldn't see: an unreliable source, a mistake I had failed to pick up, or my inability to recognise my own confirmation bias.

When Gordon died, I turned even more to Chris Masters as my journalistic and ethical guide.

The two of us spent days labouring over each line in the stories we planned to publish about Roberts-Smith. In truth, I wasn't sure I would have written a word without Masters beside me. It wasn't just his journalistic experience and special forces knowledge and contacts, but knowing he would be there if it all turned bad. It was also quietly reassuring that Masters was willing to potentially piss off his long-time senior military sources, or even friends, who didn't want negative coverage about the nation's armed forces. If he was willing to risk friendships, it was another sign the journalism was worth doing.

Still, it didn't stop me touching the photo on my desk or whispering my Mickey Gordon mantra on the evening of 7 June 2018.

The next day, *The Age* and the *Sydney Morning Herald* planned to splash with a story headlined 'SAS Day of Shame'. It would reveal the contents of a supposedly secret report by Samantha Crompvoets. Twenty-fours hours after that, for the Saturday editions, Chris Masters and I had written a lengthy feature about a soldier we called 'Leonidas', revealing he had kicked an Afghan by the name of Ali Jan off a small cliff in the village of Darwan. A day later again, we planned another front-page story alleging that on Easter Sunday 2009 while on a mission, Leonidas had blooded a rookie soldier, encouraging him to execute a prisoner, and himself executing a second prisoner.

* * *

The identity of Leonidas was immediately clear to Brendan Nelson. It was the man the former defence minister had so fiercely promoted as the face of the Australian War Memorial. Those closest to Roberts-Smith had also picked him as Leonidas.

We described Leonidas as a warrior-like soldier in a clique of SAS troopers who bore 'tattoos and devotion to the Hollywood movie *300*, which glorifies the fighting prowess of the ancient Spartans'. Roberts-Smith had a tattoo of a spartan helmet on his right ribcage. After Darwan, some soldiers had called him Spartacus.

'It's not true,' Roberts-Smith told anyone who asked of the allegations hitting the news stands. 'It's utter bullshit.'

The Roberts-Smith whom Brendan Nelson believed he knew so well, the courageous living embodiment of the modern Anzac spirit and the very epitome of human strength, sounded distraught when the former defence minister called him. Nelson reassured him – 'I believe you, Ben' – before asking him about how he was holding up.

'I know who's behind this. I know what's motivating them,' Roberts-Smith said. Nelson now recognised another emotion in the soldier. He was angry.

That same weekend, Emma had also been inundated with calls from friends and family. Her parents had called, confused and upset, worried about the impact on Emma's children. First the affair, now this.

Our first article – the detailed story about the Darwan mission – had left Roberts-Smith reeling with shock, 'betrayed and humiliated'. He told people he felt that everything he had fought for was at risk of slipping away; he'd fought for his country over and over again, only to be attacked 'from the shadows' by cowards. Ever since leaving the military, he had been looking only forward and getting on with it, trying 'very hard to live a good life'. Now, a couple of reporters were trying to 'steal' everything he had earned, to rip it all away from him.

The call from Nelson was one of half-a-dozen Roberts-Smith received immediately after the articles were published. Among those he spoke to were his trusted old comrades Neil Browning and Vincent Jelovic. They both assured him they had his back.

They also both agreed with Roberts-Smith that it was likely blokes in the SAS like Boyd Keary, Nick Simkin, Dean Tilley and Brian McMurray who were stirring shit up. And maybe someone closer to home, Jason Andrews. This is what worried Roberts-Smith the most. Andrews knew more of his secrets than anyone in the SAS.

Late on Saturday, between the story about Darwan and the Sunday front-page article about Easter Sunday, Roberts-Smith found himself in a familiar pose: staring into the dark into the early hours of the morning, consumed with anxiety and paranoia. But this was worse than ever. He had suffered severe heart palpitations. Every hour he would refresh his phone, waiting for the next story to appear. As he waited, he felt as if his very soul was at risk of being crushed.

'It's all bullshit,' he'd told Emma. The journalists were 'using smears from people' who were jealous of his achievements to try to paint him as a war criminal. They would all live to regret it. Anyone else who had had the temerity to ask if any of it was true had received the same impassioned response.

'It's all lies.'

To illustrate this, Roberts-Smith had also pointed out a fact that no one could dispute. The Brereton Inquiry had been launched in May 2016. Two years had passed since then, and Roberts-Smith hadn't as much as heard a peep from the judge. If the ex-soldier was responsible for kicking an Afghan prisoner off a cliff, surely someone from the inquiry would have hauled him in for an interview by now?

* * *

As Roberts-Smith dealt with becoming front-page news, a small group of federal agents were planning their next move. Most of these investigators could have passed for accountants. The plain-clothes detectives of the Australian Federal Police had their own uniform. For the male officers, it was a dark suit, white shirt, cheap tie and short-back-and-sides haircut. Dressing down was sneakers, jeans and a t-shirt. The female detectives also favoured dull corporate attire or the same low-key casualwear. The only thing that differentiated them from Canberra's other public servants were the guns sometimes strapped to their belts.

While every covert probe handled by the AFP's special operations division was classified, these investigators' assignment was even more secretive than usual. They were investigating three suspects, including one of the most high-profile and well-connected targets in the AFP's history. This was why the agents had been read the riot act by senior command. They'd been told not to breathe a word of anything to anyone.

Success was dependent on Ben Roberts-Smith and his two co-accused, Neil Browning and Vincent Jelovic, remaining blind to the fact that they were under covert investigation by police for alleged war crimes committed in Afghanistan. This would give police at least a fighting chance of gathering evidence. If the suspects knew they were being probed, they would likely stay off open phone lines, for fear of tapping, and stay away from emails, for fear of a raid. But if they thought no one was watching or listening, maybe, just maybe, someone would slip up on the phone.

The detectives had learnt of the identity of their quarries one week earlier, on 3 June, in a secure room behind the vast grey concrete walls of the AFP headquarters. Compared to the agency's often sluggish processes, the decision of the federal police to commence an investigation into Roberts-Smith was made with lightning speed. It had been prompted by a letter from the chief of the Australian Defence Force, Air Chief Marshal Mark Binskin, to the Commissioner of the AFP, Andrew Colvin.

Colvin had swiftly approved the launching of the inquiry. He had also been briefed on a secondary probe, which had been referred to the AFP's Canberra office by detectives in Melbourne. A woman was alleging that Roberts-Smith had struck her. While the domestic violence allegation was to be referred to the AFP's local policing division, the war crimes allegations were kept within the confines of AFP headquarters.

Binskin had sent his letter on the advice of Justice Brereton. By the end of May 2018, Brereton had grilled several soldiers who had served with Roberts-Smith. They included three men known within the SAS to hold highly damaging information about him: patrol commanders Boyd Keary and Brian McMurray, and the SAS scout from the Easter Sunday mission, Dean Tilley.

Brereton had also summoned two men regarded within the SAS as Roberts-Smith's closest friends: Neil Browning and Vincent Jelovic. One other man had been summoned, a soldier who served both at Darwan and on Easter Sunday 2009 and who was suspected in the SAS to have badly fallen out with Ben Roberts-Smith: Jason Andrews.

What these soldiers had told Brereton was highly classified, but the testimony provided by at least some of them had prompted the judge to do something no one in the defence force had envisaged when he was first appointed to begin his probe two years earlier. While Brereton had huge powers, he had no ability to launch a criminal investigation that could land a soldier before a jury in a courtroom. Under the Australian system, that was the duty of the federal police.

On 28 May, Binskin received a classified briefing outlining how Brereton had received credible information that warranted a referral to the federal police for criminal investigation. The offences Brereton suspected may have occurred included the 'war crime of cruel treatment' and the 'war crime of murder'. The key suspect was named as Australia's most famous soldier, Ben Roberts-Smith.

* * *

In the days after the articles ran, Roberts-Smith's phone had continued ringing with support from the good and great of Australian society. Mark O'Brien had fired off another legal threat on behalf of his client to *The Age* and *Sydney Morning Herald*, this time also demanding the papers provide a written undertaking never to identify Roberts-Smith as 'Leonidas'.

But in the depths of Roberts-Smith's despair, someone unexpected reached out. The man explained that he was an associate of the former head of security for Channel 7, who had given him Roberts-Smith's number.

'Mate, I've been dealing with the media for a long time,' this caller had told Roberts-Smith. 'If you ever want to have a cup of coffee or you just want to get away from those things for a while, happy to be there.'

The caller was Mick Keelty, a man with unrivalled contacts in Canberra's defence and intelligence establishment. In Keelty's mobile phone were the numbers of many officers still serving in the federal police, including the senior officers overseeing the secret Roberts-Smith police inquiries. The reason for his impressive network was simple: Keelty had previously served as the Commissioner of the Australian Federal Police.

CHAPTER 25

GOING DARK

Far North Queensland, mid 2018

A neatly dressed woman with blonde hair drawn into a tight ponytail walked into JB Hi-Fi, welcoming the air-conditioned respite from the stifling North Queensland air outside. It would be brief relief, though, for her shopping list was short: sim cards and two mobile phones.

The store was a few hundred metres from the coastline hugging the Great Barrier Reef and, beyond that, the Coral Sea. It was also an eighteen-and-a-half-hour drive north from the Roberts-Smith family home.

The distance was ideal. Ben Roberts-Smith didn't want anyone to connect the woman's shopping trip to him. Danielle Scott, an astute businessperson who also happened to be Emma Roberts-Smith's oldest friend, was surely far enough away to perform the errand without scrutiny. Danielle had met Emma before either of them could talk. The pair had been best friends since then.

Ben Roberts-Smith took a calculated risk in asking Emma's best friend to acquire two burner phones and post them to him. It guaranteed he could use the phones without fear of interception from any snooping police, but only if Danielle never told anyone about it.

But Danielle's loyalty lay with Emma, not her husband. After the discovery of Ben Roberts-Smith's affair, it was Danielle whom Emma had confided in, seeking advice and counsel.

The revelation of Roberts-Smith's infidelity twigged a long-dormant suspicion for Danielle. She'd felt wary of Roberts-Smith from the first time she'd met him. She considered Emma a catch, bubbly and gorgeous and with a burgeoning career, while at the time Roberts-Smith seemed to her a man not only ill-at-ease with those around him, but someone uncomfortable in his own skin.

She'd watched the couple's roles reverse over time, after Roberts-Smith joined the SAS and became famous. Her friend had lost her lightness as she described how her husband had become all-controlling and arrogant, characteristics that Danielle put down to his old insecure self. Even as the most renowned soldier in the land, to her Ben Roberts-Smith still seemed unable to quite fit in.

Danielle knew Roberts-Smith presented as an eloquent hero in front of refined company, but, after a few wines he'd curse, snarl, put Emma down and belittle those around him. Danielle was one of the few people Roberts-Smith dropped his guard around, maybe because they went back so long, or maybe because he assumed her loyalty to Emma would extend to him.

The decision to buy the sim cards and phones appeared to affirm this belief. Danielle and Roberts-Smith had even agreed on their own code word. When she called him on his regular line, the burner phones were to be called 'handbags'.

'I want to be able to contact the guys in the unit without our phones being tapped,' he had told her.

The request for burner phones seemed at odds with Roberts-Smith's assurances that he didn't fear scrutiny because he had done nothing wrong, but he assured Danielle that its purpose was to counter the conniving or malign forces trying to incriminate an innocent man. He convinced her that lying, jealous soldiers were setting him up.

He'd been telling Emma the same thing, but she also confided in Danielle that Roberts-Smith wasn't acting like a man with an unburdened conscience. To the contrary, Roberts-Smith was obsessed with the Brereton Inquiry, as well as the activities of his enemies in the SAS and the two journalists who wouldn't leave him alone. In WhatsApp messages, Emma described to Danielle a man under siege, drinking heavily and spiralling into frequent bouts of panic and anxiety.

While Danielle had never met them, she was becoming familiar with the names of the men Roberts-Smith was convinced might be undermining him before Justice Brereton. Emma had also told her about a phone call from Roberts-Smith's former patrol commander, who revealed he had bumped into one of these men outside the Brereton Inquiry interview room. Information given to Roberts-Smith suggested that someone in the SAS had put the Victoria Cross recipient in the frame for war crimes.

Roberts-Smith portrayed his request for burner phones as merely a means to safeguard the good guys in the SAS in the event jealous haters convinced the Brereton Inquiry to trigger some unwieldy police investigation.

'It's utter bullshit,' he said of the suggestion that he'd ever murdered a prisoner. War was ugly, and terrorists had been killed, but it was all above board.

His passionate protestations of innocence and insistence that he was the subject of a witch-hunt resonated with Danielle. She knew the army was riven with rumours, rivalry and jealousy. Her father had been a sergeant and she'd grown up around veterans who had instilled in her an abiding respect for the notion of military service embedded in the Anzac legend. If she was dubious of her best friend's husband at times, she still wanted to believe in the military her father had served.

So she'd gone to JB Hi-Fi, selected two phones and two sim cards and paid in cash. She'd also agreed to register the sim cards in her own name and post the 'handbags' to Roberts-Smith.

She also did one thing Roberts-Smith didn't request. Whether it was due to her habit of running a small business, or the niggling suspicion about Roberts-Smith that she couldn't shake, Danielle made a record of the two sim card numbers and filed them away.

* * *

Emma watched her husband as he walked into their house carrying a grey shopping bag, making a mental note to check its contents. If outsiders viewed their relationship as intact as 'Brand BRS', those closer to the couple knew otherwise. They were still together, but one thing had irrevocably changed. Emma no longer trusted her husband. She was no longer sure when Roberts-Smith was lying or telling the truth.

In the days after the discovery of the affair he'd been on his best behaviour, asking for her forgiveness. But the remnants of his lies laid everywhere, like a stain that couldn't be washed away. Every unusual past behaviour was imbued with new meaning, from the unexpected nights away for work, the multiple mobile phones, the constant cash withdrawals, the times where her calls went straight to his message bank.

Was he with her?

The future was also stained, and not just with the dread of an article that might plunge his private shame into the public square. Emma no longer knew if it was her he was fighting to keep, or the pretence of a happy family life that was part of Ben Roberts-Smith's public narrative. If that was the case, then the marriage was as good as over.

She also noticed he was preoccupied with something else. He feared another war crimes media exposé, one that named him directly. He'd begun building a wall to stave off the next assault, be it from Brereton or the media. Not only was he constantly on the phone to his mates Browning and Jelovic, but he had begun talking to a public relations adviser. The adviser was a former commercial television journalist, Ross Coulthart, who had been placed on the payroll alongside O'Brien Legal.

A tall, skinny man in his sixties with thin hair and spindly limbs, Coulthart had written a bestselling book about Australian soldiers who'd fought on the Western Front. 'I may well do a book about the Roberts-Smith story myself,' Coulthart had more recently mused.

Despite the public relations advice, Emma watched her husband descend into a deeper fervour of panic and paranoia. The single bottle of red in the evening had turned into two. The shower and mirror pep talks continued, but he'd also taken to walking around the house, muttering to himself, as if rehearsing for a play.

He was also constantly re-watching *Lone Survivor*, an action film about the heroic efforts of a four-man team of US Navy Seals who were overwhelmed by a much larger Taliban force in the Korangal Valley in eastern Afghanistan. Only one of the team survived the fierce battle, a feat that saw him awarded a Navy Cross and Purple Heart.

Something about the film and its title obviously resonated with Roberts-Smith. It was an account of the bravery and valour of American special forces, but the Navy Seal survivor's memoir that inspired the film had since become a contested account, dogged by allegations of exaggeration and embellishment.

If there was a pattern – albeit unsettling – to Roberts-Smith's obsessive traits of working out, excessive drinking, self-talking and strategising, the arrival of her husband carrying a grey shopping bag was an unexpected sight for Emma. Australia's most famous war hero very rarely did his own shopping.

This was why she decided to take a peek at the bag's contents: a ream of white A4 printing paper, a packet of envelopes and some gloves. A few hours after he unpacked the shopping bag, Roberts-Smith asked Emma for an address. He wanted to know the number of the post office box used by the SAS on the other side of the country.

* * *

A few days later, at noon, Brian McMurray checked his pigeonhole at the Campbell Barracks in Perth and discovered an envelope addressed to him in unfamiliar handwriting. McMurray immediately felt alarmed. His name, rank and SAS Squadron details were written on the envelope. All were meant to be classified, known only to those inside the regiment.

The sergeant carefully opened the envelope and took out a single piece of A4 paper. As he read the typed letter, the feeling of alarm increased. The letter was a threat.

McMurray read it once and then a second time. 'You and others have worked together to spread lies and rumours to the media and the Inspector-General's inquiry,' it said. 'You have one chance to save yourself. You must approach the inquiry and admit that you have colluded with others to spread lies.' It was signed a 'friend of the regiment'.

McMurray felt ill. A few weeks earlier he'd given his testimony to the Brereton Inquiry. What he'd told the judge had appeared to spark intense and immediate interest, for he'd been summoned back for another interview.

Whoever sent the letter knew of his military history, including supposed secret information about the squadron to which he had been posted, but also the fact of his appearance before the judge. This wasn't just a threat to his safety, thought McMurray. His family lived nearby in Perth. The threat extended to them as well.

'Hey, mate,' he barked out to a patrol team member nearby. 'I want you to witness this. I've just been sent a threatening letter in the mail. I want you to observe me handle it from here on in. I'm going to take it to the regimental troop headquarters, report it and bag it.'

McMurray's well-honed instincts were kicking in. Back in Afghanistan, he'd been assigned the task of collecting evidence from the bodies of those killed in action, recording critical details about how and where they had died and bagging any items they carried that could be of forensic value.

It was the job he'd done on Easter Sunday 2009, the mission that had recently been causing Roberts-Smith intense angst and had prompted similarly intense scrutiny from Justice Brereton.

A short time later, McMurray handed the letter to the Regimental Sergeant Major, who placed it in a plastic evidence bag. McMurray then wrote a statement outlining how he'd found the letter minutes before. Then he waited for the police to arrive.

* * *

Roberts-Smith pressed the button on the burner phone and watched the screen light up. The 'handbag' was one of two burners that had arrived by post from north Queensland and no one, save for Emma and her best friend, knew of their existence. The phones were registered in the name of Danielle Scott.

Next, he installed two encrypted communication apps, Signal and Telegram. The encrypted apps added an extra layer of protection as they couldn't be tapped by law enforcement. Roberts-Smith knew that even the intelligence services couldn't intercept encrypted technology.

His decision to activate the phone in early July had come after an intense few weeks. Not only had fallout from the media's Leonidas story continued, but he'd also sat down with the man who used to run the Australian Federal Police.

Mick Keelty was craggy-faced, with a gentle manner and rasping voice. Along with his policing and Defence contacts, Keelty had also forged strong ties in the business community, becoming a security adviser to wealthy families and companies.

'Ben's not doing too well,' Keelty had been told.

Roberts-Smith was wary of the ex-commissioner's calls and offer to meet. He'd never met the ex-police chief before and his motives seemed opaque. Beyond doing a favour for Seven's former security boss, it seemed odd that Keelty was making the effort to catch up with a man he didn't know.

Yet Roberts-Smith agreed to meet face to face after Keelty explained he'd had his own dealings with investigative journalists.

Unbeknown to either man, the same question troubling Roberts-Smith about why Keelty was eager to sit down with him was also being asked at the federal police headquarters. This question had been prompted by Keelty's behaviour.

In preparation for his meeting with Roberts-Smith, the former police chief reached out to his senior federal police contacts and queried if the agency had any active interest in Ben Roberts-Smith. Someone in the agency not only spoke to Keelty, but advised him of something that was never meant to have left the thick concrete walls of the Edmund Barton Building. Keelty was told that Roberts-Smith had recently been the subject of two official referrals, police speak for criminal complaints lodged by external parties and, depending on how they were assessed, which could trigger a full-blown inquiry.

A short time after receiving this information, Keelty dialled the number of the commander in charge of the special operations division responsible for war crimes investigations. Keelty didn't know it, but this commander had placed his call on speaker phone and urgently called in the officer heading the federal police's anti-corruption division.

There was no suggestion that Keelty was acting in any way that was illegal, but both officers scrawled notes as Keelty amiably inquired about the federal police's receipt of complaints about Ben Roberts-Smith. The commander

revealed nothing about Brereton's war crime referrals or
the allegation of domestic violence, but the damage had
already been done by someone else in the agency.

Keelty knew the AFP had been referred what were
meant to be confidential complaints about Roberts-Smith.
Now he was planning to meet with the war hero.

Keelty's phone calls triggered a wave of panic throughout
the AFP's executive command, including among officers
who had previously spent years serving under him. Keelty
is certainly not corrupt, and these police didn't believe that
he was, but they suspected his desire to network within
the business community and to help an Australian war
hero had led to a potentially catastrophic and unforgivable
scenario.

The AFP's number-one war crimes suspect was at risk of
finding out about the agency's secret interest in him from
none other than the police force's former top cop. By the
time Roberts-Smith sat down with Keelty over coffee, the
federal police had activated a covert surveillance operation.

The AFP was no longer only looking for evidence of
war crimes. Police also wanted to find out who in the
organisation had tipped off Mick Keelty about the agency's
interest in Roberts-Smith. In the pair's meeting, Keelty
had spoken gently and reassuringly to Roberts-Smith.
The Victoria Cross winner appeared to Keelty to be under
enormous pressure and he listened patiently as he lashed
out at the media and his enemies in the SAS.

Keelty also offered up some of what he'd learnt by
reaching into the AFP.

Twenty-one days later, Roberts-Smith made his first call
on one of the 'handbags'. The AFP's covert monitoring
teams missed this call, as they were blind to the existence
of the burner. But they did notice something unusual.

Roberts-Smith had stopped using his mobile phone to speak to certain contacts. There was a police term for a suspect altering their communications routine to avoid interception. It was called 'going dark'.

Barely a month into one of the toughest criminal investigations in AFP history, police were already falling well behind their main suspect.

CHAPTER 26

NOTE OF CONCERN

July 2018

I pressed my toes into the sand and my phone to my ear as ex-AFP commissioner Mick Keelty told me something I was struggling to comprehend.

'You did what?'

Yachts bobbed in the water in front of me and backpackers and grey-haired tourists were turning different shades of pink stretched out on towels nearby. I was on a short holiday on Magnetic Island, off the North Queensland coast, but my plan to put work aside and switch off for a few days was failing as Keelty explained to me how he was trying to help Ben Roberts-Smith.

As he described his interactions with the ex-soldier, I was bewildered. In quick succession, Keelty revealed how he'd called up his contacts in the federal police, been briefed on the existence of two referrals to the policing agency about Roberts-Smith and had then met with the ex-soldier to offer him support and advice.

'Mick, nobody is meant to know about the police referrals. They are meant to be secret,' I'd told him. 'If Ben Roberts-Smith is the subject of referrals, it means he's a potential police target.'

The police chief responded as if he hadn't realised what he had wandered into. He seemed not to have considered the risk of tipping off Roberts-Smith. Keelty was not a close contact or a friend, but I'd become acquainted with him years earlier, in 2008, when he was police chief, and his organised crime squad and I were investigating the same mafia syndicate. My interest in the mafia was confined mostly to its political influence, but Keelty's detectives had sought my help in investigating a massive drug importation.

I'd politely declined the federal police's suggestion to work with them but had given the agency some leads about criminals I would later implicate in a major political bribery scandal.

Keelty called me and requested a meeting to thank me for my assistance. He asked the-then Federal Attorney-General, Robert McClelland, to do the same.

Keelty projected genuine interest and warmth when we'd met, but there was something about him that also reminded me of … well, of a reporter. I'd wondered if he had been charming me in the same way he had charmed other journalists, television producers, politicians and business leaders who might yet serve some useful future purpose.

Keelty had a love–hate relationship with the press, having been lauded for his role in transforming the AFP into a vastly expanded agency that, post the September 11 attacks in America, had helped solve the Bali bombings. But journalists had also savaged him over the botched arrest of an overseas doctor falsely accused of extremism, and for his agency's role in tipping off the Indonesian police about young Australian drug smugglers who were later executed.

The Keelty I'd met in 2008 was still wounded by this media assault, yet seemingly eager to keep trusted journalists close and build new relationships. I'd marvelled at his ability to casually name-drop. He seemed to know everyone worth knowing, and my instincts told me he had me earmarked as a young reporter he might be able to work with.

A friend of mine who'd served under Keelty at the AFP laughed when I described our first meeting. He told me that Keelty was renowned for his Irish charm and penchant for networking. It had enabled him to maintain influence within the AFP while becoming a well-paid consultant to wealthy families, companies and government agencies. Long after he had handed in his badge, Keelty was still mentoring high-ranking AFP officers.

Keelty's instinct for checking in with old friends and making new ones seemed to be at the heart of his decision to engage with Roberts-Smith. He professed only a genuine desire to help a famous stranger, and yet his explanation that he was concerned with Roberts-Smith's 'welfare' made little sense given the pair weren't even acquaintances. Keelty had quickly dismissed the notion he was doing a favour for someone in Kerry Stokes' empire.

The comment of one ex-SAS soldier who had joined the corporate world flashed into my mind as Keelty told me he was simply performing a civic duty in reaching out to Roberts-Smith.

'Everyone wants to get near the SAS flame,' the veteran had said, describing the allure of decorated special forces soldiers to those in boardrooms and politics. Keelty wasn't just near the flame. He was at risk of getting burnt.

I'd never been anything but deferential to the former police chief, but I could feel the tension in my voice as we spoke and I queried his decision to cosy up to Roberts-Smith.

'If you have told Roberts-Smith about what you have learnt from the AFP, you might have tipped off a criminal suspect,' I told him bluntly, feeling simultaneously like a student telling off a school principal but also justified in stating what I thought.

Did Keelty really think he could clear up serious questions raised by the media and possibly address the authorities' pursuit of an alleged war crimes suspect with a chinwag and a few phone calls?

He stressed that he had urged Roberts-Smith to contact the AFP to discuss the allegations. To this, I screamed in my mind: *You are still missing the point!* It was for the federal police investigators assessing the allegations about Roberts-Smith to decide when to alert their suspect he was under investigation or to request an interview. Not an ex-police chief flying blind.

My bewilderment at Keelty's actions was now eclipsed by something approaching alarm – these actions could arm Roberts-Smith with the information he needed to avoid police scrutiny. Chris Masters and I had confirmed through confidential sources that the AFP had launched a full-blown secret war crimes investigation into Roberts-Smith, but we had consciously not reported this or told anyone so as not to tip him off. The last thing I'd ever imagined was a former police chief unwittingly doing what we had so studiously avoided.

Keelty sounded worried as he hung up the phone. While it was certain he had told Roberts-Smith he was the subject of police interest, what was uncertain was the impact of this on a covert police inquiry that would almost surely be relying on phone taps.

As I walked away from the beach along a strip of bitumen melting in the midday sun, I called my friend who had once worked for Keelty. I wanted someone to make a note of my concern.

'Keelty has tipped off Roberts-Smith,' I blurted out. 'The police's job just got a hell of a lot harder.'

* * *

I arrived back in Melbourne tanned but tired. I'd been investigating Ben Roberts-Smith for over a year, painfully piecing together eyewitness testimony and other accounts of his alleged involvement in prisoner executions.

I'd also been attempting to corroborate the claims of Roberts-Smith's lover, Amanda, that Roberts-Smith had punched her. The allegation seemed to fit with previous claims about Roberts-Smith's bullying and bastardising of smaller soldiers. The domestic violence allegations were still largely her word versus his. But Amanda had met with the police, providing an account of her claim in circumstances in which she could be charged for making a false complaint if it was untrue.

The months of digging had also revealed a pattern of alarming threats made towards those alleging Roberts-Smith's involvement in prisoner executions on Easter Sunday 2009 and at Darwan in 2012.

McMurray had, by early July, been sent two anonymous threatening letters warning him to recant his testimony to Justice Brereton or face the consequences. Simkin had been raided. Keary and Andrews had both been pressured to keep their concerns quiet. Defamation threats had been sent to Tindell and Nueling. Even Amanda had been sent a legal threat from an anonymous account.

Those who had challenged 'Brand BRS' had received blowback, either anonymously or in the form of legal threats, but the AFP and the defence force seemed powerless to identify who was behind the most malicious acts of intimidation. The AFP had fingerprinted the letters sent to McMurray, but no match was found. And they had referred the false complaint prompting the raid of Simkin to the Brereton Inquiry, but the identity of the mysterious complainant, Blowerw2, was still unconfirmed. Motive and circumstantial evidence all pointed one way, yet now that Roberts-Smith was aware that police were on his tail, the chance of him slipping up seemed remote.

Other forces were also at work. A day after I returned from my holiday, I had a run-in with Ross Coulthart, the former TV investigative journalist who was now working as a public relations consultant. Having previously helped Coulthart when he was a reporter, I'd decided to call him after journalists warned me he was working closely with Roberts-Smith and lawyer Mark O'Brien. One reporter told me that Coulthart had personally briefed the editor of *The Australian* that the scrutiny of Roberts-Smith was unwarranted.

When Coulthart answered his phone, I asked him outright if he was working for Roberts-Smith. He refused to say, instead claiming he might be doing no more than undertaking his own journalism or researching a book. His Twitter account stated he was an 'investigative journalist', so I couldn't help wondering why he seemed to be using the cloak of his former profession to undermine those still in it. In our conversation, he claimed he had found out about the identity of one of Chris Masters' sources and said he knew him to be unreliable.

I'd snapped back, demanding he tell me if he was a journalist or a hired gun on the Roberts-Smith payroll. He couldn't be both. He'd refused to answer and it sounded like he was taking satisfaction from my exasperation. After I hung up from the call, I felt adrenalin coursing through me.

It made sense that Roberts-Smith would come at me with all he could muster, given what I was digging up. I could cop legal warfare from the likes of Mark O'Brien, because that was his job. Understanding Keelty's actions was not so easy, but perhaps the ex-cop simply wanted to help a high-profile Australian he genuinely believed was copping unfair media heat, just like Keelty had a decade before. But Coulthart was at his core an investigative reporter. He was one of us, with an entire public persona and career built around the noble pursuit of finding hidden facts and confronting powerful interests.

If he'd been cagey about telling me of his true relationship with Roberts-Smith, Coulthart had been less restrained when texting my company's chief editor, James Chessell. Chessell was the ultimate gatekeeper, the editor with the power to back or block reporting in the *Herald* and *The Age*.

I was to learn that Coulthart had appealed directly to Chessell.

'I understand that you have to back your journalists but there are key issues that you need to understand. As you probably know, I was confronted by a very angry Nick McKenzie yesterday demanding to know who I was working for,' he had texted Chessell. 'Yesterday's unwarranted aggression from Nick McKenzie pissed me off because I was actually offering to help him. He took that to be me arrogantly dismissing his journalism.

'I was bemused by his belligerence because, as I pointed out to him, I'm perfectly entitled to investigate the very serious claims he's raised in the media about SAS with Chris M[asters].'

He'd told Chessell it was 'no secret' he was working as a public relations adviser, but that he was also 'writing books and making films'. It was why he had so 'many SAS contacts – who've been reaching out to me since the stories started appearing'.

'I am very confident, based on numerous interviews with serving and former SAS operators and other sources here and OS, that the allegations against BRS would be strongly and credibly disputed by numerous credible direct witnesses.'

To inject further doubt into Chessell's thinking, Coulthart claimed I'd been sloppy by only recently approaching a former US soldier who had served in Roberts-Smith's patrol team on his first deployment to Afghanistan. 'Privately, I am surprised that Nick has not approached this witness before because he should have,' he'd written.

In his eagerness to ensure any future story was spiked, Coulthart revealed what I took to be an indication of just how firmly embedded he was in the Roberts-Smith camp. The US soldier I'd only recently called was a Roberts-Smith loyalist whose knowledge was limited to a patrol in 2006 that I had long believed had involved no explicit war crime. The soldier could cast no light on events that occurred years later at Darwan or on Easter Sunday.

In my earlier discussion with Coulthart, he appeared to know little about the controversial missions from 2009 and 2012. Yet he was indignant and insistent to Chessell that Masters and I were pursuing an innocent man. 'I do strongly believe that the paper's line on BRS is completely false and that your sources are malign or have misled themselves,' his lengthy text to my boss had opined. 'I'm happy to sit down with you for an off-the-record chat but I don't want to get yelled at by Nick McKenzie just because I'm doing him a favour by offering to help fix a looming disaster for him and the paper.'

* * *

The intervention by Keelty and Coulthart signalled that Roberts-Smith was stepping up his efforts to shut down our reporting. In response, I began working far more closely with Chessell, a bright and brusque business journalist and European correspondent who'd risen rapidly up Fairfax Media's executive ranks.

Some of my fellow journalists at *The Age* were wary of Chessell, not because of any specific dealings with him but believing he was a symbol of a new corporate era that old school reporters like Michael Gordon had worried might be an anathema to journalism. At that time the Channel Nine company takeover of Fairfax Media seemed a near certainty, which made it likely Chessell and the executives he answered to would be even warier of an unpopular story that could spark an expensive lawsuit. If Chessell backed a story that cost tens of millions in a trial and defamation payout, it would imperil his own career.

Those at the Fairfax mastheads viewed Nine as suspiciously as Seven. Despite also being funded via advertising, albeit supplemented by subscriptions, newspaper reporters were notoriously snobby when it came to their commercial television counterparts. Some of it was deserved – the worst of tabloid TV was cringe-worthy – but most Seven and Nine journalists took their job and commitment to the truth as seriously as newspaper reporters. In turn, they sneered at their print rivals' intellectual elitism.

The financial pressures on our industry had bonded us all through a shared goal: survival. It wasn't that I seriously doubted the bosses at Nine would believe the Roberts-Smith story unworthy of publication. Rather, I doubted anyone on the company's board would want the firm to pay for the fallout if Roberts-Smith carried out his threats to sue.

After Coulthart's intervention, I was directed to brief Chessell in detail about what our confidential sources had told us of Darwan, Easter Sunday and the alleged assault of Roberts-Smith's former girlfriend. Chessell drilled me intensely and, as he did, I felt despondent. He was forensic, exacting and appeared intent on picking holes in our reporting, echoing some of what Coulthart had said to him. After an hour, I fell silent, waiting to be redirected to another project. Instead, Chessell told me he wanted to reflect on our discussion. He called back an hour later.

'It might seem unpleasant, but it's my job to test you. I've heard enough. I'm going to back you, Nick. This is too important to bury. Truth in war is why we exist,' he said.

He continued: 'Sit down with Coulthart for his off-the-record briefing. Work with the lawyers. If the eyewitness testimony stands up after that, you can name him.'

I was momentarily confused. 'Name him?'

'You can name Ben Roberts-Smith.'

* * *

Twenty-four hours later, I fashioned a polite text message to Ross Coulthart. If he had gained information while working for Roberts-Smith that could persuade Chris Masters and I we'd been fed falsehoods, I wanted to have it.

Coulthart agreed to a face-to-face meeting in Sydney and I booked my flights, wondering what he might have told Roberts-Smith about the impending meeting and what, in turn, would be provided to me. Coulthart was, in effect, acting as a middleman for an alleged war crimes suspect, but I was genuine about hearing him out.

Every previous offer I'd made to Roberts-Smith to sit down and discuss the allegations had been rebuffed, and met instead with legal threats from O'Brien. I'd always been open to any information, but Roberts-Smith and his supporters hadn't been eager to supply it.

I'd even sat down with Keelty in a plush hotel lobby in Sydney. Keelty had, by then, met with Roberts-Smith twice, only to cut ties with him, claiming he'd told the war hero he couldn't engage with him further given the AFP's interest in his activities. Keelty also had little to offer in the way of evidence pointing to Roberts-Smith's innocence, beyond mentioning that the Victoria Cross recipient believed jealousy was behind the false allegations.

After I packed a bag and arranged for a taxi to take me to the airport for my rendezvous with Coulthart, the former reporter texted me. He no longer wanted to meet. I immediately called Chessell.

'Coulthart doesn't want to talk,' I said.

'You'd better start writing,' he replied.

* * *

As I walked through the ballroom looking for Chris Masters, I stared at my shoes, avoiding all the reporters in tuxedos and colourful gowns. We had been invited to a journalism awards night, the Kennedys, having been nominated for an award for investigative journalism over our earlier reporting on 'Leonidas' and the death of Ali Jan.

It should have been a night for a few casual beers, but I felt panicked. Leonidas had taken us to court. Our carefully written story identifying Roberts-Smith as the subject of credible war crimes allegations and outlining a domestic violence allegation had been published online just hours before. It was due to be printed in hard copy papers that evening, featuring on the front page of Saturday's *The Age* and *Sydney Morning Herald*.

But an hour or so before I'd arrived at the journalism event, I'd been told Ben Roberts-Smith had sought an urgent injunction in the Federal Court to block publication. His lawyers were apparently set to argue we'd been leaked classified Defence information. Our own lawyers had raced to the court to fight the action.

The story Roberts-Smith was now seeking to censor had been crafted meticulously and, because it named him, was far less powerful than the Leonidas story that had described executions on Easter Sunday 2009 and the death at Darwan in 2012.

For this latest story we'd described how, during a 2012 'training exercise in Perth involving the mock capture of an Afghan prisoner, three SAS soldiers witnessed Roberts-Smith instruct a young trooper to pretend to execute the detainee'. The story also stated that 'four defence insiders have alleged that they observed patrols under Roberts-Smith's direct or deputy leadership severely mistreat unarmed Afghans on four occasions'.

The reason Masters and I had been so careful was to avoid a lawsuit. We believed Roberts-Smith knew he was, in fact, implicated in far more shocking conduct than we had described, and so had made the judgment that he'd avoid defamation proceedings that would risk the complete story coming out.

Our copy also carefully described how a woman with whom he'd had an affair had made allegations to police. Amanda wasn't named in the story, but her allegations were carefully described. Roberts-Smith had taken her to a Parliament House event, after which 'she stumbled and fell down some stairs'. Again, we had used careful language, avoiding an explicit mention of the alleged punch to the face.

'Police have been told that by the time the pair arrived back at the Realm Hotel, Roberts-Smith was allegedly furious and she was subjected to an act of domestic violence.'

Roberts-Smith had punched young soldiers in the face when they had irritated him. He'd bullied and belittled those smaller than him. He'd pressured a junior soldier to execute a prisoner and done so himself. When Ali Jan had smiled at Roberts-Smith, he'd kicked him off a cliff and overseen his murder. The Father of the Year was now accused of assaulting his girlfriend.

The start of the awards night passed in a blur. I was focused only on the injunction proceedings unfolding in a Sydney court a few kilometres away. This wasn't a defamation action, not yet at least, but an attempt to prevent any further publication in the next day's papers of a story that was already online.

When Masters and I heard our names called, signalling we had won the award for our story on 'Leonidas', I momentarily froze in panic. The last place I wanted to be was on a stage in front of my colleagues. I forced myself to stand up, walk briskly to the stage and receive a glass statue, then made a beeline back to my dessert.

By then, I'd received word that Roberts-Smith's injunction attempt had failed, but also that his lawyers had signalled that a defamation action was a near certainty. Roberts-Smith had also released a public statement: 'The article contains a catalogue of lies, fabrications and misrepresentations. It is the culmination of many months of malicious and highly damaging allegations, all of which will be vigorously defended.'

I left the awards night early and took a cab back to a cheap motel near the airport. Stretched out on the top of the bed, still in my suit, I tried to sleep, but couldn't. After a few hours of tossing and turning, I pulled out my phone.

The Australian newspaper had scrambled to print its own story, alongside a photo of Emma and Ben Roberts-Smith standing side by side, looking pained. The pair had told the paper that they had been separated at the time Roberts-Smith was seeing the woman who alleged she had been punched by him. Relative to the allegations of war crimes and domestic violence, the claim that no affair had occurred was insignificant. But it was clear it had been placed front and centre in the article to cast doubt over the credibility of our entire story, which hadn't mentioned any separation. The reason we had omitted this was because it was false. I'd seen dozens of text messages proving that Emma and Roberts-Smith had not been separated.

Roberts-Smith had roped his wife into his damage control, I told myself. If Emma was prepared to defend her husband in a later defamation case, it would be even harder for us to win. It was also clear that Murdoch's News Corp press was already digging into the same trench as Roberts-Smith. Coulthart's briefing may have failed to convince Chessell, but it was informing the counter-narrative.

I pulled up *The Age*'s website. The headline 'Beneath the Bravery' was still leading the site. I felt proud of our story, yet I also knew there was every chance I was only just entering the most difficult stage. If Roberts-Smith sued, the only way to defend the allegations would be to convince witnesses to take the stand. That loomed as a near-impossible task, given how hard it had been just to convince our SAS sources to meet us for coffee. There was also no doubt that Seven and News Corp would defend Roberts-Smith to the hilt, and every chance my new corporate masters at Nine would lack the stomach to see out a legal stoush.

The only thing going for Chris Masters and me was the weight of evidence we knew existed. We had ended our story by describing how 'SAS insiders aware of some of the adverse allegations about Roberts-Smith or the conduct of his patrols say credible evidence has already been placed on record and on oath'. Questions had 'dogged Ben Roberts-Smith from a time well before he became supersized by expectation, responsibility and pride in the spirit of the Anzacs'.

This wasn't about jealousy or medal envy. No one was making any allegations about other Australian VC winners. Afghan villagers hadn't somehow colluded with those in the SAS to invent a story about a prisoner being kicked off a cliff.

This was about the truth.

PART 3

CHAPTER 27

LEGAL WARFARE

September–October 2018

Lawyer Dean Levitan sat quietly as I sketched out the village of Darwan. I was using a whiteboard on the wall of the twentieth floor of the Rialto, a skyscraper that was once the tallest in Melbourne.

To Levitan's left was a large glass window that offered a stunning view of Port Phillip Bay. The view was meant to impress the merchant bankers and business types who were the mainstay clients of corporate law firm MinterEllison.

Minters also had a small media practice led by one of the firm's former chairmen, Peter Bartlett, a legendary lawyer who had represented *The Age* since the eighties, and who had advised more than a dozen editors. It was the grey-haired septuagenarian who called Levitan that morning and told him to abandon his plans to attend a legal conference.

Levitan didn't need any encouragement. He found himself half-running, half-walking along the path snaking along the bank of the Yarra River back to the office. As a junior associate who'd spent less than a year in Bartlett's media practice, Levitan had been hoping to be assigned a role in *Ben Roberts-Smith v Fairfax Media*. A Federal Court writ had just been lodged with thunderous triumphalism by Roberts-Smith and was already being described by lawyers and the media as the defamation case of the century.

The young Levitan was an idealist. The more he had worked on company mergers, insurance files and contractual disputes, the more he had yearned to work on cases that mattered beyond a client's bottom line. Between high school and law school, he'd spent a year in Israel and begun to obsessively follow the debate swirling around the use of force in the occupied territories.

Proudly Jewish, Levitan had flirted with joining the Israeli army, but he was also acutely conscious that even a military he had been taught to respect as a child could cross the line. Allegations of atrocities should be weighed on the strength of the evidence, not whether the accused or accuser was wearing a uniform or whether they were Israeli or Palestinian. Truth and justice mattered for the wronged, no matter who they were fighting for. It was why he had selected the law instead of military fatigues.

Roberts-Smith was suing the newspapers and their reporters over the Leonidas story as well as the articles that had named him. If it actually made it to trial, the case would pit a war hero against a storied Australian media company. Its executives would have to decide whether to plead a defence of truth or a defence of qualified privilege. A judge would then decide if Roberts-Smith was a war criminal who had conned a nation, or a war hero so badly wronged that his payout would be historic.

Levitan considered the chances of an historic court victory for the newspapers slim at best. Neither defence theoretically available to the journalists could be easily mounted, which made it more likely than not that the newspapers would fold and issue a grovelling apology.

The defence of qualified privilege was theoretically open to reporters who had acted reasonably in publishing a matter of public interest, but Levitan wasn't aware of any occasion it had been successfully deployed in a courtroom by a mainstream media outlet, no matter the quality of the journalism.

That left the truth defence. To rely on it, the newspapers would need to prove what they had reported about Roberts-Smith murdering defenceless prisoners, bullying his comrades and punching a woman were true. If a single execution could be proven, the papers would win the case on the basis that a murderer had no reputation to defend.

But believing something was true or reaching the newspaper standard of proof to publish didn't go anywhere near providing the detailed defence required in a courtroom.

That wasn't to say Levitan did not believe what he'd read. The reporting appeared to Levitan to be robust.

Yet war crimes were notoriously hard to investigate, even for police.

Levitan's initial gut instinct was that the prospect of building a winning truth defence was negligible. Roberts-Smith's decision to sue suggested he thought the same.

An early glimmer of good news lay in the standard of proof, which would be far less onerous in a defamation trial heard by a judge alone. A civil court judge needed only to conclude a disputed allegation was more likely to have happened than not to determine it true, whereas the standard of proof to be reached by a criminal court jury was 'beyond reasonable doubt'.

Most of the news, though, was bad. There was good reason why Sydney had been labelled the defamation capital of the world by *The New York Times*. The difficulty in constructing a defence meant it was often impossible for Australian reporters to fight back when sued, especially if the litigant was cashed up.

It was why Levitan did not believe the Roberts-Smith litigation would ever make it inside a courtroom. In the end, it would likely boil down to a financial decision – it was vastly cheaper to settle and apologise than to fight, even when a paper had it right. Many editors chose to cave in rather than hire barristers to gown up. Roberts-Smith had already sourced some of Sydney's most expensive silks, an indication that he was fully financed for a legal war, no doubt backed by billionaire Kerry Stokes. In contrast, *The Age* and the *Herald* were waiting to be taken over by new corporate owners at Nine. There couldn't be a worse time to convince a company's executives and board to embrace a court process that could cost millions.

* * *

One thing apparent to Levitan from spending just a few minutes in the meeting room with me was my raw intensity. I could feel him looking at me oddly, like I was a man possessed. He'd comment later that he'd never met someone so focused.

Levitan watched on silently as I made crude strokes on the whiteboard. I'd sketched out a dry creek bed at the base of a steep embankment lined with compounds. Talking quickly, I'd described the final moments of an Afghan villager's life.

'Ali Jan was taken prisoner by Roberts-Smith's patrol team here,' I said, marking the last compound on the ridge with an X.

'And this is where we think he was kicked over the edge. He was dragged across the creek bed and killed here, under a mulberry tree.'

I wrote the names of the SAS soldiers who were at the last compound with Roberts-Smith, a deputy patrol commander named Jason Andrews and a soldier named Vincent Jelovic.

'Jelovic is loyal to Roberts-Smith, but Andrews is his own man,' I said, pausing for effect. I knew Andrews had already reported the cliff kick to two other soldiers, Brian McMurray and Boyd Keary.

'If we can get these three to court and if they tell the truth, then we have a chance,' Bartlett said. 'Will any of them help us?'

Levitan observed a sudden despondency wash across my face.

'Not willingly. No one wants to confront Roberts-Smith in court.'

'Will the woman who made the police complaint testify?'

I hesitated again. 'If SAS soldiers are scared of taking him on, I'm not sure a lone woman will be keen.'

Levitan said nothing, but now it was his face that was talking. It betrayed his scepticism.

'There are *some* soldiers willing to help,' I offered. 'If we subpoena them to the stand and they take an oath, they will tell the truth.'

Levitan tried to gauge if he was hearing blind optimism or the beginning of a truth defence. We had less than four weeks to submit it to the Federal Court if we were going to fight the war hero's writ.

I wiped the board clean and began sketching compound Whiskey 108. This was the supposed site of the Easter Sunday 2009 mission in which two prisoners were dragged from a tunnel and executed. McMurray was also on this mission, as was Andrews, who I believed had been ordered to execute one of the detainees before Roberts-Smith murdered the other.

Next, I wrote a single word, explaining that it described a practice in which junior soldiers were pressured to execute a prisoner to claim their first kill. If the practice had garnered its own term, then maybe it wasn't just Andrews who had been subjected to it.

I then underlined it.

'<u>Blooding</u>.'

* * *

A fortnight later, Levitan was back in the twentieth-floor meeting room, waiting. He turned his chair to face the glass window, his eyes following a colourful container ship moving across the horizon. He'd barely left work since that initial meeting. On this morning, he felt both nervous and excited.

The former SAS soldier I had told him would appear at MinterEllison was running late.

Levitan had spent the past fortnight helping Bartlett organise barristers and drafting a truth defence. It had been an exhausting blur. Not only had Bartlett placed Levitan on the case, but he was assigned the role of lead solicitor.

As his work hours ballooned, so did his self-doubt. After dozens of briefings from me and Masters, and hours spent reviewing documents, Levitan was confident that our reporting was, on paper at least, sound. But days out from the deadline to file our truth defence in court, a move that would signal to Roberts-Smith how we planned to defend the case and the people we wished to summon to court, I wasn't confident that we had any guaranteed witnesses. Instead, Masters and I had sought promises that certain soldiers would show up if they were subpoenaed. None were given lightly and all were qualified, usually with the rider: 'I'll come, but only if I'm forced to.'

As one day rolled into the next, Levitan had developed a nagging feeling that he was too young, too green and too lacking in trial experience.

It didn't help that the barristers on the case, scarred by years of fighting against notoriously plaintiff-friendly defamation laws, were relentlessly pessimistic. Bartlett had settled on Sandy Dawson, SC, a charming and eloquent silk from Sydney regarded as a brilliant court performer. It was Dawson's sister, Katrina, who had been killed in the Lindt Café terrorist siege that had, four years before, led an SAS commander to reach out to Crompvoets, ultimately sparking the Brereton report.

Dawson's junior barrister was Lyndelle Barnett, a hardworking advocate respected for her mastery of defamation law. Both appeared to believe Masters and I might struggle to defend our reporting.

In truth, the choice of the pair was part process, part theatre. A defence had to be filed within twenty-eight days of Roberts-Smith's writ, no matter how weak it was. Selecting a high-profile senior counsel and a respected junior to draft the defence was intended to project confidence and strength.

So far, Masters and I had been mostly unsuccessful in trying to convince witnesses to talk directly to our legal team.

'They don't trust lawyers,' was the initial response we delivered to Bartlett and Levitan.

We had an impressive amount of forensic detail about what we claimed witnesses would say about events at Darwan and on Easter Sunday. I had also finally booked a ticket to Afghanistan, in the hope of meeting Ali Jan's family and finding eyewitnesses.

If our legal team was to embrace the case theory they would have to argue before a judge, they needed more than the say-so of two reporters. They needed living, breathing witnesses. This was why today's meeting was so important.

Levitan waited another twenty minutes, watching the container ship become a disappearing fleck on the horizon. Finally the receptionist rang.

'Your guest has arrived.'

Levitan walked out into the law firm's lobby and spotted an unremarkable man wearing a baseball cap and backpack. As he shook the former SAS soldier's hand, he realised he'd been expecting another Roberts-Smith. Instead, this ex-soldier was of average height and medium build, albeit with the lean, angular face of an athlete.

I had warned Levitan that this veteran would be intensely guarded. He liked lawyers even less than journalists. The Afghan veteran and the young lawyer sat awkwardly in the meeting room while Levitan explained how legal privilege would ensure their discussion remained confidential.

'What do you want to know about him?' the ex-soldier said. The 'him' was Ben Roberts-Smith.

'Tell me everything.'

* * *

Weeks later, on 19 October, a serving SAS soldier sat in the café of the East Hotel in Canberra waiting for the most famous alumni of his regiment to appear. The meeting had been arranged as a friendly catch-up, but the timing suggested otherwise. Everyone in the SAS knew that Roberts-Smith was rallying his supporters, having sued the newspapers who had written about him. Days earlier, Dean Tilley heard from Roberts-Smith via an encrypted application. His message was anodyne, flagging that Roberts-Smith would be in Canberra and suggesting a coffee catch-up. Tilley had responded and they arranged to meet.

'No problem,' he'd texted.

The SAS soldier's guard was up, though. Tilley had received no defamation threats or anonymous letters in the mail, but he was mates with those who had.

He was also one of the two dozen or so witnesses Fairfax Media wanted to subpoena because they had been on the Easter Sunday mission. Tilley was like most of these soldiers. He didn't want to testify for the media, nor did he want to jump into the witness box for Ben Roberts-Smith. He wanted nothing to do with the case at all.

Roberts-Smith was taking no chances. That morning, the Victoria Cross winner had given an interview to the Murdoch-owned Sky News channel in which he'd blasted the newspaper reporters he was suing. Our claims were 'completely untrue', Roberts-Smith told the Sky News reporter.

In the interview, Roberts-Smith also savaged the truth defence our barristers had just filed in the Federal Court: 'We are talking about scenarios of battle that have been twisted and in many cases falsified to resemble the allegations that Fairfax are reporting.'

The filing of the truth defence was what had prompted him to reach out to Tilley. Our defence document indicated to the court we intended to call multiple witnesses to testify about executions committed on Easter Sunday 2009. One of them was Tilley.

Roberts-Smith wanted to test the loyalty of his old comrade. While Fairfax's defence document indicated who they intended to call as witnesses, it gave no indication about whether they were actually cooperating with Fairfax.

This was why Roberts-Smith had told Sky News he was abundantly confident of being vindicated. Even so, Roberts-Smith needed to know for sure that Tilley would be on team RS.

When Tilley spotted the large soldier, he rose from his seat and extended his hand.

'How're you going?'

The men greeted each other with a strained casualness, which continued through a few minutes of small talk. It vanished, overtaken by a frosty formality, when Roberts-Smith brought up the true purpose of the meeting. He pulled out a copy of the newspaper's truth defence like a prosecutor brandishing a murder weapon before a jury.

Tilley had never seen the file before. 'I'm not signing anything mate,' he said, momentarily confused.

'I'm not trying to get you to sign anything. I want you to read it. I know it's not … I know it's not you,' Roberts-Smith said, before adding: 'I know we will be all good.'

Tilley didn't respond, but began scanning the document. The journalists' lawyers had placed him as one of a few soldiers with a clear line of sight to the execution of an Afghan prisoner outside compound Whiskey 108 on Easter Sunday 2009. Someone close to Tilley must have spoken to them.

Tilley glanced up at Roberts-Smith and looked him square in the eyes. 'Well ... actually ... that's how I remember it ... You were pretty loose at Whiskey 108. You did a lot of things in front of the young guys you shouldn't have.'

Roberts-Smith appeared shocked. 'You can't get in trouble for perjury if you legitimately don't remember,' he told Tilley.

Tilley was resolute in his response. If he was subpoenaed to the Federal Court or to the Brereton Inquiry, he would be telling the truth. 'I'm not going to lie on the stand. The truth is the only thing that will protect me.'

The large ex-soldier then changed tack. Tilley couldn't be a witness to something he hadn't actually seen. 'Your patrol team was on the other side of the compound,' Roberts-Smith said.

But Tilley was in no doubt where he was located on Easter Sunday. He remembered the drizzle in the air, the thickness of the poppy crop that had swallowed him up, and the mud and grass he'd dived into when a burst of gunfire exploded near him.

The whole mission was burnt into his brain because he'd expected he was going to be killed and, instead, he'd taken a life. An Afghan had popped out from a wall and, believing he posed a risk to the Australian soldiers creeping up on Whiskey 108, Tilley had shot him.

Tilley also remembered clearly what happened after this, in the fading light. A large soldier with paint on his face and who was holding a machine gun had stepped outside the compound walls and thrown a large dark mass to the ground. Tilley later discovered it was an Afghan man with a prosthetic leg.

Across the café table, Tilley held Roberts-Smith's gaze again. 'Come on, mate ... You machine-gunned that guy,' he said to him.

'Ben, there's no way I am going to get up on a stand and lie. And I hope no one else does.'

Tilley watched his old comrade as silence descended over the table. Roberts-Smith turned to look outside the café window. He appeared lost in his own thoughts. Thirty seconds passed until Roberts-Smith turned back to face him.

'I don't even know what to say,' Roberts-Smith said stonily.

Tilley responded by rising from his chair. 'Thanks for the coffee,' he said to Roberts-Smith. He then turned and walked away.

CHAPTER 28

AFGHANISTAN

April 2019

As I walked up the side of the ancient Afghan fortress, my security guard, an ex–British army infantryman, trailed behind me. After hours spent moving slowly in our armoured car through bustling streets lined with hawkers, shopkeepers and men guarding checkpoints, I'd welcomed the chance to stretch my legs with barely another person in sight.

The walk up the steep incline had also given me time to think. After three days in Kabul, I'd achieved none of what my fixer, Rashid, had promised to deliver before I'd left Australia. I had met no witnesses to the Ali Jan cliff kick, nor was I even sure if Rashid had located them. And while he said he had arranged for some of Ali Jan's relatives to make the perilous trip north to meet us, they hadn't showed either.

Instead, I'd marinated in my worsening mood in a secure concrete compound that doubled as our accommodation. To pass the time I chatted with aid workers and private security staff in a small fortified yard outside our sleeping quarters. Those new to Kabul still spoke with hope about Afghanistan, but anyone who'd been there for longer than twelve months despaired.

It was one of those jaded observers who had suggested I climb Bala Hissar, an ancient city citadel with thick, stone-coloured walls and round towers.

'Watch how many military helicopters pass overhead,' the tour guide said. To him, the choppers were markers of a city on edge. 'No one knows when the next bomb will go off,' he'd said forlornly.

Almost two decades had passed since Australia had joined the US-led invasion of Afghanistan. The Taliban government had been quickly toppled, but the insurgency had persisted, with militants capitalising on the decision in 2014 to hand over security responsibilities to local Afghan forces backed by a remaining contingent of American soldiers.

Suicide bombings and attacks by gunmen remained a regular feature of life here. My fellow security compound lodgers were still talking about a wedding party that had just been targeted by a suicide bomber. The Ashraf Ghani–led government was weak and ineffectual.

My plan to travel to Darwan had been blocked by Nine's security advisers because parts of the country's south were considered strongholds of the Taliban's estimated 60,000 fighters. That left Kabul. My trip to the capital city had been made for two purposes. Dean Levitan had been pushing me for weeks to locate Darwan witnesses for our court case, a task which I had assigned to Rashid. I had also convinced my new bosses at Nine to send a cameraman with me in the event we could capture an eyewitness on film or interview Ali Jan's family.

The executive producer of Nine's flagship program *60 Minutes*, Kirsty Thomson, didn't flinch when Masters and I met with her to propose a program on war crimes. As alumni of the public broadcaster's *Four Corners* show, both of us were wary of *60 Minutes*. It was partly media snobbery, but Nine could be unashamedly tabloid. Yet it could also cut through to a mainstream audience in a way the ABC couldn't. *60 Minutes* had the best ratings in the country and producers and reporters just as capable as anyone at the ABC. It wasn't as flush as the old days, but the program retained a modest budget for international travel.

'Go for it,' Thomson had urged us. 'Leave the bean counters to me.'

A pattern was emerging. Roberts-Smith's decision to sue and publicly attack us was intended to shut down our reporting. But when we briefed our editors on our research and sources, they almost always fired up, finding their own ways to convince their own bosses of the need to take an expensive risk. There was something else at play. Reporters-turned-managers like Kirsty Thomson and James Chessell relished a journalistic chase and fight. Backing us meant putting their own careers on the line, but that was one of the reasons I believed they did it. For those odd beasts who truly loved the news industry, there was nothing quite like having skin in the game when the stakes were high and it really counted. Roberts-Smith's full frontal attempt to suppress the truth was having the opposite effect. Now I just had to repay their faith.

After waiting for forty-eight hours in our secure Kabul compound, it wasn't looking good. Rashid had delivered bleak news. No witnesses could be located and he was also unsure if Ali Jan's wife and children would show.

The evening after receiving this news, I found myself next to an open fire in the courtyard drinking from the bottle of Scotch I'd intended to give to our security team. Three glasses later, I no longer felt as bad. I was getting used to bad news.

Several months had passed since we had filed our truth defence. Much of it centred on one man: Jason Andrews.

He was one of several witnesses our lawyers hadn't spoken to, but who, through a network of defence sources, Masters and I were confident held critical evidence. It was Andrews who we believed had witnessed Ali Jan being kicked off the cliff and who had witnessed two executions, partaking in one himself, on Easter Sunday 2009.

I had contacted Andrews personally, politely imploring him to help us, but had heard nothing back. He'd assured others in the SAS that he would tell the truth if subpoenaed to any court, but his lawyers had also repeatedly rebuffed our approaches. My offer of a brief introductory chat under the protection of legal privilege was met with silence.

It hadn't all been bleak. Before flying out of Melbourne, I'd had one potential breakthrough. I'd met a former SAS medic whom I had bonded with almost immediately, first over a few meals and drinks, and then over a twice-weekly punishing fitness regime. My friendship with Dusty Miller had flourished as I had shared with him how my anxiety could become paralysing, plunging me into cycles of overwork, excessive drinking and destabilisation in my home life.

Dusty had in turn revealed his own pain, far greater than mine. On a mission in early 2012, Miller had been treating an Afghan farmer with a non-fatal bullet wound when a senior soldier had taken custody of the prisoner and allegedly murdered him. Miller had never recovered from failing to intervene to stop a defenceless man having his life snuffed out. He'd cycle 100 kilometres in the morning, run in the afternoon and polish off a bottle of vodka in the evening.

We'd talked for hours, first about Afghanistan and the SAS, and then about our childhoods and partners and dreams and fears. I'd encouraged Miller to contact the Brereton Inquiry, but it had reached him first. Miller's moral trauma had nothing to do with Roberts-Smith, but he'd told me about one of his close friends, an SAS medic called Jimmy Stanton. Stanton had served on a mission with Roberts-Smith in which Stanton had searched a Toyota HiLux with four Afghans, including a male who looked about sixteen.

The four men had been detained after the SAS discovered weapons in the car boot, and Stanton recalled the chubby sixteen-year-old shaking in terror as he was led away by Roberts-Smith's patrol team for questioning. Twenty minutes later, Stanton heard Roberts-Smith over the radio, announcing 'Two EKIA.'

Stanton hadn't witnessed what became of the sixteen-year-old so he asked Roberts-Smith about the young detainee a day or two later. The answer had shocked Stanton.

'I shot the c*** in the side of the head,' Stanton remembered Roberts-Smith telling him. 'I blew his brains out and it was the most beautiful thing I've ever seen.'

We added him to our list of witnesses. Unlike most of the other men in the SAS, Stanton hadn't prevaricated when asked if he would appear in court.

'I don't want to be there but I'll tell the truth if I'm called,' he'd said.

I was sweating by the time I reached the top of the fort. It offered sweeping views of Kabul, a city of old white and grey towers and mosque domes. But my guide was right. The helicopters were everywhere.

* * *

An armed guard outside the hotel entrance patted me and the cameraman down, before opening a reinforced door and herding us into a small antechamber where another guard stood. Once the door behind us was bolted shut, another door was opened and we walked through into a large terracotta-walled courtyard lined with tired pot plants. Ali Jan's wife, three of their children and her brother-in-law were waiting, along with Rashid, my now triumphant fixer.

Bibi Dhorko, thirty-four, was wearing a bright green shawl that covered her head and most of her face. Her two sons wore traditional Afghan shirts, each also a different shade of green, while her daughter was dressed in a bright, colourful tunic. As I spoke, thanking them for making the journey from Oruzgan, Rashid translated slowly.

The children stared at me, eyes wide, but when I looked back at them, they averted their gazes nervously. I guessed I was one of the few foreigners they had ever met. Bibi avoided eye contact, as was the custom, but I occasionally caught her glimpsing at me with wariness. Her face looked worn, her eyes dark and sad.

Rashid ushered us to a room and when we were seated on an old carpet, he filled our cups with sweet tea. My conversation with Bibi was slow, stilted and solemn, lightened only by the giggles of Ali Jan's children as they played with marbles. They could have been any children in any part of the world, I'd thought before correcting myself.

They were undoubtedly children of Afghanistan. Where else did life count for so little?

One of the SAS soldiers who'd been at Darwan the day Ali Jan died had told me something just before I'd made the trip to Kabul. I'd thought about it ever since. Ali had lived a relatively meagre existence confined to a few villages, a cluster of kin and a daily struggle to survive. Once the story of his death was published in our papers, it had viscerally exposed the barbarity of those few Australian soldiers who had gone rogue. In failing to value Ali's life, Ben Roberts-Smith had laid bare not only his belief in the cheapness of Afghan blood, but the undeniable absence of his own moral code.

In death, Ali had reinforced to my war-bitten source the sanctity of human life, even in a conflict. This was why the laws of war mattered. Maybe that was Ali's ultimate legacy.

With the camera rolling, I asked Rashid if Bibi could tell me what had happened on the day Ali was meant to return to his home a three-hour donkey ride from Darwan. As she spoke, Bibi dabbed her eyes with her green shawl.

She explained that she had finished the morning chores and was preparing lunch to be ready for Ali's return. Bibi had taken her time. No one was in a rush. The kids had their playground of rock crevices and mountain paths to explore. She had supposed Ali would ramble up one of these with his donkey at any moment.

But then an hour passed. And then another. Bibi was at first unconcerned. Ali was a man who avoided trouble.

'He didn't side with anyone and never had a gun,' she told me. 'He was living in the mountain and doing his work, only going occasionally to the village if we needed any supplies.'

Another hour had passed. It was well into the afternoon when Bibi finally heard someone approaching. It wasn't Ali, but a young boy from the village, sweating and panting, who raced up with the news.

'I started crying, shouting,' Bibi said. 'My legs were numb. I couldn't breathe.'

Bibi may not have seen what happened to her husband. But she said she still remembered clearly the last time she saw Ali alive, and the last time he'd seen his children: Guldasta, eight; Rashida, seven; Sidiqa, four; Muzdalifa, three; and their two babies, Mohmmadullah and Nematullah. She remembered him telling her to tend to their plot of land while he was gone. She remembered how Ali then turned to face her and wished her goodbye.

She also remembered dashing, many hours later, down the rocky path towards Darwan, retracing her husband's last steps, until she was finally convinced by relatives to turn back home. It was too late, they told her.

She remembered seeing blood on the floor of her hut and realising she'd badly cut her feet while running but had not noticed the pain. She was pregnant at the time with her seventh child, a girl who would never meet her father.

Before the interview ended, I asked Bibi if she had a message for Australia. While I couldn't understand her words until they were interpreted, her quiet anger needed no translation. She said she wanted the Australian government to tell her how and why her husband died.

'I want justice because I have been widowed ... my children are now helpless,' she had told me.

Life without the family's breadwinner was now even harder. Her children did not go to school and often went without food or proper clothes. Seven years after Ali was murdered, she was still in mourning, clinging to old memories. In her interview, she recalled Ali's donkey, led by a relative, returning home after his death.

The shoes for his daughter that Ali had promised to bring back from his trip to Darwan were strapped to the animal's side.

CHAPTER 29

DEADLINE

July 2019

As one winter day rolled into the next, bringing Roberts-Smith closer and closer to his first major pre-trial court deadline, those around the Channel Seven executive watched him will himself into a state of near-constant intense focus. He was running part of Kerry Stokes' Seven West Media empire under the shadow of a police inquiry, clinging to a marriage marred by his infidelity, and suing the biggest media company in the land. He told a confidant his fellow executives considered it a miracle he was keeping it together.

Exercise was his saviour. He would lift weights or run until he was heaving and drenched in sweat. Those close to him wondered if these workouts were the only time he was fully in control. There were other times, though, when he appeared a man engaged in relentless battle, ricocheting around like a ball in a pinball machine as he obsessed over a growing list of enemies and drank himself to sleep.

The pressure was mounting. The judge had finally come calling. Had the AFP known of the existence of his burner phones, they would have seen a spike in Roberts-Smith's use of encrypted applications in the days prior to his much-anticipated interrogation by Justice Brereton. But they were in the dark.

Roberts-Smith arrived at the Brereton Inquiry's offices flanked by lawyers and barristers, all paid for by his employer, the Kerry Stokes–owned Seven. The judge slapped a suppression order on what he had quizzed Roberts-Smith about, but it was no secret he was investigating the allegations we first reported in mid-2018: the suspected executions by Roberts-Smith and Jason Andrews of two Afghans on Easter Sunday 2009 and the killing of Ali Jan in September 2012.

Despite fuelling his stress, the ongoing defamation case provided the ex-soldier a vehicle to promote his denials of wrongdoing. He did so at every chance.

Nine's decision to back the war crimes' reporting surprised many in the media, given the potential costs of the court case if it ever went to trial and the fact that Nine, as the new owner of *The Age* and *Sydney Morning Herald*, had no loyalty to either masthead or any stories published well before the corporate takeover.

For Roberts-Smith and his team, Nine's funding of our defence created a useful narrative. The adverse allegations about him could now be dismissed as the product of corporate rivalry. According to this logic, the defamation case was a proxy war between two old commercial television rivals. This case wasn't about two newspaper journalists fighting for the truth, it was about Nine trying to best its television industry rival, Seven, no matter the pain inflicted on a celebrated war hero.

The court-issued deadline closing in on Roberts-Smith required his lawyers to lodge paperwork detailing how he intended to rebut the allegations he'd participated in prisoner executions. The war hero also had to scuttle our claims he'd bullied his Special Forces colleagues and punched a woman in the face.

But that wasn't all.

Our lawyers had significantly upped the ante when they had lodged the initial defence of truth, flagging we intended not only to prove the existing allegations of murder published in 2018 but also seek to convince the court that Roberts-Smith had committed other heinous war crimes. Our defence claimed he'd issued a gruesome confession to a medic, Jimmy Stanton, about executing a terrified Afghan teen who'd been taken prisoner on a mission in late October 2012.

We were also alleging that Roberts-Smith had, on another mission, directed an Afghan partner force commander named Ismail to execute an Afghan farmer. If just a single murder allegation was proven in the Federal Court, then we could claim victory. But each allegation added to the pile could also increase the size of Roberts-Smith's damages in the event none of the execution claims could be proven. If he won, it would be an historic payout. Victory would simultaneously imperil our careers and any prospect of a successful police war crimes inquiry. It was three for the price of one.

There was no way the war hero was going to withdraw his writ. Roberts-Smith wanted his day in court. Our expanded truth defence left open more potential weak spots for the ex-soldier to exploit in order to convince the judge it was Roberts-Smith who was telling the truth.

Take medic Jimmy Stanton. Stanton had not actually witnessed the claimed execution of the young prisoner. Rather, he alleged Roberts-Smith had bragged about it after the mission in question, a proposition the war hero dismissed as fanciful.

Roberts-Smith insisted it beggared belief that a person would boast about the beauty of watching another person's brain explode from the side of his head, but this is what Stanton was saying. The Victoria Cross recipient simply didn't talk like that. He was a corporate executive and the face of the Australian War Memorial, not some psychopath.

Roberts-Smith and his team also believed they had uncovered a potentially fatal problem with Stanton's allegations. Roberts-Smith wasn't on any mission with Stanton on the date detailed in the newspapers' court filings. If he wasn't there, he could hardly have executed someone. It was just one of many catastrophic errors Roberts-Smith thought he had picked up as he and his team had deconstructed our defence.

Little wonder that he still had the backing of Brendan Nelson. Kerry Stokes still believed in him. His wife, Emma, appeared less certain, but she had her own reasons to doubt him.

He also had another person firmly in his corner.

* * *

Roberts-Smith had no greater supporter in his legal team than Monica Allen. In her early forties with a bob of curly hair and a penchant for colourful designer suits and shoes, the Sydney lawyer had become the engine room of the Roberts-Smith litigation team. She appeared to observers to be as impassioned as the war hero about the injustice of his ordeal.

'She's protective of him,' was one lawyer's assessment.

She had taken the key role at Mark O'Brien Legal in marshalling those in the SAS who Roberts-Smith had said would back him to the end.

Allen was also helping prepare a killer legal blow. Executed well, it would demolish not only the allegation Roberts-Smith had ordered Commander Ismail to execute an Afghan. It would also destroy the credibility of a critical witness the newspapers appeared determined to subpoena and who, like Jason Andrews, posed a serious danger to Roberts-Smith.

* * *

Dean Tilley had already indicated to Roberts-Smith that if he was subpoenaed, he would testify that he'd witnessed an execution on Easter Sunday 2009. Tilley had more recently been listed as a potential witness regarding the claim Roberts-Smith had ordered Commander Ismail to execute an Afghan.

Roberts-Smith believed he'd found another grave error in the addition of the Ismail allegation, one which would destroy Tilley on the stand. He'd already rung around several of his mates in the SAS. Each of them had agreed with the same proposition. Ismail had been banned from working with the SAS because he'd shot a dog several weeks before the October mission in which the execution order was supposedly issued to Ismail. If Ismail's sacking could be proven in court, then it would appear Tilley had conjured up a lie and his credibility would be in tatters.

Roberts-Smith carefully laid the groundwork for this knockout blow. In a document set to be filed in court, he revealed how he 'had previously been informed ... that

Ismail had been stood down and replaced as Commander …
after he shot at a mongrel dog'.

This statement omitted the fact that Roberts-Smith
himself had no independent recollection of Ismail being
sacked or whether it was another Afghan commander.
In reality, he didn't know Ismail 'from a bar of soap'.
Roberts-Smith was basing his account on the say-so of
others in the SAS.

Monica Allen helped with bolstering it, collating outlines
of evidence from others who also claimed knowledge of
Ismail's sacking. She helpfully offered up Ismail's name to
one of these supporting SAS witnesses. This same witness
would go on to express doubt to Roberts-Smith about
whether it was, in fact, Ismail who had been sacked. Yet,
when his statement was filed in the Federal Court, it was
unequivocal.

'I recall that early in our deployment, in about late July/
early August 2012, the Commander of the ANA, Ismail,
was removed from participating in missions with the SASR
after he shot at a dog.'

At final count, Roberts-Smith had mustered four SAS
witnesses ready to back the claim Ismail was sacked at
least two months before he allegedly executed an Afghan
on the war hero's orders. Roberts-Smith believed he had
discovered the Achilles heel of the newspapers' defence.
Those he'd sued just didn't know it yet.

* * *

As Roberts-Smith's lawyers filed his response in court to
our defence case, one uncertainty loomed large. It came in
the form of his old comrade, Jason Andrews. The question
of whether Andrews would appear in court was still an

unknown. He'd long ago gone cold on the Victoria Cross recipient, not returning his calls, but the word from the regiment was that he was also refusing to deal with our lawyers. If Andrews didn't turn up, the claim about an Afghan kicked off a cliff could be comprehensively exposed as the lie Roberts-Smith insisted it was.

Whenever he'd been asked about this allegation, Roberts-Smith's deep voice would quiver as he vehemently and passionately described it as false. If Andrews had said otherwise to Boyd Keary or Brian McMurray, Roberts-Smith reasoned it was either down to medal envy or mental health problems. Or maybe both. Whatever the reason, he continued to state it was untrue. Keary and McMurray might come to court and disclose that Andrews had uttered these allegations, but this would be mere hearsay.

If Jason Andrews was blowing in the wind, Vincent Jelovic was solid. His recall of events at Darwan was diametrically opposed to the version in the offending news reports. According to Jelovic, no one had been taken prisoner in the last compound on a ridge above a stony, dry creek bed. Instead, he and Roberts-Smith had stumbled across an insurgent holding a radio in a cornfield on the other side of the creek, a short walk from the cliff. Jelovic and Roberts-Smith had done what they had to. They shot the Afghan in keeping with the rules of armed conflict.

The allegation that, earlier in the Darwan mission, Roberts-Smith had unlawfully executed an insurgent he'd hunted down after wading through the Helmand River was also disputed. There was not a single living witness to this engagement besides Roberts-Smith, who insisted he'd discovered the armed Afghan hidden among some rocks before shooting him dead, wrapping the man's gun and radio in a dark coloured shawl and wading back across the river.

Roberts-Smith was 'particularly disgusted' that this allegation of murder had made it into our truth defence. It was a justified killing he was rightly 'proud' of, not least because he'd risked his own life to try to catch an Afghan who he only later discovered wasn't Hekmatullah.

Roberts-Smith and his team believed this was precisely the sort of weak allegation that could drown the entire defence in a sea of doubt.

CHAPTER 30

JOURNEY TO KABUL

August 2019

Justice Paul Brereton didn't want his team to know it, but he was feeling as dejected as they looked. Four days had passed since he'd walked through Kabul Airport to be met by an Australian security team. The airport was teeming with Afghans in traditional garb and Westerners wearing wraparound sunglasses and cargo pants.

Brereton and his small team had been fitted with body armour before being whisked into an armoured vehicle and driven to the Australian embassy. The security precautions initially felt like overkill. The bustling streets of Kabul appeared relatively sedate and the fortified embassy even more so. It was only the occasional distant thud of bombs that served as a reminder the country Australia had sought to help pacify remained an unpredictable volcano, quiet for long stretches but still capable of erupting.

The main risk the judge faced was that the whole trip would be in vain. Brereton's team had spent weeks arranging meetings with villagers from Darwan, who investigators hoped could tell them about the last few hours in the life of Ali Jan. If finding these potential witnesses had been a remarkable feat, getting them to the Australian ambassador's compound seemed increasingly impossible. As mornings blurred into days and nights, it appeared the witnesses were not coming.

Ever since Ben Roberts-Smith had become a major target of his inquiry, Paul Brereton had not breathed a single public word about its progress. Very few people outside of his tight-knit team knew of his building interest in the war hero. They included a small number of federal police and a few high-ranking military officials, and they were all sworn to secrecy.

Roberts-Smith was also acutely aware of Brereton's interest in him. The judge had already secretly grilled the soldier and had been engaged in paper warfare with Roberts-Smith's lawyer, Mark O'Brien. The correspondence was the result of a formal complaint lodged by O'Brien on behalf of Roberts-Smith against one of the judge's staff, an unnamed lawyer, for allegedly making derogatory comments about the war hero in a social setting to an acquaintance of Roberts-Smith. This Brereton Inquiry lawyer was accused of telling the war hero's acquaintance, a Queensland doctor called Mark David, that if he knew 'anyone looking to go into business with BRS, tell them to be careful'.

O'Brien asserted these comments were not only a vicious slur, but evidence that Brereton's inquiry was corrupted. 'The comments made by the lawyer are defamatory, embarrassing, demonstrate bias against our client and, again raise serious concerns about the integrity of the Inquiry,' O'Brien had written to Brereton. 'It is highly unsatisfactory that our client has been the subject of defamatory gossip by members of the Inquiry's staff.' O'Brien demanded an investigation and an 'apology to our client'.

The allegations about the mystery lawyer were also aired in court by Roberts-Smith's barristers and published on the front page of *The Australian* newspaper under the headline: 'Lawyer's smears against SAS hero'.

Brereton launched an investigation into the complaint, only to quickly find it backed by 'no evidence whatsoever'. All the parties identified by O'Brien as potentially holding evidence about the alleged misbehaviour denied making the comments that O'Brien attributed to them.

Dr David told Brereton's investigators that he was 'adamant' he had never spoken to any war crimes inquiry lawyer. He also said no one had ever told him not to go into business with Roberts-Smith, but rather this was a decision he had made of his own accord.

The inquiry lawyer singled out by Roberts-Smith actually appeared not to exist and when the judge sought more evidence from Roberts-Smith's lawyers to back up their claims, they fell silent.

Brereton published a thirteen-page report on the defence force Inspector-General's website concluding that 'there is no evidence whatsoever that any lawyer or other person working for or associated with the Inquiry made any statement to the effect alleged, or anything like it'. The judge had been careful to stress in his report that he wasn't holding the flimsy complaint against the credibility of Roberts-Smith, given it may have been the product of faulty assumptions and surmising by O'Brien or Roberts-Smith's other lawyers.

The only thing the judge would rely on was evidence. The search for that evidence was why he'd made the journey to Kabul.

* * *

After five days of waiting, Brereton finally received word that a small group of Darwan villagers were en route to the Australian ambassador's compound. This was what the inquiry staff had worked so hard for.

Brereton's team had taken over the ground floor of the diplomatic residence. They had laid a carpet on the floor with cushions and plates of dried fruits and nuts.

It was mid-morning when the security detail at the front of the compound responsible for vetting visitors noticed the approaching Afghan men. Two of them looked like farmers, wearing worn robes and tunics. Their bearded faces were deeply tanned and lined. The third was an urbane-looking Afghan who appeared to be about forty-five years old, cleanly shaved and wearing an odd blend of Western attire and Afghan clothes. At the embassy entrance, he confidently introduced himself as Ahmad and explained he was there to see 'the general', a reference to Brereton's military rank.

Ahmad had been working with Brereton's team for the last few months, risking death in doing so. The Taliban insurgency viewed anyone who collaborated with Western defence officials as a traitor, spy or both.

Each of the Afghans was searched and scanned with a metal detector before being escorted towards the ambassador's residence. To succeed in getting the villagers to drop their guard, Ahmad knew the judge would have to build a rapport with the two men. Ahmad planned on bringing more witnesses in over the following days, including two women and an elder from Darwan. It was this man, aged in his sixties, who was most vital to get onside.

If the two elders, the Australian judge and the old Darwan farmer, could build some level of trust, the other

Afghans might talk more freely to the white man seated awkwardly on the colourful carpet.

Ahmad knew the villagers had powerful stories to tell, but didn't know exactly what the Brereton Inquiry was searching for and had taken care to say little about any particular event involving Australian soldiers. He was under strict instructions not to pollute the pool of potential witnesses.

Yet some of the villagers had freely offered to Ahmad what they claimed were accounts of a raid by foreign men years before. One man in particular, a young Afghan farmer called Hanifa, described how he'd been taken prisoner by these foreign soldiers. Detained with him was his uncle, Ali Jan.

* * *

Boyd Keary hesitated before he reached for his phone. I'd called him earlier without notice and reintroduced myself. We'd briefly met a year or so before, at a gathering in Melbourne that Chris Masters had organised to enable Keary, a passionate rugby league fan, to meet Masters' brother, Roy, a former legendary coach of the Western Suburbs Magpies.

Keary had met Chris Masters in 2016 after the defence department had given the green light for SAS soldiers to be interviewed by Masters for his book *No Front Line*. Keary trusted Masters, regarding him as a friend and source of wisdom on the soldier's biggest passions, Rugby League and military history. I was an unknown. The night of our first meeting, I sat quietly alongside the Masters brothers, excusing myself after a beer and disappearing into the Melbourne night.

My unexpected call to Keary had come with a request. I had travelled to Afghanistan and located the family of the man who Jason Andrews had claimed had been kicked off a cliff by Roberts-Smith. I explained that I was preparing a report for the Nine news program *60 Minutes* about the allegations Roberts-Smith was facing.

I had a proposition for Keary: that he appear on camera, his face and voice disguised, to be interviewed about Roberts-Smith and the war crimes allegations being investigated by Brereton.

'Not interested mate,' Keary had said politely, hanging up the phone.

Still, my call to Keary had got him thinking. There were so many blokes who'd been adversely affected by Roberts-Smith. As early as 2017, Keary reckoned his old comrade had been behind a campaign of intimidating and threatening soldiers who'd stood up to him. There was Roberts-Smith's legal threat to Keary's mate, Keith Nueling. Nick Simkin had copped a police raid on his family home after an anonymous email campaign designed to smear him.

Dean Tilley had been called to a meeting in Canberra where Roberts-Smith tried to persuade him to stay silent. Brian McMurray had received anonymous letters in the mail. Roberts-Smith was also using the media to disparage those challenging his version of events as jealous or driven by medal envy. He'd labelled his critics as 'cowards in the shadows'.

It seemed clear to Keary that Roberts-Smith was counting on men in the regiment staying silent through fear or peer pressure. Keary could be a voice from within who challenged this, and tell the public that not everyone in the regiment thought that scrutiny of the war hero was undeserved. He dialled my number.

CHAPTER 31

SHAKEN

September 2019

I watched as Dusty Miller and Jimmy Stanton guided their horses along a muddy fire track, past tall gum trees and scrub until they disappeared over a ridge and into the Victorian high country. In the cold air, my breath formed puffs of mist. A *60 Minutes* camera crew had followed the two former SAS medics into the bush to film them as they participated in an outdoor therapy program for veterans designed by Dusty and a military pyschologist.

Since I'd returned from Afghanistan after meeting Ali Jan's wife and children, I'd flown across Australia, building my television story about the SAS and Roberts-Smith. I'd confirmed several critical facts, including that Justice Brereton and members of the AFP had travelled to Kabul and found the Darwan eyewitnesses who had eluded me on my own journey. The mere fact of these trips was remarkable. Few in the Defence community had expected Justice Brereton or war crimes detectives would ever make the journey.

That they did suggested both the judge and police were serious about testing the allegations surrounding Australia's most revered Afghan veteran. But that didn't make for meaningful television. I needed people on camera.

At first, no one in the Defence community wanted to be interviewed, but as days and weeks passed, serving and former members of the SAS offered growing support. Two serving members agreed to be interviewed without seeking approval from command, despite the grave risk to their careers if they were caught doing so. The soldiers met me in Perth on different days at a warehouse we had hired. One of the men wore a wig and both wore hats to disguise their faces. Even then, we filmed them in silhouette and hired actors to revoice the interviews.

Neither SAS soldier interviewed knew the identity of the other soldier. Both of them described allegations that Roberts-Smith was involved in executions of Afghan prisoners, including Ali Jan.

'A hero is not someone who harms innocent individuals,' one of them told me as I'd asked him about war memorial chief Brendan Nelson's strident defence of Roberts-Smith.

Both had called for accountability of what they described as a 'dirty' element in the SAS who 'thought they were above the law'.

'I think they actually thought they were not going to be caught. That it was a free for all,' one of the soldiers said in his interview.

Andrew Hastie, who was three years into his political career, had also reluctantly appeared on camera. After weeks of my polite badgering, he'd agreed on the proviso that I would ask him about no individuals, including Roberts-Smith. He intimated to me off camera that he was deeply uncomfortable with his famous former comrade, but wouldn't say why.

Hastie viewed his role in the *60 Minutes* program as advocating for public scrutiny of the SAS, including via the Brereton Inquiry, as well as backing the whistleblowers. Both Hastie and I were unsure whether the public would listen to SAS soldiers challenging a war hero, but Hastie wanted to try to explain why Australians should.

'There are two forms of courage in war: moral courage and physical courage. I think moral courage is greater, so these guys have shown that, and the Australian people should be glad, going forward, we have men of that calibre in the SAS,' he'd said in his interview.

Hastie also agreed with me that we needed to challenge the narrative being pushed by people such as Brendan Nelson that the Brereton Inquiry and the media were judging acts carried out in the fog of war. Kicking a handcuffed man off a cliff had nothing to do with a split-second decision taken in the heat of battle.

To draw the distinction between prisoner executions and fog-of-war incidents, Hastie recounted a mission in which he called in an air attack on approaching Taliban soldiers. US helicopters misjudged the coordinates and fired missiles at the wrong target.

As the camera rolled, Hastie's eyes welled with tears as he described learning that his order had led to the death of two young boys.

'My heart just sank, like it just dropped through the floor. We went out there, and there were two little bodies, six and eight years old.'

This genuine fog-of-war blunder prompted the SAS captain to offer his resignation. Instead, Hastie was flown to a meeting with the boys' grieving family. Hastie had told their uncle, 'I'm the one who gave the order, and I'm sorry.' The reply from a grieving man of different faith had stayed with him.

'I forgive you,' the uncle had replied.

I thought about stopping the interview at this point, such was the pain on Hastie's face, but he composed himself and pressed on. The interview was the first time I realised the depth of Andrew Hastie's conviction. He was willing to risk his political future, and the fury of those who supported Ben Roberts-Smith, to call for justice for Afghan families whom Hastie had idealistically gone to war to protect.

I'd wondered if it was these deaths that were driving him. As I'd spoken to more and more Afghanistan veterans, it seemed clear that many wanted accountability, not for fog-of-war incidents, but for those soldiers suspected of war crimes that crossed a clear line.

Something else was also evident. Those who witnessed or knew of atrocities, such as Dusty Miller and Jimmy Stanton, were desperately searching for their own peace. The suspected murder of Afghans who had briefly been in their care, either as a patient or a detainee, was eating away at both medics. As I waited for the pair and camera crew to return on horseback, I walked into the scrub, following their path. It was eerily quiet and misty.

Stanton hadn't agreed to an interview about Roberts-Smith's apparent confession to killing a young Afghan the medic had earlier helped detain. He was on horseback being filmed only to support Dusty. But he appeared to have made up his mind to testify in the defamation court case about his suspicion that Roberts-Smith had executed the young prisoner.

Stanton and I had also both agreed to check in on Dusty every week or so as he battled his demons.

Dusty's encounter with an alleged war crime had nothing to do with Roberts-Smith. But his story of another SAS soldier who had taken an injured Afghan from Dusty's care and allegedly executed him was powerful evidence of the lines that were being crossed in Afghanistan by the supposed good guys. Moving further down the sodden track, I wondered if Dusty's decision to go on national television was about seeking a form of redemption.

'I fucking hate myself for not doing more to help that man,' he'd told me.

Months before he agreed to the interview, Dusty had invited me to a dinner at an upmarket seafood restaurant in Melbourne's CBD. I was quietly chuffed by the offer. As I had with Hastie, I'd begun to count Dusty as a genuine friend, someone I could drop my guard with and reveal my true self.

The morning before the dinner, Dusty had been awarded a prestigious military honour, the Conspicuous Service Medal, for his work setting up a new training centre for Australian soldier medics. A ceremony was held at Victoria's Government House, where state governor Linda Dessau pinned the medal on his chest.

Few in attendance at this ceremony knew that, weeks earlier, Dusty had checked himself into Ward 17, the Melbourne psychiatric unit for veterans. After his celebratory dinner, he'd caught a taxi back to the ward.

Dusty was still an inpatient when an official from the Brereton Inquiry called to tell him the judge wanted to talk. By now, Brereton was investigating dozens of war crimes and Dusty's case was among them. It was during a meeting with Brereton that Dusty learnt the name 'Haji Sardar'. He was the Afghan who had been taken from his care and killed. He learnt another fact, too. 'He had seven children he didn't go home to,' Dusty told me, his voice breaking.

'Like, I'm a father. Can you imagine that?'

Dusty also disclosed occasions when he was overtaken by uncontrollable rage fuelled by feelings of helplessness and self-loathing. One night he'd punched himself in the face, going to work the next day with a black eye. When the swelling subsided, he did it again. After he'd been diagnosed with post-traumatic stress disorder, Dusty had decided to launch an outdoor therapy program for veterans like him, plagued by an endless loop of intrusive, distressing memories. Dusty hoped his appearance on *60 Minutes* would help connect him with other veterans who wanted to ride into the wilderness with him as part of a healing process.

Ahead of me, I saw two men on horses emerge through the mist. Dusty and Jimmy Stanton rode in single file, as silently as the gum trees standing like soldiers at a funeral.

* * *

My legs shook as I stared down the barrel of the camera, trying to conjure up authority. An hour before, I had agreed to be interviewed by a panel from the current affairs show *The Project* about my *60 Minutes* program that had aired the evening before.

Now, one of the panellists, a Sydney radio shock jock, was grilling me about whether it was fair for the media to judge acts committed by a soldier in the fog of war. I knew this line of questioning would be coming. Our reporting had divided Australians, with some urging for scrutiny of alleged war crimes, others labelling it an unjustified and cowardly attack not only on a war hero but on the nation's Anzac foundations.

I'd taken to ignoring threats on social media because they were arriving so often.

'Nick McKenzie. Pity someone doesn't break his fucking neck as he tried to take down an Australian war hero Ben Roberts-Smith. McKenzie a gutless asshole with a pen someone should shove up his arse.'

Tweets like this were not uncommon.

I responded to the shock jock's questioning by pointing out that I wasn't judging anyone. It was Roberts-Smith's own comrades in the SAS who had raised concerns, which we had in turn corroborated via eyewitness accounts. I knew of at least three direct witnesses to Ali Jan's assault.

Roberts-Smith had already appeared on the Seven Network to dismiss the allegations about Ali Jan's treatment and death aired on *60 Minutes*.

'Their story is simply false,' he'd said sombrely, wearing a tailored suit.

The war hero had also released a media statement drafted by his PR agent to *'categorically deny the allegations made against me'*.

'I have filed comprehensive evidence in the Federal Court which clearly demonstrates that these allegations are false and should not have been made let alone repeated. I will not be intimidated. Let me be clear: I have never committed any of the acts alleged in the 60 Minutes broadcast. I have never contravened any laws of war. I am proud of my military service and I believe I can demonstrate, with the support of numerous witnesses, that I have acted honourably at all times in my military service. I am appalled that the service of my colleagues and my service to my country and my regiment is being traduced in such an irresponsible way. Nine has recklessly allowed its journalists to slur my reputation by calling

*me a war criminal and by slurring the SAS I have been so
proud to serve.'*

I learnt later that Roberts-Smith had been taken by
surprise by the *60 Minutes* program. It wasn't until an old
SAS comrade texted him – 'It's about you!' – that he turned
on the television. He spent the next few hours glued to the
phone, workshopping the identity of the two silhouetted
SAS soldiers, proofing his media release and, I am sure,
cursing me. At midnight, he was still awake, texting his
lawyer Monica Allen.

Allen had gifted Roberts-Smith a small Ganesha
elephant-headed doll she'd bought in India along with a
typed letter explaining how the deity 'plays a dual role of
supreme being powerful enough to remove obstacles and
ensure success'.

According to Allen, the spirit of Ganesha could help the
ex-soldier 'create obstructions for those whose ambition
has become destructive (i.e. Nick McKenzie)'. Her letter
compared me to a 'mouse' who 'is most always depicted at
the feet of Ganesha'.

After *The Project* interview finished, the cameraman
spoke to me. 'You held up well, mate. That was a good
interview.'

As I thanked him and walked off, I wondered if he'd
seen my legs shaking.

CHAPTER 32

THE DIG

14 March 2020

Emma Roberts-Smith bent over and picked up a rock that was sitting under the hose reel. Her best friend, Danielle Scott, stood beside her. Emma's two children were watching a movie inside, unaware of the drama unfolding a few metres away. Ben Roberts-Smith was interstate.

Next, Emma loosened the earth underneath the rock with a pitchfork. She was increasingly certain this was where her husband had buried something. Emma suspected it was cash he'd been using for a secretive purpose, but didn't know for sure. When she felt the pitchfork hit something hard she pushed her hand deep into the loose soil, encountering smooth plastic. She found an edge and traced her finger along it until finding a corner. Emma then eased the object out of the dirt. It was one of her twin daughters' clear lunchboxes, rimmed with pink clips. Inside was a snap-lock bag filled with USBs.

It was Danielle who, the evening before, had urged on the fossicking after Emma had described Roberts-Smith's increasingly bizarre behaviour in the preceding months, as the defamation trial drew closer and the Brereton Inquiry rolled on. She told Danielle she'd seen Roberts-Smith bent over outside near the hose, trying not to be seen.

'He is out in the garden burying things,' Emma said.

Emma witnessed other strange acts, too. Roberts-Smith drilled through a laptop and set it on fire, and was still withdrawing large sums of cash from ATMs without explanation. He also asked John McLeod, the private eye he used to carry out certain tasks, to send Danielle a copy of some footage for safekeeping. This video opened up its own can of worms.

In early 2018, Roberts-Smith had asked McLeod to covertly film Amanda, the woman he'd had an affair with, as she left a Brisbane hospital. He wanted to confirm whether she'd fallen pregnant with his child and had an abortion, as she claimed.

Roberts-Smith also asked Danielle to purchase more burner phone sim cards and post them to him as he'd prepared for a second interview with Justice Brereton in late 2019. By then, Danielle had already supplied Roberts-Smith with two 'handbags', regularly topping up their credit, so he could call his mates without fear of telephone tapping.

After the interview with Brereton, Roberts-Smith seemed to Emma to be under even more pressure than before, if that was possible. He, Emma and the twins had crisscrossed the globe to allow him to catch up with those he'd served with in the SAS. Roberts-Smith had insisted it was merely a family holiday to take in the mountain air of New Zealand and the snowfields of Colorado, where Kerry Stokes had a ski lodge they could visit. A short time after coming home, Roberts-Smith travelled alone to Perth.

But if it was just a holiday, it was one that coincidentally enabled Roberts-Smith to have face-to-face meetings with those who were the cornerstones of his defence to the war crimes allegations at the centre of the Brereton Inquiry and the defamation proceedings. The ex-SAS soldier he met with in New Zealand was the man Masters and I were alleging had entered the tunnel on Easter Sunday and discovered the two Afghans who were later executed by Roberts-Smith and Andrews. In the US, he met with Neil Browning, the patrol team commander who allegedly oversaw these executions and boasted of having blooded Andrews.

In Perth, Roberts-Smith met with Vincent Jelovic, the man we alleged had been at the final compound in Darwan with Roberts-Smith and Andrews when Ali Jan was kicked off the cliff in 2012. According to information we'd received, Jelovic was with Roberts-Smith when Ali Jan was executed.

But it wasn't just the Brereton Inquiry or the defamation case that Emma believed was causing Roberts-Smith to act so strangely. She'd told Danielle that on Christmas Eve, on the way back from the US, she spied a text message her husband had sent his lawyer Monica Allen.

'I know what I'd be doing if I was with you on Christmas,' the message said. Emma suspected Roberts-Smith had grown too fond of another woman.

As a result of her husband's secrecy, Emma expected to find something buried in the back garden confirming an affair, like a stash of cash Roberts-Smith was hoarding for their trysts. Instead, she'd found six USBs.

The discovery triggered a memory. Months before, Roberts-Smith had told Emma that several SAS soldiers would be sending him USBs in the mail.

'Give them to me,' Danielle said calmly to Emma as the pair stood in the garden. Emma's childhood friend then walked inside the house, checked that the twins were still occupied, and retrieved her laptop. She copied each of the USBs onto a hard drive. Danielle was worried Emma was being subjected to more and more pressure by Roberts-Smith as their relationship collapsed. She wanted her friend to start taking precautions to safeguard her future. The USBs appeared to contain thousands of photos from missions in Afghanistan. Many showed Australian soldiers on patrol or drinking beer from a prosthetic leg.

Others showed dead Afghans covered in blood and missing limbs or with gaping head wounds. One particularly gruesome photo stood out. It was of a dead, blood-smeared Afghan. Two SAS souvenir coins had been placed on his eyes.

After the files were downloaded, Danielle handed the USBs back to Emma, who put them back in the snap-lock bag and placed it in the lunchbox. She then walked outside and carefully reburied it so her former husband would not suspect anything.

CHAPTER 33

THE AFGHANS

April 2020

Dean Levitan sat waiting, perched on a chair in front of a small screen that was beaming vision from the Kabul office of Kakar Advocates, the law firm hired to manage potential witnesses.

The purpose of this teleconference was to drill down into the stories of Darwan villagers who claimed to be eyewitnesses to the September 2012 mission, and who I had finally tracked down with the help of Afghan journalists in late 2019.

The most impressive of these Darwan locals had been identified as the nephew of Ali Jan, a young man called Mohammed Hanifa Fatih. I'd been told Hanifa had a detailed memory of events back in September 2012, including the presence of a 'big soldier' with green eyes, a sharp, handsome face structure and a uniform that was wet and sandy. The description matched the Victoria Cross recipient; it was only Roberts-Smith who had waded through the river on the day of the Darwan mission.

Other details that Hanifa was said to recall also matched what SAS soldiers had told me or Chris Masters about what had happened that day, down to the number of helicopters – six – that had arrived, including where they landed. His description of how the troops swept through the village during the first part of the raid matched that of SAS soldiers who'd been there. And Hanifa's description of how he and Ali had tried to leave the village with two donkeys matched an account made by an SAS observation post overlooking Darwan.

Roberts-Smith and his loyal patrol team member Vincent Jelovic described finding no Afghans in the last compound, yet Hanifa was said to be insistent that he, Ali and an Afghan called Man Gul had been detained in this same compound and interrogated by the big soldier with green eyes.

Continuing to watch the empty teleconference screen, Levitan heard the Pashto chatter grow louder before Hanifa came into view. He sat cross-legged on a seat and stared at the camera.

* * *

Levitan would wake up thinking of the Darwan mission and go to sleep doing the same. So, too, would barrister Sandy Dawson SC and defamation law specialist Lyndelle Barnett. A former war crimes prosecutor, Chris Mitchell, who was recruited later to join the barristers' team, would ultimately become its Darwan specialist. Levitan wondered if Mitchell ever slept, such was his relentless focus on the mission.

Where Dawson could be almost theatrical, to the point where Levitan wouldn't have been surprised if he pulled out the colourful silk pocket square he wore and waved it for dramatic effect, Mitchell was stubbornly no glitz, no glamour. But he was also quietly brilliant, and at times endearingly obsessive. He frequently dropped unexpected one-liners, which were usually dark, dry and very funny. The junior advocate had initially joined the newspapers' defamation team to help Dawson challenge an effort by Roberts-Smith to get Masters and me to hand over documents that could reveal the identity of our sources.

Mitchell played a crucial role in prompting the court to rule against Roberts-Smith, preserving our sources' confidentiality. The winning argument was simple enough: our intention to call SAS soldiers as witnesses did not indicate that these same soldiers had ever been a confidential source for any story, despite Roberts-Smith's claims to the contrary. Of the growing list of SAS witnesses we intended to summons to court, the only known journalistic source was Andrew Hastie, the ex-officer turned politician who had appeared on *60 Minutes*.

After the Federal Court rejected Roberts-Smith's effort to unmask sources, the journalists' union had called it a 'huge victory for public interest journalism and the public's right to know'. I was worried that Roberts-Smith would make further attempts to identify the sources to destabilise our case, despite the fact that the war hero was now a media executive responsible for his own stable of reporters with their own confidential sources.

I could refuse to hand over documents, as I had already done, but any secret journalistic source who was also a witness might still face intensive questioning on the stand about contact with me or with Chris Masters.

There was already a witch-hunt underway about the identity of the two silhouetted SAS soldiers I had interviewed on *60 Minutes*. Roberts-Smith would likely come at our suspected sources again and again.

Dawson, Mitchell and Barnett had already spent days building the truth defence, but I knew that very few SAS soldiers would be willing witnesses. I expected that some of the two dozen or so SAS witnesses we had hoped to call would try to be deployed overseas or use some other tactic to avoid a subpoena.

With key witnesses uncooperative, the case needed to be built on small details that we believed would be confirmed as facts in the event that our witnesses actually turned up to court.

Levitan regarded Mitchell's strength as his obsessive, exhaustive forensic approach to every facet of the case. Mitchell had filed away in his mind every small detail that each of the cooperating SAS sources had told me or Masters. He had been assigned the task of proving or disproving Roberts-Smith's contention that Commander Ismail could not have been issued an execution order because he'd been sacked from serving with the SAS. Roberts-Smith appeared to have multiple witnesses supporting this contention but we didn't buy it. For one thing, we had photos of Ismail in Afghanistan with Australian SAS soldiers in October 2012, months after Roberts-Smith and his witnesses were alleging Ismail had been dismissed for shooting a dog.

Mitchell made it his mission to find the real story.

Mitchell, who had prosecuted Balkan war criminals at The Hague, had also painstakingly matched every detail provided by the potential Afghan witnesses with the details provided our sources in the SAS. He would regularly phone Levitan at 5am with a slew of suggestions. Levitan had been left wondering if the barrister ever slept.

Despite only being in his early forties, Mitchell had the cynical, pessimistic air characteristic of many of the elders of the bar. He feared that the Afghan witness testimony could only get them so far, no matter how detailed and precise. One thing the Afghans would struggle to do is positively identify Roberts-Smith. They didn't know his name, rank or role, just some physical characteristics. Only someone from Roberts-Smith's patrol team from the mission could provide a definitive ID.

Even though the Afghans seemed willing to testify, there was a logistical problem. The case was taking place in the Federal Court in Sydney and Hanifa and his neighbours lived in southern Afghanistan.

Roberts-Smith was sure to oppose any application to have their testimony heard by video link. Another lawyer in Levitan's team was responsible for applying for Australian visas for Hanifa and the other potential witnesses, but the prospect of securing them seemed remote. Hanifa didn't have a passport and was unsure of his date of birth.

The mere act of tracking down the Afghan witnesses, let alone getting them from Darwan to the Kabul offices of Kakar Advocates, was a minor miracle, but this was only a further cause for pessimism. To win we needed the Afghans in a Sydney court and at least half-a-dozen SAS eyewitnesses on the stand and testifying about war crimes that some of them were possibly implicated in or might have helped cover up.

Mitchell's Bosnian Serb war crimes cases had succeeded because one of the co-accused had confessed to his own crimes while testifying about his fellow comrades. This was why securing Jason Andrews as a cooperative witness was so crucial. I was confident that Andrews had not only witnessed Ali Jan's final moments, but that he had been directed by Roberts-Smith to execute one of the two Afghan men captured in a tunnel on Easter Sunday in 2009.

Andrews' legal representative, a lawyer called Alisdair Putt, was refusing to return Levitan's calls, giving every indication that Andrews would do all within his power to avoid giving testimony.

All we could do was keep calling.

Levitan tried the same tactic with another potential SAS witness whom Andrew Hastie believed had also been blooded by Roberts-Smith. Chris Masters and I had gone hunting and found information to corroborate this suspicion, including the fact that this soldier had confessed to executing an Afghan to others in the SAS. It gave us enough of a basis to lodge a court filing describing how this soldier, given the legal pseudonym 'Person 66', had been blooded by Roberts-Smith during a mission 'on about 18 to 20 October 2012', around five weeks after the Darwan operation.

Our court documents alleged that Roberts-Smith had 'stood behind Person 66 and ordered him to shoot' an Afghan and then later boasted that 'he had blooded Person 66'.

But like Jason Andrews, Person 66 had ignored Levitan's attempts to make contact.

We knew that to defeat Roberts-Smith's defamation action, soldiers such as Andrews or Person 66 would need to testify.

If Andrews ever made it to court and told the truth along with the Afghan witnesses, we stood a chance of overcoming Roberts-Smith's and Jelovic's insistence that no Afghans were ever taken prisoner in the last compound and interrogated, and that Ali Jan was never kicked off a cliff and murdered.

Finding out more detail from Hanifa and the other Darwan witnesses could therefore make or break the

Darwan component of the case in the event the legal team could actually get Andrews to court.

**

In the days after talking with Hanifa, Levitan fell into a deep funk. After meeting with Hanifa, our lawyers filed an outline of evidence with the Federal Court that reflected what we hoped Hanifa would say if he ever appeared in court. This document described how Hanifa had encountered a 'big and tall soldier' aided by a translator who had interacted with both himself and Ali after the pair were detained with a third Afghan.

As Hanifa was interrogated by the 'big soldier', the translator had barked at him: *'Look at him when he is talking to you but listen to me and talk to me.'*

The document filed with the court described the big soldier becoming vicious, kicking Hanifa 'twice hard in the chest'. He was punched hard in the upper body, blows that still ached in the morning. The Afghan farmer described the military translator working with Roberts-Smith at Darwan as a young man, maybe in his late twenties, dressed in Australian military fatigues but who spoke both English and Pashto.

If Hanifa's outline of evidence was to be believed, the translator was also involved in the abuse of detainees.

'He hit me hard in my face with a pistol and called me a Talib,' Hanifa's outline of evidence stated.

'I said to him, "I am no Talib."'

It was his description of a translator with a pistol that had emerged as a serious problem and the source of Levitan's despair. Translators were strictly prohibited from carrying weapons.

If Hanifa ever testified, Roberts-Smith's barristers would surely point out this anomaly to undermine the Afghan's credibility.

Levitan's dark mood was lifted by Mitchell. The barrister seemed to relish the opportunity to solve a problem, especially if it involved copious amounts of detail others would find mind numbing. It explained why Mitchell could spend countless hours with his son building and sorting Lego.

Among the thousands of pieces of evidence Mitchell and Barnett were responsible for sorting through – from detailed mission reports to soldiers' performance reviews – were a few photos I had obtained. They appeared unremarkable, but Mitchell had still catalogued each image in his mind. It was why he had the answer to our problem. One of the photos showed a young, grinning man with a mullet haircut and dressed in an Australian military uniform. It was the Afghan translator from the Darwan mission. In the photo, he was posing for the picture at the SAS base in Tarin Kowt.

A pistol was strapped to his leg.

CHAPTER 34

THE BARRISTERS AND THE JUDGE

June 2020

A quarter of a century before Queen Victoria created the Victoria Cross to recognise acts of valour during the Crimean War, her tenth cousin, Queen Elizabeth 1, appointed the world's first silk. The famous English philosopher and statesman Francis Bacon was made Queen's Counsel in 1597, a designation that recognised his status as a distinguished advocate. Upon their appointment, Queen's or King's Counsel, which from 1993 in New South Wales were renamed Senior Counsel, were said to 'take silk' in reference to the silken black gowns worn by these elite barristers.

Just as the men of the SAS distinguished themselves from regular soldiers, the leading silks of the New South Wales bar occupied an elite and rarefied pocket of the legal industry where they could charge north of $10,000 a day for their services.

It was perhaps why Roberts-Smith's key silks appeared to get along so well with their client. Arthur Moses SC,

Bruce McClintock SC and Roberts-Smith VC no doubt considered themselves standouts in their fields and had the post nominals and pay packets to prove it.

McClintock and Moses may have had healthy egos, but they were no fools. They also knew it would come down to the details, big and small, and to each side's ability to get credible witnesses to court. This all suited Roberts-Smith just fine, because the ex-soldier had a good answer for every ridiculous allegation the newspapers had thrown at him and a witness to back him up.

His two senior barristers never missed a chance to point this out to Federal Court Justice Anthony Besanko, the judge selected by the Chief Justice to preside over the blockbuster defamation case. While the case was still in its preliminary stages, Roberts-Smith's two silks had already created an impression of strength and success when they appeared in various pre-trial hearings to decide what allegations would be tested before Justice Besanko when the trial commenced.

Moses had radiated the same confidence when, in February, he and lawyer Monica Allen travelled with Roberts-Smith to the AFP headquarters in Canberra to meet with his federal police pursuers. The AFP had written to Roberts-Smith to inform him detectives had 'conducted inquiries in Afghanistan and obtained statements from a number of current and former ADF personnel', including eyewitnesses, about allegations he had subjected Ali Jan to cruel and degrading treatment before participating in his execution.

Moses had been assigned the task of safeguarding Roberts-Smith's interests in a formal interview with these officers. Moses had risen through the legal ranks and become president of various legal bodies. He'd flirted with a career on the conservative side of politics, but he'd stayed at the bar. He'd built his profile with big cases, including representing the-then Liberal premier of New South Wales, Gladys Berejiklian, in a corruption inquiry.

The decision to give a police interview had come at a time when Roberts-Smith was not only dealing with war crimes allegations being lobbed from three directions – the AFP, the Brereton Inquiry and by our newspapers – but after he'd also finally separated from his wife.

In such a stressful environment, a lesser man might have exercised his right to hold his tongue. But not Roberts-Smith. The AFP interview presented another opportunity to convincingly protest his innocence.

Moses knew Roberts-Smith's version of events almost as well as the ex-soldier. He also appeared as convinced as his client about the injustice that the Ali Jan murder allegation had even been made.

With Moses in the police interview room, flanked by Allen and a second barrister, the federal police would have been left in no doubt that Roberts-Smith was not only confident of his position, but had backers who were equally convinced.

A month later, after Masters and I heard about this AFP interview, we called Mark O'Brien seeking comment. Roberts-Smith and his legal team moved quickly to manage the news. Before The Age and Herald could publish, The Australian's defence writer Paul Maley released a story online quoting Ben Roberts-Smith confirming the police interview had taken place but claiming he had volunteered for it. The story created the impression that Roberts-Smith was a good guy wrongly accused, rather than a police suspect identified by eyewitnesses on different continents as a war criminal.

* * *

On 2 June 2020, as Bruce McClintock readied for another day of courtroom sparring with his barristers' robes flowing from his shoulders, the aim was to create a similar impression. He exuded aggression and confidence, the product of many years as one of the bar's most pugnacious and successful defamation silks. When he'd represented the famous actor Geoffrey Rush in a defamation case against the *Daily Telegraph*, McClintock had theatrically savaged 'gutter journalism' and the state of reporting in Australia, helping his client win a record $2.9 million in damages. The Roberts-Smith case was on another level.

McClintock was renowned for taking to his feet in court like an ageing heavyweight fighter, his eyes sparkling with intent as he jabbed a pointed finger towards the witness he was cross-examining.

If a witness became confused, McClintock wouldn't hesitate to scoff openly, his quick-fire questions dripping with incredulity. To judges, though, he could be charming, sharing jokes and asides with a genteel bonhomie.

What wedded McClintock and Moses was their fondness for courtroom theatrics. Where McClintock was blustery and bellicose, Moses adopted a different persona and tone, one that to me came across as sneering and supercilious. Our barrister Sandy Dawson also had a flair for the theatrical, but he could often make light of himself with a charm that was more than skin deep.

In contrast to all three senior barristers, Justice Anthony Besanko was quietly spoken, preferring stern brevity to courtroom soliloquies. He looked to be in his late sixties, was serious, unflappable and razor smart.

Justice Besanko had devoted his life to the law, having presided over criminal trials as a judge in the South Australian courts before his elevation to the federal jurisdiction. He didn't interject as much as many other judges, but he didn't need to in order to assert authority. When he spoke, everyone in the court listened. He somehow balanced gravitas with humility, so was admired, respected and, for the ill-prepared barrister, feared.

'Are you sure you don't want to develop that point a little more?' he would quietly ask a counsel, a sign that not only was the judge unconvinced, but that the barrister before him had missed a precedent or otherwise stumbled and would be wise to request a brief adjournment to conduct some panicked legal research.

Grandstanding in the court by a defendant or barrister would be met with an arched eyebrow. Given the judge's usually unreadable face, this was rarely a good sign.

By midway through this particular day's hearing, it seemed evident there would be no shortage of theatre. True to form, Justice Besanko had said little, coolly observing as Dawson and McClintock argued over whether the newspapers could add more witnesses and allegations to their truth defence.

Square-jawed, lithe and with his hair impeccably styled, Sandy Dawson described to Besanko how our legal team had tracked down four Afghan eyewitnesses to events at Darwan. The most important of these witnesses was a man called Hanifa.

'Each of them, as Your Honour will have seen, are eyewitnesses to aspects of the Ali Jan incident, including, for Hanifa, witnessing the kick that we say that Ali Jan suffered at the hands of, or perhaps I should say at the feet of, the applicant, which sent him over the cliff and ultimately led to his death,' Dawson told the court.

Dawson also detailed how the murder of the Afghan farmer had been covered up. His plasticuffs had been cut off and near his body was planted the radio Roberts-Smith had retrieved from the dead insurgent he had earlier waded through the Helmand River to hunt down.

Dawson conceded to Justice Besanko that none of the Afghan witnesses had seen which soldier had fired the bullet that killed Ali Jan after Roberts-Smith kicked him off the cliff. Speaking in a crisp, careful manner, the barrister then moved to matters of the law. He explained to the judge that a recent criminal case had established a legal precedent that meant the newspapers only needed to prove that Roberts-Smith was part of a joint criminal enterprise.

The precedent-setting case involved a 2016 murder trial in which the accused, a notoriously corrupt ex-cop Roger Rogerson and his accomplice Glen McNamara, both blamed each other for killing a drug dealer. 'They were both convicted of his murder on the grounds of a joint criminal enterprise,' Dawson said. That case had clear parallels with the contested allegations now before Justice Besanko.

'It doesn't matter if Mr Roberts-Smith directed Jelovic to pull the trigger. It doesn't matter if it was Mr Roberts-Smith or Jelovic who fired the fatal shot,' Dawson extrapolated.

Dawson had also tried to convince Justice Besanko that the newspapers should be permitted to introduce new evidence about the 'blooding of Person 66' in late October 2012. The barrister stepped through what he said his clients, me and Masters, had asserted were the facts of this allegation.

Person 66 was a soldier who had answered to Roberts-Smith on the mission in question and had yet to kill any

Afghan in the field of war. Determined to 'blood' him, Roberts-Smith had directed Person 66 to take an Afghan detainee to a field and shoot him in the head.

'After that had occurred, the applicant [Roberts-Smith] said that he had "blooded" Person 66,' Dawson said.

He spoke matter-of-factly. These allegations were so grave they required no colourful emphasis by Dawson. 'Blooding ... is the process by which a young soldier is directed to kill for the first time, and is therefore blooded,' the barrister said.

* * *

Roberts-Smith had instructed McClintock to attack the new allegations and witnesses, and he obliged. The war hero's barrister had the air of a man personally offended at having to deal with scurrilous claims made by incompetent reporters, as if it was beneath him. He argued to Justice Besanko that the newspapers were making it up as they went, revising their truth defence as Roberts-Smith pointed out flaw after fatal flaw.

'It's a *new* case, Your Honour – it's a defective case,' McClintock told the judge, sounding exasperated as he urged the court to disallow the changes the reporters were seeking to make to their original court filings. These efforts to amend the truth defence amounted to another 'cruel strain' inflicted on an innocent man.

'Yes, he's won a Victoria Cross, yes, he's a soldier, yes, he saw a considerable amount of action, yes, there can be no question about his courage,' McClintock told the court.

'But he's still a human being, your honour, and to confront allegations like this, put forward by a large and powerful media organisation, in circumstances where, it turns out, what they actually said in the articles is insupportable, and now they want to change position.'

McClintock seized upon the attempt by us not just to add the Afghan villagers and Person 66 to our witness list but to revise what he said were crucial details of other allegations. He went on to say we had originally claimed that it was a mission in late October after which medic Jimmy Stanton had allegedly heard Roberts-Smith boast of executing a young prisoner Stanton had earlier detained.

But after Roberts-Smith pointed out he was on no such mission on the date nominated, Dawson revised the mission date to 5 November 2012. Dawson fired back at McClintock's efforts to claim this showed the newspapers' case was a shambles. Stanton may not have been sure of the day of a mission eight years before, but the core allegations – taking an Afghan detainee shaking like a leaf and handing him to Roberts-Smith's patrol team only to hear the soldier later boast about how beautiful it was to murder him – were unchanged. That is what mattered, Dawson argued.

Not so, McClintock thundered. The newspapers kept repainting their canvas because their claims of murder were fundamentally baseless. 'The enormous emotional stress my client has been facing is compounded by this new case and changing the date of the one already alleged. The dates matter.'

McClintock also claimed Masters and I had invented the Person 66 story because we were 'worried about Darwan' and 'the unreliability' of our Afghan witnesses. The failure to identify who pulled the trigger and killed Ali Jan was supposedly another fatal weakness that exposed our case as an emperor with no clothes. Furthermore, Dawson's effort to plead the Ali Jan allegations as a joint criminal enterprise case was yet another indicator of the flimsy foundations of the truth defence.

As the two barristers jousted, Justice Besanko remained inscrutable. He gave no indication about whether he would allow the Person 66 allegations to be added to the truth defence or permit Hanifa and the three other Darwan villagers to testify. He would deliver his ruling later, he told the court.

McClintock left the judge in no doubt of the high stakes of this pending decision. Australia's most decorated Afghan veteran had suffered greatly when the initial truth defence had been lodged by the reporters. By rejecting their proposed amendments, Justice Besanko could use his power to confront a fresh injustice.

McClintock's ultimate contention was clear. We had gathered a hundred jigsaw pieces only to find that none of them fitted. Adding more pieces would only add to the mess.

'I ask your honour to imagine the strain on anyone, including a man with the supreme courage of my client, of having to put up with a case, which, every time he shows it's false, they change it,' McClintock pleaded to Justice Besanko.

If the judge was moved, he didn't show it. No one watching on – not Roberts-Smith, me, Dawson or McClintock – knew who had won the day.

CHAPTER 35

PAIN, HEALING AND A NEW SOURCE

July 2020

In a darkened hotel room in July 2020, I placed a hand on Dusty Miller's shoulder, trying to offer him some comfort. He was about to come face to face with the adult children of Haji Sardar, the Afghan farmer he'd treated for a minor bullet wound eight years before, only to have the man taken from his care by another SAS soldier and allegedly murdered.

As we waited for the children to appear, the fifty-year-old ex-SAS medic was sweating and grinding his hands into each other. Occasionally his face winced, as if being tortured by an invisible force. Despite my suggestion that Dusty prepare a short, written statement he could rely on if he panicked, he hadn't prepared a script – or indeed any words at all – for the young Afghan men who would soon appear on a computer screen in front of him.

Until this moment, the idea of retracing the clandestine SAS mission that changed Dusty's life had been driven by something he couldn't easily put into words. He told me he was worried he'd fall short. What do you say to the sons

283

of a father whose brutal killing you feel partly responsible for? Will they hear you out? Will they want revenge? And if they're willing to listen, will you fail them again?

My journey with Dusty Miller to meet the children of Haji Sardar had started weeks before. Dusty had been crucial in helping me win the trust of Jimmy Stanton, the medic who had agreed to appear as a witness in the Roberts-Smith case. Both Dusty and I had watched Stanton quietly struggle as he recounted detaining the young Afghan he suspected Roberts-Smith had later executed. While Stanton wasn't thrilled with the prospect of appearing in court and testifying against Roberts-Smith, he'd still spoken passionately of the need to address past wrongs instead of burying them.

'I'm a medic. I'm meant to save lives,' he'd said.

Dusty had never served directly alongside Roberts-Smith and his suffering had nothing to do with the famous ex-soldier. The soldier Dusty accused of murdering an injured Afghan had served in a different SAS squadron, one with its own history, culture and characters.

As Dusty watched Stanton's quiet resolve to confront Roberts-Smith's involvement in a suspected murder, I realised he hoped he might find his own sense of purpose in confronting the death of Haji Sardar.

Dusty asked me if I could track down Sardar's children. Next, he asked me if we could travel to Afghanistan to meet them. He had at first struggled to explain why, other than saying going back might make him feel like he felt before everything changed.

'I want to say sorry,' he told me one night. 'And to tell them that I should have done more.'

It had taken a few weeks, but eventually Rashid, the freelance Afghan journalist working with me on the

Roberts-Smith case, tracked down a tribal elder who knew Sardar's family.

A security company run by ex-Australian soldiers advised it would be dangerous for Dusty to travel to Sarkum, where the family lived. The Taliban still controlled the village and were gathering more power and territory as the group negotiated a power-sharing agreement with the US-backed Afghan government.

If news of Dusty's impending arrival leaked, it would make him a prime kidnap target. Sardar's family might also want revenge, the security advisers warned, but said they could make a meeting safer by changing location at the last minute and checking for weapons.

Dusty told me he'd take the risk and packed his bags. Two of Haji Sardar's seven children agreed to make the dangerous journey from Sarkum to Kandahar, a city where our security advisers believed they could minimise any threat to our team. We booked tickets in early 2020, and had aimed to fly in the first half of the year.

Dusty gave me a refresher course on how to use a first-aid kit. He seemed focused, intense, a master with his tools, but I knew this about him already. I'd spoken to several SAS soldiers who described Dusty as the best medic they had ever worked with, and one of the bravest.

In the days before we were due to leave, Covid-19 began sweeping the world and roadblocks were set up in Afghanistan's south as cases emerged in the region. Dusty's mental health also appeared to have deteriorated. The bruises on his face suggested he'd been punching himself again, and he quietly confirmed this was the case. When I told him the trip was off he was deeply affected.

'Is there another way I can see them?' he asked me quietly. I told him there was a chance our security company could set up a video connection with the sons. I also tried to lighten the mood. Everyone is meeting on computers now, I told him.

'It won't be the same,' he responded.

'Let's see,' I said.

* * *

Months later, I sat with Dusty and an Afghan translator in a dark Melbourne hotel room, our faces illuminated by a laptop screen. The sun was shining brightly outside, dancing on the surface of the nearby Albert Park Lake, but I felt as if I was somewhere else entirely, a netherworld of memory, death and regret. I'd spent days and days with Dusty in the weeks before this, but I'd never seen him so anxious. A slight stutter had crept into his speech. He was sweating from the brow. He looked a mess.

While Dusty was worried he'd not know what to say or how to say it, I was not even sure Sardar's sons would want to talk to him. Hours before, the tribal elder told Rashid that he, the elder, would do the talking rather than the sons. I'd wondered if the elder would demand compensation.

'The boys are coming now,' our fixer said over the video link.

The faces of two young Afghan men almost filled the screen. Hazratullah Sardar was twenty-two, but he looked younger, wide-eyed, boyish. His older brother, Abdul, thirty-four, sat next to him, more serious. The tribal elder was also in the frame.

For a moment, there was silence. Then Dusty took control. He spoke with precision and care, and no trace of a stutter. He explained that he arrived in their village with the

SAS in March 2012 and was handed their injured father. He said he examined his wound and bandaged his leg.

'I made him as comfortable as I could,' he said. 'I knew the injuries your father sustained were not immediately life-threatening. We were going to leave with your father and take him back to get treated.'

Haji Sardar's sons had never heard an Australian talk about their father's final minutes. Dusty told them how a senior soldier took Haji from his care, and that this soldier came back minutes later and told him the Afghan had died.

I noticed Hazratullah staring downward, as if in quiet mourning, while Dusty explained how his father could not have died of the gunshot wound he had been treating, but must have been murdered by this senior soldier.

'Something very bad had happened to your father. And it was wrong,' Miller said.

I watched on silently as the former medic's eyes filled with tears. As the Afghan men stared intently at him, Miller pressed on.

'I want you to understand that I was very disturbed and troubled by what happened. I am very sorry for what happened to your father. And I wish I could have done more.'

Miller wiped his eyes. His utter anguish was so palpable, I wondered if they could feel it in Kandahar.

The sons appeared to me to be transfixed by Dusty's face. He paused, drew in some breath, and apologised again. 'You shouldn't have lost your father that day. And I am so sorry that happened.'

There was silence before the sons responded.

What they said was not what Dusty or I had expected. There was no anger, no thirst for revenge, no demand for money. They spoke quietly and with dignity via their interpreter, taking it in turns to thank him.

They told us they had noticed the bandage on their father's leg when they washed his body and knew someone had cared for him before he was killed. The older son asked Dusty if he knew who stomped on their father's chest. While disclosing no name, Dusty explained that there was an inquiry in Australia and that he'd fight to see them get some form of justice for their father.

Justice Brereton's inquiry was expected to be finished in months. I expected the judge would refer a small number of soldiers alleged to be involved in executions of Afghans to the federal police, and recommend sweeping reforms to the Special Forces.

But I had no way of knowing if Brereton had found enough information about the soldier at the centre of Dusty's story, or about Ben Roberts-Smith, to ever warrant a criminal prosecution.

After Haji Sardar's sons heard Dusty's promise, they thanked him again. The quiet gratitude from the sons of a murdered man struck me as bewildering. Dusty told them again, as if he had thought they failed to understand the first time, that he should have done more to save their father.

I watched on as the sons responded that he had done all he could in the circumstances and that they granted him their full forgiveness. Their words, the tone in their voices and the look in their eyes suggested they not only felt Dusty's anguish, but that it had lessened their own suffering, too.

'I am very thankful to Dusty for his help. And getting in touch with us and telling us what he did,' Hazratullah Sardar said as the call neared its end. Before the power cut the connection, he said: 'Please tell Dusty to look after himself. He has suffered enough.'

* * *

A fortnight after a story I wrote about Dusty was published in the *Good Weekend* magazine, I received an email. The sender used the alias 'Delta Charlie' and had set the email to self-destruct after it was opened. The message stated that Roberts-Smith had been spotted holding the hand of his lawyer Monica Allen, during what looked like a date at a swanky restaurant. 'Delta Charlie' had left no clues as to their identity, but I guessed they were perhaps an old regiment friend of Roberts-Smith with a conscience or one of his Channel Seven colleagues. By now, secretive messages from the SAS were coming in thick and fast.

Another SAS source had recently delivered me journalistic gold: an outline of a classified briefing that the new commander of Australia's Special Forces, Major General Adam Findlay, had delivered to the soldiers of the SAS at Perth's Campbell Barracks.

A seething Findlay indicated he'd spoken to Justice Brereton and, as a result, the senior officer believed a small number of SAS soldiers had betrayed the regiment by committing war crimes. Not only did those few soldiers taint the reputation of those who had served with honour in Afghanistan, their historical conduct was now at risk of besmirching the reputations of SAS recruits who had never deployed overseas.

'I spent two years of my life in Afghanistan and I don't feel validated and you shouldn't either,' Findlay told the regiment. He warned the soldiers assembled before him that Brereton's findings would be so bad, it would take the SAS ten years to rebuild trust with the Australian community and government.

'Prepare for the long haul,' he'd fumed, claiming a rotten culture had developed due to 'weak' leadership and poor moral values.

'You gotta develop your moral compass. You gotta develop your moral courage ... you gotta have something that tells you what is right and what is wrong when nobody is over the top of you,' he implored the soldiers.

I filed away details of the Findlay speech for a future story just as the message from Delta Charlie arrived. I would have disregarded it, if not for the fact that my *60 Minutes* producer, who lived in the same apartment block as Allen, told me he'd twice seen Roberts-Smith leaving Allen's apartment complex in his exercise gear in the morning.

I wasn't remotely interested in Roberts-Smith's love life, but if he'd hooked up with his lawyer it raised the prospect that Emma may not be prepared to testify on his behalf during the defamation court case. Or at least not prepared to testify untruthfully.

I already knew of one significant lie in the statement that Roberts-Smith's lawyers had filed on behalf of Emma in the defamation case. This 'outline of evidence' indicated that Emma would potentially say on oath that she and Roberts-Smith were separated when he had been seeing Amanda. I knew this to be false, because Amanda had shown me messages from Roberts-Smith clearly showing he and Emma were together when he'd been secretly dating Amanda.

Was Roberts-Smith pushing Emma to lie on his behalf?

* * *

Days later, a friend texted me a photo of the front page of the *Courier-Mail* newspaper. It was splashed with a story about Roberts-Smith and Allen. The pair had been photographed by a News Corp snapper holding hands after leaving Roberts-Smith's Brisbane apartment.

A short time after that, Allen's boss, Mark O'Brien, tried to hose down the story by telling reporters that it was 'interesting that in 2020 people make assumptions about friendships between adults'.

In the same breath, O'Brien appeared to acknowledge the pair's relationship had grown too close. 'She and I agree that it was unwise to spend some time socially with him,' O'Brien said.

Perhaps the ex-soldier and Allen were simply friends holding hands, but distraction or not, the revelation of their relationship left open a door.

We have to find out if Emma had hired her own lawyer, I thought to myself. And try to make contact.

CHAPTER 36

THE REPORT

November 2020

Justice Paul Brereton was dressed in his khaki ceremonial military uniform. Large gold buttons ran down the front of his jacket, two epaulets indicating his rank as a major general sat on each shoulder. His facial expression was sombre.

Brereton was flanked by four other lawyers who had helped him run his inquiry over the previous four years, led by a barrister and wing commander, Matt Vesper. He, too, was wearing his ceremonial uniform.

Throughout the inquiry, Vesper had often played good cop to Brereton's bad. A surfer with a laid-back manner and an easy laugh, Vesper had quickly won the trust of the reluctant SAS soldiers he gently coaxed to open up. In contrast, Brereton could switch from quiet formality to bouts of masterful, intensive cross-examination. SAS witnesses remarked how the gentle judge could instantaneously transform into a brow-furrowed unrelenting inquisitor.

Today, even Vesper's face appeared grim as he stood to attention next to Brereton. The pomp and ceremony in the office of the Inspector-General of the Australian Defence Force, Jim Gaynor, was to mark the formal conclusion of one of the most sensitive, secretive and exhaustive inquiries in military history.

Brereton, Vesper and a small team of lawyers and investigators interviewed 423 witnesses, most of them soldiers and officers of the SAS and Commandos who had served in Afghanistan. To supplement these interrogations, they reviewed more than 20,000 documents and 25,000 images and travelled to Afghanistan to find corroborating information.

The only soldier to be identified publicly as an inquiry suspect was Ben Roberts-Smith, but the judge had also been probing other, unnamed veterans. They included the soldier Dusty Miller had identified as the suspected killer of injured Afghan father, Haji Sardar, and a soldier who was captured on body-cam vision, leaked to the ABC, shooting dead an apparently unarmed Afghan lying in a wheat field. Prior to pulling the trigger, the soldier was recorded asking a colleague: 'Want me to drop this cunt?'

Very few senior officials knew what information Brereton had gathered about war crimes and what findings, if any, he would make about individual and command responsibility and the need for broader reforms to Australia's most elite military units.

There were good reasons to be doubtful of Brereton's prospects. Inquiries into war crimes in the US and UK had both collapsed while facing political pressure, including that brought by President Donald Trump. In Canberra, Defence had a well-founded reputation for burying bad news.

After eighteen months of finding very little, Brereton's inquiry had begun to gradually gain momentum. Those the judge intermittently and carefully briefed sensed this.

They included defence force chief Angus Campbell and successive defence ministers Marise Payne, Christopher Pyne and Linda Reynolds, as well as the-then attorney-general, Christian Porter.

The politicians didn't know the details of any suspected war crimes the inquiry may have uncovered, but were told enough to know Brereton and his team had been making progress, slowly at first and then, like an avalanche, building into something that even if they wanted to, they could not stop.

The judge had kept the inquiry's detailed classified findings a secret from all but Campbell and Gaynor for good reason. Not only did the law require it, but what he had dug up was far more incendiary than anyone in Defence had ever imagined.

* * *

For many months, Brereton had faced increasing pressure to finalise his inquiry. So too had the chief of Australia's military. In the more than four years that had passed since he'd appointed Brereton as war crimes investigator, Angus Campbell had been promoted from army chief to the general in charge of the Australian Defence Force and had faced growing calls to expedite Brereton's work.

Leading the media attack on the length of time the Brereton Inquiry was taking was *The Australian*'s Paul Maley, a Defence reporter who, it appeared to me, had become Roberts-Smith's journalist of choice. Unable to dig up any information from the close-knit Special Forces community about the war crimes allegations occupying Brereton, Masters, me and the AFP, Maley had run with Roberts-Smith's counter-narrative.

His newspaper gave Roberts-Smith a consistent platform to respond to the ongoing adverse revelations in our stories, as well as to critique the Brereton Inquiry. Maley would receive press releases prepared by Roberts-Smith's public relations agent or his lawyers, which *The Australian* would then run as 'exclusive' news stories.

One particular article written by Maley led with: 'Australia's most decorated soldier, Ben Roberts-Smith, has labelled the fight to clear his name of war crimes allegations his "most important" battle, accusing Nine newspapers of engaging in a commercially motivated campaign to tear him down.'

The story quoted Roberts-Smith as saying: 'I want Australians to know that I absolutely deny these hurtful allegations. I believe Nine's continued publication of these false claims is malicious and commercially motivated.'

At times Maley appeared personally invested in Roberts-Smith's fortunes. 'Guilty or innocent, the treatment of VC recipient Ben Roberts-Smith has been demonstrably unfair. My feature on this most unseemly saga,' Maley had tweeted about a lengthy article he'd written savaging the Brereton Inquiry's failure to wrap up its work.

The article contained a ferocious attack on the ADF for defending the time Brereton was taking to collect his evidence. 'Ask the Defence Force why it is taking so long and you'll get an answer about the complexity of the inquiries, the transnational nature of the inquiry, the fact the material is secret,' Maley wrote. 'Don't believe a word of it.'

Roberts-Smith chipped in directly with an appearance on Sky News that warned young Australians not to enlist in the army because the military leadership didn't support veterans. Brereton was not mentioned directly, but most observers in Canberra viewed Roberts-Smith's supposed care for veterans as a Trojan horse to attack those in the military command who were backing the judge.

Justice Brereton also copped threats on social media. One internet warrior posted the names of his children, leading to a police investigation. Brereton remained unfazed. He had a job to do. He ignored the white noise. His critics were swinging in the dark, unaware of the lengths to which he had gone to defeat the tactics of rogue soldiers trained in secrecy and counter-surveillance.

His inquiry had 'intentionally not given a specified timeframe in which to report'. Those with a deep understanding of the Special Forces brotherhood knew it would take 'considerable time' for Brereton 'to gain the confidence and trust of members of an organisation that does not readily welcome engagement or scrutiny by outsiders'.

So it had proved. The judge had 'encountered enormous challenges in eliciting truthful disclosures in the closed, closely bonded, and highly compartmentalised Special Forces community'. He'd come up against a code in which 'loyalty to one's mates, immediate superiors and the unit are regarded as paramount, in which secrecy is at a premium, and in which those who "leak" are anathema'. Those from the SAS and Commandos he had interviewed had frequently employed 'resistance to interrogation' techniques.

In Brereton's mind, it was 'hardly surprising' that it had 'taken time, opportunity, and encouragement for the truth to emerge'. Sometimes it was only on the second or even third interview when the truth would finally spill from a soldier's mouth and their conscience would 'prevail'.

But the truth had spilled out. Again and again and again. By the end of 2019, multiple Special Forces operators had secretly confessed to Brereton that they had executed prisoners. Throughout 2020, fresh confessions were still being made.

It wasn't until October 2020 that the full scale of the Brereton Inquiry's findings began to be shared in classified briefings to senior ministers and Defence top brass. The complete compendium of secrets Brereton had uncovered was detailed in an eight-volume report that now sat in Inspector-General Gaynor's office.

After a brief speech in which the judge acknowledged the tireless work of his staff and the extraordinary scale and seriousness of what they had finally uncovered, Brereton and his team walked out into the Canberra air. Now it was up to others to ensure Brereton's work was taken further.

* * *

Wearing a light-blue tie, white shirt and dark suit, the Australian prime minister spoke slowly and gravely about his nation's proud military history. Amid constant clicking of the cameras of the Canberra press gallery, Scott Morrison invoked the legacy of the Anzacs, noting how twenty-four hours earlier the nation had paused to remember and honour veterans who had served and died in conflicts.

'Our serving men and women are deserving of the respect and admiration in which they are held by the Australian people,' Morrison said. 'They have earned it. They have demonstrated it.'

The prime minister then moved to the reason for his press conference. The high pedestal the Australian public placed its military upon also necessitated deep scrutiny when things went bad.

'When you have such standards and respect such standards ... this requires us to deal with honest and brutal truths, where expectations and standards may not have been met.'

The Brereton Inquiry was still secret, with none of its contents, even in redacted form, having been released to the public. Morrison was one of the few briefed on Brereton's findings. The prime minister moved quickly in response to what he had learnt.

While it would be military chief Angus Campbell who would choose how much to tell the Australian public about the findings once he had fully considered his report, the prime minister had called the press conference to announce the creation of a new agency, the Office of the Special Investigator (OSI), to handle the information unearthed by the judge.

The OSI would supplement the work of the federal police in assessing whether Brereton's discoveries should prompt further investigations aimed at gathering evidence that, unlike the judge's inquiry, could be used in potential criminal prosecutions.

Morrison's announcement was made with little prior discussion with Campbell. To political and Defence watchers in Canberra, it seemed a hastily made political solution to a grave national problem that had yet to be explained in any detail to the public. Morrison had placed the horse before the cart.

No one outside the dozen or so officials who had received Brereton's classified report knew the breadth and scope of what he had discovered. The prime minister knew, but he was leaving the grim task of making it public to Campbell.

A new independent agency was Morrison's answer to a looming scandal that would reverberate not just around

Australia but around the world if Campbell decided to reveal the shocking details in Brereton's report. The prime minister's announcement would enable the government to sidestep questions about political accountability by simply referring to its creation of the OSI and explaining that to comment would be to risk ongoing investigations. Morrison's desire to keep politically powerful veterans and Defence groups onside while bowing to Australia's Anzac tradition was obvious as he fielded questions.

When a journalist asked him if the overuse of the Special Forces in Afghanistan by political leaders may have contributed to the problems Brereton confronted, Morrison responded with praise for Australian soldiers. 'Whether that is those that [sic] are based over there [in Perth] as part of the Special Air Services Regiment or indeed the 2 Commandos, not far from where my electorate is in southern Sydney, we ask an extraordinary amount of them and we always do,' he said.

The public reckoning over the suspected executions of prisoners and civilians Brereton had uncovered had yet to occur, and the prime minister was already paying homage to Australian military exceptionalism.

'I stand in awe of those who choose to put on a uniform,' he said.

* * *

A short time after Morrison delivered his address, Roberts-Smith released a statement. It was aimed squarely at the Brereton Inquiry, but also included a barb aimed at hostile media. Roberts-Smith said he welcomed the announcement by the prime minister that 'for the first time accurately clarified that it was not part of' Brereton's remit to 'make any findings of fact in relation to rumours'.

'It is heartening to hear that these matters, which have been the subject of rumours for years, will now be examined by a Special Investigator's Office with expertise and experience to consider evidence, not rumours, and make decisions based on evidence rather than unsubstantiated rumours … It is regrettable that the IGADF Inquiry took such an extraordinarily long time to be finalised. I am hopeful that this next phase will be completed as expeditiously as possible so that all current and former Special Forces soldiers who have been deeply impacted by the Inquiry process can move on with their lives.'

Roberts-Smith finished his statement with a pot shot at me. It blamed my reporting for engineering the police investigation into him over the Ali Jan allegations, despite the fact that the federal police had written to his lawyer Mark O'Brien, disclosing how its inquiry into Roberts-Smith had been triggered by a referral in May 2018 from the-then chief of the ADF, Mark Binskin.

The intention of Roberts-Smith's statement was obvious. He wanted the public to believe that Brereton had been meandering around hopelessly for years, lost in a fog of rumour and innuendo, while I had somehow convinced the federal police to launch a baseless and costly probe into a war hero.

That both these claims were false didn't seem to matter.

* * *

'Those talking are dogs.' The words were spat out by a soldier of the SAS at a meeting of Afghan veterans still serving at the regiment's Perth base. Another muttered the word 'rats'.

If the imminent release of the Brereton Report had caused a political scramble in Canberra, internal tensions were in overdrive at the SAS headquarters. Roberts-Smith's few remaining loyalists had become openly hostile to the soldiers they suspected had spoken either to Brereton or the media. As these men saw it, the problem wasn't executions or torture. It was blokes who Roberts-Smith and his mates reckoned were talking out of school who were the problem.

The unknown SAS member's leaking to me of a classified briefing by Major General Adam Findlay about Brereton's anticipated findings had sparked a fresh round of accusations over who was talking. After I published Findlay's comments, the most senior soldier on the base, the Regimental Sergeant Major, had asked everyone at Findlay's briefing to sign a document stating it wasn't them who was the leak. He also called a meeting of the SAS's Afghan veterans to clear the air.

Brian McMurray was there, as was Boyd Keary and Dean Tilley. All three were known in the regiment to hold grave concerns about Roberts-Smith's involvement in war crimes. As a result, the trio had been subjected to a quiet campaign of isolation by Roberts-Smith's backers, a cold war with no end in sight.

Jason Andrews was missing, having taken extended leave, but by now it was an open secret among the more experienced SAS soldiers that he had likely broken his silence to Justice Brereton. Exactly what he had told the judge was not known, but the fact that he had cut ties with Roberts-Smith suggested it wasn't in keeping with the war hero's version of events about Darwan and Easter Sunday.

Vincent Jelovic had also quietly disappeared from the regiment, but was known to still be close to Roberts-Smith. So was an older SAS soldier in the meeting called by the Sergeant Major. It was this soldier who, among those hissing about dogs, rats and snitches, spoke most vehemently against the veterans suspected to have broken ranks.

Those airing the SAS's dirty laundry were not looking after their mates, the Roberts-Smith loyalist had said. The comment incensed Keary.

'Looking after your mates doesn't mean just looking after blokes you like,' Keary snapped.

For years, Roberts-Smith had bullied those in the SAS who were weaker than him. It was now also an open secret, at least among the group assembled in the room, that he was also accused of blooding more junior soldiers, scarring their careers and mental health. His supporters in the regiment had stood by silently. There was nothing courageous about falling into line behind a bully.

Keary wasn't finished: 'In the SAS, looking after your mates means looking after everyone in the regiment.'

CHAPTER 37

RICOCHET

November 2020

Dr Samantha Crompvoets sat in front of the camera, watching as I fired question after question at her. For two years, I had hassled her politely, requesting she consider conducting an interview about the reports she'd written back in 2016, and which were the catalyst for the Brereton Inquiry.

She'd always politely declined, while urging me to keep digging. But days before, Crompvoets had been called by Campbell and told the reports he'd commissioned her to write on alleged war crimes would be released along with a redacted version of the Brereton Inquiry.

Ever since leaked excerpts of the reports had been published by me and Chris Masters, Crompvoets had been the subject of stories and online commentary. Some of it was supportive, but much of it was vitriolic. She was savaged on social media and in some mainstream outlets, accused of being a left-leaning feminist cultural warrior. The irony was that she was in fact a conduit for the concerns of battle-hardened soldiers.

Still, she had stayed silent. Even when former defence minister turned war memorial director Brendan Nelson inferred that the crimes under scrutiny were 'fog of war' incidents rather than summary executions, she held her tongue.

Through it all, I had stayed in touch with Crompvoets, urging her to explain to the public why she had documented such serious allegations and then urged Campbell to embrace further accountability. Crompvoets was bracing for more blowback once her complete set of reports were released with the Brereton Report.

She would be blamed for triggering the scandal and attacked again as a woman with no wartime experience, a view that conveniently ignored the fact that all Crompvoets had done was steadfastly document the stories of Special Forces insiders who *had* experienced incidents they could no longer stay quiet about.

Her realisation that it was finally time for her to have a voice was why Crompvoets accepted my latest offer to go on camera. She was still a little wary of me, but she had listened when I'd spoken about my deep connection to some who'd served with the SAS. I also revealed my deep anxiety that I might lose the Roberts-Smith case because witnesses wouldn't show, an outcome that would inevitably lead to claims that war crimes had never occurred, and that would cast a shadow over her own work and that of Brereton.

As Crompvoets spoke to the camera about the work she'd finished five years earlier, she was amazed at how visceral and clear it still seemed. The disclosures from the Special Forces soldiers came to her slowly at first. Some spoke of killing as a 'sport'. Others of shame suffered in silence. As word spread among the secretive community of Australian soldiers and spies who had served in

Afghanistan, information arrived with more urgency. Some men spoke matter-of-factly; others broke down. One thread bound many of them: their belief that small cliques of their fellow Special Forces soldiers had turned bad with impunity, enabled by a bystander culture festering in the Special Forces. Crompvoets was still in touch with soldiers shattered by what they witnessed and, sometimes, their own failure to challenge more powerful colleagues or officers who were later rewarded with medals and promotions.

'I spoke to people who did call out bad behaviour and who were basically belittled and left broken,' she said. 'We're not talking about a couple of fog-of-war events that were, you know, perhaps confusing to understand,' Dr Crompvoets recalled. 'This is deliberate, repeated patterns of behaviour.

'One of the most disturbing things for me was people saying the phrase, "It happened all the time,"' she said, knowing her words would ricochet around Australia.

***

In the hours before General Angus Campbell strode to a lectern to brief the Australian public, he called his Afghan military counterpart, General Zia. He told him that he wished to apologise to the people of Afghanistan, sincerely and unreservedly.

Campbell repeated this apology in front of the Australian media scrum in words he knew were being beamed live across the nation and into military bases where soldiers and officers had been ordered to watch. Campbell revealed that Brereton had uncovered 'credible information' that thirty-nine Afghans had been murdered by nineteen current or former Special Forces soldiers.

He had recommended most of these soldiers face criminal investigation and the possible stripping of their medals. The thirty-nine unlawful killings included the execution of handcuffed prisoners. Brereton had also documented the torture and cruel treatment of prisoners.

Brereton described patrol commanders 'blooding' young soldiers by forcing them to shoot a prisoner to achieve their first kill, and carrying 'throw downs' – weapons to be placed with bodies so that in photographs they appeared as combatants. None of these alleged crimes was committed during the heat of battle. The victims were prisoners or civilians: Afghan fathers and farmers who had died for no other reason than being in a village or cornfield at the wrong time.

The alleged executions and mistreatment of civilians and detainees had 'profoundly disrespected the trust placed in us by the people of Afghanistan, at a time when they had asked for our help', Campbell said. He spoke calmly and with authority imbued with sadness, explaining how the actions of a few dozen Australians had 'devastated the lives of Afghan families and communities, causing them immeasurable pain and suffering, and put in jeopardy both our mission and the safety of our Afghan and coalition partners'.

'Today the Australian Defence Force is rightly held to account for allegations of grave misconduct by some members of our Special Forces community on operations in Afghanistan,' he said. 'To the people of Australia, I am sincerely sorry for any wrongdoing by members of the Australian Defence Force.'

As the General spoke, Crompvoets watched it all unfold live on television. She had been invited to Canberra by Campbell and given the Brereton Report the day before.

As the most senior officer in the land delivered his carefully prepared remarks, Crompvoets felt a sense of relief. Campbell wasn't holding back. He'd picked the most powerful parts of Brereton's report and was methodically listing them on national television.

The culture in the SAS had turned rotten as some within the regiment had come to foster a self-centred 'warrior culture', prioritising prestige, status and power at the expense of the regiment's heritage of quiet humility. As units became consumed with preparing for and fighting the war, much of the good order and discipline of military life fell away. Cutting corners and bending and ignoring rules was normalised.

Campbell also revealed how Brereton had determined that this distorted culture was embraced and amplified by experienced, charismatic and influential senior soldiers and their proteges, who fused military excellence with ego, entitlement and exceptionalism.

'Not correcting this culture as it developed was a failure of unit and higher command.'

There was nothing 'fog of war' about the incidents Brereton had catalogued. Instead, General Campbell described a 'disgraceful and a profound betrayal of the Australian Defence Force's professional standards and expectations'.

'In this context it is alleged that some patrols took the law into their own hands: rules were broken, stories concocted, lies told and prisoners killed.'

* * *

In his speech, Campbell did not identify any alleged perpetrators by name. Neither did the redacted version of the Brereton Report released online. Instead, Brereton had issued suppression orders preventing the naming of any suspects whose identity could be deduced via reference to the detailed contents of the publicly released report.

Suspects would be named if and when the federal police and the Office of the Special Investigator had conducted their own inquiries and the Director of Public Prosecutions (DPP) ruled there was sufficient evidence to lay a charge.

The exception was Ben Roberts-Smith. In his pre-trial defamation hearings, he'd been outed in court as both a Brereton Inquiry suspect and a target of a federal police investigation.

Among the reforms revealed by Campbell was that the SAS's 2 Squadron would be struck off the army's order of battle following the devastating revelations. Roberts-Smith was 2 Squadron's most famous and highly decorated former member. Campbell had also revealed that consideration would be given to cancelling medals of individual recipients.

Roberts-Smith may have hoped his denunciation, days earlier, of Brereton's pursuit of 'rumours' would cripple the impact of his report. Instead, the head of Australia's military had apologised on live television to two nations because of the information Brereton brought to light.

Winning the defamation trial was now more important for Roberts-Smith than ever before.

CHAPTER 38

BALLS IN A VICE

A new year – early 2021

'For God's sake, Peter. Offer to fly over to Perth to meet him. We are stuffed without Andrews.' I could feel the panic and exasperation running through my voice as I spoke to Peter Bartlett, the most senior lawyer on our defamation case team and Dean Levitan's boss.

The 'him' was Alisdair Putt, the solicitor working for Jason Andrews.

'Yes, boss,' Bartlett said curtly to me. This was Bartlett's code for: 'Stop being a rude prick, Nick. We are doing all we can.'

I knew I was being aggressive, even hostile, but the way Bartlett maintained a genteel, patrician air even when things were turning to shit drove me mad.

'If I lose this case, my career is over, a war criminal gets off and Ali Jan's family get no justice. But all the lawyers will get is another beach house,' I snapped.

I regretted my words as soon as I'd uttered them. Bartlett cared deeply for journalism and for me. At seventy-two, the case would bookend his career as the finest media lawyer of his generation. He didn't need money or the stress of defending Masters and me. He was in it for the right reasons.

He'd built a small and dedicated team to service the endless demands of the impending trial. Bartlett oversaw Levitan, who had taken on the role of lead lawyer, a human engine room driving a small team of even younger solicitors: the whip-smart Tess McGuire wasn't afraid to challenge the pale, stale and mostly male lawyers who ran MinterEllison; there was Dougal Hurley, a studious and serious lawyer itching for more responsibility; Jeremy Forbes, a softly spoken young lawyer whose fierce work ethic was matched by his intelligence; and Dylan Dexter, the youngest of the team with an earnestness that gave him the air of a 24-year-old Atticus Finch.

Still, it wasn't Bartlett's balls in the vice. That privilege belonged to the named defendants. It was Masters and me who would go down in history as the authors of the most expensive journalistic disaster if we lost the case. Also at seventy-two, Chris Masters was an Australian Media Hall of Fame inductee who had a decorated career set in stone and built over five decades. I wasn't starting out, but I wasn't even halfway through my career.

'You've got more to lose than Chris,' Bartlett had once said to me, blind to the anxiety the comment was sure to induce.

General Angus Campbell's press conference and the release of the Brereton Report had led to plenty of newsroom backslaps and colleagues describing our vindication in pursuing the war crimes story. There was no doubt in my mind that Roberts-Smith's alleged criminality dominated the still-classified and unreleased full Brereton

Report. But the redacted public version didn't name anyone and provided us with nothing we could use to bolster our truth defence.

To win the case, we needed Jason Andrews, the linchpin witness of the Darwan and Easter Sunday allegations, to come and tell the truth. And yet we couldn't get a return call from his lawyer, let alone him. Nor had we had any luck making contact with another allegedly blooded SAS soldier, Person 66.

Given both Andrews and Person 66 were suspected of murdering prisoners on Roberts-Smith's orders, they both had powerful reasons to avoid appearing in our trial. We could ask the court to grant them special certificates ensuring any admission they made about their own criminality could never be used against them in another legal proceeding. But there was no guarantee the court would provide this protection and, if it didn't, we may not be able to compel them to give self-incriminating evidence.

I wondered if a moral appeal to Andrews might work, if we ever managed to speak with him. This seemed increasingly unlikely.

We knew that other SAS eyewitnesses would come to court and tell the truth about Roberts-Smith if we subpoenaed them, but none would come voluntarily. The risk to their careers and the animosity they would face inside the regiment going up against one of its most famous sons was simply too great.

In the weeks after Campbell apologised to the nation, the success of our case depended on a series of uncertainties. Would Andrews ever make it to court and, if he did, would he tell the truth?

Would others who had witnessed alleged war crimes or misbehaviour – Person 66, Dean Tilley, Boyd Keary,

Brian McMurray, Nick Simkin and Keith Nueling – do the same? Would they even be in Australia when we dispatched a process server to hand them a subpoena warning that they could be arrested if they didn't show? Would the act of compelling them to court in this manner turn them against us?

It wasn't all grim news. Having earlier convinced Justice Besanko to allow us to expand our initial truth defence to include more allegations and witnesses, our lead barrister, Sandy Dawson, had scored a stunning legal victory in one of the pre-trial hearings.

Roberts-Smith and Justice Brereton had sought to prevent us getting access to what was known as a 'Potentially Affected Person' (PAP) notice. Every person accused by Brereton of war crimes had been sent a PAP notice, giving them an opportunity to respond to the judge's draft findings prior to the finalisation of his still-classified report.

Dawson had performed magnificently as he argued to the court that the PAP notice served on Roberts-Smith would likely contain potentially vital descriptions of SAS eyewitness testimony that, if replicated in our trial, could determine its outcome.

The Federal Court's decision to order the release to us of a redacted version of Roberts-Smith's PAP notice had briefly filled us with an electrifying hope, given it could lead to new witnesses and evidence. But it was just a hope. The PAP notice wouldn't arrive for weeks as it needed to be redacted and there was every chance it would be full of blacked-out sections.

We achieved another potential breakthrough. We used a legal discovery order to demand any documents that Roberts-Smith held relating to what we suspected was an acrimonious separation between the war hero and his wife.

While Dawson's junior counsel, Chris Mitchell, had taken the lead on the Darwan part of our case, Barnett had been assigned the task of unpicking the Easter Sunday killings. She'd also been given the job of liaising with Amanda, the woman who alleged Roberts-Smith had punched her.

Barnett was forensic, pedantic and possessed a human touch that meant she gently but firmly reassured potential witnesses that we would do all within our power to protect them. She also seemed willing enough to put up with anxious, late-night calls from me.

When Roberts-Smith's legal team resisted the order, we pressed the case and threatened court action if need be. Then an email appeared in Levitan's inbox from Roberts-Smith's legal team a few days later.

Emma had revealed in a sworn statement in another court proceeding that Roberts-Smith had told her to lie to support the falsehood that he had been temporarily separated from her three years earlier when he'd begun his affair with Amanda. But as with the news of Dawson's PAP notice victory, any high point was quickly swamped with bad tidings.

Emma was still rebuffing our efforts to make contact. She might have busted up with the Victoria Cross recipient and been distressed by photos of him holding hands with his lawyer, but Emma Roberts-Smith was no friend to us.

In contrast, her husband still had his best mates to count on. There was every indication Vincent Jelovic would stay loyal to the war hero, not only because of their long friendship but because we suspected he was also implicated in the death of Ali Jan. Neil Browning was similarly bound to Roberts-Smith through friendship and alleged involvement in the Easter Sunday murders.

Roberts-Smith's employer, Kerry Stokes, was also showing no signs of walking away from his senior executive. The billionaire media mogul was still lending Roberts-Smith the funds to go to legal war. In return, the war hero had given his Victoria Cross medal, worth an estimated $2 million, as collateral. Stokes' newspaper, the *West Australian*, was also backing Roberts-Smith.

The seeming strength of the war hero's position and the minefield we had to walk through to secure a legal victory was why Peter Bartlett had sent O'Brien a letter with an offer to settle the case and avoid going to trial.

If Roberts-Smith dropped his defamation proceedings, Bartlett told O'Brien that the newspapers wouldn't pursue him for our vast and still-growing legal costs. Bartlett had tried to exude confidence in his letter, highlighting how the release of the redacted Brereton Report had vindicated our journalism and that access to the PAP notice would help us build an already powerful truth defence.

I knew it would be read, and probably scoffed at, by Roberts-Smith, so Bartlett included a line that made it clear that Masters and I weren't afraid of going all the way.

'We wish to make this plain: Nick McKenzie and Chris Masters are eager to see this matter play out at trial,' Bartlett had written at my urging.

The truth was that I was less than eager to see the matter proceed, at least not while such ambiguity surrounded the question of whether we could get our key witnesses into court, and to testify honestly.

Andrew Hastie was one of the few potential witnesses willing to walk into court, but even he appeared to be getting cold feet. I'd reassured him that our case was progressing slowly and surely, and appearing on behalf of me and Masters wouldn't blow up his political career, but I could tell he found my words hollow.

Now it was me who sent him a Bible quote. It was the same message he had sent me months before: 'Be on your guard; stand firm in the faith; be courageous; be strong.'

Hastie hadn't responded.

I wasn't religious, but I'd taken to whispering that line to myself when I felt a panic attack closing in. It wasn't faith in any god that I was clinging to. It was faith in the truth. This was why I believed Roberts-Smith had powerful reasons to walk away from the case and use our offer to do so in a blaze of PR.

If we lost the case because Andrews and other key eyewitnesses were no-shows at the trial, I would lose my career. Even if Roberts-Smith was triumphant, police could still pick over the information aired during our trial to attempt to strengthen their own case.

While Andrews wasn't helping us, I'd heard from multiple sources he had agreed to help the federal police. While I doubted our capacity to win in court, I had no doubt that Andrews and Person 66 were telling the authorities the truth about being blooded.

Bartlett had spelled out Roberts-Smith's predicament in his letter to O'Brien, writing that the federal police and OSI would welcome a defamation trial as it would serve as a prosecution 'dry run' in the event Roberts-Smith was ever charged.

'We would have thought that your client could materially benefit from focusing on the criminal processes rather than the costly and heavily involved civil matter, which we plan to ramp up in intensity in the coming weeks and months,' Bartlett's offer of settlement had concluded.

It had taken O'Brien three weeks to send back Roberts-Smith's response. His letter contained just four paragraphs. It began with a slight. 'Thank you for your judgmental letter.' He then stated that his client rejected the offer to reach a settlement.

In doing so, the letter had bluntly highlighted what was also my chief concern: that Andrews and Person 66 would not support our case against Roberts-Smith 'for fear of self-incrimination'. Roberts-Smith's legal team was 'convinced' his 'evidence will be accepted as credible, corroborated and consistent'.

'If so, he must succeed,' O'Brien wrote. The letter also aimed a pointed barb at me and Masters. I wondered if it was Roberts-Smith who had sought its inclusion. The letter acidly observed the reaching of a 'consensus' on one of the points made by Bartlett in his letter. O'Brien had written: 'Roberts-Smith, like Nick McKenzie and Chris Masters, is eager to see this matter play out at trial.'

* * *

My phone lit up with Levitan's name. Seeing it usually triggered a pang of anxiety. We spoke to each other at least twice a day, sometimes more. In most weeks over the past two years, news had arrived that was in some way consequential, be it bad or good.

I'd sought advice from a retired public prosecutor about dealing with these highs and lows. 'A trial is like a tennis match,' he'd told me. 'You'll gain and lose witnesses in the lead-up. Evidence you thought strong will melt away but you'll find new leads as well. Your heart will be in your mouth every other day. But it's not won on points or even sets. You must have it in you to last the distance.'

It felt like we had already played a few full-length matches, but December 2020 brought more twists and turns and some devastating news. *The Guardian* published two pictures it said were supplied by a freelance reporter I knew was close to Roberts-Smith. The pictures featured two SAS soldiers skylarking in the Fat Lady's Arms with the prosthetic leg of the insurgent allegedly executed by Roberts-Smith on Easter Sunday. Their faces were blurred, yet one of my sources called me up within minutes of the article being posted.

'It's Tilley and Simkin,' my source said.

Rumours had been circulating for months about the existence of hundreds of photos depicting dozens of SAS soldiers and officers at the same Tarin Kowt military base bar also posing with the leg. Why were these specific pictures leaked and published? I suspected it was because both men were slated as potential witnesses in our matter.

I emailed the freelance reporter but he refused to answer questions about why he'd singled out two SAS soldiers known to be prepared to testify against Roberts-Smith.

Two weeks after *The Guardian*'s article, the *Daily Mail* took up the story. It ran the same photo but also wrote that both Tilley and Simkin were 'facing the sack' from the SAS. The assertion was false. Tilley had in fact been recommended for promotion by the Brereton Inquiry for his bravery in exposing alleged war crimes.

That was not the devastating news, though. 'What is it, mate?' I asked Levitan, fearing a fresh article aimed at smearing our witnesses may have been published. I could tell from his voice he was shaken.

'It's Dawson. He was getting headaches in court so he had a scan. He has a brain tumour. It looks pretty bad. He has to have urgent surgery.'

He paused. 'It's not looking good.'

After I hung up the phone, I closed my eyes, resisting the urge to cry.

Weeks before, I'd watched Sandy Dawson on his feet in court, an Errol Flynn in barrister's robes and a vision of colour and life. It was his flawless advocacy that had won us the right to amend our truth defence and to access Roberts-Smith's PAP notice. Both courtroom wins had saved us from near-certain defeat at the trial. But what were all of Dawson's efforts really for? Was the looming trial no more than an insane piece of theatre?

A brilliant man in his prime was now facing the fight of his life. I couldn't stop thinking about him and his family.

I also continued to obsess about the situation I'd found myself in. Was my desire to prove our reporting correct just about my ego? I remembered a friend of mine, a barrister, telling me how defamation cases rarely achieved anything that resembled justice. The litigant who claimed their good name had been slandered invariably muddied their reputation even more by going to trial, while the defendant could spend millions trying to prove an issue that would have long ago faded from memory had the case never been brought. It was usually not the stuff of life and death.

The truth was, had Roberts-Smith never sued me, our stories would have been long forgotten as a footnote to a war hero's glittering corporate career within Kerry Stokes' media empire. By launching the defamation action and refusing to settle the case, Roberts-Smith had forced us to fight him in the defamation trial of the century.

My mind still whirred. Our case wasn't without real meaning. We were arguing that innocent Afghans had been murdered and that Roberts-Smith was one of the greatest liars in Australian history rather than a modern embodiment of the legend of the Anzacs. We were fighting for truth in war.

A victory in court by two journalists wasn't going to bring tangible justice to the wife and children of Ali Jan. That could only come with a police inquiry and eventual prosecution. Yet, if we won, our case would help police and prosecutors gather and assess evidence. It provided a path to justice. Sandy Dawson had helped give us a fighting chance of holding to account a man I believed to be one of Australia's most notorious war criminals.

As I opened my phone to text Dawson, I scrolled up through my previous messages. 'Bravo today Sandy. You killed it. Really fantastic,' I'd written after I'd watched him jousting with Bruce McClintock and Arthur Moses. 'Gosh you're good.'

I typed my message slowly: 'Hi Sandy, not sure when you'll get this but I'm thinking of you. I know you'll get through it because you're bloody incredible. I'm giving the legal team grief as always. I know you wouldn't have it any other way! Nick McK.'

I then called Dawson's junior, Lyndelle Barnett. Before either of us spoke, I heard her quietly crying.

CHAPTER 39

BURIED TREASURE,
FILES AND PHOTOS

February 2021

Anxiety-inducing adrenalin surged through my stomach as I double-clicked on the folder. Hundreds of thumbnail images appeared. I double-clicked on the first photo thumbnail, and an image filled my screen. It was of Ben Roberts-Smith's patrol team resting in dappled shade on the edge of a cornfield. I then clicked on the next image.

The swirling mix of excitement and nausea was familiar. I'd felt much the same before a football match when I was a teenager. I was an ordinary footballer, but what I lacked in skill I'd tried to make up for in determination and preparation. I'd spend hours by myself at my local park in the days leading up to each Saturday-morning game, kicking and running until it was dark. Even with all my pre-game work, I couldn't shake the anxiety that grew until the opening bounce. Then, I would just go as hard as I could all game, free of nerves. In my final two seasons I was knocked out twice, broke my nose and spent two days in hospital with severe concussion, all in the service of a most unremarkable football career.

As a cadet journalist, I applied the same exhaustive approach to work to try to stave off the fear of failure. I broke big and high-risk stories that brought me more success than I'd ever envisaged, but which also led to searing scrutiny in defamation cases and from rival publications. Now, fifteen years into my career, I was still trying to outrun that pang I felt every morning that told me I needed to do more, achieve more, be more.

The approaching trial had brought this fear of finally being exposed as a fraud into sharp relief, and was the backdrop to that familiar, deep-in-the-guts queasiness I felt as I began my digital deep dive, hoping desperately it might deliver something, anything, for my legal team to use.

The confidential source who had supplied the files told me they comprised the contents of USBs that Roberts-Smith had buried in the backyard of his Sunshine Coast home a year earlier. If he was hiding the USBs, he must be doing it for a reason. There had to be something on the devices he didn't want discovered.

These were the same USBs Emma Roberts-Smith and her best friend had copied and then reburied. The copied contents had then been covertly seized by the federal police war crimes taskforce. Detectives had also secured evidence showing Roberts-Smith had later retrieved the USBs and taken them away, presumably to his new bachelor pad, unaware they had already been discovered by his estranged wife and federal agents.

The war hero also had no idea that a source had provided them to me.

With our key witnesses still non-committal and Sandy
Dawson fighting for his life, we needed a breakthrough.
Maybe, just maybe, the pictures on the buried USBs would
provide it.

Within weeks, Roberts-Smith would be the first witness
in a trial expected to last months. His legal team was
oozing confidence while ours was without its captain.
Sandy Dawson's diagnosis had hit everyone hard, and he
now had an even bigger battle on his hands.

But we couldn't stop. We had to keep preparing. The
most urgent task was the search for a new senior counsel
to lead our defence. The person we landed on would be
the chief advocate for our case in front of Justice Besanko,
responsible for signing off on all major legal strategies and
also for grilling Roberts-Smith along with several dozen
SAS soldiers all trained in resisting interrogation.

My earliest choice was a young senior counsel, David
McClure, not only because he was said to be a razor-sharp
emerging star of the Sydney bar, but because he had served
in Afghanistan as a special forces officer. McClure would
be able to speak the jargon of witnesses and would not be
cowed by decorated veterans.

'Too late,' Peter Bartlett told me when I mentioned his
name. McClure had only months earlier been appointed
by the Commonwealth Director of Public Prosecutions
(CDPP) to lead any courtroom prosecution of Roberts-
Smith. The prospect of Roberts-Smith being charged had
been an unknown but as the defamation trial drew closer
the deafening silence from the CDPP and the federal police
made it clear the authorities wouldn't act until our matter
was decided.

Masters and I were being sent into a minefield. If we
won, the Commonwealth might consider charging Ben

Roberts-Smith. If we lost, we'd be blown up, along with any chance of a prosecution.

Bartlett suggested various commercial law barristers, the type of silks who charged $20,000 a day to represent magnates and multinationals. While ours was a defamation case on paper, it was actually more like a murder prosecution without a jury. I wanted a criminal law barrister, someone who had defended or prosecuted serial killers and gangsters. Ideally, they would have done both for both. I suggested the name Mark Tedeschi, a veteran prosecutor renowned for his aggression and ability to persuade juries of an accused's guilt.

'He'll alienate Besanko,' said Bartlett. The judge already had to put up with Arthur Moses and Bruce McClintock. The paddock couldn't fit a third bull.

'Nic Owens is our man,' Bartlett told me after a few more days of searching. 'He's young but he's brilliant.'

I immediately googled the name, wary. Bartlett was a blueblood of the law, who I thought leaned towards barristers who enjoyed golf and first-class lounges as much as he did. This could pay handsome dividends in the right legal matter, but the Roberts-Smith case was in a league of its own.

Nicholas Owens was a commercial silk in his forties with a mixed law practice, minimal public profile and an impeccable résumé. He'd won every award at Adelaide University Law School, studied at Harvard, worked for a governor-general and the chief justice of the High Court and, after a brief stint at a New York corporate law firm, joined the New South Wales bar.

On the day of the September 11 2001 terror attacks that would lead to Roberts-Smith's deployment to Afghanistan, Owens was in the offices of Ivy League law firm Sullivan

& Cromwell, a few blocks from the World Trade Center. He raced to an underground carpark to take shelter with his fellow junior lawyers.

Owens was appointed silk after working as a junior for some of Sydney's finest senior counsel (SC), joining a small chambers on the fifth floor of St James Hall with just five barristers, all of whom were SCs and recognised as leaders in their areas of legal advocacy.

Owens would have faced off in court with many businessmen in suits and ties, but we were accusing Roberts-Smith of punching a woman and murdering multiple people. Owens hadn't appeared in a single criminal case or a defamation hearing.

I called around the senior barristers I knew in Sydney. Each of them said the same thing: 'You must get Owens.'

Geoffrey Watson SC, a delightful and mischievous barrister, was effusive in his praise. 'He talks quietly but I've never seen a young barrister be so incisive with so few words,' he said of Owens. 'They call him whispering death.'

I liked the sound of that. If he was as good as the hype, he might be just the silk we needed.

* * *

I clicked on more thumbnails. One photo that filled my screen was of Roberts-Smith staring at me, the hint of a smile on his camouflage paint–smeared face.

I doubted he or any of his patrol team members would have been foolish enough to photograph explicit evidence of a war crime, but I'd reasoned the photos might still provide clues. The metadata of the photos included time and location stamps.

There was another key reason the photos could be important. If any of them related to missions relevant to the defamation case, Roberts-Smith was facing strict court orders to pass them to my lawyers. If he hadn't done so, it could suggest he was covering up potential evidence in breach of his court obligations. Not a smoking gun, but a potentially powerful blow to his credibility. In the absence of committed witnesses, I was focusing on finding anything that could expose the real Roberts-Smith.

One new avenue of inquiry came about via several anonymous emails sent to Roberts-Smith's ex-lover Amanda from a false email address. I assumed Roberts-Smith was the sender, not only because the emails appeared designed to advance his interests, but also because the language used in them was similar to the other emails I suspected he had sent. Anonymous threats seemed his modus operandi. I had no proof, but I was convinced he was behind the anonymous emails about Simkin that led to the police raid.

The emails to Amanda were from 2018 and appeared designed to scare her off from contacting Roberts-Smith and into staying silent. Whoever had sent them had ensured their identity was obscured. But whoever it was had made a mistake. They hadn't completely covered their tracks. The emails had left small digital clues that led to a name: Danielle Scott. I'd already heard it before, via other sources. She was Emma Roberts-Smith's best friend.

In making inquiries about Danielle, I'd learnt something else. The federal police had already been in contact with her, having discovered that she'd supplied Roberts-Smith with several burner phone sim cards she'd registered in her own name.

I made a mental note to call Dean Levitan and ask him to add Danielle Scott to our subpoena list as well as the major phone companies who sold pre-paid sim cards.

Subpoenas that required a person to hand over documents or testify had emerged as a potential lifeline in our case. Ignore a subpoena and a person could be charged.

My hope was that if we called possible witnesses and explained we had little choice but to force them into court to explain their role in Roberts-Smith's conduct, they might see it in their best interests to help us willingly. At the very least, their lawyers might engage with us.

Our approaches were yet to yield any fruit, but perhaps Danielle Scott was the way in. My sources had told me she'd begun cooperating with the federal police since helping to dig up the USBs. This suggested she was no longer in the Roberts-Smith camp, even if he had directed her to send emails to Amanda using an alias.

Over time, I'd become a lightning rod for sources willing to help us in our case. There was no shortage of people who'd had adverse experiences with Roberts-Smith, from soldiers to colleagues at Seven. These sources had not only been left shaken by various interactions with Roberts-Smith, the wounds had cut so deeply they'd picked up the phone to a reporter they didn't know. Once I'd assured them I'd go to jail before revealing their identities, some of these same informants had opened up.

It wasn't only men, including hardened Afghan veterans, with stories to tell, but young women who'd felt bullied or belittled by the war hero. Their stories were linked by a common thread. Roberts-Smith's sense of entitlement meant that if he didn't get his way, he was prone to vicious outbursts and demeaning put-downs. When things went wrong in Roberts-Smith's world, everyone but him was always to blame.

This dynamic was evident in recordings leaked to me by one source who had secretly taped Roberts-Smith while the war hero confided in him. There was an irony in this betrayal. Roberts-Smith had covertly taped his former SAS comrade Keith Nueling back in 2018, when he suspected the soldier had turned against him. Now, someone had played the same trick on Roberts-Smith.

Listening to Roberts-Smith talk gave me a deeper sense of a man I'd never met. He sounded fiercely determined, intensely self-absorbed and viciously vengeful. And very, very mean.

Few were spared. Roberts-Smith criticised everyone. His fellow executives at Seven were incompetent. The staff under his command were conniving or weak, or both. Women were not pretty enough to be on television. Politicians and those in the SAS who had sought to undermine him were cowards now firmly in his sights.

The only person Roberts-Smith spoke highly of besides himself was Kerry Stokes. 'I talk to Kerry about life,' he'd said.

His greatest hate was reserved for me and Chris Masters. On the tape he made it clear he would do anything to bring us down.

* * *

Forty or so photos in, my eyes were immediately drawn to a name: 'W108'. It had to refer to 'Whiskey 108', the compound central to the Easter Sunday execution allegations.

Bingo.

The photo depicted a section of a muddy, bomb-
damaged compound. It was almost certainly the site
where, according to our case theory, two Afghan men were
discovered in a tunnel, detained and separately executed by
Roberts-Smith and Jason Andrews. I checked the metadata
of the photo. It was taken on 12 April 2009. There was
no doubt this photo should have been handed over by
Roberts-Smith to our lawyers.

I forged on, clicking on files until I came across a video
taken by a military drone with a classified marking. It may
have been illegal for any ex-soldier to possess this video, let
alone bury it in their backyard. It was potentially unlawful
for me to have possession of it. I made a mental note to
contact the federal police.

Another hundred or so photos in, I froze as Roberts-
Smith's face appeared. He was in a picture with
Commander Ismail. The metadata revealed it was taken in
early October 2012, well after Roberts-Smith was claiming
Ismail had been sacked. If he was still serving with the SAS
in October, the allegation that he had executed someone
on Roberts-Smith's orders might still be in play. This was
another photo that not only should have been handed
over to our legal team but contained potentially critical
evidence.

The next photo that seized my attention was of a patrol-
room door. On the door was a board bearing the names
of Roberts-Smith and his patrol members. However, the
name of one of the patrol team members was listed as
'rookie fuck'. Another potentially important clue.

I knew Roberts-Smith's witnesses would be claiming in
court that the terminology 'blooding the rookie' had never
been used. According to these witnesses, not only was no
one ever 'blooded', but junior soldiers had never even been

referred to as 'rookies'. The photo of the patrol-room door suggested this latter denial was false.

Scanning onwards, another image appeared on the screen. I swore under my breath. A dead Afghan man was lying on his back. On his bloodied face, someone had placed two SAS souvenir coins on his eyes. It looked like a trophy kill. While the time stamp suggested it wasn't from one of the missions that formed part of our defence, it was still from a mission in which Roberts-Smith's patrol team had been accused by others in the SAS of war crimes.

It may not help our case, but it did provide a powerful illustration about what had gone wrong in Afghanistan. The Geneva Conventions required soldiers to treat the dead with respect, not dress their corpses up for photos.

It wasn't the only file on the USB that pointed to an off-the-books photo and video industry that was running in breach of official protocols. I found a video that had been edited into a short home movie, with snippets of photos and drone vision from the missions Roberts-Smith undertook with his patrol team in 2010. The video featured the patrol team members from that year: Jason Andrews, Neil Browning, Ben Roberts-Smith and Brian McMurray. The markings on parts of the video suggested it, too, had been created using classified vision unlawfully obtained by whoever had edited the film. I turned the volume up to hear the soundtrack. It was 'Scotland the Brave'. My mind immediately turned to Browning, a Scotsman and Roberts-Smith's former patrol team commander, who was set to play a key role in the upcoming trial.

Not only did this video raise questions about the unauthorised exchange of potentially classified footage, but it also suggested Roberts-Smith had been gathering photos and videos from his witnesses. Witnesses were not meant to be exchanging information because it could taint their evidence.

A sub-folder from the USB material suggested another key witness for Roberts-Smith – an ex-soldier from New Zealand called Tim Douglass – had curated an album on one of the buried USBs. This folder contained hundreds of photos of Douglass in Afghanistan and Australia. Our case alleged that Douglass was the soldier who had discovered the two men – including the man with the prosthetic leg – in the tunnel on Easter Sunday and handed them over to Roberts-Smith. Douglass was being called as a witness by Roberts-Smith to state that he'd found the tunnel empty. Had Douglass also shared a USB with Roberts-Smith to help him prepare for the trial? Were they workshopping their evidence?

After another hour spent scouring the photos from the Douglass folder, I came across a series of party pictures from the Fat Lady's Arms. I immediately recognised the photo of Tilley and Simkin with the prosthetic leg. It was the photo that had been leaked to *The Guardian* and the *Daily Mail* in an effort to smear the pair. Was the leaker of this picture Roberts-Smith or the person who sent him the USBs?

If so, they were sitting on hundreds of other damaging photos from the bar the SAS would assemble at after missions in Oruzgan.

The leg also appeared in several dozen photos taken at an SAS fancy dress party hosted at the Fat Lady's Arms. Scanning through these shots, my eyes were drawn to a soldier wearing a pointed white hood and robe, the uniform of the American white supremacist group, the Ku Klux Klan.

His face was obscured by the hood, leaving only his intense eyes. In one of the pictures, this pretend KKK member was also holding forth a noose and a flaming cross while surrounded by two dozen other soldiers. In the back row, I picked out Roberts-Smith's grinning face, his arm held aloft triumphantly.

Other photos showed Roberts-Smith appearing to cheer on another soldier as he drank from the prosthetic leg taken from the man who, on both our and his own account, the war hero had killed. War crime or not, it wasn't pretty.

The pictures were at odds with claims made by Roberts-Smith's barrister Bruce McClintock, who had argued in a pre-trial hearing that his client was utterly disgusted by the use of the leg as a drinking vessel. McClintock had stressed in court that Roberts-Smith 'never drank from that thing ... because he thought it was disgusting to souvenir a body part, albeit an artificial one from someone who had been killed in action.'

Roberts-Smith didn't look at all disgusted in the photos. He looked positively gleeful, fist-pumping as a soldier swilled beer from the leg. In a second photo, Roberts-Smith was grinning, with his arm draped around another soldier wearing a cowboy hat who was posing with the leg.

After three hours of scrolling, I had counted dozens of photos and several videos that Roberts-Smith should have disclosed. The files didn't only reveal scenes from Afghanistan. One of them was a video of Amanda entering a cab outside a Brisbane hospital. I immediately recalled Amanda telling me that Roberts-Smith had warned her he could have her tracked if she ever crossed him.

Not only had Roberts-Smith been concealing this photographic evidence instead of handing it over, the pictures raised questions about both his behaviour and that of his key witnesses. The pictures also told a story about the SAS's R and R on the base at Tarin Kowt.

The Fat Lady's Arms had been constructed by some handy soldiers as a place where members of the SAS could decompress over a few beers after an arduous mission, despite a rule banning alcohol. The bar wasn't authorised by senior command but there was no way it would have been a secret to any half-smart officer on base.

Having a beer hardly seemed a hanging offence, but in some of these photos the soldiers looked blind drunk, were urinating in public and simulating oral sex on each other.

Was the bar one of an assortment of nods and winks to a regiment whose leash was becoming longer and longer? Why did no one say anything when their comrades desecrated a dead man, used classified vision to make a home movie, or dressed as a white supremacist in a country where Western soldiers were already regarded with intense suspicion?

I'd previously seen a photo taken by an official army photographer of Roberts-Smith wearing a Christian crusader cross patch on his uniform while on patrol in Afghanistan. On one view, it was a harmless piece of iconography but, in a Muslim country, it could also risk inflaming the local population.

All of these images brought to mind a letter Andrew Hastie had given me recently. He had written to the former head of the special forces, Major General Jeff Sengelman, five years earlier. The first time I read the letter, I thought it was a little puritan. Hastie was equating 'binge drinking and other reckless behaviour' with a betrayal of the 'moral obligation' meant to be upheld by those touted as the finest soldiers in the country.

But maybe Hastie was right. Did a small number of soldiers in the SAS believe they were not only entitled to a longer leash, but were no longer tethered to any moral code at all?

At that moment, I resolved to do another *60 Minutes* program. Australians deserved to see what was going on in their name during and after missions. The pictures could tell some of the story, and audio recordings could be broadcast in a manner that allowed me to protect my source's voice.

Having been placed on a national pedestal as an exemplar of public service, leadership, bravery and fatherhood, Roberts-Smith was still promoting himself as the gracious and noble representation of a country at war. That was just 'Brand BRS'. The real story spoke of a man taken to burying evidence in his backyard and who railed and plotted against his enemies like King Lear in a storm.

CHAPTER 40

'YOU WEAK DOG'

March 2021

Emma Roberts-Smith wasn't sure if she felt sick because she was mildly hungover or because of the meeting that was about to occur. Perhaps it was both.

The previous twelve months had been among the hardest of her life. As Ben Roberts-Smith's wife, she'd been his dutiful sidekick as he'd found fame and fortune, only to see their lives plunged into controversy. The whole experience had been a struggle, but they'd forged on together and she'd found joy in their children.

For the last year, however, Emma had been alone, a single mum with no job negotiating over assets and parenting rights with a war hero turned highly paid corporate executive used to getting what he wanted. It was divorce lawyers at ten paces, curt emails and snide remarks during pick-ups and drop-offs.

And yet, Emma was finally free. To do what, beyond being a mum, she wasn't quite sure. She knew it involved finding financial independence and, hopefully, a sense of contentment in herself that had eluded her during much of her marriage. Her hope for a future without media scrutiny seemed unlikely, though, especially given the meeting that was about to take place.

Her best friend, Danielle Scott, had convinced her to sit down with me, Dean Levitan and Peter Bartlett.

We had obtained a statement Emma had made in a separate proceeding that revealed how Roberts-Smith had pressured her to lie about being separated when he'd had his affair with Amanda.

I had also made contact with her. 'Dear Emma,' I'd texted. 'I'm sorry for troubling you and I hope you are holding up ok. I'm sorry that you are stuck in the midst of all of this. It can't be easy. If you ever want to talk – confidentially – please let me know … if this message and reaching out causes stress, I'm truly sorry.'

I didn't sound to Emma like the devil that Roberts-Smith had conjured up. 'You might as well meet him and his lawyers. If they are going to subpoena you anyway, you can find out what they want,' Danielle had told her.

Throughout it all, Danielle Scott had been a source of stability, support and black humour for her friend. Before Emma separated from Roberts-Smith, and even though Danielle had never much liked him, she'd helped Ben deal with various crises. She'd bought him burner phones; sent emails from an anonymous account to Amanda that Roberts-Smith had dictated; and as an ex-postal system worker, offered advice to the ex-soldier about whether letters could be tracked back to the sender. Danielle didn't know the true reason for Roberts-Smith's sudden interest in the mail system. In reality he was planning to send anonymous letters to an old SAS friend who had turned hostile, Brian McMurray. The person who'd placed the letters in a postbox over the state border was Roberts-Smith's private eye, John McLeod.

Emma had discovered her husband's letters plot after I revealed the anonymous threat-by-post scandal in the *Sydney Morning Herald* and *The Age* in 2018.

'What the fuck have you done,' Emma had asked Roberts-Smith. He responded that he'd 'written the letters, saved them on a USB, printed them at the Seven office, sealed them in the envelopes and given them to John McLeod to post'.

I also revealed in my reports that the police had been called in, but their investigation quickly stalled. No arrests, no raids, just an article that raised suspicions but little else.

After the separation, Danielle had only one project. She devoted her energy to keeping Emma's head above water.

'I reckon we put our heads together and we get you as financially sufficient in the next two to three years as possible,' she wrote to her friend. 'And it doesn't matter what happens to him or what jail cell he rots in.'

With her blinkers removed, Emma now felt detached towards Roberts-Smith in a way she'd never thought possible. She observed him from a distance as something of a sad oddity, a foreign object that cared only for itself. In her darker moments, she confided in Danielle that he was nothing but a 'lying, cheating' excuse for a human.

Between the two of them, Emma and Danielle knew enough about Roberts-Smith's psyche to predict his next steps. He was a narcissist who had to have the last word, a man who both loved and loathed himself but who lacked the insight to know why.

They guessed it was Roberts-Smith who had leaked the photos of two of the potentially opposing witnesses, Tilley and Simkin. Emma made her own direct inquiries – when

Roberts-Smith came by their former matrimonial home, she said to him: 'Nice article in *The Guardian*.'

He replied, 'Fuck them. They can take some of the pressure for once.'

It was Danielle who instructed Emma to photograph the rock and earth under the garden hose after Roberts-Smith emailed her one morning to say he was coming over to gather some of his remaining personal items. The 'before' shot revealed the ground undisturbed prior to Roberts-Smith's arrival. In the 'after' photo, the rock had been moved and dirt disturbed, exposing the hole where the USBs had been buried.

She warned Emma to stay clear of Roberts-Smith's ship in the event it sank. In reply, Emma texted Danielle: '#titanic'.

Despite the banter, Emma didn't want her ex-husband to lose everything. He was the father of her children. If he won the defamation case and stayed out of jail, life would be simpler – the school fees would be paid and her girls would face fewer questions from their friends.

It was Roberts-Smith who launched the defamation case and asked Emma to back him up by lying. He'd picked the fight with me and Masters and walked away from an offer of settlement. She wasn't going to go to jail for perjury for him. Maybe the old Emma would have, but she would no longer be defined by her ex-husband.

This is why she decided to change her name to 'Emma Roberts'. A small thing perhaps, but it was a statement of quiet resolve nonetheless. And it was why she agreed to meet me.

* * *

Once he made up his mind, John McLeod wouldn't be changing it. He knew where he had to go on this particular day and he wouldn't back out. The broad-chested ex-cop eased his car onto the road, scanned behind him for anyone following and began to drive towards an office he knew well. On the passenger seat next to him was evidence of a possible crime he had unknowingly helped to commit.

Three years had passed since Ben Roberts-Smith asked him to pop some letters in a postbox. It had never sat right with him. It wasn't what a mate did to a mate, at least not in McLeod's world. Before they'd stopped talking, the ex-cop turned private investigator had done Roberts-Smith a host of favours, from the mundane to the more curious.

He'd filmed a woman leaving a hospital, eavesdropped on guests at Roberts-Smith's house while posing as a barman and sent a bunch of anonymous emails written by Roberts-Smith that concerned an SAS soldier called Nick Simkin. Roberts-Smith had told him that Simkin was trafficking assault rifles.

McLeod was initially happy – helping to get guns off the street was noble stuff. This was reflected in the address McLeod chose for the anonymous email account used to contact the federal police, journalists and a politician. Blowerw2 stood for whistleblower, which was what McLeod thought Roberts-Smith was at the time.

Not anymore.

Three years before, he'd met Roberts-Smith at a Bunnings hardware store. The war hero passed him a blue folder containing four sealed envelopes, along with scraps of paper bearing unfamiliar names.

'I'm under the pump, mate,' Roberts-Smith told him.

That night, Roberts-Smith called with an address McLeod was to write on the envelopes, along with the names he'd earlier handed over. It was the address for the SAS barracks in Perth. McLeod posted two of the letters a short time later.

A few days after that, Roberts-Smith asked McLeod to meet him in Brisbane. As McLeod approached the war hero, Roberts-Smith barked: 'No phones, no phones, no phones.'

After McLeod put his phone in his car, Roberts-Smith quizzed him about whether he'd read the story I'd written revealing how threatening, anonymous letters had been mailed to an SAS soldier in Perth. 'They're not f***ing threats, it was just a touch-up,' he'd told the ex-cop.

This was when the penny finally dropped for McLeod. Roberts-Smith had compromised him.

'[You'd] better get me a f***ing good lawyer,' McLeod told Roberts-Smith, warning him that 'the cover-up was always ten times worse than the offence'.

Roberts-Smith responded by instructing McLeod to take the rap if the police ever twigged he'd sent the anonymous threats. 'Tell them ... you're a supporter of mine and you were sick of the way I was being treated,' Roberts-Smith demanded.

That was when McLeod snapped: 'F*** that, you weak dog.' The private eye then spun around and walked away. He never spoke to Roberts-Smith again.

In the intervening years, the incident had played on his mind, fading but never dying out. It wasn't just the memory that was alive, though. McLeod had kept some of the scraps of paper Roberts-Smith gave him, along with two sealed envelopes that had never been sent and which Roberts-Smith had asked him to destroy. It was this paperwork that was now on the seat next to McLeod as he searched for a parking spot near the offices of the Australian Federal Police.

* * *

Dean Levitan thought back to advice I'd given him. Something about equating a trial to a tennis match. Witnesses would come and go, new leads would be found, and so on. He'd found the analogy trite at the time but, ever the diplomat, he'd acknowledged it as sage and changed the topic.

After three years, he'd learnt how to manage me. He knew I was relentless, an open-all-hours store of ideas, demands, complaints and energy. As far as he was concerned, dealing with me was the tennis match. It was exhausting.

He'd learnt to pick his battles and, when necessary, firmly shut down my wilder ideas. Of late, one of them involved seeking a court order to enable us to arrive at Roberts-Smith's Brisbane apartment unannounced to search for items he had failed to hand over, in potential breach of his court obligations. The idea was sparked by the discovery of the buried USBs.

Levitan knew I'd never stop digging, like a runner in a never-ending marathon. Where new leads could be found, there was hope for the court case, even for the side without committed key witnesses. This was the upside of my relentless nature. Among the chaff, wheat also grew. He saw how I found fresh witnesses, new allegations and more evidence.

At first Levitan had found my intensity intimidating, then grating, but he'd come to understand and, mostly, appreciate that, when it wasn't annoying, my passion could be contagious. I believed with every fibre of my body that Roberts-Smith had done what he'd been accused of doing. It wasn't based on gut instinct, but exhaustive journalism conducted over many years. I would remind the barristers they were fighting for Ali Jan's children as well as the entire journalistic profession, praising them for courtroom wins, attacking them for perceived missteps and urging them to fight harder. If they were to fail in court, I'd told Levitan often that I would hang up my journalistic boots.

My faith in the ability of journalism to do what it was meant to do – hold the powerful to account – was on trial. But I wasn't the only one with a lot to lose. Levitan had in turn discovered that his faith in the law as a vehicle for justice was also in the dock. Backed by a billionaire, Roberts-Smith had used the law to shut down his critics, first with legal threats and later by launching the defamation case. With the trial approaching, he'd flouted his legal obligations in failing to hand over the USB photos and other key documents.

We didn't back down. I fought back with my own weapon: media revelations. *60 Minutes* aired a program about the classified information and photos of questionable conduct buried in Roberts-Smith's backyard. The program also linked the threatening letters sent to McMurray directly to Roberts-Smith.

In response, the federal police announced fresh investigations into Roberts-Smith's handling of classified files and possible witness intimidation. The fresh scandal prompted the ex-soldier to release a statement denying the allegations outright.

'The allegation that he threatened any witness or potential witness ... to stop them giving evidence is false. The allegations that he buried USBs in his backyard is false. This simply did not happen.'

Roberts-Smith's lawyers had also stepped up pressure on me in the Federal Court. Barrister Arthur Moses used a pre-trial hearing to accuse me of 'potential unlawful conduct' by obtaining classified images stored on the USBs his own client had been withholding. It was a ridiculous allegation. After being provided with the USB material by a confidential source, I had contacted the AFP to alert them.

A day after Moses' sniping in court, Bruce McClintock launched a second attack, claiming that I was responsible for 'procuring' the federal police's interest in the war hero. 'My client imperatively wants to get into the witness box and say what happened in Afghanistan. Something that he actually looks forward to,' McClintock told Justice Besanko.

McClintock also savaged Chris Masters' and my defence. It was a house of cards, he said: our witnesses who would not appear or, if they did, would not say what we were counting on. 'We don't know who the respondents [McKenzie and Masters] will be calling in these proceedings. We know the respondents have not actually spoken to a number of people for whom they have put on outlines of evidence. At least in one case we know the person in question says, "No, I'm not going to say it,"' McClintock said.

Levitan knew that beneath the puffery, McClintock was partly correct. Levitan was confident that if Andrews and the other SAS witnesses we were hoping to call to court actually appeared on the stand, there was a chance of proving the allegations of war crimes.

It was getting them to court that was the problem. McClintock not only knew it, he appeared to be goading us about the weakness of our case. No witnesses, no chance.

Roberts-Smith not only had his SAS mates lining up to testify, but the good and the great of Australia still in his corner. McClintock told the court that the former governor-general of Australia, Quentin Bryce, the woman who had pinned the Victoria Cross on Roberts-Smith's chest back in 2011, would be appearing to give character evidence on his behalf. No wonder Team Roberts-Smith was so cocky, his barristers preening in court like peacocks.

In contrast, Nic Owens was quiet and gentlemanly. His advocacy before Justice Besanko was sharp and decisive, but it wasn't evident to me that he was sufficiently fired up or had the measure of Moses and McClintock.

I called Levitan pondering this very point. Was Owens too polite and courteous to take on the legal war machine of a Victoria Cross winner?

Extreme times demanded extreme methods. Levitan had come to realise that he was engaged in a form of guerrilla warfare against an opponent who wouldn't willingly hand over anything that might disadvantage his own case, whatever his legal obligations. Instead, important evidence was being literally unearthed.

He'd listened to me analyse every moment of the case and complain bitterly if I didn't think things were being handled in the way I thought was best. Nic being too polite was one of those complaints. 'Maybe tell Owens you're pissed,' Levitan said to me. 'And tell him why.'

I drafted a text message. 'Nic. I'm deeply disappointed you didn't protect me in court today. You are my advocate. I'm a real person. Yesterday I was falsely accused of criminal conduct. Today I was falsely accused of initiating the police war crimes inquiry. I need you to have my back when it counts. Nick.'

After I read it to Levitan, he said to me: send it.

* * *

Levitan found Nicholas Owens SC something of a complex character. The silk seemed increasingly despondent at the struggle to win the support of key witnesses.

But while Moses and McClintock might be raging bonfires, all colour and light, Owens' cautious, careful style belied a ruthless determination.

'The blue flame burns hottest,' Levitan told me once he'd got Owens' measure.

Before he left the case, Sandy Dawson's pre-trial courtroom wins had delivered Owens legal manna from heaven. The 'potentially affected person' (PAP) notice served on Roberts-Smith by Justice Brereton the year before proved to be a treasure trove of new leads. The document was heavily redacted and could only be viewed in a secure room designed to hold classified information. But when Levitan had first read it, his heart had begun racing.

'You gotta come in and see this,' he told me.

'Oh fuck … oh fuck … oh fuck …' I whispered intermittently after I'd raced to the secure room and started reading. In the document were the names of new and potentially critical SAS eyewitnesses to the events of Easter Sunday.

Within days, Mitchell, Barnett and Owens were also locked up and reading the PAP notice in tense silence. Owens then spent the next few days with his two junior advocates devising a legal strategy built around the new information.

Revising the defence for a third time was a long shot given it was the eve of the trial and any amendments were sure to be fiercely opposed by Roberts-Smith's legal team. But we called for an urgent court hearing before Justice Besanko to argue that the contents of the PAP notice necessitated a ruling that allowed more SAS witnesses to be added to our truth defence.

Owens also argued that three more civilian witnesses should be summonsed to court to cast light on the disputed facts: Emma Roberts-Smith, Danielle Scott and John McLeod. The attempt to add the trio prompted what was by now the inevitable public relations counterattack. *The Daily Telegraph* ran a front-page story smearing McLeod with false claims. Emma's and Danielle's names also appeared in unflattering tabloid articles. It didn't take a genius to wonder who'd encouraged the adverse press.

Roberts-Smith's legal team again arrived in force to convince the judge that the bid to call more witnesses was a last-ditch, eleventh-hour throw of the dice by desperate defendants. In response, Owens firmly impressed upon the judge that the new information was not in fact new at all. Roberts-Smith had known of the contents of the PAP notice ever since Brereton had served it upon him months before. It was only us who'd been in the dark. To disallow the appearance of new witnesses would deny the court potentially critical evidence. We had also decided to withdraw one of the murder allegations made against Roberts-Smith in our initial defence outline, that involved the man killed after Roberts-Smith waded across the river at Darwan.

Levitan also sought to issue a series of subpoenas to uncover information Roberts-Smith wouldn't hand over without a fight. For weeks, I'd been pushing Levitan to subpoena telecommunication companies to hand over any burner phone records subscribed in Danielle Scott's name. It was a long shot.

Owens had not only backed this idea but pursued an aggressive strategy to demand Roberts-Smith deliver his laptop to the court. The hope was that the laptop may hold further photos from Afghanistan or metadata that could cast light on whether it was the war hero's witnesses who had sent him the USBs.

In response, Roberts-Smith's lawyers advised that he had wiped his laptop four days after the *60 Minutes* program that had exposed the hidden USBs. But he had no control over the burner phone records. The telco subpoena uncovered four pre-paid mobile phones subscribed by Danielle Scott and each used for a period of several months. An initial analysis suggested the records were useless. While Levitan suspected the burners had been used by Roberts-Smith to collude with his witnesses, all the records revealed was that whoever was using the phones had been relying on encrypted applications that left no clues about incoming or outgoing numbers, information that could have confirmed the phones were in Roberts-Smith's possession.

'Look harder,' Levitan demanded of one of his younger legal team members. The encrypted applications had left a trail of digital breadcrumbs revealing the location of the phone towers the burners had been near when the encrypted applications were used and the approximate duration of calls.

There was a pattern. The burners had not only been most often used near the cell tower close to Roberts-Smith's house but had bounced off towers at interstate locations that matched Roberts-Smith's travel and holiday movements. The use of the encrypted applications on the phones had also spiked in the hours before and after Roberts-Smith appeared at the Brereton interrogation hearings.

There had also been slip-ups. One of the burner phones was used to make a quick call to an American number. Overseas records linked the number to a name: Neil Browning. It was Roberts-Smith's alleged Easter Sunday accomplice.

* * *

Even before the judge ruled on whether the new Easter Sunday and civilian witnesses could be called, Levitan sensed Owens had won the argument. Roberts-Smith might appear to have the stronger overall case and large sections of the media cheering him on, but Owens hadn't shied away from the fight. He just didn't need to shout in court to make a point.

While wary at first, I had arrived at the same conclusion after I'd needled him about whether he was prepared for the legal fight of his life and if he cared about the case as much as Levitan and his solicitors, me and Masters, and the two barristers who'd worked so closely with Sandy Dawson. For months, Mitchell and Barnett had woken up thinking about the war hero and gone to bed doing the same. Even as he recovered from brain surgery, Dawson had offered advice and encouragement.

The trial itself would begin soon, and it would be Owens alone who would be going head-to-head with Roberts-Smith. The legal team could help prepare him – Mitchell and Barnett had already spent weeks preparing the cross-examination – but once Roberts-Smith hit the witness box and Owens rose to his feet, it would be one man's wits pitted against those of the other. The Harvard-trained lawyer versus a soldier willing and trained to endure excruciating conditions to destroy his enemy.

Owens responded to my query about his commitment to the case with his trademark brevity: 'I can only emphasise that you have my assurance that I am devoting and will devote, my every fibre to ensuring you prevail.' This was all I needed to hear. Willing witnesses or not, Owens was ready to go to war.

CHAPTER 41

THE FIRST BATTLE

June 2021

Ben Roberts-Smith held his chin high and with a taut smile strode through the throng of journalists and photographers. His dark, tailored suit was pressed and flawless, his hair impeccable, and his body language unambiguously confident. This was a man who appeared very much in control.

The war hero had arrived alone. The symbolism was unmistakable. Here was an ex-soldier fighting a rapacious media company to clear his name of smears so shocking that not even a judge's damning denouncement of his journalist persecutors and a multimillion-dollar payout would ever fully clear the taint. But it would help. Roberts-Smith had already told those close to him about how he would spend his multimillion-dollar winnings.

He'd never been in doubt. He may have arrived alone, but Roberts-Smith's small legal army was already assembling on Level 18 of Sydney's Federal Court building. His team comprised eight barristers and lawyers. For the most part they, too, looked confident, exchanging jokes and smiles.

Roberts-Smith's audience for the next few months wasn't only to be Justice Anthony Besanko. The defamation 'trial of the century' would be covered by every media outlet in the country. It would be the journalists and, through them, the Australian public, who Roberts-Smith and his legal team were aiming to win over.

These efforts had begun weeks before, with *The Daily Telegraph* releasing a story that highlighted how Jason Andrews had never spoken to our lawyers and yet was slated as our key witness. The article sought to describe the flimsiness of our planned defence, to make it appear we were on a wing and a prayer. The *Daily Telegraph* also ran an article smearing private investigator John McLeod, falsely implying he'd been paid by Nine and had secretly taped Roberts-Smith. Both claims were false but the message to potential witnesses was unambiguous. Appear for the journalists in court and go down with their sinking legal ship. Or end up in the press, attacked and belittled.

In the days before the trial was due to start, Roberts-Smith's parents released a carefully prepared statement to favourable media outlets. 'The allegations have not only destroyed Ben's life but have affected us every day for the last several years,' it said. 'We never expected that our son would be unfairly attacked in this manner after he served his country in Afghanistan with distinction and risked his life.'

It was published in the *Daily Mail*, along with pictures of Roberts-Smith working out in public. It seemed to me no accident that a photographer had documented the war hero exercising – he'd surely provided the tabloid outlet with advance notice of where he'd be. Midway through his exercise routine, Roberts-Smith had stripped off his singlet, leaving him only wearing a pair of black tights. The photographer duly snapped away.

The article had included a quote the war hero had given, glistening with sweat, muscles rippling. 'I'm feeling good mate, looking forward to finally setting the record straight,' he'd told the *Daily Mail*, whose reporter added that he'd made the comment after he'd finished 'a set of one-legged push-ups'.

The article had also rounded on Roberts-Smith's ex-wife, describing how Emma had 'flipped' sides and would be called 'a "liar" at trial' and accused of 'airing the family's "dirty laundry"'. The *Daily Mail* breathlessly described how Roberts-Smith had also launched a separate legal action against his 'tense' wife to accuse her of improperly accessing his emails via a shared company account. This legal action was doomed to fail, but there was no sense of this in the article, nor did the story cast any light on the reason Roberts-Smith had sued his ex-wife.

The catalyst for this lawsuit was Roberts-Smith's earlier decision to subpoena Emma in our case. Rather than provide documents that undermined her credibility, Emma had answered the subpoena by releasing to the court a document that Neil Browning had emailed to Roberts-Smith in 2018. It contained Browning's detailed defence to the claims of murder on Easter Sunday and exposed the possibility that he and Roberts-Smith had been colluding to defeat the allegations.

The utter dissolution of Emma and Roberts-Smith's relationship was illustrated by the photos published in the *Daily Mail* story. In contrast to her ex-husband, Emma had no advance warning that a paparazzo would be dispatched to photograph her. The shots the *Daily Mail* published were unflattering, showing Emma looking concerned and forlorn.

Her photos were positioned underneath the staged pictures of Roberts-Smith wearing a singlet that barely covered his tattooed and bulging chest and on which was printed the words 'embrace the pain'. The reporter had described Roberts-Smith appearing 'every bit the determined warrior'.

The photos of Emma showed her taking out the bins.

* * *

McClintock opened the case for Roberts-Smith in his typical style. There were no shades of grey, no subtleties at play, to lessen or explain the sheer injustice perpetrated on a hero to whom Australia owed a debt of gratitude. Roberts-Smith was everything Masters and I, and our cast of uncertain witnesses, were not.

He embodied 'courage, devotion to duty, self-sacrifice and perhaps, most important of all, surpassing skill in soldiering'. Roberts-Smith was 'highly organised; disciplined; a leader; resourceful; and exceptionally brave'.

In contrast, McClintock described 'credulous' reporters who had embraced 'dishonest journalism, corrosive jealousy, cowardice and lies'. In doing so, we had spun a 'ridiculous' story and transformed an Australian legend into an 'ostentatious psychopath'.

The SAS witnesses we were hoping to call to court were 'failures as soldiers' driven by 'corrosive jealousy' because of the medals Roberts-Smith had received for bravery they could never emulate. He'd done what his nation had asked of him: kill Taliban insurgents in a chaotic conflict where violence, death and the confusion of battle lay in wait around every compound corner.

'The simple fact is that some who have reported on matters concerning my client have forgotten that fact, the violence of war, in their rush to tear him down,' McClintock said.

As McClintock spoke, the windows to his left provided a view of Sydney's harbour. When it emerged through the grey winter sky, the sun danced on the water. It couldn't be further away from the dust, mud and gunfire of Oruzgan.

* * *

Before Roberts-Smith entered the witness box to deliver his version of events guided by his barrister – known as a witness's evidence-in-chief – Nic Owens was granted a short right of reply. The much younger silk didn't deviate from his style. His task was to tarnish the picture McClintock had painted and he did so with ruthless efficiency.

The case he was intending to argue was diametrically opposed to that which the war hero's barrister was positing. It had nothing to do with split-second battlefield decisions. The evidence, said Owens, would show that Roberts-Smith was complicit in six executions, none of which were carried out in the fog of war. Once an Afghan was in the custody of an Australian soldier, they couldn't be summarily executed.

It mattered not if they were 'the most brutal, vile member of the Taliban imaginable'. The truth was that Roberts-Smith was a ruthless executioner of prisoners. The truth was that Roberts-Smith was a liar. The truth was that a war hero could also be a war criminal.

Where McClintock had spoken for hours, Owens took just fifteen minutes.

* * *

The 42-year-old war hero's sonorous voice filled the courtroom as his large frame filled the witness box. 'I solemnly and sincerely declare and affirm that the evidence I shall give will be the truth, the whole truth and nothing but the truth.' Roberts-Smith had been preparing for this moment for three years.

It wasn't really a moment at all. For the next four days, the famous soldier would have centrestage as McClintock led him through his decorated career and the allegations he said had ruined it.

It began the only place it could: with the Anzacs. 'I have three descendants [who] landed at Gallipoli,' he told the court with sombre gravity. 'I learnt from a very young age the value of service, and that there is, in fact, something much greater than ourselves in relation to the freedom of a country.'

Next, Roberts-Smith impressed on Justice Besanko how, even though every killing he conducted was lawful, some deaths weighed on his mind. 'I saw things in Afghanistan and did things in Afghanistan, like having to engage adolescents, that I am not proud of. And I live with that.'

The point Roberts-Smith was making for the judge was obvious. He was no psychopath, but rather a man with a conscience. 'I did everything that I was supposed to do, and I followed the rules.'

The court and the watching media didn't need reminding of Roberts-Smith's status as Australia's most decorated Afghan veteran, but McClintock stepped him through every medal he had gained, from minor clasps to the Victoria Cross. Battle by brave battle, the barrister was leading him to Tizak.

As he recounted the fight that transformed him into a national icon, Roberts-Smith was telling a story he'd told dozens of times before, sometimes charging up to $20,000 for the privilege. Still, he spoke with a visceral and captivating intensity.

As he did, the courtroom became smaller. Every person watching could feel the bullets hitting the earth and the shadow of death closing in as Roberts-Smith posed the questions that would change his life. He recounted them for the court.

'Could you go home and face their families if you didn't do anything and they were to get injured or killed? Or do you go and potentially get injured or killed yourself?'

With his fellow soldiers pinned down by machine-gun fire, Roberts-Smith had surged forward towards danger, eliminating the enemy with no regard for his own safety.

'The decision that I made was that ... I could die knowing that I've done the right thing by them and their families,' he recalled.

For Roberts-Smith, Tizak not only allowed him to set the character bar as high as it could go in a case that was ultimately about reputation. It also created the motive for those making the false allegations against him: medal envy.

McClintock led him there seamlessly. 'After the Victoria Cross, did you observe a change in attitude towards you?' the barrister asked the war hero.

'Absolutely. It put a target on my back.'

* * *

For four days, Roberts-Smith performed. The slight nerves of his first morning in court, if they were ever there at all, were gone. His self-assurance was stunning. He was gracious to the judge and thanked the court staff for handing him exhibits.

Each major allegation was dismissed confidently, from the claims of executions said to have been raised by men such as Stanton, Person 66, Andrews and Tilley, to the claims of punching a woman and sending threatening letters.

Roberts-Smith conceded some ground on relatively minor matters, such as punching a junior soldier in 2012, but he mostly downplayed these admitted misdemeanours.

None of the most serious of the claims were true.

None of them.

Roberts-Smith maintained he was separated from Emma when he'd begun seeing Amanda. It was her obsession with him, after he'd decided to return to Emma, that spurred her to invent false claims of violence that had in turn been lapped up by me.

The only reason he'd asked a private investigator to film Amanda outside a hospital was because she was probably lying about being pregnant after she'd shown him a positive pregnancy test. He wanted to see for sure if she'd actually had an abortion.

'They're very easy to fake, pregnancy tests, and I had no idea whether she was or she wasn't,' he told the judge.

Emma was also a liar. The USBs were never buried in the back garden, nor dug up by her. He'd simply left them in his desk only to later overlook the need to hand them over to his opponents' lawyers in the legal discovery process.

As Roberts-Smith dismissed and dissected the claims of his detractors, Justice Besanko watched on carefully but impassively. Occasionally he nodded ever so slightly, as if to signal he'd absorbed a point, but it was never clear if it was to register agreement or something else.

Justice Besanko's unflinching impassivity remained in place as, guided by McClintock, Roberts-Smith traversed his account of what happened at the final set of compounds on the Darwan mission. This was where it was alleged he'd detained some Afghans, including Ali Jan, and interrogated them with a translator.

This couldn't be so, Roberts-Smith said calmly. Not only were these compounds empty, he had sent his translator to help another patrol team well before Roberts-Smith arrived at the site.

There was no interrogation with a translator. No smiling Ali Jan. No cliff kick and no subsequent execution. Roberts-Smith didn't even remember seeing a cliff, he told the judge.

A man did die near the end of the mission, but he was never a detainee. Roberts-Smith and Vincent Jelovic had fired on an Afghan insurgent carrying a radio whom they'd stumbled across in a cornfield. Jelovic had fired the first shots from a distance of just two metres.

It was a similar set of denials issued in connection to the Easter Sunday allegations. No men were pulled out of a tunnel inside the courtyard of compound Whiskey 108. No Afghans were detained. And there were no executions involving Roberts-Smith or Andrews.

Instead, an insurgent with a prosthetic leg, running while carrying a weapon, was shot dead by Roberts-Smith after he ventured outside the compound walls. The second dead Afghan found near the first was also an insurgent gunned down only seconds after Roberts-Smith had engaged the prosthetic-legged man.

Both shootings were not only lawful. The brave soldier who had killed this second Taliban fighter had likely saved Roberts-Smith's life. It was an act of quiet heroism.

'To have somebody tell you that that is now somehow kind of a criminal act or a war crime, it makes me angry,' the war hero said. 'Makes me really angry.'

* * *

Having guided Roberts-Smith through the mountains and valleys of Afghanistan, then through his personal life, McClintock closed his evidence-in-chief by asking the ex-soldier how our reporting had made him feel.

The mood in the court changed to one of quiet sorrow. 'I was wracked with anxiety and wanted to stay at home,' Mr Roberts-Smith said. 'I was worried about my children. I was worried … what people might say to them, what someone might do to them.'

McClintock prodded his client gently onwards. 'How do you think people see you now, Mr Roberts-Smith?'

When he answered, the war hero's voice sounded different. His eyes welled with tears as the courtroom fell silent. The giant of a man who Australia had come to love and revere no longer knew what people were whispering when he walked by. 'That's the problem. I don't know.'

CHAPTER 42

FACE TO FACE

17 June 2021

I launched my board out into the Bondi surf, pulling my arms through the water and feeling the cold spray sting my face. An eerie dawn mist cloaked the water's surface, enveloping the dozen or so surfers already out the back. I wanted to feel cleansed and energised before I put on my suit and caught the bus to the Federal Court.

This morning would be the first time I would come face to face with Ben Roberts-Smith.

It surprised me, but I was looking forward to Owens' cross-examination and to eyeballing the ex-soldier at close quarters. I'd tried to meet Roberts-Smith on several occasions prior to the lawsuit, but each time he'd responded through his lawyers or not at all.

Over the previous week, I'd been stuck in Melbourne due to Covid, missing the start of the trial and instead watching online as Roberts-Smith was rolled softball questions by McClintock.

After four years of researching him, I felt as if I knew Roberts-Smith. I didn't underestimate his cunning or determination, but I also believed him deeply flawed. He couldn't seem to recognise his own failings or handle criticism. Everyone else was always to blame when things went wrong.

His arrogance, the bullying and violence he inflicted on those who dared to challenge him, and his ability to charm those who served a purpose, all pointed to a narcissist. This presented us an opportunity in court. A man who believed his own lies, or thought himself above scrutiny, might be prone to mistakes.

One comment from someone who had closely observed Roberts-Smith had stuck with me: 'He's always been a winner.'

It was his hubris, cheered on by self-interested enablers, that had propelled Roberts-Smith to launch a court case in which he hoped he would triumph in glorious fashion. It was as if he couldn't see the risk he might also destroy himself. Or maybe he didn't care? I cast my mind back to his words that he'd either be famous or infamous. Still, he'd dragged me to this precipice with him.

Only one of our livelihoods would survive the trial. I wasn't confident it would be mine, but nor was I sure he had it in the bag quite yet.

While we may not have had committed witnesses rushing to trial, none had officially pulled out either. Our subpoenas had been prepared and we'd decided to issue them far and wide, minimising the chance of witness no-shows. The only way witnesses could lawfully avoid giving evidence was to plead that they were mentally unfit or claim that to testify would force them to incriminate themselves and therefore they should be excused.

Roberts-Smith and his legal team's confidence seemed predicated on our witnesses never materialising. The story he had chosen to tell the court was one of broad-stroke absolutes. There were not only no executions on Easter Sunday, but no Afghans ever found in any tunnel. Ali Jan was not only never detained and executed, but the final set of compounds at Darwan were empty. Roberts-Smith was not a bully. Emma was lying. Amanda was lying. McLeod was lying. The SAS soldiers were lying. The Afghans were lying.

The only person telling the truth was Roberts-Smith himself.

For his version of events to be believed, he would need his own witnesses to stick to stories we considered inventions and for our witnesses to either lie on the stand or avoid coming to court at all.

As I pushed the nose of my board under a surging wall of white foam, feeling it pass over me, I thought back to Owens. He'd been sleeping four hours a night, reading transcripts and refining his planned cross-examination.

Owens had already warned me not to expect any major blows to be landed during his cross-examination. Roberts-Smith wouldn't dramatically fold or make any key concessions. He'd already made a series of minor ones while being led by his own barrister, McClintock, in order to deal with inconsistencies, appear more humane and give the appearance of honesty. The only mission he'd recounted, blow by blow, was that in which he'd earned his Victoria Cross, but it had nothing to do with our war crimes case.

What Roberts-Smith hadn't done was to respond in detail to the missions that would determine the trial's outcome. If the last compound at Darwan was empty, why did the records from that day suggest he spent such a long time there? What was he doing as the minutes ticked past?

Owens' plan was to go slowly. He knew Roberts-Smith would be shaping for a fight, so Owens just wanted to get him talking, to commit to more and more detail.

Owens had taken to repeating a mantra: every lie he tells serves a purpose. The trick was in spotting the lie and its utility, then exposing it to Justice Besanko. Roberts-Smith claimed that, during the Darwan mission, he had sent his translator away prior to reaching the final compound. This story appeared designed to undermine the anticipated testimony of the Darwan villagers about a translator who taunted and struck them in the end compound.

His recollection of having his life saved on Easter Sunday by an SAS soldier who'd shot dead an approaching insurgent helped explain why not one, but two, dead Afghans were found near the compound courtyard. This lie could be potentially exposed by pressing Roberts-Smith on the identity of the mysterious soldier who had saved his life, and then dragging him to court to testify.

Not that any of it would be easy or immediately fruitful. Owens had dampened my expectations about something else. Even if he landed a few blows in the cross-examination, if we didn't get a bunch of decent witnesses to court, we were still doomed. I could tell Owens was gravely concerned about this. So was I.

This was the other reason I was in the surf. The ocean was the one place I felt no anxiety, although I'd rarely go for a paddle without thinking about my old friend, surfing companion and mentor, Michael Gordon, and his yelps of encouragement that echoed well after his death.

I wanted to eyeball Roberts-Smith, if only to show him that I believed we had a chance, but we were still swamped by problems. The trial had already begun, and Jason Andrews was still missing in action. Person 66 was the same. Our other SAS witnesses were using lawyers to field our inquiries, and their commitment was mostly lukewarm. We had eight or so core witnesses onboard, but we needed at least double that.

Covid border controls around Australia were further complicating our ability to fly even willing witnesses interstate, and providing an excuse for others to avoid court. Our Afghan witnesses were in a safe house in Kabul, but the Taliban were now sweeping through the country. If Afghanistan's capital fell, it would destroy our chances of hearing from the villagers.

With the trial upon us, we had run out of time.

As the swell rose, I turned the board to shore and paddled like hell. I slid to my feet, carved through the base of the wave, upwards towards the lip, then back down the line, thinking of nothing but flying across the smooth grey blue before me.

'Go, Nicky, go!'

* * *

Chris Masters and I walked through the court entrance, past the bank of cameras. We had started this journey together, never really believing it would end in a courtroom. We had assumed that Roberts-Smith wouldn't take the risk of having his war service scrutinised. And yet here we were. Perhaps it was us who were the fools for publishing without certainty of victory in a defamation court.

Masters always had a calm response to my second-guessing. 'Was it in the public interest? Did Australians have a right to know? And was it true?'

The answer to all these questions was, yes, whether we could prove it in court or not.

'Then hold your line, Nick,' Masters would reassure me. Today, though, he looked as nervous as me.

'I'm shitting myself, Chris,' I said.

'Me too.'

* * *

Roberts-Smith's cross-examination began slowly, just as Owens predicted. There were no early fireworks, only brief, clipped answers from the Seven executive, who appeared to be offering up as little detail as possible.

Roberts-Smith was believable and confident. I hated to admit it, and it was early days, but he was a good witness.

Owens seemed hesitant. I wondered if Roberts-Smith observed this. It was only after an hour or so of questioning, during a brief break, that Roberts-Smith appeared to notice me. We locked eyes and I held his gaze before I looked away.

After a couple of hours, Owens had settled into a rhythm, rocking back and forward ever so slightly. He was polite, measured and at times even deferential to the war hero. But I knew he was playing a long game.

Mitchell and Barnett had spent weeks examining military documents, debriefing SAS soldiers and poring over the photos from the buried USBs.

Owens was using this painstaking research to slowly force Roberts-Smith to commit to detailed accounts of the missions in question. If McClintock's examination of the war hero was scant of detail, Owens was aiming for the opposite, question by question, hour by hour, day by day.

Many of the questions seemed meaningless. Had a stranger wandered into court, they would have wondered if Owens was lost in the weeds or hoping to grind Roberts-Smith into submission by wearing him out.

But he wasn't. He was inducing Roberts-Smith to weave an intricate web whose anticipated structure was known only to those familiar with the evidence we were hoping to use later in the trial.

The war hero may have been too confident to realise it, and perhaps some of his legal team were the same. I watched as Moses giggled, rolled his eyes and whispered, as if Owens was flailing and Moses enjoying the show.

I overheard McClintock chuckle during one court interlude: 'Well, that didn't go very well for Mr Owens.' During another adjournment, one of the journalists covering the trial said to me: 'Geez, this is boring.'

But Justice Besanko was listening intently. He appeared to be absorbed in the picture being painted, even if it eluded others.

If our witnesses came and told the truth, the web Owens was encouraging Roberts-Smith to weave would shimmer into view. It was all a big if. But *if* it happened, Roberts-Smith would be trapped in the threads of his own lies.

* * *

Along with Masters, my companion in court during day after day of cross-examination was Sandy Dawson. He sat next to me, watching the cross-examination he should have been delivering. He looked gaunt and was wearing a hat, which I guessed was to hide the scars from his brain surgery.

A mutual friend told me his cancer was terminal, but Dawson never let on. He was cheery, gracious and seemed to relish the role of ringside commentator. Because of his previous role in the case, Dawson knew why each line of questioning had been cast and whether Owens had snagged what he was fishing for.

'He's becoming angrier,' Dawson whispered to me about Roberts-Smith as he'd weathered a barrage of questions aimed at extracting a blow-by-blow account of his movements at Darwan. 'The detail is what will get him. It may not seem like much now, but it will matter in the end.'

The timing of Roberts-Smith's Darwan story simply didn't add up. Owens got the ex-soldier to lock in an account that involved him directing a translator and patrol team member to help another SAS team well before Roberts-Smith had arrived at what he claimed was an empty final compound.

The military records from the day didn't tally with these claims. An hour or more was unaccounted for and Roberts-Smith had no convincing explanation as to what he was doing at a supposedly empty compound during what Owens claimed was a vital window of time.

The logical conclusion was that the translator and fourth patrol team member had in fact made it with Roberts-Smith, Vincent Jelovic and Jason Andrews to the final compound and, once there, had helped Roberts-Smith interrogate Ali Jan, as Hanifa and our other Afghan witnesses were claiming.

Owens pushed the issue of timing again and again. There was nothing even remotely resembling a confession, but Roberts-Smith's scoffing and robust ripostes no longer seemed quite as self-assured. Or was I imagining it?

Owens showed Roberts-Smith a photo of Ali Jan's bullet-riddled body and asked him to focus on wounds and blood smears that, the barrister explained, appeared to match injuries one would expect if a handcuffed man was shot while facing his executioners. It showed nothing of the sort, Roberts-Smith responded firmly.

The trauma on Ali Jan's face supported the claim he'd gone headfirst into a rock after being propelled over the cliff, said Owens.

Roberts-Smith not only dismissed this, but denied the existence of a cliff at all.

Owens pushed on, drilling down into the ex-soldier's semantics.

'Will you agree with me, then, that even if you wouldn't call it a cliff, this is a very, very steep incline up which one could not walk?' Owens asked him.

'I would say it's a steep incline. You could walk down that; it would just be difficult.'

'Why didn't you say, "Well, I wouldn't call it a cliff, but I accept there was a very, very steep incline."?'

'I mean, a cliff is a cliff, and that is not a cliff to me.'

Owens kept trying to close in and as he did, I felt the dynamic in the court shift ever so slightly. Roberts-Smith was still cocky, but Owens looked more alive.

He pushed on.

In his evidence-in-chief, Roberts-Smith had deftly sought to abandon his earlier claim that Commander Ismail had been sacked from the SAS before the mission in which Tilley alleged that the war hero ordered Ismail to execute an Afghan.

The sacking story had been exposed as false because the photos on the USBs proved that Ismail was on the mission in question. The problem for Roberts-Smith was that he and four of his witnesses had all implied in statements that they had first-hand knowledge of Ismail's sacking.

I felt myself tensing up as Owens reeled Roberts-Smith in slowly. First, the barrister got him to confirm that he knew that witnesses were meant to offer only their independent recollections of events. Next, Owens needled Roberts-Smith as he tried to explain how he had so confidently described Ismail's sacking when he never actually had an independent recollection of it. Roberts-Smith twisted himself in knots as he tried to justify how a story told to him by others had transformed into his own memory.

Owens kept prodding, confirming how after Roberts-Smith was warned that it was another soldier who was sacked rather than Ismail, he had initially stayed quiet and stuck to his story.

Why was this so? Owens politely demanded of the war hero.

Once again, Owens never extracted an explicit admission from Roberts-Smith. He denied having embellished the story of the sacking to shake off one of our war crime allegations. But the barrister forced the ex-soldier to admit his 'recollection' was in fact a false story relayed to him by his mates in the SAS, which Roberts-Smith had in turn adopted because 'it fitted'.

These concessions came sporadically but, with each one, Roberts-Smith's credibility suffered. The web was being woven.

Owens exposed him for failing to hand over the USBs to our legal team as required under court discovery rules. Buried or not, the photos were in Roberts-Smith's possession and played a potentially vital role in determining contested issues.

Roberts-Smith blamed the failure on an inadvertent oversight, but the explanation rang hollow. He did the same when Owens demanded he explain why he'd failed to hand over the 2018 email from Neil Browning detailing Browning's strategy to defeat the Easter Sunday murder allegations. It was critical evidence and yet it had been hidden from the court.

The email showed that Roberts-Smith and Browning were colluding to come up with lies about a double murder, Owens told the court.

Roberts-Smith scoffed again, denying this.

As the judge watched on, Owens' cross-examination took an unexpected turn. He demanded Roberts-Smith and his legal team hand over any other emails between the war hero and his lawyers that referred to Browning's statement.

As Moses and Roberts-Smith's lawyers sought to fight further disclosure, Owens held firm. He pushed and pushed. Soon, more documents were being handed up.

They revealed that Roberts-Smith had also sent Browning's Easter Sunday statement to a senior executive known to be Kerry Stokes' right-hand man at Seven. Roberts-Smith had also told his lawyers in writing that Vincent Jelovic would be preparing a similar statement.

I watched as Justice Besanko scrawled something in his notebook, his brow furrowed. Browning and Jelovic were Roberts-Smith's key witnesses. Had the trio put their heads together, colluding to defeat our case?

It was at this point that Dawson leaned over to me with a glint in his eye. 'Owens has found his mojo,' he whispered, his gaunt face trying to disguise a smile.

'If I was Roberts-Smith's lawyers, I'd be shitting myself,' Dawson said.

But there was no sign of that. It wasn't quite high fives among the Roberts-Smith legal team, but they still regularly joked, giggled and traded notes. They seemed as confident as their client and I couldn't work out why.

* * *

As Owens began to unpick Roberts-Smith's account of the Easter Sunday mission, I noticed Dawson inching forward in his seat. Owens had run with Dawson's theory that Roberts-Smith had invented a series of lies to explain the presence of two dead Afghan men we alleged had been pulled out of a tunnel in a compound courtyard and executed.

Find the lie, expose its purpose.

Lie one was Roberts-Smith's claim he'd shot an armed man with a prosthetic leg 'running in a crouch' several metres outside the Whiskey 108 compound. Lie two was that his life had been saved by an SAS comrade who, moments later, had shot dead a second darting insurgent.

Once again, Roberts-Smith's story didn't quite fit. Photos that Mitchell and Barnett had spent countless hours examining pointed to a different tale. In one picture, the dead prosthetic-legged man could be seen lying next to the compound wall. This suggested he hadn't been shot by Roberts-Smith metres outside the compound, but had fallen much closer to its walls.

To explain this away, Roberts-Smith told the court that he'd dragged the dead insurgent five metres or so towards the compound courtyard after killing him. This was lie three.

He'd then doubled down with lie four. He recalled how the SAS soldier who killed insurgent number two had also dragged his body until it, too, lay near the Afghan killed by Roberts-Smith.

Question by question, Owens sought to lay bare these concoctions. Why did Roberts-Smith feel the need to drag the prosthetic-legged man in the first place when there was no obvious reason to do so?

Not so, said Roberts-Smith. He'd dragged the dead man because to leave him and his weapon may have posed a safety risk.

If the second insurgent had also been dragged towards the compound, why did the photo of his body show a pool of blood and brain matter that indicated his body came to rest at the precise location where he had been shot?

Why did another of the photos show this man tagged with an evidence bag bearing the word 'tunnel', which suggested he'd been found in the tunnel and detained prior to his killing?

And if the SAS soldier who had killed the second insurgent in the heat of battle had indeed saved Roberts-Smith's life, what was his brave comrade's name?

Roberts-Smith responded forcefully, holding his ground. He'd been confused, he'd told the court. He'd slept on it and returned to court to change his testimony. The second insurgent's body was never dragged.

Owens pounced: 'Why were you prepared to give such a specific account if it's not true?'

'Because the events we're referring to happened over a decade ago. I've had six deployments to Afghanistan. I've had multiple engagements. I realised that that was not what happened at that exact moment,' Roberts-Smith answered defiantly.

As he spoke, Justice Besanko's gaze was locked on Roberts-Smith. I noticed everyone in court was doing the same.

Owens, though, wasn't finished. What was the name of the soldier who shot dead this second enemy gunman as he advanced on Roberts-Smith?

The Victoria Cross recipient had no answer. He claimed he simply couldn't remember who it was who had saved his life.

After days of watching Roberts-Smith battle Owens, I had to admit that I marvelled at the ex-soldier's persistent confidence. Even when his answers seemed implausible, Roberts-Smith imbued them with self-belief.

'It's an interesting spin, Mr Owens, but it's completely wrong,' he would offer the silk with the air of genuine grievance. 'You've gone the wrong way with it.'

Even though I was convinced he was often lying through his teeth, he was good at it. He didn't seem to get exhausted. He never seemed to go to the bathroom. When he strode into court each day, he did so with purpose. Roberts-Smith was a man on a mission.

He brushed off blows that I hoped would stun him, leaving me wondering if they had landed at all. Somewhere, out of sight, he must have been hurting. Several of his explanations were so tortured or bizarre that they were ending up on comedy websites and as internet memes.

He admitted to dousing his laptop with petrol and setting it on fire to ensure its data could never be recovered, but resisted the suggestion that this was suspicious. The burner phones he explained away as necessary to prevent the press from tapping his phone calls, while dismissing the proposition he wanted to sidestep scrutiny from those who actually had the power to bug phones, the police.

Dawson's commentary had kept my hopes up and yet I couldn't shake the feeling that Roberts-Smith knew something that we didn't. He was being grilled about his claim of being separated from Emma while having an affair – the most obvious of all his lies albeit not the most serious – when Levitan whispered in my ear to follow him into a small room adjacent to the court.

It took me a few moments to absorb the news. Jason Andrews had fallen ill. He was not mentally well enough to testify. The linchpin of our case and the key to our success would not be coming to the Federal Court in Sydney.

My thoughts raced. All hope wasn't lost, I told myself. We could fight for the Afghans to appear in court urgently by video link on the basis that the Taliban could take Kabul at any moment. Other witnesses identified in the PAP notice might still come to court, even if they were reluctant.

'We need more time,' I whispered to no one in particular. But even with more time, there was still no guarantee Andrews would ever be well enough to come to court. He was carrying immense trauma, a brave but broken man who had spoken out to authorities about Roberts-Smith but had no interest in helping a media company.

And why would he? He had no obligation to us, no interest in supporting some far-flung notion of a free press and the public's right to know. He was like many of our other SAS witnesses. They had wives and children, lives they wanted to get on with. Revisiting a past they probably preferred buried was hardly appealling.

The last place any of them wanted to be was in courtroom 18D. And I didn't blame them.

The social media accounts run by bitter military veterans that were previously preoccupied with attacking people like me, Samantha Crompvoets and Dusty Miller had now turned their sights on our witnesses. #IstandwithRS was a hashtag.

Having wanted to eyeball Roberts-Smith on day one of his cross-examination, I suddenly wanted to be anywhere else but in the Federal Court. The fear I'd carried for three years had been realised, and there was nothing I could do.

Our most important witness had finally abandoned ship, if he was ever onboard at all.

CHAPTER 43

A MESSY BUSINESS

June 2021

Brendan Nelson stood solemnly in the witness box as Bruce McClintock listed the high points of his glittering career in medicine, politics, diplomacy and defence. The fact that there were so many of them explained why Nelson had received a medal reserved for exceptional Australians.

'And you are an Officer of the Order of Australia as well, aren't you?' McClintock asked, rhetorically.

A simple yes could have sufficed, but Nelson was never one for keeping it short.

'Privileged to be so and surprised to be so,' the former defence minister answered, with an air of grave humility.

Ever since Nelson had emerged as the highest profile defender of Ben Roberts-Smith besides Kerry Stokes, he had worn his loyalty to his friend as a badge of honour. This is what exceptional men did. They weathered the storm together.

Nelson's decision to attend court and testify about Roberts-Smith's impeccable character was in stark contrast

373

to some others. The former governor-general Quentin Bryce indicated to her advisers that she no longer wished to be called as a character witness as more and more Australians had begun to wonder if there might be a hint of truth to the war crimes allegations.

Even a surprise visit to her Brisbane home by Roberts-Smith bearing flowers hadn't changed her mind. It was a damning disappearing act given McClintock had earlier flagged to Justice Besanko that Bryce was among the good and great of the nation willing to vouch for the war hero.

Nelson had never wavered. The optics of having the now ex-head of the Australian War Memorial backing an alleged war criminal appeared not to bother the ex-politician. Nor had the fact that Nelson's ultimate overseer at the war memorial, its chair Kerry Stokes, was also the employer of Roberts-Smith.

'Mate ... I have stood up publicly for him and will continue to do so,' he'd written of Roberts-Smith to a veteran back in late 2018, months after the war crimes allegations had first hit. '[The] most highly decorated soldier in fifty years. He needs support, mate, from people who can see through this.'

'Unless there have been the most egregious breaches of laws of armed conflict, we should leave it all alone,' he told journalists around the same time. 'War is a messy business.'

Nelson had shrugged off controversy surrounding his support for Roberts-Smith, landing a lucrative executive position at arms manufacturer Boeing shortly after he'd departed the war memorial in late 2020. If his professional life had prospered, those calling for war crimes scrutiny had endured a different fate. As Nelson was giving his testimony, Samantha Crompvoets was fighting for her career. After a brief high following her appearance on *60 Minutes*, Crompvoets had crashed back to earth. The threats on social media had escalated.

'Something might happen to you if you keep speaking up,' a senior SAS officer had warned her, before adding: 'One woman can't change everything.' She'd felt confused, threatened. In a coffee shop at Defence headquarters in Canberra, Crompvoets burst into tears after meeting a senior official. 'Do I need to be worried about my safety?' she had asked.

Days before, the new federal defence minister, Peter Dutton, had publicly warned his government might no longer hire Crompvoets to conduct research. Dutton was seeking legal advice about whether she had improperly used information she gained as a Defence consultant to publicly expose alleged atrocities. The military should not be 'distracted by things that have happened in the past', he said.

'I am unapologetic about raising issues that I see as significantly jeopardising the reputation and capability of defence,' Crompvoets had countered in a speech on the eve of the Roberts-Smith trial. 'And for those who wish to silence me and my work I say this – I won't be bullied or intimidated. Cultural change needs to happen.'

Nelson was waging a different war, at least when it came to Roberts-Smith. The failure, as Nelson saw it, was with those who had sought to tear the war hero down and rewrite the history that Nelson had helped shape.

The defamation trial was Nelson's chance to highlight this. 'Ben Roberts-Smith VC, MG was the most respected, admired and revered Australian soldier in more than half a century,' Nelson informed the court. 'I'm happy to go on.'

McClintock didn't need convincing. 'Please continue.'

Nelson obliged, his voice rich with emotion as he described the awe with which he regarded Roberts-Smith. 'Men and women of everyday life would want to be with him, to shake his hand, perhaps to have a photograph … In some cases at the Australian War Memorial, I saw people fall into his arms, very emotionally describing their experiences and that of their families of war.'

This 'immensely courageous and strong man' had been savagely wronged, which was why Nelson called him after Masters and I published the first articles. 'He was clearly hurt. It has been devastating, the impact on him,' he said.

Nelson recounted how he had comforted Roberts-Smith, telling the Seven executive of 'my support for him, my belief in him'.

That wasn't all, Nelson recalled. 'The overwhelming majority of Australians' also believed in him. In embracing the war hero, Nelson was merely channelling the nation.

* * *

Mohammed Hanifa settled into his seat and faced the computer screen. It was early morning in Kabul. He'd risen at 4am, dressed in a traditional olive-green tunic and long black waistcoat, prayed and made his way to the legal offices of Kakar Advocates.

He'd been waiting for weeks in a safe house to tell the Australian court about his uncle, Ali Jan. At times, Hanifa and the other Afghan witnesses weren't sure if they would ever appear in this Australian court. As each day passed, the Taliban had inched closer to the capital. Fear and death were, once again, everywhere.

Final confirmation had arrived days before. The grim-faced Australian judge now sitting in the right corner of the screen had agreed to allow Hanifa and three fellow Darwan villagers to testify urgently via video link due to the risk Kabul would soon fall to the Taliban.

The Darwan farmer would be questioned by one white man in a black robe, and then another. The judge would watch on, perhaps asking his own questions.

A translator would interpret both ways. The translator would log in from Canada, because no one in Australia with sufficient language skills had security clearance. This complication was one detail too many for the farmer who couldn't read or write and measured distance by his arm, time by the seasons and wealth by the bounty of a harvest, be it 'wheat, corn, kidney beans, tomatoes'.

Hanifa's core task was simple. Tell the truth.

Ali Jan had died nine years before, but when he was asked about when the military raid that led to the death had occurred, Hanifa wasn't really sure. He estimated about eight years had passed, but also explained to Owens that his measure of the passage of time was imprecise. 'I understand the days of the weeks. I know the names of the months. But I don't know the years.'

But he told the court he was certain Ali was not a fighter or an insurgent. Ali was a simple, impoverished farmer and labourer, like himself, making do from season to season to feed his family while trying to avoid the trouble that refused to take leave in southern Afghanistan.

From his home in the nearby village of Baag, Ali used a water spring for irrigation, tended to crops and cattle and collected wood that he sold to supplement his meagre income.

'I grew up as a child with him,' Hanifa explained. Ali Jan's family 'used to come to our house. We used to go to their house.'

Hanifa explained that his memory of the day in question, the last day he saw Ali alive, wasn't bound to any specific date. It was tied to cascading actions, each more shocking than the one before, culminating in a needless and inexplicable death. And it was bound to one soldier in particular.

This man stood out, Hanifa explained, not just because of his brutality. He was bigger than the other men and wet, with traces of river sand on his uniform. It was this 'big soldier' with 'blueish eyes' who had set his sights on Ali.

Hanifa's account of the day matched the account he had given months before when his outline of evidence was prepared. Six helicopters had thundered into Darwan, and soldiers had swept through the village. He and Ali sheltered in a guesthouse in the final set of compounds on a ridge that ran to a small cliff.

Hanifa described how he and Ali had their hands secured behind their backs and were assaulted by the 'big soldier' and the interpreter. Hanifa remembered a dog wearing goggles with the soldiers, a sight he had never seen before. The villager had no way of knowing it, but his description matched the protective glasses worn by the working military dogs that were with the SAS that day.

Hanifa's recollection of the big soldier being wet and covered in river sand matched another independently verifiable detail. Roberts-Smith was the only soldier who had waded through the Helmand River.

It was this big soldier, Hanifa told the court, who took an intense dislike to Ali during the interrogation. 'I told Ali Jan, don't laugh or don't smile, because they do not like when you smile or when you laugh,' Hanifa recalled.

But Ali couldn't suppress his smile. Hanifa watched him being moved to the edge of the small cliff.

'Ali Jan was kicked,' he recounted. 'The soldier kicked him, not with the sole of his feet, rather with the, the toes.

'He was rolling down, rolling down until he reached the river.'

Hanifa recalled his terror as he glimpsed two soldiers drag his wounded uncle across the dry creek bed into a clump of vegetation. He then heard gunfire.

* * *

As Bruce McClintock began his cross-examination of Hanifa, his voice was laced with something between incredulity and disdain. Whether this was because of the need to translate his words, or the fact that he was talking via a video screen on another continent, McClintock's questioning served only to prompt Hanifa to give further and firmer detail.

'Mohammed Hanifa, the evidence you've given about seeing the big soldier wet is completely untrue, isn't it?' McClintock barked.

'Whether you call it a lie, that's up to you, but I have seen this person with my own eyes.'

'It's also a lie to say that there was sand on his uniform?'

'Sand, sand, sand from the river. If you call it a lie, that's up to you. Sand from the river.'

'Now, has someone suggested to you that you should say that the big soldier was wet in your evidence?'

'No. I'm the one who is saying that, because I saw him with my own eyes.'

'The reason why you've said that Ali Jan, or the man you call Ali Jan, was not a Talib was that you know that you won't get compensation if he was a Talib. That's correct, isn't it?'

'He is not a Talib. He is not a Talib. He is a labourer. He is a labourer.'

McClintock finished without laying a glove.

But Hanifa wasn't ready to go. The continual challenges to his honesty and suggestions that Ali Jan was a terrorist had offended his honour. As Justice Besanko began to instruct that he could now leave, the Afghan stared down the camera and gave one last address to the Federal Court.

'Look, brother, I am a witness, I am not afraid of anybody, even if I die I will tell the truth,' Hanifa said. His voice rose as he continued. 'This is the Pashto customs. It is the tradition. And this is the law. If you witness something like a crime, you have to testify about it. Even if somebody wants me to go to Australia or to the US or to any other country in the world, I would go there. And I would testify.'

* * *

Dean Levitan silently counted the steps in the room that had become his office, bedroom, exercise space and eating quarters. It was five steps in width and six in length. Five days into his mandatory quarantine period, he'd taken to pacing it in rectangles, like a prisoner going slowly insane.

In June 2021, Covid lockdowns and border restrictions had forced Justice Besanko to stall the trial until witnesses could travel, possibly for months.

There were two ways to look at it. On one view, it had simply delayed execution day, when Owens would be forced to announce to Justice Besanko that Jason Andrews wouldn't be coming to testify, all but signalling Roberts-Smith's victory in connection to a core part of the case. The second view was that Levitan and his team had been smiled upon by the legal gods. They now had an opportunity to go back to the drawing board and devise strategies to ensure their line-up of reluctant witnesses attended court when the trial resumed in several months' time.

One, two, three, four, five.

One, two, three, four, five, six.

There was no suggestion that Person 66 was unwell or overseas, so he was still a live prospect. Given he had been allegedly blooded, he alone could win the case. But he needed to agree to testify under the cloak of a Federal Court immunity certificate. The granting of a certificate meant that if he confessed to being ordered by Roberts-Smith to execute an Afghan, this admission couldn't be used against him in any future criminal proceeding.

Person 66's other option was to fight any move to force him to court by arguing the immunity certificates didn't do enough to protect his legal rights. If he chose this path, Levitan had no idea of the outcome.

One, two, three, four, five.

One, two, three, four, five, six.

If Person 66 indicated he would support them, he'd be the ideal first witness. Roberts-Smith had never made any adverse allegations about Person 66. He wasn't said to be jealous and they hadn't served together long enough to develop any known animosity.

This was in stark contrast to Nick Simkin, who Roberts-Smith had repeatedly blamed in court for stoking rumours and resentment about him. Simkin had raised at least one formal complaint about Roberts-Smith and was open about his intense dislike for him.

Levitan had decided not to haul Simkin to court, thereby denying Roberts-Smith his chance to claim our witnesses were motivated by hatred. This is why it was so crucial to secure the witnesses whose names had been uncovered by winning access to Roberts-Smith's PAP notice. They were mostly known to be indifferent to Roberts-Smith as a person. They had no desire to come to court and testify but had still witnessed him engage in suspect battlefield acts.

One, two, three, four, five.

One, two, three, four, five, six.

The most important of these newly identified witnesses was a soldier called John Langmore. Langmore was on the Easter Sunday mission, was said to have been close to Roberts-Smith and Andrews when the two Afghans found in the tunnel were handed over to the pair as detainees.

Given his vantage point, if anyone had seen what had gone down, it would be him. If Langmore backed up the anticipated testimony of other SAS witnesses from the day, such as Dean Tilley, then they had a chance of proving that Roberts-Smith and Andrews had executed two prisoners. If Tilley and Langmore both got a case of sudden-onset amnesia in the witness box, it would be for nought.

Levitan had come to realise that getting witnesses to court was only half the battle. With the trauma and chaotic nature of war, and because they were trained to withstand interrogation, many of the proposed SAS witnesses could very likely convincingly plead memory loss or some other malady if they wished to stay silent. Or they could say they were simply looking the other way.

The challenge for Levitan was twofold. Get them to come to court, and encourage them to testify honestly and openly.

Jason Andrews appeared intent on doing neither. Without Andrews, we had no Australian witness to corroborate the three Afghan witnesses from Darwan.

One, two, three, four, five.

One, two, three, four, five, six.

Hanifa had been better than expected in the box. He'd given detailed, authentic and raw testimony, and had avoided McClintock's attempts to confuse or anger him. So had the other villagers.

It had become clear, though, that Roberts-Smith's legal strategy was to deny the very fundamentals of their evidence, hoping that no Australian would ever step forward to corroborate what the Afghans had testified had happened.

According to Roberts-Smith's version of events, there were no humans at the last compound save for him, Andrews and Jelovic. There were no detainees, no translator, no military working dog with goggles. There was no cliff, no cliff kick and certainly no execution. Roberts-Smith wasn't even conceding that it was Ali Jan he had gunned down with Jelovic in the cornfield. It was simply an unknown Taliban insurgent with a radio.

Roberts-Smith wouldn't even concede our village witnesses came from Darwan. To him, they were Afghans looking for a payday whom Masters and I had rustled up in some Kabul back alley.

It's why Andrews was even more critical than before when it came to proving the Darwan allegations.

So how to get him into the witness box?

One, two, three, four, five.

One, two, three, four, five, six.

The weight of albeit untested evidence pointed to two things. The first was that Andrews had been blooded on Easter Sunday 2009. The second was that Andrews would do everything within his power to avoid testifying about it. This left open a small window.

Would Jason Andrews come to court if it was guaranteed that he would only be compelled to answer Owens' questions about the events at Darwan in 2012, where there were no allegations of criminality that involved him?

One, two, three, four, five.

One, two, three, four, five, six.

CHAPTER 44

MORAL COURAGE

Witnesses for the newspapers:
February–April 2022

Six months after Justice Besanko paused the trial, I sat in the back row of the court and waited for our first SAS witness to appear. I had no idea if he would actually say what we so desperately hoped he would. Sitting a few metres from me, Ben Roberts-Smith was also in the dark.

It was 2 February 2022, and the lead-up to the resumption of the trial had seen no respite in drama. Person 66 had been slated as witness number one, but had made it clear he would do his utmost to make himself unavailable, subpoena or not.

Our witnesses from Perth still faced the prospect of forced quarantine if they crossed their state border, so they were unavailable. Roberts-Smith's Perth-based witnesses, due to appear in the witness box after ours, faced a similar problem.

A few weeks earlier, the case had invaded my life in a different way. My fixer and translator for the stories that got us sued, Rashid Ghulam, called me in a panic after the fall of Kabul. Because he'd assisted Western journalists, he was at risk of retribution from the newly ascendant Taliban. I'd helped him and his family apply for urgent visas to Australia, but they couldn't make it onto a plane. Desperate Afghans had swarmed Kabul Airport, which had become a target for suicide bombers. Rashid was waiting there with his wife and children when a bomb ripped through the crowd, killing an estimated 170 Afghans. He fled towards the Pakistan border in a minivan as hope of making it to Australia had faded. But four weeks before the resumption of the trial, in late December, I took Rashid and his family to the beach in Victoria. They'd finally made it to the country that would become their new home. When we arrived at the foreshore, his wife waded into the water, still fully clothed and wearing her hijab. She sat in the shallows grinning like a toddler, the cold water lapping against her. She stayed there for half an hour. When I asked Rashid if she was bothered by the cold, he told me it was the first time she had been in the ocean.

The family's safe passage had helped me reflect on the trial. The stakes were incredibly high, but no one was at risk of imminent death if we lost.

The outcome was now firmly out of my hands, and up to our legal team and witnesses. The quarantine and border restrictions in Perth forced the decision to call our first witness from another state. We had settled on John Langmore, an SAS soldier from Victoria, where Covid restrictions had eased. I'd never laid eyes on Langmore. And yet I was relying on him to save the day. No wonder I was wracked with nerves.

Arthur Moses was at the front bar table with a second barrister, looking primed. A book titled *The Law of Armed*

Conflict sat in front of him, along with thick folders of transcripts and the questions he'd prepared for his cross-examination of Langmore once Owens had finished leading him through his evidence-in-chief.

Moses was the witness attack dog, aided by Monica Allen and a second solicitor. McClintock sat behind Moses, whom he would replace as cross-examiner when our non-military witnesses took the stand.

I watched as Roberts-Smith huddled with McClintock, who guffawed at some joke made by the war hero. They didn't appear the slightest bit worried, which made my mouth feel even drier. It was grey outside, ghostlike, and I watched the water in the harbour and the black turret of a submarine

Dean Levitan sat in front of me. He appeared restless, stapling documents together and ordering his pens. At the bar table in front of him sat Owens, whom I'd earlier approached and squeezed on the shoulder in a silent gesture of support. One row behind Owens was a young, bearded barrister looking nervous. It was Langmore's advocate, there to argue the SAS soldier's case if Owens or Moses attempted to get him to talk about anything he wished to remain silent about.

After Justice Besanko entered the room and the tipstaff announced the court was in session, I watched Owens rise to his feet, hands loosely crossed. He looked poised and confident but then I noticed him reach for a handkerchief and wipe a thin layer of sweat from his brow.

'I seek to call John Langmore,' he said.

My heart was now racing. I scanned the room again. It had fallen silent. Moses sat with his hands clasped in front of him. McClintock was no longer grinning. I turned to Roberts-Smith, who was back in his seat in the far corner of the room, occupied with his mobile phone. He looked up at me and I caught his eye. He appeared to grin behind his black Covid face mask, but I wasn't sure.

Langmore would be entering through a door to the left of the judge. If he was staring ahead as he opened the door, the first person he would see would be his old SAS comrade.

I wondered if this was why Roberts-Smith had chosen to sit in the back corner, and decided to stare at him as fixedly as he was staring at the door. If he was going to try to eyeball our witnesses, I wanted him to know I'd be watching him do so.

The door opened and John Langmore strode into court, missing Roberts-Smith's gaze completely and walking straight towards the witness box. With a sharp jaw and short hair, he appeared wiry but strong. Classic SAS.

As Owens guided Langmore through his early army career, I felt my anxiety building and stomach swirling. I was glad I'd skipped breakfast.

I glanced over at Roberts-Smith again. He was absorbed with his mobile phone, busily texting someone.

Langmore calmly described the start of the Easter Sunday mission, directing his testimony to the judge. He recounted entering the Whiskey 108 compound and observing Ben Roberts-Smith, Jason Andrews and Neil Browning in the courtyard surrounded by rooms and which also contained a hidden tunnel that an SAS soldier had unexpectedly uncovered. I inched forward in my seat. Did he see two Afghans led out of the courtyard tunnel as prisoners?

Fuck, I thought to myself as he described entering one of the adjoining rooms. There was no mention of prisoners leaving the tunnel. Maybe he'd describe seeing them once he had walked back into the courtyard.

As Owens gently prodded Langmore onwards, asking him to explain to the court what happened next, Langmore's young barrister leapt to his feet. He told Justice Besanko he would be seeking an immunity certificate to protect Langmore from any disclosure that might involve his own misconduct. Levitan had warned me this was likely to occur if Langmore had any part in what we were alleging was a double execution.

The barrister's concern loomed as both a good and bad sign. It suggested Langmore had seen at least some of what had gone down in the courtyard and maybe even played a small role. But it also meant he wouldn't be giving further evidence if the judge couldn't be persuaded to grant the certificate.

This is what Roberts-Smith desperately wanted.

Langmore's barrister was hesitant as he referred to legislation and legal principles. Justice Besanko looked mildly annoyed. Moses was grinning.

I watched Owens rise to his feet, eloquently intervening as the judge nodded. Then Justice Besanko spoke the words I was desperate to hear. He would grant the certificate.

Next, the judge addressed Langmore. 'Are you willing to give the evidence?'

The SAS soldier nodded. 'Yes, Your Honour.'

I breathed out and looked at Roberts-Smith. He was still staring at his phone, but his body was rigid. Every person in the room was staring at Langmore except for Roberts-Smith as the soldier transported the court back to compound Whiskey 108.

He described hearing a commotion in the courtyard and stepping out of the room he was searching to encounter Roberts-Smith and Andrews to his immediate left. He noticed an older Afghan man dressed in a traditional loose top and clothing, light in colour, squatting against the compound wall near the tunnel entrance.

Then Andrews and Roberts-Smith approached their comrade. 'They said, "Hey, Langmore. Can we borrow your suppressor?" I thought it was a bit of a strange request at first, but I complied.'

As Langmore recounted watching Andrews fit the suppressor to his M4 rifle, I realised why he had sought the certificate. He was worried that by supplying the silencer, he might be accused of being party to the event he was about to describe to the court.

I glanced again at Roberts-Smith. He had finally stopped texting and was staring at Langmore. Roberts-Smith's head was slightly cocked to one side as Langmore described watching the war hero and Andrews walk back towards the squatting Afghan male. As he continued, I noticed Justice Besanko take a quick look at Roberts-Smith before returning his gaze to the witness.

'I then thought to myself, I think I know what's about to happen here, so I just stood there for another few seconds and watching,' Langmore said. 'RS then walked down and grabbed the Afghan male by the scruff of the shirt, picked him up, marched him a couple of metres forward ... he then kicked him in the back of the legs behind the knees until he was kneeling down in front of Andrews. He pointed to the [Afghan] and said to Andrews: "Shoot him."'

Yet again I glanced at Roberts-Smith. He was now glaring at Langmore, shaking his head as the soldier pressed on, telling the court how he stepped briefly into a room adjacent to the courtyard to avoid seeing what he feared was about to happen next. Seconds later, Langmore recalled stepping back into the courtyard to see Andrews standing over the dead body of the Afghan man.

'I walked up to Andrews. I don't believe anything was said. He removed the suppressor from his rifle. And he gave it back to me. When he handed it to me, it was warm.'

* * *

Every eye remained glued to Langmore as he continued his testimony. In a state of shock, he spotted Roberts-Smith holding another 'Afghan male by the scruff of his clothing'.

It was the man with the prosthetic leg. Roberts-Smith 'had a machine gun in his right hand'. He was 'sort of frog-marching the Afghan by the scruff of the neck with his left arm'.

Instead of stepping away as he'd done with Andrews and the older Afghan, Langmore remembered turning directly towards Roberts-Smith as he threw the detainee to the ground.

'I observed him lower his machine gun and shoot approximately three to five rounds into the back of the Afghan male. After he'd done that, he looked up and saw me standing there and looked at me, said, "Are we all cool? Are we all good?"'

Langmore walked away, only to bump into another SAS soldier who quizzed him: 'Do you know what happened to those two blokes that they pulled out of the tunnel?'

It was only then that Langmore 'realised where those two Afghans had come from'.

Before Owens finished his examination-in-chief, he asked Langmore a final question. He wanted the court to know why Langmore never reported what he'd witnessed on Easter Sunday.

'I was a new trooper; my very first trip with the SAS, so I just wanted to toe the line,' Langmore responded. 'It's sort of an unwritten rule ... you just go along with whatever happens.'

* * *

Masters and I walked silently out of the courtroom towards Owens' chambers. Once inside, I hugged Masters amid a flood of utter relief.

Moses' cross-examination of Langmore had gone nowhere very slowly. At times it appeared as if Moses was lost, peppering Langmore with question after question in the hope of provoking anything even slightly resembling a slip-up. It never came.

Langmore was calm and resolute in his answers. He only appeared to lose his composure once, after Moses repeatedly put it to him that he'd given false evidence.

He clenched his jaw and spat back: 'I know what I saw.'

As Moses sought to undermine Langmore's testimony on the basis that he'd invented the story to cover up his own cowardice, Langmore responded: 'Not a coward, sir, no. I was happy just to put that in the back of my memory and carry on with the rest of my life.'

After our embrace ended, I said to Masters: 'One witness down. Twenty more to go.'

* * *

The next few weeks passed in a blur. As each Easter Sunday witness strode through the door, Roberts-Smith would attempt to stare them down and I would in turn stare at him.

I watched on excitedly as two more witnesses took to the stand and, to differing degrees, corroborated Langmore's account of Roberts-Smith executing a detainee. They, too, told the court they had seen an Afghan machine-gunned.

Four other SAS eyewitnesses told Justice Besanko of Afghans being discovered in the courtyard tunnel and detained. Some of our SAS witnesses delivered only small pieces of the puzzle, but they were still vital.

Brian McMurray was a member of the patrol team led by Neil Browning. While Roberts-Smith and Browning had for years denied this team had taken any Afghan prisoner, McMurray recalled a detainee in the courtyard. 'I still can remember him having his cuffs on his wrist ... I just remember he was dressed in white.'

His description matched that given by Langmore of the older Afghan he claimed had been executed by Andrews on Roberts-Smith's orders.

But it was a few other lines of testimony about a photo that our legal team believed could prove so crucial. The photo was one of the thousands from Afghanistan that Chris Mitchell had carefully scanned and mostly discarded.

This picture, though, had become central to our case theory. It showed the body of the older Afghan man. This was the Taliban fighter Roberts-Smith had insisted was lawfully shot by an unknown SAS soldier as the Afghan raced towards him from the fields and scrub outside the compound.

It was this mysterious hero who Roberts-Smith initially claimed had then dragged the older Afghan's body towards the compound courtyard, only to later discard the dragging story.

By Roberts-Smith's account, the older Afghan was shot dead outside the compound where he was then photographed, but the photo suggested something else. I'd spent hours analysing this image, convincing myself that the picture in fact showed a body *inside* the compound walls that surrounded the tunnel.

At times, I wondered if this was due to confirmation bias. But there were clues backing up my belief. The dead Afghan could be seen in the photo lying near items that would tend to be found inside living quarters, including cooking structures and a container of palm oil. Near the man was some chopped grass matching that used to hide the tunnel entrance. Most significantly, affixed to the dead Afghan's body was an evidence bag marked with the words 'NW CORN Tunnel'.

McMurray was the man we all hoped could explain what these words meant, because he had written them. He was clinical in his evidence. He explained to Justice Besanko that he had used the words 'NW CORN Tunnel' because the body he photographed was located 'inside the compound … roughly near the tunnel entrance'.

As he uttered this sentence, I saw Mitchell turn to Barnett and quietly nod. He'd been right all along.

* * *

Dean Tilley started in the witness box nervously, but quickly settled, delivering a spellbinding account of his role as lead scout heading towards compound Whiskey 108 on Easter Sunday. He vividly described the drizzle in the air and the changing light, the fear he might die and the flash of an enemy darting behind compound walls. I felt my own body tense up as he spoke of his split-second decision to kill an enemy soldier.

When he described witnessing a large soldier shooting a dark body mass that Tilley later identified as the Afghan with the prosthetic leg, Tilley unexpectedly mimicked the sound of the machine gun.

'*Brrrrrrrr*,' Tilley exclaimed loudly and suddenly. Others in the court flinched with me.

Next, he described how he'd heard Neil Browning hatch a plan 'to blood the rookie', and then returned from the Easter Sunday mission boasting about having achieved this goal.

'I finally blooded the rookie,' Tilley testified he had heard Browning say.

When Owens asked Tilley who he understood the rookie to be, he responded, 'Jason Andrews.'

After hours spent describing the Easter Sunday mission, Tilley testified about the allegation involving Roberts-Smith, Afghan Army Commander Ismail and an order to execute a farmer on a different operation.

'Shoot him or I will,' Roberts-Smith demanded of Ismail, according to Tilley's account to the court. Tilley then watched an Afghan soldier under Ismail's command murder his countryman.

Moses took to Tilley more savagely than he had to Langmore.

The barrister had obtained Chris Masters' detailed notes, provided to the court under compulsion, that revealed how Tilley had told the reporter of the war crimes allegations. As I watched Tilley being quizzed by Moses, I realised the soldier was oblivious to the fact that my fellow reporter's notes were in Moses' possession. Moses appeared to be drawing Tilley into a trap so he could accuse him of lying about his dealings with Masters.

Over an hour's adjournment for lunch, Masters and I both spiralled into despair. We had subpoenaed Tilley, forcing him to court, and now a single meeting held years before threatened to blow up his credibility.

When no one was around, I punched a wall and swore repeatedly. If Tilley was disbelieved, it wasn't fatal to our Easter Sunday case given we had multiple witnesses. But it would weaken it.

The news was bleaker for the Ismail allegation. Despite the weeks of work that had gone into proving Ismail hadn't been sacked from the SAS, this allegation would likely be lost if Tilley didn't do something to rescue his credibility.

After lunch, Tilley resumed testifying with a fervour I hadn't previously seen. Whether he'd sensed the imminent attack by Moses or had simply refreshed his memory, the soldier took a markedly different approach to describing his meeting with Masters. With each detail he recounted, he was circumventing Moses' impending attack.

As he neared the end of his evidence, I wondered if Tilley had begun to enjoy the joust with Roberts-Smith's barrister. He had started returning fire, calling the silk 'Mr Moses' with just the hint of a smile on his face.

* * *

There was something I found particularly irritating about Arthur Moses' courtroom theatrics. As Owens contested a point of law or questioned a witness, Moses sometimes leant back in his chair, rolled his eyes or arched his brows, grinning or whispering audibly.

The barrister seemed to have little regard that he was at risk of annoying the one person he needed to please: Justice Besanko. While the judge was mostly as expressionless as a stone-faced poker player, I'd heard him more than once address Moses like a schoolteacher chiding an errant student.

It seemed to me Moses would labour points that went nowhere, only to tell a witness 'I'll come back to that', as if an aimless question would improve like a wine in a cellar.

I also repeatedly wondered why Moses did not effectively challenge our witnesses on critical points of disputed evidence, an apparent Law 101 error.

For instance, when McMurray described how he'd found the old Afghan's body inside the courtyard near the tunnel, Moses never accused McMurray of invention or put to him an alternative theory.

In contrast, Moses never missed a chance to advance the theory that our witnesses were lying because they were cowards or envious of Roberts-Smith's medals. I found it a discombobulating line of attack. These witnesses may not have been awarded a Victoria Cross, but most had served repeated tours of Afghanistan with distinction.

The whole thrust of Roberts-Smith's case – that our witnesses invented murder allegations because they were jealous – had always sounded inherently implausible to me, no matter how seriously it was described in articles written by journalists close to Roberts-Smith. Would veterans really lie about prisoner executions because they were envious?

McClintock had tried his best with this claim when he'd theatrically launched the first salvos of the trial in his opening remarks, but even then it sounded hollow.

As the trial progressed under the stern and unrelenting eye of Justice Besanko, the allegations of medal envy sounded even flimsier. As our witnesses swore oaths to tell the truth and presented in the stand as decent men who'd served their country honourably, I felt the jealousy motive had morphed into something nearing a conspiracy theory.

It imbued Roberts-Smith's case with an air of desperation, especially as it became evident that some of our witnesses admired Roberts-Smith as a soldier far more than they wished to come to court and help out two newspaper reporters they'd never met. One of the SAS eyewitnesses to the killing of the prosthetic-legged man told the court he believed Roberts-Smith had performed an 'exhibition execution'.

'He wanted people to see that he was going to kill someone out there in front of everyone,' this witness testified. But this same witness was clearly furious we'd forced him to court to testify about the Victoria Cross winner. He didn't believe there was anything wrong with executing a Taliban member.

According to this witness, Roberts-Smith had nothing to justify or explain. 'I still don't agree with the fact that BRS is here, and he's under an extreme amount of duress for killing bad dudes who we went over to kill,' he told Justice Besanko.

As I watched witness after witness firmly rebut Moses' claims they were jealous haters, or that their mental health had muddled their memories, I understood why our legal team had decided to call them to the stand while benching other potentially helpful witnesses.

Nick Simkin was the most prominent of these. His absence in court guaranteed the 'hater' claims Moses desperately wanted to air were given less oxygen. With no Simkin to question, Moses' efforts to portray him as an arch villain fell limp.

So did Moses' battle with Tilley. The pair sparred for hours until both seemed to run out of puff. Tilley might have lost a little skin by initially hesitating to accept propositions that Moses put to him. But the barrister's subsequent high-camp denouncements of Tilley's integrity were totally overblown.

Tilley knew it. As he left the witness box, I saw him lock eyes with Roberts-Smith and give him a salute. I interpreted the gesture as a message that he wasn't intimidated.

Roberts-Smith responded by opening up his arms in a cocky gesture, as if to say: 'Go to hell.'

* * *

By the time Boyd Keary had entered the witness box, Moses had taken to repeatedly playing my *60 Minutes* programs to witnesses, and asking them if they were one of the anonymous SAS soldiers who'd appeared on the show. He'd been met with denial after denial.

But Moses appeared to believe he would be onto a winner with Keary.

As Owens led Keary through his evidence, Moses seemed, at least to me, to be itching to have his turn.

As Keary delivered his evidence-in-chief with confidence and clarity, Moses theatrically raised his eyebrows. I couldn't be quite sure, but it appeared as if Moses was also trying to get the judge's attention, as if to draw him in on some inside joke.

Justice Besanko studiously avoided catching Moses' gaze, with eyes only for Keary as he described to the court a series of ugly encounters with Roberts-Smith: the war hero had bullied his fellow soldiers; he'd bashed a petrified, unarmed detainee; on a pre-deployment training exercise he'd instructed a junior soldier to conduct a mock execution; he'd told Keary how he wanted to 'choke a man to death with my bare hands' and 'watch the life drain out of his eyes'.

Keary also claimed to have raised the cliff kick allegation up the chain of command, only to have it fall on deaf ears.

The soldier left nothing back as he testified. He was open about his scepticism around some of Roberts-Smith's awards, including the Victoria Cross. He, too, had raised his concerns about the awarding of certain medals with his superiors, including the Regimental Sergeant Major (RSM). Like the war crimes and bullying complaints, Keary said no one senior wanted to challenge Roberts-Smith.

'At one point the RSM said to me, "What are you hoping to get out of this?",' Keary told the court. 'I said, "It's not what I want to get out of this. It's what needs to be done."'

When Owens asked Keary if he'd had unapproved contact with the media, Moses broke into a smile and stared directly at the judge. I froze, feeling the familiar stomach churn. If Keary chose the same path as Tilley, he, too, would face a sustained attack on his credibility.

Keary sought and was given an immunity certificate for breaking defence force rules. He then continued testifying without hesitation. He told the judge that he was one of the two anonymous SAS soldiers interviewed by me for *60 Minutes* and justified his decision to do so because he wanted to push back against a campaign of intimidation he believed Roberts-Smith was waging. McMurray had been sent anonymous letters, Simkin had been raided, Tilley had been warned.

As Justice Besanko continued silently observing Keary testify, the judge looked serious and absorbed. In contrast, Moses was grinning.

It was obvious what was coming next. Almost as soon as he'd leapt to his feet, Moses launched into Keary over his interactions with me. Just as immediately, the barrister's attack appeared to fall short. Keary had steeled himself for the onslaught. If Moses' questions were designed as punches, they did not land on an unflustered Keary.

Levitan passed me a note that said of the soldier: 'He has brought his A-Game.'

As Moses' cross-examination began to dissolve into repetition and Justice Besanko glanced at the clock, I started a tally on how many times Moses said: 'I'll come back to that.'

Something else was also happening. Moses' voice was beginning to rise.

As Keary pushed back calmly and firmly, the barrister was becoming shrill. The judge interrupted him. 'Just pause,' he told Moses, his brow furrowed. 'Mr Moses ... I won't tolerate raising the voice to the extent that you did in this court.'

Moses: 'Yes, your Honour.'

Justice Besanko: 'All right.'

Moses: 'I won't do that.'

Justice Besanko: 'Thank you. Please ask your next question.'

If Moses had sought the judge's attention earlier, he had it now.

I watched as the barrister repeated a question about Keary's dealings with the media. As Keary again held his ground, Moses snapped: 'That is a nonsense answer, isn't it?'

Owens leapt to his feet to object but he didn't need to. The judge again intervened.

'I don't know that it adds much to the questions that you've previously asked,' he told Moses, while also leaving the door open for him to ask it again. Moses strode through it.

'That was a nonsense answer, wasn't it?' the silk asked a second time of Keary.

'No, it wasn't, Mr Moses,' the Afghan veteran replied matter-of-factly.

When pressed further on his decision to call out Roberts-Smith on national television, Keary gave what seemed to me a thoughtful answer. 'It was a mistake. I know that because it was against defence policy,' Keary said. 'I'm not proud of it. However, I can't say I regret it.'

As I watched the war-hardened soldier leave the court, I thought back to Andrew Hastie's appearance on *60 Minutes*, in which the captain-turned-politician had described his own decision to be interviewed. Hastie explained he wanted to stand by the few soldiers who had also chosen not to stay silent, despite knowing the career kiss of death in the regiment that came with confronting wrongdoing. Hastie believed their actions represented the ultimate form of moral courage.

If this was so, Keary had it in spades.

* * *

So, too, did SAS medic Jimmy Stanton. I watched him testify for hours. He was an impeccable witness: thoughtful, composed and genuine. He radiated honesty as he spoke about the mission in which he'd detained a young Afghan trembling uncontrollably and passed him on to Roberts-Smith's patrol team, only to hear Roberts-Smith later boast of executing him.

'I shot the c*** in the side of the head,' Stanton told the court Roberts-Smith had said to him. 'I blew his brains out, and it was the most beautiful thing I've ever seen.'

Stanton's testimony alone seemed unlikely to reach the standard of proof we required, especially given Stanton had never claimed to have actually witnessed an execution. But when shown a photo of one of the Afghans shot dead during the mission in question, Stanton told the court it appeared to be the young, trembling man he'd taken into custody.

His testimony added to other circumstantial evidence. While the official records from the mission described four men being detained, the official photos of these detainees only showed three men. Each had a number on their shirt, yet the numbers on these three detainees were out of sequence. A number had been inexplicably skipped.

It suggested that one of the four detainees had disappeared. Had they been released, contrary to policy? Or had they been executed?

Maybe I was too invested in our case, but I couldn't see any reason why Stanton would be disbelieved. The judge might decide that there wasn't enough evidence to prove an actual murder, but I believed he would find Stanton a truthful witness.

Moses' ultimate strategy in attacking Stanton seemed to be aimed at implying he lacked the mental fortitude to deal with the rigours of war.

Whether it was because he was acting on Roberts-Smith's misguided directions or had come up with the legal strategy himself, Moses appeared to have failed to read the room in pursuing this line of questioning.

'And did observing dead Afghans cause you any anguish or trauma?'

'It's never nice to see a dead person regardless of whether they're an Afghan or Australian.'

'It's something that is hard to look at?'

'I don't think it's enjoyable.'

Moses also tried to attack Stanton over his relationship with me, asking if he'd broken military rules by talking to a journalist. Stanton countered with the truth. He'd shared nothing with me I didn't know already. We'd stayed in touch only because we were looking out for our mate, Dusty Miller.

'We had a mutual friend who was having some health troubles,' Stanton replied. 'We would check in on him, and if he didn't respond to either one of us, we would contact one another to see if one of us had had contact with him to ascertain he was okay.'

It was at this point that Masters leant over to me and whispered: 'This is suicidal for Moses.'

When Stanton regrouped with our legal team in an empty courtroom after he'd finished testifying, he was visibly exhausted. Owens gently tried to comfort him. But he couldn't offer Stanton a prediction about whether Roberts-Smith would ultimately be held to account. It was too early to speculate about what Justice Besanko might conclude.

We had more witnesses to call and more evidence to gather in order to reach the bar Justice Besanko would need to find in our favour. Roberts-Smith's witnesses were also yet to appear. If they performed well, our witnesses' testimony could all be for nothing in terms of the final outcome.

That was our problem. For his part, Stanton had done all that was humanly possible. 'That was some of the most powerful witness testimony I've ever seen,' Owens told the ex-medic. 'You were incredible.'

It wasn't clear if Stanton registered what Owens was saying. He'd broken down and was softly sobbing.

CHAPTER 45

FLOWER OF TRUTH

Witnesses for the newspapers:
February–April 2022

Emma Roberts was riddled with anxiety as she waited in the witness room to be called. It was 14 February and she was wearing a dark dress on which she'd pinned a white flower brooch. In her handbag was a small, smooth stone she'd picked up months before in the sand at Byron Bay. It was a good luck charm. If she survived the ordeal that confronted her, she'd return it to the ocean.

It wasn't just the prospect of giving evidence about her former husband. This was only part of a long process that was entirely out of her control, one she could not avoid and which offered only bleak outcomes. She'd been subpoenaed, so had no choice but to come to court.

If Roberts-Smith won the case, he'd be escaping accountability for his lies and misbehaviour. If he lost, there was every chance the police might move on him. In the end, it was their children who would suffer either way. Her daughters were all that Emma really cared about.

Emma knew he had a long-term affair and had lied about it. She knew he had buried USBs in their backyard. He had set fire to laptops. He had used burner phones. He had engineered the sending of anonymous letters and emails to scare off potential witnesses. And he'd brought on this whole mess by going to court in the first place.

Roberts-Smith had described Emma in his own testimony as 'extremely bitter'. 'She has done things along the way that have been detrimental to my family, and particularly to me, because she thinks it will hurt me,' he'd said.

But Emma didn't want to hurt him. Her life had moved on. New surname, new boyfriend, new job, new home. When her mind turned to Roberts-Smith, she pitied him. But he invaded her thoughts less and less.

Emma had no idea if Roberts-Smith had executed Afghans. Of the allegation he'd punched his former girlfriend, she had no firsthand knowledge. But she knew him as controlling and a compulsive liar who, having had his affair exposed by his girlfriend, had pushed Emma to help him cover it up by inventing the story that they were separated when he was in fact cheating.

Now, in the neighbouring courtroom, through a wall a few feet away, Roberts-Smith was seated with his parents awaiting her arrival.

The man who would guide her through her evidence-in-chief, Nic Owens, waited quietly at the bar table.

'I'm very nervous for her,' he'd earlier said quietly to me and Dean Levitan.

'She's about to get monstered by Bruce.'

Bruce McClintock was known for his, at times, overbearing manner in court. It was he who would be cross-examining Emma based on Roberts-Smith's instructions.

'I seek to call Emma Roberts,' Owens said.

'This way please,' the tipstaff told her.

* * *

The night before he was due to take the stand for the first time in the Federal Court, Andrew Hastie called his father and asked if they could pray together. Nerves were creeping in and the politician was uncertain of what was to come when he entered the witness box.

The regiment he loved had been ripped apart by the release of the Brereton Report sixteen months earlier, yet it had also started to reform and heal. After being promoted to Assistant Minister for Defence shortly after Brereton tabled his report, Hastie had aided this process only to see the Roberts-Smith trial plunge his old workplace back into the headlines.

Old enmities between comrades once only whispered about at Campbell Barracks were now in the public domain. So, too, were the atrocities Hastie suspected had occurred. The witnesses had been forced to relive trauma when they were hauled before court and, as their testimony hit the press, the Australian people were once again wondering if they could trust the most elite military regiment in the country.

Hastie prayed with his father for the courage to tell the truth. He also prayed for Roberts-Smith and his family. The soldier he once admired appeared consumed by hate and revenge. If the testimony of others in the SAS was to be believed, Roberts-Smith was also a war criminal.

It was terrible for Australia. It was terrible for the SAS. And no one, least of all Hastie, wanted to see it. But until the truth was there for all to witness, Australia couldn't move forward.

Hastie felt no malice. His goal in testifying was only to speak honestly. But not even prayer could shake his feeling of deep sadness. The ex-SAS captain told himself something else. It would be lonely and hostile when giving evidence. Roberts-Smith's barrister would come for him. And when he did, Hastie would punch back.

* * *

Owens addressed Emma gently, asking her question after question as he guided her through the wreckage of the last few years: the affair; the distressed woman at her house with a black eye who disclosed she had been pregnant with her husband's child; the pressure Roberts-Smith had placed on Emma to lie to the press in 2018.

'Ben had suggested that the only way we would survive [was] that if we said we were separated,' Emma told the court. 'I didn't want to lie. There were enough lies.'

Emma said he'd left her no choice. 'He pointed to our children sitting in the loungeroom, and he said, "If you don't lie, you will lose them."'

She explained to Justice Besanko that she had gone ahead and lied. She'd also appeared on the front page of *The Australian* to help Roberts-Smith rebut what was in fact a valid claim by the newspapers he was now suing: that he'd cheated on her with Amanda.

In the lead-up to this newspaper article, Emma told the court Roberts-Smith had become increasingly agitated. When she read media reports about the anonymous threats posted to an SAS soldier, she confronted Roberts-Smith, demanding to know if he was behind the intimidation.

Emma told Owens what she'd previously observed had fuelled her suspicions. She had watched as Roberts-Smith arrived home one day with gloves, envelopes and paper. He also asked her to check the postal address for the SAS's Perth headquarters.

'He told me he had written the letters, had printed them at the Seven office, had sealed them in the envelopes, addressed them, and had given them to John McLeod to post.'

Emma kept herself composed throughout Owens' examination, but that was the easy part. McClintock started fiercely and never gave up. He had plenty of ammunition. Emma and her friend Danielle Scott had been compelled to hand over hundreds of private messages they exchanged as Emma's marriage imploded.

'He's a lying cheating cunt,' Roberts had lashed out in one of her messages.

The picture McClintock painted was of a scorned woman, hell-bent on revenge. Yes, she was emotional, Emma conceded, but her life was spiralling out of control.

'I was very frustrated with Ben at the time. I was very frustrated in a bitter divorce.'

As the questions continued, Emma found she couldn't contain the emotions welling up in her. When McClintock queried if it was true that one of her daughters had asked her, 'Why does Dad not smile anymore?', Emma found her voice disappearing.

As the court fell silent and Justice Besanko gently called for a brief adjournment, Emma felt tears streaming down her face.

* * *

'I don't dislike Mr Roberts-Smith at all,' Hastie told the court. 'I pity Mr Roberts-Smith. I pity this whole process. I don't want to be here.'

Hastie felt emotion wash over him as he spoke. He may not have directly witnessed a war crime, but he knew enough to know bad things had likely happened.

'My ambition has been to preserve the SAS regiment and the way we do that is by coming clean on some of the mistakes of the last fifteen years,' he testified.

Those mistakes included some patrol teams embracing a 'pagan warrior culture'. 'In the warrior culture that was being emphasised at the time ... killing became a sacrament in itself.'

But it wasn't just rogue elements of the SAS, or a rotten culture, that were to blame, Hastie said from the witness box. It was those at Parliament House who also needed to shoulder the blame. 'Politicians were sending us over there ... and it was bloody ridiculous some of the stuff they were asking us to do.'

There was also a need for individual accountability. When he was pressed about what he thought had happened to the soldier known as Person 66 on a mission in 2012, Hastie said he believed something terrible had occurred and suspected one man was to blame: Ben Roberts-Smith.

'It's my view that Person 66 was blooded,' Hastie told the Federal Court.

**

Emma had no way of knowing it, but while McClintock accused her of lying again and again, another witness who would corroborate much of her story was preparing to come out of hiding.

John McLeod had become increasingly paranoid, worried about getting photographed again by the tabloid paparazzi. But he, too, had been subpoenaed by our legal team. The ex-cop had no choice but to come to court and tell the judge how Roberts-Smith had used him to send threatening letters and anonymous emails. In McLeod's mind, he'd been Roberts-Smith's patsy, a fall guy trusted to keep his mouth shut.

And he had, for three years. Right up until the moment when he'd walked into the federal police offices in Brisbane and confessed to his role in Roberts-Smith's campaign of witness intimidation. He vowed to do the same in the Federal Court.

Emma only learnt of McLeod's corroborating testimony when it appeared in the media.

Where he had backed up her account, Emma's testimony would in turn corroborate the testimony of another witness. Emma had initially helped discredit Amanda's allegations by going along with her husband's separation lie, but she abandoned this falsehood under oath.

Emma's testimony about her ex-husband's intense scheming and dishonesty had the effect of undermining his claims in court that he should be believed over Amanda.

It seemed undeniable that both Amanda and McLeod were more Roberts-Smith roadkill, victims of a man used to getting what he wanted, disposing of people when they no longer served a purpose and coming after those who stood in his way. That was not Emma's life anymore. She'd made that decision when she'd ditched the 'Smith' from her surname.

As she walked out of the court for the last time, Emma was again chased by photographers, who snapped away.

On her final few hours in the witness box, McClintock had done the same. 'You would like to see my client lose this case, wouldn't you?' he'd asked. 'In fact, you're here to inflict as much damage upon him as you can?'

Emma remained resolute. 'I hope Ben survives this nightmare,' she replied.

In the photos of Emma on the front page of the nation's papers the next day, she appeared grim faced and stoic as she'd exited court. The white flower pinned to her breast stuck out against the black dress. No one in the press had picked it up, but it was a chrysanthemum. Emma Roberts had chosen it because it was the flower of truth.

* * *

After Hastie was finally excused from the witness box, he returned to his Sydney hotel room and lay on his bed. He was exhausted.

Hastie had done what he had set out to do: tell the truth, whatever the impact on his political career. He had even gone in to bat for those less popular than politicians – he told the court that the reason he had spoken to me was that he believed journalists had played a vital role in the war crimes scandal.

'My view is that the system failed, which is why public interest journalism is important,' he had told Justice Besanko.

Hastie knew many voters still supported Roberts-Smith and would do so until the moment Justice Besanko concluded he was a war criminal. If the judge found otherwise, Hastie would be mercilessly attacked.

This was why Hastie believed that Person 66's anticipated evidence about his alleged blooding was so important. And it was why Hastie had been shocked to learn that Person 66 had successfully fought the move to have him testify.

Nic Owens had described his potential evidence as a path to outright victory for us as he'd urged Justice Besanko to force Person 66 to answer questions, albeit with the safeguard of a certificate of immunity.

But Person 66's barrister convinced the judge that he should not answer questions on the grounds of self-incrimination. A certificate wouldn't provide enough protection, he warned. 'If that evidence were given ... then it would have the tendency to incriminate the witness,' Person 66's barrister said from the bar table. 'The offence ... would be an offence of murder.'

Without Person 66, our prospect of victory was far less certain. We were still relying on witnesses such as Jason Andrews – a man who once considered Roberts-Smith as close as kin – to defeat Australia's most famous soldier.

CHAPTER 46

WHAT DID HE SAY?

Witnesses for the newspapers:
February–April 2022

As I waited for Jason Andrews to be called to the stand on 28 February, I once again turned to face Roberts-Smith. We hadn't said a word to each other, despite sitting only metres apart for days on end. Instead, we exchanged occasional stares and facial gestures.

On this morning, as we locked eyes, I raised my brows and he did the same, mimicking me. But something had changed. For the first time, I recognised in Roberts-Smith something I had not seen before.

He now appeared to me as an oversized boy in a suit who, having made his vow of innocence to Kerry Stokes or his father or whomever else it was he had lied to about what he'd done in Afghanistan, was too arrogant or proud or scared to back down. He'd walked himself to the edge of a cliff. If Andrews' testimony pushed him over, his lies would be exposed. I almost felt sorry for him.

Then my mind turned to the man actually kicked off a

cliff, Ali Jan, and his donkey loaded with flour, wood and shoes for one of his children, whom I'd met in Kabul three years earlier.

On day one of the trial, Bruce McClintock had used a very descriptive term referencing Roberts-Smith's alleged actions. It was perfect. Ben Roberts-Smith VC, MG *was* an ostentatious psychopath.

I was certain of this because of everything that had preceded Andrews' impending appearance in court. It wasn't just the years of journalism or what I'd learnt about the Brereton Inquiry and federal police investigation. Contrary to the expectations of Roberts-Smith's legal team, our witnesses – civilian and SAS – had shown up in droves, save for Person 66.

They had to be forced to court with subpoenas, but once in the stand they had nearly all exceeded our expectations. I thought Arthur Moses and Bruce McClintock had largely been ineffectual. Their jocularity and guffawing faded as the days passed.

The senior Seven executive who had spent the first few days of the trial chummy with lawyer Mark O'Brien was no longer coming to court, possibly watching online instead. Monica Allen now seemed nervous when she entered the court, staring at her shoes. Moses still appeared smug, but it was clear that his client's great hope regarding Jason Andrews would not be realised. Roberts-Smith's worst nightmare was taking shape. Andrews had arrived at the court.

The heart of the journalism that had landed us in court in the first place, and the core of our war crimes defence against Roberts-Smith's lawsuit, was what happened in Darwan. It was why we had spent the best part of four years battling to get Andrews to testify.

The breakthrough had come only recently, with Andrews' lawyers finally paying serious heed to Levitan's suggestion: Would Andrews come to court and testify about Darwan if Owens gave a guarantee not to ask him about his alleged blooding on Easter Sunday?

We booked plane tickets for Andrews and his wife from Perth to Sydney. But until I saw him enter the courtroom, I wouldn't breathe out. And even then, it all depended on what he said. Would he back up his old friend, the man he once regarded as a brother?

Usually Owens would tell me about the nerves of jittery witnesses he had to prod forward as they testified, but prior to court that day he disclosed it was he who was feeling nauseous.

'I've never felt so nervous,' he said.

If I hadn't already spent weeks watching Owens on his feet in court, I might have been worried. But he had performed flawlessly, week in week out. Essentially, though, the question of whether Andrews would testify honestly was outside of Owens' control.

For weeks, I'd sought to gather intelligence. Were Andrews and Roberts-Smith still not speaking? Had anyone got to Andrews? Had they secretly conspired to defeat our case?

The witness door opened, and a suited man with a greying beard strode in.

* * *

I found the building tension almost too much to bear as Owens guided Andrews through his memory of the Darwan mission on 11 September 2012. He began with the arrival of the SAS and moved to the decision of Roberts-

Smith to cross the Helmand River to hunt down an insurgent armed with a rifle and radio. Owens was slowly leading Andrews to the final compound on the ridge, the place where Roberts-Smith insisted there were no Afghans.

It wasn't just me who looked anxious.

The whole courtroom was on edge. Levitan turned around to look at me and nodded. This was the moment of truth. Our case about Darwan would rise or fall on what happened next.

Andrews took three sips of water and continued, directing his answers to Justice Besanko.

According to his recollection, the far compound wasn't empty. He recalled an Afghan male and a donkey draped in a red rug. The donkey man was detained by Roberts-Smith's patrol team. A translator was then called for and an interrogation commenced.

I tried to make notes, but I was squeezing my pen so hard my hand cramped. Andrews was already drastically diverting from the account given by Roberts-Smith. Along with the man and the donkey, Andrews recalled at least one other Afghan detainee in the compound that Roberts-Smith insisted was empty.

I stopped writing and focused on Andrews, my heart pounding.

The soldier questioning the donkey man with the help of an interpreter was Roberts-Smith, Andrews said; he then described moving outside of the compound 'down a rocky slope' as the interrogation continued.

A short time later, he watched as another patrol team member, Vincent Jelovic, moved 'towards a large drop-off'.

Andrews sighed audibly, and his face looked pained. Gently urged forward by Owens from the bar table, he pressed on.

Jelovic wasn't alone. He had guided the handcuffed man to the edge of the cliff and was holding him still, his hand upon his shoulder. Andrews described the Afghan to the court using the military terminology for a detainee in Australian custody: a 'person under control'.

'Which person under control are you talking about?' Owens asked quietly.

'The individual that had arrived with the donkey ... the person under control had his back towards the large slope,' Andrews answered.

Next, Andrews 'noticed Ben Roberts-Smith'. 'He had walked to a position, maybe three or four metres away. And as I was trying to understand what was happening, he turned around, walked forward and kicked the individual in the chest.'

The donkey man was 'catapulted backwards' over the cliff edge. As he fell, Andrews 'saw the individual's face strike a large rock'. 'He knocked out a number of his teeth, including his front teeth.'

Andrews described feeling shocked, but still followed Roberts-Smith and Jelovic as they manoeuvred down a track towards the creek bed where the donkey man had landed.

'Might be an obvious question, but why were you in shock?' Owens asked.

''Cause it was something I've never encountered before,' Andrews replied, his face ashen.

'When you say you'd never seen this before, you're referring to someone being kicked off a cliff?'

'Absolutely.'

The three soldiers found the donkey man lying in the dry creek bed, dazed and bleeding from the mouth, his hands still bound behind his back with plasticuffs.

'He attempted to sit up and then fell back down again,' recalled Andrews.

'Was he still handcuffed or not?'

'Yes.'

Andrews described Roberts-Smith ordering him and Jelovic to drag the donkey man to the base of a large tree and the pair following the command.

Next, Andrews testified that he walked away from the tree, searching for other members of the SAS. Then he turned back in the direction of the donkey man. The Afghan was now standing, still in handcuffs, so Andrews looked away again. He didn't want to see what happened, but he knew it had been done when gunshots rang out.

He turned back again, this time to see Jelovic 'still in a position with his rifle in his shoulder'. The donkey man was dead.

'And did you observe anything about it that struck you?' Owens asked.

I'd never seen the courtroom so still. Justice Besanko watched Andrews like a hawk as he described noticing a radio had appeared next to the donkey man's body.

It 'was slightly wet', he recalled. It was then Andrews realised the radio had been taken from the insurgent Roberts-Smith had earlier waded across a river to kill.

But the cover-up wasn't complete. After they returned to the base, Andrews recounted how Roberts-Smith met with his small patrol team in their room and invented a false story about killing a Taliban member in a cornfield.

'He came back into our room and said, "This is what the story is …" Your Honour, it was words to the effect of "the story is that we engaged a spotter".'

* * *

As I waited for Moses to rise to his feet to begin the cross-examination, I wondered what else might fall out of Andrews' testimony. I also slipped off my suit jacket. It was convention to keep it on in court, but I'd been so anxious I'd been sweating,

During the proceedings Moses had already drawn out information that had helped, or at least hadn't harmed, our case. He wouldn't disappoint with Andrews.

Moses pushed Andrews on his relationship with Jelovic, pointing out that he'd been the best man at Jelovic's wedding.

'And he's upset with you, is that right?' Moses asked.

'I guess so.'

'Do you know that he's upset with you because he feels that you have, in effect, accused him of being a murderer?'

'I'd suggest so.'

I watched this line of questioning in bewilderment. It seemed to serve no purpose other than reinforce the discomfort Andrews so evidently felt in testifying.

The same occurred when Moses accused Andrews of being jealous of Roberts-Smith's Victoria Cross. He'd fought alongside Roberts-Smith at the famous battle of Tizak, but Andrews had won a Medal for Gallantry, a lesser, albeit still revered, medal recognising bravery. Roberts-Smith had found fame and fortune, but Andrews had left the army a relative nobody.

So what? I thought. Again, the questioning seemed to fall well short of its intended mark, highlighting only the anguish faced by Andrews in entering the witness box.

'I loved him as a brother,' he said to Moses. 'There's no resentment there.'

'But now you hate him, don't you?'

'Of course I don't hate him.'

'And it's the case, isn't it, that you're jealous of him?'

'Believe me … I'm not jealous of him.'

* * *

To highlight the incongruity of Andrews' claim that Roberts-Smith had boasted about the cliff kick after trying to cover it up, Moses pushed the Afghan veteran to recall what precisely it was Roberts-Smith had uttered.

'Is that what he said, "I kicked the individual off the cliff?"' Moses asked.

'No, he didn't say that.'

'What did he say?'

'I kicked the cunt off the cliff.'

I noticed a Commonwealth lawyer wince as Andrews recalled the words.

Most in the courtroom had now watched my *60 Minutes* story, care of Moses' decision to repeatedly replay it on a screen to various witnesses. As a result, they knew the executed donkey man had a name. They knew the 'cunt' kicked off a cliff had a wife and several children.

Andrews knew it too.

As Moses forced him to watch the program featuring Ali Jan's family calling for justice, Andrews wept silently.

CHAPTER 47

HAVE WE WON?

Witnesses for Ben Roberts-Smith, April–June 2022

'Dean … you've got to check this out.'

Tess McGuire, one of the youngest lawyers on the team, sounded excited. It was 10pm and McGuire's face was lit up by her computer screen at the MinterEllison offices in Sydney. The city skyline blinked in the darkness out the window, a sea of lights stretching to the harbour. But McGuire was focused only on the screen in front of her. She was scanning through the Instagram account of Tim Douglass, a witness for Roberts-Smith due to appear in the Federal Court the next day.

In the days before testifying, Douglass had 'liked' a number of posts denigrating me, Chris Masters and members of the SAS known to have spoken out against war crimes or testified against the Victoria Cross winner.

Now it was Levitan's face being lit up by the screen.

I had earlier spent an evening scouring the images on the USBs. They'd confirmed a small but useful fact. The SAS soldier who had dressed up as a member of the Ku

Klux Klan at the party at the Fat Lady's Arms mostly had his white hood on when photographed. But in one shot, the KKK soldier could be seen in the far corner of the bar with his hood off. It was Douglass.

As Levitan scoured the Instagram page, he realised it not only confirmed Douglass was one of those who helped erode the culture in pockets of the SAS. It also made it plain he was fiercely loyal to Roberts-Smith.

Douglass had liked a post that listed 'Fun Facts' about Ali Jan: including that he was a 'terrorist p3do'. The post included the hashtag: #nothingofvaluewaslost. He'd also endorsed social media posts describing whistleblowers in the SAS as 'rats' and 'snitches'.

Based in New Zealand, Douglass was one of the soldiers Roberts-Smith visited on his international tour of SAS mates as the Brereton Inquiry had closed in. The two others he'd seen were Neil Browning in the US and Vincent Jelovic in Perth.

The pair, along with Douglass, were among Roberts-Smith's closest mates. They, along with one or two other witnesses also known to be Roberts-Smith loyalists, comprised the core of his witness list. This was a major weakness for Roberts-Smith, as long as Owens could expose it effectively in court.

Whereas almost all of our witnesses had to be forced to court with subpoenas and had no bonds of any note with me or Masters, Roberts-Smith's witnesses were not only his good mates but, in many cases, also facing war crimes allegations.

Jelovic was Roberts-Smith's co-accused in the 2012 murder of Ali Jan. Browning was commander of Roberts-Smith's small patrol team when the war hero and Jason Andrews allegedly executed prisoners on Easter Sunday 2009.

We had earlier uncovered that both Jelovic's and Browning's legal fees were being paid by Kerry Stokes' publicly listed media company, Seven West Media, an arrangement no doubt organised by Roberts-Smith. As Levitan had written to Roberts-Smith's lawyers and Seven demanding more information about these legal fee payments, Seven had been replaced as the company funding the two soldiers by a private firm owned by Kerry Stokes and his family.

It seemed an odd arrangement – the two men could have been given defence department–funded lawyers free of charge, as was the case for all of our SAS witnesses. It was also strange that Stokes and his companies would be willing to fund suspected war criminals. (These legal fees were belatedly paid by Stokes' private company, not Seven.)

Douglass wasn't accused of involvement in any executions himself, but we suspected he was prepared to testify, along with Browning and two of Roberts-Smith's other witnesses, about the tunnel being empty on Easter Sunday. Douglass's story would potentially carry more weight, though, given he was the soldier who had searched the tunnel. His legal fees were also being paid for by Seven (which were also later repaid by Stokes' private company).

The legal fees arrangement was another indicator that he was bound to Roberts-Smith, not just through ties of friendship, but bonds of financial support. Would that be a motive for him to lie?

Owens just needed to lay it all out in the courtroom.

* * *

The barrister didn't prevaricate. Just moments into the cross-examination, a hint of crimson washed over

Douglass's face. Owens had asked him from the bar table whether he was an active follower of 'several Instagram pages that post commentary on this trial'.

'I do follow those pages,' Douglass said from the witness box.

Levitan knew what was coming next. He looked at Tess McGuire and nodded.

'Now, do you remember this?' Owens continued. 'Do you remember that one of the posts that you liked yesterday morning, before court, started off with this: *"When some fuckwit in a suit starts questioning your integrity and using his fucktard snake logic he learned getting his tonsils bruised by some lecturer's spotty dick at their non-binary law school, remember one thing: that this cunt will be one of the first to be held down and drowned in a muddy puddle for his fancy jacket when society crumbles".'*

Douglass looked uncomfortable. Next, the silk pushed Douglass on whether it was Owens who was the fuckwit in a suit in question.

'Who did you understand the comment in that post to be referring to?' the barrister asked.

'I have no idea,' Douglass responded.

Owens: 'It was me, wasn't it?'

Douglass: 'Sorry, I don't follow. Why would it be you?'

'Who else would it be?'

'I don't know.'

Time and time again, Owens pushed Douglass into corners, exposing his preparedness to lie if it suited Roberts-Smith.

Douglass was one of the soldiers who had provided Roberts-Smith with a statement falsely claiming that Ismail had been sacked after shooting a dog. On the stand, even after Roberts-Smith had himself abandoned the sacking claim, Douglass grimly hung onto the falsehood.

We hoped this apparent willingness to lie would taint what Douglass had earlier told the judge when Moses guided the witness through his evidence-in-chief. As anticipated, Douglass testified about finding a tunnel empty of any human form. If the judge believed the tunnel was empty, then he would find no prisoners were ever captured or executed.

Douglass had also sought to pre-empt the KKK revelation, by offering up to Moses that it was he who had worn the white robe and hood. 'It was the easiest costume to manufacture on short notice,' he explained of his decision to dress up as a member of the notorious white supremacist group.

'I knew one other person was coming in blackface, so I thought it would be funny if I come [sic] as a Klansman … probably just make fun of, like, the actual Klan itself.'

'I actually won the fancy dress competition that night.'

* * *

As Roberts-Smith's witnesses began to cycle through the courtroom, Levitan told me he noticed something strange happening. He was sleeping better and feeling lighter for the first time in a long time. Gone was the impending sense of doom. He no longer shuddered when I called to probe him about whether he had fixed one mishap or another.

It wasn't that he thought we had won the case. It was far too early for that. Douglass had done poorly, but if Roberts-Smith's other witnesses performed well, Levitan thought the case would come down to the wire.

Levitan's sense of contentment stemmed from the knowledge that he had done all that he could do over several years, and this effort had appeared to have paid dividends. Our witnesses had not only shown up after multiple false starts, but they had told the truth and mostly performed well. Owens had been brilliant, Mitchell and Barnett the same.

If Kabul had fallen earlier, or the Covid adjournment hadn't happened, or if Andrews had remained unwell, or the PAP notice had never been released and Langmore never discovered, or if Emma hadn't been so brave, or Amanda hadn't shown up to court and delivered her evidence about her treatment by Ben Roberts-Smith with such courage, there was every chance we would have been annihilated.

The one thing Levitan knew we always had on our side was the truth. It just needed a few major delays to rise to the surface.

This realisation had struck him in the strangest of circumstances. In the days before Roberts-Smith's legal team had begun calling his witnesses to court, Levitan was at the gym next to the Meriton Hotel when he spied the war hero on the step machine, dripping with sweat. Levitan had quietly slipped out, wanting to avoid a confrontation. That evening, at around 8pm, he bumped into Roberts-Smith again. This time it was in the foyer of the Meriton and Roberts-Smith was stumbling, blind drunk and reeking of booze.

Roberts-Smith had also been spotted drinking alone at a Sydney inner-city pub on Anzac Day. Usually on Anzac Day he would have been a subject of adulation and adoration, leading celebrations alongside notable Australians at the war memorial in Canberra. The sighting of the forlorn ex-soldier drinking alone, or heavily intoxicated in a hotel lobby, might have meant nothing. But it didn't scream of a man in firm control of his destiny. The man Levitan saw waiting for the lift wasn't celebrating. He was drowning.

Nic Owens also seemed far more confident. He hadn't left his manners at the courtroom door, but he'd also ramped up his aggression.

When Neil Browning stepped into the box, Owens barely drew breath before hitting him straight between the eyes. He opened his questions by asking the ex-SAS soldier: 'How many allegations of murder are you aware of have been made against a patrol of which you were the patrol commander when Ben Roberts-Smith was your 2IC?'

'Three,' Browning responded icily.

Owens peppered Browning with questions, methodically getting him to paint a picture for the judge that showed that the former patrol commander, like Douglass, had motive to lie. In Browning's case, he wasn't just protecting his good mate, but himself.

'You've in fact come here to give a deliberately false account of events at Whiskey 108 because you think it will be to your advantage in deterring prosecuting authorities from pursuing you in relation to those charges?' Owens put to him calmly.

'That is not true,' Browning shot back.

Curiously, Browning claimed he had only found out that Seven was paying his legal fees just a few days before being called as a witness and did not know why, despite the fact they were over $65,000.

While Browning stuck to the general Roberts-Smith script – no men in the tunnel, no executions – his story deviated from Roberts-Smith's when it came to the two armed Taliban aggressors supposedly shot dead outside the compound. He described hearing gunfire while he was at a patrol team commanders' meeting inside the compound, then dashing outside to find Roberts-Smith and Andrews had just lawfully shot dead two insurgents. Yet not a single other witness at this meeting recalled the event. Only Browning remembered it.

The two men had been shot while running away, said Browning. This also appeared at odds with his comrade's account. Roberts-Smith described the men as running towards the compound, not away from it.

In court, the ex-patrol commander was openly hostile about those in the SAS he suspected had assisted me and Masters. Browning denied war crimes had occurred, but said that if they did, soldiers should alert their officers, no one else.

'Then the chain of command decides where that goes, that's how it should happen. You don't go through the *Sydney Morning Herald* to get it done,' he said.

Under cross-examination, Browning also denied he'd used the term 'rookie' to describe junior soldiers while patrol commander. Owens questioned him about whether this denial was an effort to undermine our case that he'd boasted of 'blooding the rookie'. 'Rookie' simply wasn't a term he used for his junior patrol team members, Browning insisted. After locking Browning into his story, Owens challenged him about an image of a piece of paper stuck to his patrol room's door in Tarin Kowt in 2010. It was from the buried USBs. It listed the most junior member of Browning's patrol team in 2010 as the 'rookie fuck'.

'I don't remember that,' was all that Browning could muster in response.

By the end of his cross-examination, the often combative Browning seemed to me to be spent. Owens, in contrast, was beaming.

It wasn't the end of the ordeal for the former soldier, though. The next morning in court, Browning's barrister was unexpectedly absent. He was meant to be there to represent another of Roberts-Smith's witnesses, but was nowhere to be found. Even Justice Besanko queried his whereabouts.

Mitchell had a hunch. He searched the daily listings of the Local Court criminal division and found what he was looking for. Neil Browning had been arrested.

'Get someone to the Local Court NOW!' Mitchell said to one of the team.

Two hours later, Mitchell received a dispatch from a junior lawyer who'd dashed to the Local Court. A prosecutor had revealed that hours after Browning had finished testifying in the Federal Court, he had been confronted by war crimes investigators from the federal police and Office of the Special Investigator at his hotel. They were armed with a search warrant and demanded he hand over his mobile phone.

Browning appeared 'intoxicated, acting in a belligerent, unreasonable and aggressive manner,' court documents revealed. 'The accused attempted to enter the lift to leave the hotel and refused to hand over his mobile phone. When prevented from entering the lift, to prevent the destruction of evidence, being the mobile phone in his possession, the accused tensed up, clenched his fist, and shoved police to the body, constituting an assault.'

Browning had spent the night in a jail cell, charged with obstructing and causing harm to a Commonwealth official.

Within hours, the news of Browning's arrest and bailing was being reported by almost every news outlet in the country.

* * *

Owens' questioning of Vincent Jelovic followed a similar
pattern to Browning's, albeit concerned with events at
Darwan. Jelovic also stuck to the general script, but
deviated at critical junctures.

Roberts-Smith had testified watching Jelovic shoot dead
an insurgent in a cornfield at a distance of two metres. But
Jelovic claimed the Afghan man with a radio was about
fifteen metres away, separated by dense corn crops.

Owens surgically attacked Jelovic on how he was able to
see a man holding a radio through fifteen metres of heavy
vegetation that, by Jelovic's own account, stood between
five and seven feet high. With each question, Roberts-
Smith's earlier claim that the same shooting took place at a
distance of just two metres hung in the air, unspoken but
deadly.

'How is it that you could have seen an insurgent through
fifteen metres of thickly planted crops that were five to
seven feet tall?'

''Cos I could,' came the answer.

* * *

After ninety-nine days of hearings, the trial was nearly
finished, save for final submissions. Five years had passed
since I had partnered with Chris Masters to begin an
exposé that had never really ended. It had been almost
four years since Roberts-Smith launched the defamation
case that would change so many lives.

In Afghanistan, too, much was changed. The coalition
had hastily departed, and the Taliban was once again
in control, if one could use that term for a country still
marred by violence, poverty and despair. All that blood
and treasure, and for what?

Australia's defamation trial of the century had become a public spectacle that was spoken about at dinner parties and barbecues. Roberts-Smith was despised in some quarters, a laughing stock in others, and still lauded by some.

Drama continued to unfold outside the courtroom. On 18 June, I wrote a story revealing how Justice Brereton had given a speech in Sydney to the Military History Society about the need to hold a country and its soldiers to account for war crimes. Doing so was vital to preserve a nation's 'reputation and standing'. Seated in the front row of the small audience were the parents of the ex-soldier Brereton had spent so much time pursuing: Len, the former judge and general, and Sue Roberts-Smith. The pair had sat through much of the trial. Their son was the man accused of murdering a defenceless Ali Jan and other Afghans, and the legacy of the Roberts-Smith family name hung in the balance.

Their attendance at Brereton's speech may have been no more than a product of their genuine interest in its contents, but I felt it also suggested a steadfast defiance and belief in their son's innocence.

My article about Brereton's speech had also described how the multiple ongoing investigations by authorities into Roberts-Smith remained unresolved. Nobody knew if Roberts-Smith would ever be prosecuted in a criminal court, but if there was a chance of that ever happening, it seemed to me to hinge on the outcome of the defamation case. No prosecutor would be bold enough to charge Roberts-Smith if he was to beat us.

The Office of the Special Investigator (OSI) and the federal police hadn't given up on Roberts-Smith, but investigations were increasingly focusing on what one observer described to me as 'lower hanging fruit' in the SAS. The ex-soldier Dusty Miller had identified as the likely killer of an injured Haji Sardar was now a major law enforcement target, as was the former trooper filmed on helmet camera shooting dead an Afghan in a wheat field. These suspects were likely to be the first soldiers charged by the OSI, but none of the allegations they faced had anything to do with the man who had sued us.

Roberts-Smith's victory in our case would not only mean he would likely never face prosecution, but would challenge other legacies, too.

Samantha Crompvoets had resolved to wind up her Canberra business, having been effectively frozen out by Defence for publicly calling out war crimes. History would record her as the first to bravely document alleged war crimes, but her findings would fall under a cloud of doubt if Justice Besanko found in Roberts-Smith's favour. So, too, would Justice Brereton's work. Certain members of Roberts-Smith's legal team were already spreading the word that they'd won the case.

If they were hoping to end the calling of their witnesses with a bang, their client's case had finished with more of a whimper. An SAS soldier had appeared for Roberts-Smith and testified on oath that John Langmore couldn't have witnessed the Easter Sunday executions because he was searching an orchard outside the Whiskey 108 compound at the time. This unexpected evidence would have been capable of destroying a large part of our case, save for a major problem. Roberts-Smith and his lawyers had failed to make mention of the orchard story throughout the entirety of their own case. This not only rendered the testimony meaningless but gave it the air of a recent invention, a story desperately cooked up to help a mate.

Yet it made clear in my mind that Roberts-Smith would never stop fighting and his team of supporters would be backing him to the bitter end. He remained on a lucrative salary, despite taking extended paid leave from Seven, and still expected to be invited to ceremonies along with other Victoria Cross recipients.

We would all have to wait for the estimated six months Justice Besanko would take to deliver his judgment.

'What do you reckon?' I asked Levitan outside court as we walked out on the last day of the case.

'Have we won?'

CHAPTER 48

JUDGMENT DAY

Federal Court, Sydney, 1 June 2023

One murder. Just one murder.

My mind was replaying this unspoken plea as Chris Masters and I were swarmed by a throng of media cameras as we walked into the Federal Court.

One murder. Just one murder.

We needed a judicial finding of a single murder. If Justice Anthony Besanko found Australia's most decorated soldier had executed Ali Jan or another Afghan detainee, we would win the case, even if we proved nothing else.

The waiting media pack had been hoping to film Ben Roberts-Smith arriving to face judgment in the case he had brought five years earlier, but he was nowhere to be seen. The previous evening, news reports revealed he had jetted off to Bali, broadcasting pictures of the war hero sunbaking by a pool in a pair of colourful speedos.

Roberts-Smith had featured in the media less frequently in the previous few months, but when he emerged into public view, it was mostly with his trademark arrogance.

No one knew what Justice Besanko had decided, but at times Roberts-Smith appeared to be acting as if it was a foregone conclusion.

Victory was his and he was a man with nothing to fear.

When the Queen died in September 2022, all the living Commonwealth Victoria Cross recipients were invited to attend her funeral as part of a protocol the Palace had organised prior to her death. Australian diplomats were privately shocked when Roberts-Smith indicated he'd be attending, given the war crimes allegations hanging over him.

As the Queen's casket was carried down the aisle at Westminster Abbey followed by a procession of royals, including the new King, Roberts-Smith took his place alongside the good and great of international politics, military affairs and diplomacy. He sat upright, face grim in mourning, medals on the breast of his black suit, looking every inch a man who believed he was where he belonged.

Roberts-Smith wouldn't mourn silently. In a media statement he released in the hours before the funeral, he described his 'immense respect' for Queen Elizabeth. 'She was someone I admired greatly. In every interaction I had with the Queen she was warm, insightful and engaging.

'She was a magnificent monarch, a stoic leader, and importantly just a lovely lady. I feel extremely honoured to be fortunate enough to pay my respects to the Queen and humbled that she saw fit to include the Victoria Cross recipients in her funeral procession.'

To me, it seemed the ex-soldier simply couldn't resist thrusting himself into the public conversation. It was more 'Brand BRS'.

While Justice Besanko hadn't ruled one way or the other, it was an undeniable and very public fact that

Roberts-Smith remained the major suspect of an ongoing federal police war crimes investigation. Would the Queen really have wanted an accused war criminal at her televised funeral? If he did so admire Her Majesty, wouldn't it have been prudent to mourn out of the public eye?

Roberts-Smith's favoured outlet, the *Daily Mail*, wasn't interested in asking these questions. Its headline read: 'Embattled war hero breaks his silence about his special invitation to the Queen's funeral in Westminster Abbey – one of just a handful of Aussies – as his arch nemesis tweets scathing message'.

It took me a moment to realise that I was the arch nemesis in question. The *Daily Mail* was casting me as the villain of this story, because I had tweeted that Roberts-Smith remained under police investigation. Even after his own SAS colleagues had accused him from the witness box of executing prisoners, the ex-soldier was still seen by some not only as above scrutiny but deserving unquestioning reverence.

If Justice Besanko hadn't found substantial truth in our allegation that Roberts-Smith had murdered a civilian or a detainee, there was every chance this view would become entrenched. We needed the judge to rule that at least one murder had occurred for us to win the case.

Even if the allegation Roberts-Smith struck Amanda and bullied and intimidated other soldiers did not reach the evidential bar required, a finding that he had participated in the murder of an Afghan detainee would trump those relatively less serious allegations.

Surely, not even 'Brand BRS' could absorb a finding he had kicked Ali Jan off a cliff and overseen his execution.

One murder. Just one murder.

Masters and I assembled with our legal team in a small room near courtroom one, where Justice Besanko would deliver his findings at 2.15pm. Dean Levitan looked pale. So did Owens, Mitchell and Barnett. In fact, the whole team looked like mourners at a funeral.

I walked into the courtroom corridor and one of Kerry Stokes' key advisers, Seven executive Bruce McWilliam, strolled briskly past. He looked to be smiling. Days before, I'd been leaked confidential emails McWilliam had written about the view of the case from the Stokes camp.

In an email sent in January 2021, McWilliam described it as 'laudatory that Mr Stokes AC supports Ben Roberts-Smith VC with his own money'. In making this point, McWilliam positioned Roberts-Smith as a 'small guy' whom the billionaire Stokes was helping to 'stand up' against a 'big company'.

In another email, McWilliam denigrated our SAS witnesses. 'There are a few witnesses protecting themselves and blaming others, including one guy who actually has immunity even tho [sic] he is a crook,' he wrote. I guessed he was describing Jason Andrews.

The compelling eyewitness testimony of SAS soldier John Langmore had backed up our case that Andrews had been blooded under Roberts-Smith's watch on Easter Sunday 2009. If Andrews had executed a prisoner, it was done with the encouragement of the Victoria Cross recipient, the man McWilliam thought it was so noble for Stokes to support. Andrews had testified with grace and courage about watching Roberts-Smith kick Ali Jan off a cliff at Darwan, presenting as a deeply traumatised but honest veteran.

I wondered if McWilliam's flawed analysis of the case had infected Stokes' own judgment. At Seven's most recent annual general meeting, Stokes had called over a junior reporter and told them: 'Ben Roberts-Smith is innocent and deserves legal representation and that scumbag journalists should be held to account.'

'Quote me on that,' Stokes had added.

The scumbag journalists were obviously Masters and me. Still, I knew from my sources that, in private, Roberts-Smith was worried. Heading to Bali rather than facing the music suggested as much.

Roberts-Smith had told those close to him that even if he lost, there was 'nothing they could do to me'. My sources suggested this was a reference to the fact that a finding of murder in a defamation trial wouldn't land him in jail. The risk of prison time would only arise in the event of a criminal prosecution, but the chances of that happening were much higher if we proved he was involved in an execution.

My sources in various agencies with insight into the Roberts-Smith investigations by the federal police and Office of the Special Investigator told me that officials had downed tools. No agency would act until Justice Besanko issued his ruling.

One murder. Just one murder.

Team Roberts-Smith had already enjoyed a small victory, with Neil Browning avoiding a criminal conviction after pleading guilty to hindering war crimes investigators who had sought to seize his phone while he was drunk. A magistrate had described Browning's actions as those of 'a drunken fool' who had 'made a jolly nuisance of himself', but also noted his decorated military service and how, when investigators approached him, he was under intense pressure – having just exited the witness box in the Roberts-Smith defamation trial.

There was no mention that Browning was a war crimes suspect himself or that he'd entered the witness box willingly to help the case launched by his co-accused best friend. If Browning had finished his evidence in a blaze of publicity, most others from the SAS who had testified had tried to get on with their lives and avoid the spotlight once they left the courtroom.

I heard that Andrews was training in the wilderness to raise money for charity as part of an extreme endurance event, but that he had stridently refused to be featured in any publicity about the case when approached by reporters. That fitted with what I knew about Jason Andrews.

Where Roberts-Smith had insisted on seizing his chance to take his very public place among select mourners at the world's biggest funeral, Andrews was quietly grinding on with life, determined to avoid attention.

The word from a senior officer I knew in Canberra was that Boyd Keary had been promoted within the SAS to staff sergeant major, but was still copping blowback from some in the special forces community because he had dared challenge Roberts-Smith. So were the other SAS witnesses with the guts to tell the truth or confront the Roberts-Smith myth: Dean Tilley, Brian McMurray, Nick Simkin, Jimmy Stanton, William Tindell, Keith Nueling and John Langmore.

The officer also told me that when a few young troopers were overheard discussing those accused of 'ratting' on the war hero, Keary had called a meeting at the regiment. 'Anyone got a problem with me, come to my office and I'll explain why I did what I did,' he told the meeting.

No one ever showed up at Keary's office.

The nasty chatter continued, though. Some former special forces veterans had taken to social media to deny that war crimes had occurred or to label those who had exposed them as 'dogs'.

'I would spit in their face,' one veteran had written of his former comrades who had called out potentially criminal behaviour. In a photo he posted of himself next to Roberts-Smith, the ex-soldier had written: 'we gotcha back'.

Keen to draw attention, he'd also begun selling bottles of 'Whiskey 108' alongside promotional material that described how SAS soldiers had engaged in 'gangster shit' during the Easter Sunday operation and how the removal of the prosthetic leg from an allegedly executed Afghan had symbolised 'everything the Troop stood for: violence, drinking and theft'.

I knew this disgruntled veteran was in a small, noisy minority.

Most in the SAS had by now heard more than enough to harbour grave doubts about Roberts-Smith and his claims of innocence. But even the RS sceptics were waiting. Their judgment would be informed by that of Justice Besanko.

Our SAS witnesses would be forever harassed and attacked if we lost the case. A few weeks before judgment day, I'd caught up with Dusty Miller in the country town he had moved to. He was living a quiet life with his two children and wife, keeping his demons at bay by relentlessly exercising. He encouraged me to go for a swim with him. I managed a kilometre in the time he pumped out three.

'Those who have spoken up about war crimes really need this case to go your way,' Dusty told me as we shared a bottle of wine that night. 'It will show the public that what we did was the right thing. That what we said was true.'

One murder. Just one murder.

Initially, I'd counted on Justice Besanko delivering his judgment in December 2022 or January 2023. But as the New Year came and went with no word from the judge's chambers, the hope for a relatively speedy conclusion to our case faded.

The judge was taking his time.

In May, I joined Dean Levitan on a two-week trip to Poland and Israel, as part of an educational tour he was leading that retraced the Holocaust and the birth of the Jewish state.

The question of what men did in conflict, and why, hung over much of our journey, from the death camps of Poland where I mourned my great-grandparents murdered by Nazis, to the battlefields of the Arab–Israeli war, and the sites of more recent skirmishes.

The accusations now being weighed by Justice Besanko involved the Geneva Conventions, international treaties shaped after the Second World War as a check on the barbarity of battle and a means of protecting civilians and prisoners. What had struck me about most of the SAS soldiers I had grown to know while investigating Roberts-Smith, was their professionalism. For them, it was a matter of pride and honour to operate consistently with the Geneva Conventions, while also being ruthless and efficient killers of enemy combatants.

Justly, Australians had always been fiercely proud of the bravery and skill of our soldiers – but, more than that, we were proud of the fact that Australian soldiers fight fairly. Even when our nation's enemies fight dirty and break the rules, most of the men of the SAS refused to debase themselves by retaliating in kind, instead adhering always to the rules of war.

As one SAS veteran explained to me, he did this because to ignore the rules of war was to lose moral authority. Australian soldiers would never stoop to the level of Nazis or jihadis. Justice Besanko's task was to conclude whether

Roberts-Smith was an aberration in this proud SAS tradition.

One murder. Just one murder.

If Justice Besanko found Roberts-Smith was implicated in the murders of Ali Jan, the prisoners captured on Easter Sunday, or the Afghan executed after an order issued to Commander Ismail, it would be self-evident that the war hero had used legal proceedings to silence the reporting of allegations that he knew to be true.

It would also become clear that Roberts-Smith had instructed his barristers, led by Arthur Moses, SC, to make serious accusations, including claims of perjury and cowardice, against witnesses that Roberts-Smith knew to be telling the truth.

These were men who not only risked their lives in the service of their country in Afghanistan, they were men who demonstrated the moral integrity and courage that Australia reveres in its servicemen and women, by having the bravery to speak the truth about the shameful acts that Roberts-Smith carried out in Afghanistan.

But if we couldn't prove a murder, then Masters and I would go down in history as the reporters who had taken on a national icon without enough evidence to back up our reporting in court.

My former boss James Chessell had already addressed the newsrooms of the *Sydney Morning Herald* and *The Age*, telling them to hope for a win but prepare for a loss. 'Even if Nick and Chris don't succeed, we will be proud of their journalism. The company has already planned in the budget for the loss, so it won't lead to job losses.'

The tone of the reporting about the impending judgment had changed, something I had also noticed during the trial. A respected reporter, Stephen Rice, had taken over coverage of the Roberts-Smith case for *The Australian*. I'd never met him, but his journalism was always fair and rigorous. Chris Reason, a veteran reporter from Seven, had also stuck to the facts, despite Roberts-Smith's position as a senior Seven manager, albeit now on extended leave. Stokes' *West Australian* was still running what I considered propaganda, but journalists such as Reason were a reminder that many in the media cared more for the truth than their bosses.

* * *

In the second-last week of May, Justice Besanko's associate emailed our legal team to inform us His Honour would be delivering his judgment on the first day of June. After Dean Levitan called me to tell me the news, I walked into an alley and dry-retched for a few minutes.

It wasn't just my reputation on the line. If we lost, I would have let down Ali Jan's family, along with so many people dragged into the court case that Roberts-Smith had launched: the SAS soldiers who came to court and told the truth with grit and honour; Hanifa and the other Darwan villagers who had stood up proudly in the witness box; Emma Roberts and her best mate Danielle, and John McLeod, who had had been dragged into the legal mess by us, subpoenaed and forced to hand over documents or testify.

Amanda's life had been hurt by the whole legal process, but she had still shown up to court and testified with courage. Andrew Hastie had risked his political career to do the right thing.

Three days before Justice Besanko was due to deliver his ruling, Justice Paul Brereton delivered an address to a ceremonial court sitting of his fellow New South Wales judges, to announce he was hanging up his judicial robes.

Brereton had been appointed to head Australia's new National Anti-Corruption Commission.

I watched online as Brereton's voice swelled with emotion as he remembered his deceased father, Russell, the former war crimes prosecutor and judge. He then steeled himself as he spoke of his work investigating war crimes, praising General Angus Campbell for his 'great moral leadership, first in seeking and supporting an inquiry which was never going to be popular and then in courageously presenting and addressing its outcomes and recommendations, because it was the right thing to do'.

The eve before Justice Besanko was to deliver his judgment, Nic Owens called me. He had heard that Roberts-Smith's legal team was brimming with confidence. I could tell Owens was desperately nervous.

'I can't sleep,' he told me.

That same night, I got a call from a barrister who was close to the man Owens had replaced to lead our team. The barrister told me that the previous Saturday was Sandy Dawson's birthday. He would have been 51.

* * *

'Courtroom is open, guys,' someone said.

Masters and I followed Nic Owens, Chris Mitchell, Lyndelle Barnett, Dean Levitan, Jeremy Forbes and Tess McGuire into court. James Chessell walked behind us.

It was a much bigger room than that which had hosted the trial and it was packed with reporters and lawyers. Bruce McClintock wasn't there, but Arthur Moses entered grimly, along with Mark O'Brien and Monica Allen.

That morning, I had woken at 5am and run in the dark on the Bondi to Bronte track. It was a warm, slightly drizzly morning. Then I plunged into the ocean in my running shorts. A complete rainbow was in the sky, forming a perfect arc over the Bondi surfers. My old journalism mentor Michael Gordon would have loved it.

'Silence. All Stand,' the court attendant said.

'The Federal Court is now in session. Please be seated.'

Justice Anthony Besanko entered the court in his black robes, as sombre as an undertaker.

He explained he would only be reading a summary of his judgment, a scorecard of what parts of the case Roberts-Smith had won or lost. He would release his detailed, 606-page judgment four days later, after the Commonwealth requested to read through the document to check for any National Security issues before it was publicly released.

So it wasn't going to take the judge long to either deliver us an historic win or a catastrophic loss.

As Justice Besanko spoke slowly while he outlined the background to the case, I focused on breathing deeply to stop everything spinning. For a few seconds, I felt as if I might vomit on the bar table.

One murder. Just one murder.

Now I was praying to myself. These silent pleas were answered within minutes.

As the judge outlined his findings, it became clear that the complex web of evidence we believed Owens had quietly but effectively woven in court had shimmered into the clear view of the judge. And it had done so stunningly. It wasn't just one murder Roberts-Smith was found to be involved with. Justice Besanko concluded it was four. The substantial truth of the majority of our claims was proven.

Justice Besanko used dry, technical legal-speak, but the meaning of his ruling was clear. The judge had found

Roberts-Smith was a serial war criminal, a compulsive liar and a vicious bully.

After almost a year assessing the evidence, Justice Besanko had concluded that the testimony given by our witnesses was enough to prove that Ben Roberts-Smith *had* kicked Ali Jan off the cliff and participated in his execution, his hands still bound. The two Afghan prisoners found in the tunnel *had* been executed at Whiskey 108: Andrews *had* been blooded, and Roberts-Smith *had* executed the man with the plastic leg.

Dean Tilley's account of the execution involving Ismail and ordered by Roberts-Smith was also ruled as truthful by Justice Besanko. Roberts-Smith's key witnesses – Vincent Jelovic, Neil Browning and Tim Douglass – were all liars who had colluded to cover up their mate's war crimes.

In contrast, the judge found that when it came to the evidence that really counted, Jason Andrews, Dean Tilley, Boyd Keary, Brian McMurray, John Langmore, William Tindell, Andrew Hastie and Jimmy Stanton had all told the truth. Emma Roberts was declared truthful in connection to the key contested allegations, such as whether she had honestly testified about Roberts-Smith's threats to our witnesses and plots to bury evidence.

John McLeod's key evidence was also accepted by Justice Besanko. Roberts-Smith *had* directed the ex-cop to send the threatening letters to McMurray and send the emails that led to Simkin's family home being raided.

While Justice Besanko ruled there wasn't enough evidence to prove the execution Roberts-Smith had boasted about to Stanton because of the absence of an eyewitness, this didn't matter because of the evidence he was involved in the murder of Ali Jan and three other Afghan detainees. The judge still believed that Stanton was honest.

Justice Besanko ruled that the evidence didn't allow him to prove Amanda's punch allegation to the standard required by the court, yet he also concluded that this was 'contextually true' because of the court's conclusion that Roberts-Smith was a violent war criminal. The judge believed Amanda when she spoke of being threatened and intimidated by Roberts-Smith, and found he had lied in court when attempting to deny this.

As Justice Besanko told the courtroom that he was dismissing Roberts-Smith's entire defamation case, I squeezed Masters' shoulder.

'I haven't felt this good in ages,' the legendary reporter whispered to me.

Levitan turned from the bar table in front of me. His face was beaming, lined with relief. I turned behind me to see Chessell's face bearing the same expression. Owens walked towards me and we silently embraced.

As Masters and I walked out of the Federal Court, camera operators and photographers again swarmed around us. The media pack had grown in the last hour. Masters was the first to speak at the bank of microphones.

'I don't want people to think of this as a bad day for Australian soldiers. I think of those soldiers who not only had physical courage, but also moral courage. Nick and I know them well, we've spent a lot of time with them,' Masters said. 'I'm proud that they're out there.'

As I stepped forward to speak, I felt strangely calm. 'Today is a day of justice. It's a day of justice for those brave men of the SAS who stood up and told the truth about who Ben Roberts-Smith is: a war criminal, a bully and a liar.'

I heard the cameras whirring but, aside from that, the media pack was silent.

'Australia should be proud of those men in the SAS. They are the majority in the SAS, and they stood up for what was right, and they have been vindicated.'

'Ali Jan was a father. Ali Jan was a husband. He has children who no longer have a father. He has a wife who no longer has a husband. He was kicked off a cliff by Ben Roberts-Smith, and he was murdered with Ben Roberts-Smith's participation. There's some small justice for him.'

'Finally, a massive thank you to Chris ... for standing beside me in the toughest fight of our journalistic careers. We couldn't have done it without each other. And we couldn't have done ... this without the best legal team in the country.'

That evening, after dinner with Masters and the legal team, I arrived back at my Bondi Airbnb at around midnight. It was a small, simple one-bedroom unit, but I had booked it because it had a view of the ocean.

I opened the window so I could hear the waves and began drafting a story I had hoped to write if we won the case. It was about all the dirty tricks Roberts-Smith had employed to cover up his monstrous crimes.

It started with words I had never before used without a qualifying term such as 'alleged' or 'suspected'.

It began: 'War criminal Ben Roberts-Smith ...'

After years spent fighting to prove these words were accurate, it felt strange to finally see them on the page. But it also felt good.

It was the truth.

ENDNOTES

Author note: These endnotes provide a non-exhaustive summary of how some of the material was sourced for certain chapters. Where the chapters take place via my own perspective, I have provided no endnotes as sourcing is self-evident.

PART 1
Chapter 1
This chapter relies on interviews, including with confidential defence force sources as well as the wife and family of Ali Jan conducted in Afghanistan. It also draws on Federal Court trial transcripts: those of the SAS witnesses on the mission to Darwan and the Afghan villagers from the village who observed the detention, brutal mistreatment and death of Ali Jan.

Chapter 2
This chapter relies on the Federal Court trial transcript of witnesses from the Easter Sunday mission, most significantly the extensive testimony of the SAS soldier given the alias Person 14, who described in detail the events before, during and after the mission. Person 14's testimony was corroborated by the testimony of other SAS witnesses, including Person 41.

Chapter 3
Roberts-Smith's trip to meet the Queen has been the subject of extensive reporting. He has provided accounts of his meeting with Her Majesty to various journalists, including immediately after the meeting and, again, after her death. Newspaper and Defence Department reports describe Roberts-Smith's comments at various investiture ceremonies. These articles and reports formed part of the research for this chapter, as did discussions with confidential sources with insight into Roberts-Smith's personal life, upbringing and

relationship with his now ex-wife. The reference to the Tizak mission is sourced from the official citation. I interviewed ex-3RAR soldiers for their recollections about bullying at the hands of Roberts-Smith. The descriptions of Roberts-Smith's early military life and decision to join the SAS were partly informed by two speeches he delivered on Australia Day 2015 and Australia Day 2016. Material in direct quotes, is drawn from these speeches. I also spoke to former SAS comrades of Roberts-Smith who described to me their observations of the SAS recruit. The dispute about the 2006 mission that is described was canvassed extensively during the Federal Court trial, and this also formed part of the research material for this chapter as did a newspaper report flagging concerns about Roberts-Smith's bullying behaviour. The comment about being famous or infamous was sourced and confirmed via confidential sources.

Chapter 4

The material in this chapter is sourced from several accounts by soldiers provided during the trial as well as material provided by confidential sources. Person 7 gave extensive testimony in court about the incident described in this chapter. Some of this chapter was written by Chris Masters.

Chapter 5

This chapter's research relied on discussions with confidential defence sources and on the extensive trial transcript and other material released in open sessions of the Federal Court. Hanifa and other Darwan villagers testified (including some who were eyewitnesses to key events) on oath about the mission on 11 September 2012, as did SAS soldiers on the mission. The chapter relies heavily on these witness accounts, especially the testimony of Person 4 (an eye witness) and Person 7, the former providing important detail about the war crime described in the chapter. The testimony of Roberts-Smith and those in the SAS who corroborated his false account was also reviewed. I also interviewed the family of Ali Jan in Afghanistan. Some of the material used also draws on the account of this mission I researched and published in 2018 in *The Age* and *Sydney Morning Herald*.

Chapter 6

Brendan Nelson's interactions with Roberts-Smith are drawn from his own testimony about the war hero during the trial and interviews Nelson has provided to journalists about Roberts-Smith and about the war memorial. A National Press Club address given by Nelson about the role of the Afghanistan conflict at the memorial informed some of this chapter, as did an interview Nelson gave after the unveiling of a series of portraits of Roberts-Smith. The material in quotation marks about the Afghanistan conflict and Roberts-Smith is drawn from the aforementioned primary sources. The description about the 2006 mission is drawn from the citation, which Nelson in turn described during his trial testimony. The quote about Gallipoli is from Charles Bean and is featured on the war memorial website. Detail around the Shepherd Centre award was drawn from media articles and sources with knowledge of the award, including Roberts-Smith's own reaction and those of persons close to him. Confidential sources with knowledge of Roberts-Smith's personal life also informed the content of this chapter as it pertains to his relationship with his ex-wife and dealings with an SAS person described as 'Turtle'. The description of Roberts-Smith being the war memorial 'mascot' was from a 2015 article by Peter Stanley in *The Conversation*.

Chapter 7

This chapter draws on the Federal Court testimony of Person 7, Person 18, Person 4 and other SAS witnesses. Chris Masters provided some of the content about the background of soldiers. The chapter also relies on research that informed my previous reporting about Roberts-Smith in 2018 and 2019.

Chapter 8

The reference to Roberts-Smith's early-morning anxiety was described by him in an interview with the University of Queensland *Contact* magazine (Winter 2017), and this was among my sources for this chapter. I also gained an understanding of his behaviour and obsession with his accusers in the SAS from confidential sources who dealt with him, including (but not limited to) former colleagues at Seven West Media and from the military. The 'tv tonight' blog in 2015 described the *Power of Ten* series featuring Roberts-Smith. His earning capacity with RS Group was dealt with in court submissions, while his speakers' circuit bio is online. The mediation with an SAS trooper over bullying was dealt with in court, with the solider in question, Roberts-Smith and other soldiers testifying about it, and I have drawn from this testimony in describing the mediation and the allegations of bullying and threats. The Koran Gar battle was also dealt with in court and in our earlier reporting, and these are both sources for my description of events on the mountain ridge. Chris Masters also provided some of the content about the Koran Gar conflict, while the citation regarding decorations received as a result of the battle was also consulted. The information about the misleading radio reporting was sourced during reporting.

Chapter 9
This chapter was sourced from Andrew Hastie's detailed court testimony and interviews conducted with Hastie. Some of the content was also drawn from a podcast, 'Unforgiving60', which I also later discussed with Hastie. A few lines are drawn from our previous reporting, including descriptions written by Chris Masters. Confidential defence sources provided the contents of the complaint letter written by Person 6 and persons close to Person 6 also provided detailed descriptions of his attitudes and conduct which informed this chapter.

Chapter 10
This chapter was sourced from interviews with Dr Samantha Crompvoets, who also generously provided a draft of a book she is working on about her experience dealing with war crimes. I also spoke with persons who dealt with Dr Crompvoets in different stages of her life, including university. The content about the USBs is drawn from material disclosed in court and from other sources. I also obtained a copy of the USB material and examined it closely.

Chapter 11
The speech delivered by Roberts-Smith in early 2016 is available on social media, while Hastie's Australia Day tribute was posted online. I also interviewed Hastie for this chapter and reviewed material he had provided Major General Sengelman. Dr Crompvoets was also interviewed for this chapter, while her reports on war crimes

also informed my research and the contents of this chapter. Where material is in quotes, it is taken from her reports.

PART 2
Chapter 12
This chapter is sourced from discussions with sources at Seven West Media, including several Seven employees who worked with Roberts-Smith and observed his behaviour, management style and attended events he organised. A confidential source, who had extensive dealings with Roberts-Smith, also provided several recordings of Roberts-Smith that were made covertly and capture him talking about his work at Seven and other aspects of his life. The interview Roberts-Smith gave UQ *Contact* magazine (Winter 2017) was also used as a source, and some of the material in quotation marks are from the interview he gave the magazine. Other material in quotation marks is from the covertly made tapes of Roberts-Smith discussing his work life and attitude towards his colleagues and fellow executives. The chapter also relies on the testimony of John McLeod in the Federal Court and confidential sources who have had extensive interactions with Roberts-Smith and those in his inner circle at various times.

Chapter 14
My research into Justice Paul Brereton was sourced from speeches and articles about him and his father delivered by Justice Brereton or other lawyers, judges and scholars. I consulted materials including Justice Brereton's swearing-in ceremony, in which other legal heavyweights described his character, and an article written by Tony Cunneen in 2021 in the *Australian Law Journal* (95 ALJ 257), 'From Middle East Battlefields to the War Crimes Tribunals in Borneo: The War Letters of the Hon Justice Russell le Gay Brereton.' I also talked to confidential sources who know Justice Brereton and drew heavily from his official Inspector General report into war crimes, which details his methodology and approach to investigating the special forces. Justice Brereton has spoken about war crimes, including to the Military History Society of NSW in 2022, and I consulted this speech in particular and, to a lesser extent, an article he wrote in the 'The International Law of Armed Conflict: The Australian Application' in 2021 in the *James Cook University Law Review*. The reference to Brereton's description of Gina Rinehart is from his

reported judgment in the NSW Supreme Court. I also interviewed Dr Crompvoets about her interactions with Brereton.

Chapter 16
The content in this chapter was sourced from a multitude of confidential sources, previous reporting, and material aired in the defamation trial, including messages between Roberts-Smith and his ex-wife and testimony of John McLeod.

Chapter 17
This chapter was largely sourced from a covert tape recording of Roberts-Smith speaking to an ex-SAS soldier. I also conducted other research, including via discussions with confidential sources.

Chapter 19
This chapter relied on the court testimony of Emma Roberts about her interactions with Person 17 and Ben Roberts-Smith, including her recollections of conversations and her feelings as key events unfolded. I also conducted research with confidential sources with knowledge of some of the events described.

Chapter 20
The interaction between Person 18 and Person 5 outside Justice Brereton's Perth hearing room was dealt with in court testimony by various SAS witnesses and their testimony has informed some of this chapter, supplemented by additional research including discussions with confidential sources. What Persons 5 and Person 18 told the judge remains unknown to me and therefore is not dealt with, other than what was released in public court hearings during the defamation trial. Person 5 was pressed on the stand about his interactions with Roberts-Smith post his Brereton interview and I relied on his testimony in writing this chapter, as well as the testimony of persons 18, 7 and 4. The covert recording used in Chapter 17 also provided insight into Roberts-Smith's concerns about his fellow SAS soldiers and attitude towards Justice Brereton's inquiry. I also used evidence aired in court of what Emma Roberts messaged her best friend about what she had learned of Person 5's discussions with her husband after Person 5's interview with Justice Brereton. The judge's attitude towards the SAS code of silence and

the application of his powers to break it was dealt with in detail
in his final war crimes report, and this was a critical source of
information for this chapter. In his 2022 speech to the Military
History Society of NSW, Justice Brereton also described the means
by which soldiers could be compelled to disclose war crimes.

Chapter 22

My research for this chapter included conversations with confidential
media sources who have worked with Mark O'Brien and journalists
who have been sued by his clients. O'Brien's role as Roberts-Smith's
lawyer was also scrutinised in the defamation trial in respect of his
communications with Roberts-Smith and Person 5 over some of
the war crimes allegations the pair faced, and I have drawn on the
testimony and evidence dealing with this (particularly his receipt
of information prepared by Person 5 post his Brereton Inquiry
questioning). The role of O'Brien Legal and a second law firm in
representing Roberts-Smith or other SAS soldiers was examined in
detail in the defamation trial, providing content for this chapter.
I have drawn on the testimony of Person 5 and Person 11 about
this. Discussions with Hastie and Dr Crompvoets also informed
this chapter, as did extensive coverage of Hastie's parliamentary
speech on press freedom. Roberts-Smith's reaction to my questions
were described to me by a reliable source, while covert recordings
of Roberts-Smith discussing his relationship with Kerry Stokes in
respect of my reporting was also used in this chapter. Where quotes
appear about this, they are from this recording, as is his comment
about doing all he could to destroy Masters and me.

Chapter 23

This chapter relied on the extensive defamation trial testimony of
Person 17 about her interactions with Roberts-Smith and her meeting
with me. This research was supplemented by my earlier newspaper
reporting and, to a lesser extent, my recollections of my interactions
with Person 17 and discussions with confidential sources aware of
events that transpired in Canberra and elsewhere.

Chapter 24

The reactions of Brendan Nelson, Roberts-Smith and Emma Roberts
to our reporting was detailed in trial testimony of Nelson and

Roberts-Smith and where sentences are in quotes marks, they are mostly taken from trial transcripts. Person 11 and Person 5 also testified about their discussions with Roberts-Smith in respect of our reporting, while confidential sources also described how the Roberts-Smith camp reacted in the aftermath of an article. I have also used the content of covert recordings described in earlier chapter endnotes, while Roberts-Smith's public statements about the fact that he had not been contacted by authorities also informed this chapter. The referral to the federal police by the defence force chief (and the referral to the chief by the Brereton Inquiry) of the allegations against Roberts-Smith was partly detailed in a federal police document that was read out in open court by Sandy Dawson, while confidential sources provided me other details related to the police investigation into Roberts-Smith. The offences the police were referred by the ADF, as they appear in the chapter, were also contained in this document. The summonsing of SAS witnesses by Justice Brereton was detailed in open court, although the contents of their interviews with the judge have never been disclosed and so are not dealt with in this chapter or others. Roberts-Smith's interaction with Mick Keelty was described in the testimony of Roberts-Smith.

Chapter 25

The purchase of the burner phones was dealt with in testimony by Roberts-Smith and was also confirmed via in-depth reporting that informed stories I wrote in 2021. Confidential sources disclosed some details of the burner phones and the discovery of USBs buried in Emma Roberts' backyard, as well as other details about Roberts-Smith and Emma Roberts' relationship. The use of the burner phones was dealt with extensively in the cross-examination of Roberts-Smith, while his comments that encrypted apps could not be tapped was sourced from the covert recordings made of Roberts-Smith. Emma Roberts and Ben Roberts-Smith's court testimony was also consulted in preparing this chapter, including Emma Roberts descriptions of observing Roberts-Smith arriving home with material used to post anonymous letters. Roberts-Smith's frequent conversations with Person 11 and Person 5 were detailed by both men in their court testimony, while I had direct dealings with Ross Coulthart and sources who also spoke to Coulthart. The detail about Roberts-Smith's peculiar habits was confirmed by confidential

sources, while the reference to controversy around the film *Lone
Survivor* has been described in a lengthy *Newsweek* report from
May 2016. The description of Person 18 finding the anonymous
letters, and his reaction to these discoveries, was sourced from his
testimony in the defamation case and supplemented by additional
research. My own dealings with Keelty, and with confidential sources
who were aware of Keelty's actions, also informed my research. I
confirmed (via a statement provided to me by Keelty in response to
a series of questions and via confidential sources) the steps taken
by the federal police to investigate Keelty's dealings with Roberts-
Smith. Roberts-Smith also provided a detailed account of Keelty's
disclosures to him in his testimony in court.

PART 3
Chapter 27
The parts of this chapter that deal with Person 14's interactions with
Roberts-Smith in Australia and Afghanistan are drawn from Person
14's detailed court testimony. Roberts-Smith also provided the court
with his own account of the meeting in Canberra with Person 14 and
I reviewed this account in preparing this chapter.

Chapter 29
This chapter is informed by the observations of confidential sources
dealing regularly with Roberts-Smith and other key persons involved
in the defamation trial during the period described. The burner
phones use was disclosed during open court hearings, while that
fact that he was grilled by Justice Brereton and of interest to the
federal police was disclosed either in open court or by other sources
(for instance, I reported on Roberts-Smith's police interview shortly
after it occurred). However, the content of his interviews with Justice
Brereton or the AFP is unknown and not referred to in this chapter
or the book. Roberts-Smith's positioning of his case as Nine v Seven
was evident in statements he released publicly. The material about
the various allegations added to the truth defence is sourced from
the defence itself. Roberts-Smith's reaction to these allegations is
contained in his court filings and in his testimony (ie., his disgust
about the river killing allegation that was later abandoned), while
covert recordings and other source material (including his public
comments) helped me confirm his attitude towards myself and

Masters. Roberts-Smith's desire to have his day in court was also detailed in his rejection of our settlement offer. Details of his relationship with Monica Allen and her manner as a lawyer was sourced via multiple information streams, including my access to a letter Allen provided to Roberts-Smith, a phone message sent by Allen to a third party, and observations by sources of the pair's relationship. News Ltd tabloids also photographed the pair holding hands for a story which prompted public comment from Allen's boss, Mark O'Brien (referred to in Chapter 35). Allen's role in handling the allegations about the purported dog shooting and removal of an Afghan commander was dealt with in detail in open court when an SAS witness nominated Allen as the supplier of information in his outline of evidence. The descriptions of the dog shooting from this witness and Roberts-Smith was contained in their outlines of evidence, which they (and other SAS witnesses) were grilled about in detail in cross-examination. The relationship between Roberts-Smith and persons 4, 11, 7 and 18, and their respective accounts of key events, was scrutinised in detail during the defamation case, and this informs some of this chapter, as does source briefings about the relationships between various persons within the SAS.

Chapter 30

The details of Justice Brereton's trip to Kabul was sourced from confidential informants, while the judge's dismissal of the complaint lodged by Mark O'Brien is described in a detailed report released on the Inspector General's website. This chapter describes the lead up to the interviews conducted by Afghan witnesses, but the content of the interviews themselves are unknown and do not inform any part of this book. However, the Afghan witness accounts were provided in the testimony of the witnesses in the defamation case, and this informed some of this chapter and the recreation of their recollections. The description of dealings between Person 7 and me is sourced solely from Person 7's court transcript, including his recollection of a conversation he had with me. Person 7's court testimony also informs the description in this chapter of his decision to give an interview.

Chapter 31

Source information and a letter given to Roberts-Smith by Allen was used in recounting the reference to Ganesha and me.

Chapter 32

The description of the existence and subsequent discovery of the USBs is sourced from court testimony delivered by Emma Roberts and materials aired in court to corroborate her account, including photos. I also reviewed an outline of evidence that dealt with Danielle Scott's anticipated evidence. My reporting on the USBs and purchase of burner phones in 2021 informed some of this chapter, while Roberts-Smith's interstate and overseas trips to meet SAS witnesses was dealt with in detail during his cross-examination and that of those he met. Source information was relied upon to describe the relationship between Roberts-Smith and Allen.

Chapter 33

The content of Levitan's dealings with the Afghans remains subject to legal privilege and could not be relied upon to inform this chapter. Similarly, the need to maintain privilege meant other key details could not be disclosed. However, certain documents lodged in court (outlines of evidence) and court testimony provided insight into the Afghan witness accounts, and they helped shape this chapter, as did general observations of the character of our legal team and other matters that did not raise privilege concerns. Court documents and some court discussion informed the content about Person 66.

Chapter 34

The description of barristers and Justice Besanko was the product of my own observations. I also talked to several barristers about the key legal players in researching this chapter and examined Justice Besanko's career using open source material. The presence of Moses and Allen at the AFP interview was confirmed by a confidential source, while the letter requesting Roberts-Smith conduct an interview with the AFP was read into court testimony. The content of the actual AFP interview is unknown to me and did not inform this chapter or any other. The end of the chapter is sourced from court transcripts. I also observed the hearing.

Chapter 35

A long format piece I published in the *Good Weekend* in 2020 forms a large part of this chapter, as do interviews I conducted for *60 Minutes* of Miller and the Afghan family of Sadar.

Chapter 36

Confidential sources provided some of the material for this chapter, as did the public report of Justice Brereton. Several quotes that describe the judge's views are drawn directly from his report. I also consulted transcripts or video recordings of Prime Minister Scott Morrison and CDF Angus Campbell that dealt with the Brereton Report. Person 7's federal testimony also provided material in respect of the mistreatment of whistleblowers at the SAS headquarters, including Person 7's comments at a SAS meeting.

Chapter 40

This chapter is drawn from the testimony in the defamation case of Emma Roberts and John McLeod, as well as discussions with confidential sources. Both Roberts and McLeod gave detailed testimony of the anonymous letters threats, and where there are quotes in this chapter, they are drawn from this testimony or from messages sent by Roberts that were disclosed in court.

Chapters 41–47

The defamation court case transcripts provided invaluable material for these chapters. It is supplemented by my own observations in court, as well as material provided through interviews (for instance, I discussed the process of giving evidence with Andrew Hastie) with confidential and non-confidential sources. If witnesses are quoted, it is usually drawn from court transcripts. In some sections, material is sourced from what witnesses or barristers and lawyers said prior to or after court. This is not an exhaustive telling of the trial, but seeks to capture key moments through my perspective or, where possible, the perspective of certain witnesses.

ACKNOWLEDGEMENTS

I will be forever indebted to Chris Masters. It hasn't always been easy, but I couldn't have told this story without you. The barristers Lyndelle Barnett and Chris Mitchell were incredible and exhaustive and deserve their own book. Nic Owens SC and the late Sandy Dawson SC (both brilliant advocates) were both endlessly generous with their time, support and care. The entire legal team – Peter, Dean, David, Tess, Jeremy, Dougal, Dylan – gave their all. Andrew Hastie and Samantha Crompvoets gave me time, encouragement and brilliant insights. Dusty's friendship I will never forget. To the Afghans who helped me, I will be forever grateful. My publisher, Vanessa Radnidge, and editor, Jacquie Brown, were also constant and wonderful support. My editors James Chessell, Michael Bachelard and Tory Maguire were endlessly supportive when the pressure was on, as were my producers Kirsty Thomson and Joel Tozer and inhouse lawyers Larina, Kiah and Sam. My Afghan colleague (who I can't name) was always brave. Journalist Mark Willacy was a powerhouse in helping expose war crimes and has been a constant support, while reporters Dan Oakes and Sam Clark were the first to courageously start digging into the issue. My colleagues at *The Age* and *Sydney Morning Herald* and at *60 Minutes*, including all the editors, producers, camera and sound operators, helped bring my journalism to life. To my whistleblowers, I can't name you but I'll forever be in your debt. But, most importantly, I am indebted to the soldiers and support staff of the SAS who had the courage to tell the truth, despite the personal cost. I can't name most of you, but you are the real heroes of this story.

hachette
AUSTRALIA

If you would like to find out more about Hachette Australia,
our authors, upcoming events and new releases you can visit
our website or our social media channels:

hachette.com.au

HachetteAustralia

HachetteAus